Seven Demon Stories
from Medieval Japan

Seven Demon Stories from Medieval Japan

Noriko T. Reider

Utah State University Press
Logan

Published by Utah State University Press
An imprint of University Press of Colorado
5589 Arapahoe Avenue, Suite 206C
Boulder, Colorado 80303

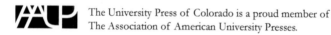

The University Press of Colorado is a proud member of
The Association of American University Presses.

The University Press of Colorado is a cooperative publishing enterprise supported, in part, by Adams State University, Colorado State University, Fort Lewis College, Metropolitan State University of Denver, Regis University, University of Colorado, University of Northern Colorado, Utah State University, and Western State Colorado University.

The paper used in this publication meets the minimum requirements of the American National Standard for Information Sciences—Permanence of Paper for Printed Library Materials. ANSI Z39.48-1992

ISBN: 978-1-60732-489-8 (paperback)
ISBN: 978-1-60732-490-4 (ebook)

Library of Congress Cataloging-in-Publication Data

Names: Reider, Noriko T., author.
Title: Seven demon stories from medieval Japan / Noriko T. Reider.
Description: Logan: Utah State University Press, 2016. | Includes bibliographical references and index.
Identifiers: LCCN 2015041220| ISBN 9781607324898 (pbk.) | ISBN 9781607324904 (ebook)
Subjects: LCSH: Demonology—Japan. | Folklore—Japan. | Legends—Japan. | Supernatural. | Spirits.
Classification: LCC GR340 .R36 2016 | DDC 398.20952—dc23
LC record available at https://lccn.loc.gov/2015041220

Cover illustration: "Minamoto no Yorimitsu slaying tsuchigumo yokai," by Utagawa Kunyoshi.

To MaryEllen and Warwick Reider

My children who are my driving engines

Contents

Acknowledgments

AGAIN, DEMONS. JAPANESE DEMONS AND OGRES IN FOLKLORE, literature, and art. Not simply pernicious, but transformative and sometimes positive, formidable in their ability to express the human experience, they have become my academic lifework. During my journey, I have met many wonderful people, and this book has benefited greatly from them. I am especially grateful to Shelley Fenno Quinn, Peter Knecht, and Mark Bender, who have been gracious in their assistance and encouragement from the beginning of my academic endeavor.

Roger Thomas of Illinois State University, a genuine scholar, and Keiko Wells of the Ritsumeikan University were immensely generous and kind to read the whole manuscript and to give valuable comments.

The draft chapters were read by Benjamin Dorman, Paul Swanson, and David White of Nanzan Institute for Religion and Culture; Cristina Bacchilega, Anne E. Duggan, and Hellen Callow of *Marvels & Tales: Journal of Fairy-Tale Studies*; and Carolyn Stevens, Rebecca Suter, and David Kelly of *Japanese Studies*. My book would have been inferior without their comments and suggestions.

Special acknowledgments are due R. Keller Kimbrough, Hank Glassman, Charlotte Eubanks, Scott Schnell, and Elizabeth Oyler for their helpful advice and comments in the process. I would also like to thank Rebecca Copeland, Michael Bathgate, Ethan Segal, Mariko Kakehi, Michael Mitchell, Richard Torrance, Clark Chilson, Gergana Ivanova, Mikiko Hirayama, and Ann Wicks for their kind support and suggestions on various stages of this project. Thomas Kasulis and the late David Chen, experts on Buddhism and classical Chinese, respectively, were very generous in helping me translate *Tsukumogami ki* (The Record of Tool Specters).

Also I have to thank Komatsu Kazuhiko, Tokuda Kazuo, Michael Dylan Foster, Raluca Nikolae, Nakano Yōhei, Kobayashi Kenji, Nagahara Junko, and Saitō Maori, whom I met at International Conference on Tradition and Creation in the Culture of Yokai and the Strange. The conference was one of the most memorable and fruitful conferences I have ever attended. Matsumura Kaoruko at International Research Center for Japanese Studies, Kyoto, was very helpful for my obtaining the illustrations used for this book. Apart from International Research Center for Japanese Studies, the following institutions kindly supplied me with illustrations for this book: Itsuō Art Museum, The Senshū University Library, Hiroshima University Library, DNP ART Communications, and Museum of Fine Arts, Boston.

The guidance of Michael Spooner, associate director and acquisitions editor at University Press of Colorado/Utah State University Press, has always been helpful and encouraging. Anne Morris Hooke, my neighbor and friend; Cheryl Carnahan, copyeditor; and Laura Furney, assistant director and managing editor at the press, were professional and patient in proofreading my English. I am grateful to the staff at museums and historical sites in Japan and the United States. Stacy Brinkman, Asian Studies librarian, the staff at the Interlibrary Loan office, and the Special Collection office of Miami University Libraries have been invaluable in obtaining the many books and articles I requested for research. My colleagues in the Department of German, Russian, Asian, and Middle Eastern Languages and Cultures, especially Margaret Ziolkowski, John Jeep, and Shi Liang, director of Interactive Language Resource Center Daniel Meyers, and the East Asian Studies Program have been always supportive and are exemplars of collegiality. Likewise, comments, friendship, and encouragement from the members of Midwest Japan Seminar are much appreciated. Discussions at Midwest Japan Seminar have been critical for my publications.

I would like to thank Miami University for awarding me an Assigned Research Appointment in the spring of 2013 that made it possible for me to research in Japan and the financial support from the Committee of Faculty Research in obtaining permission for the illustrations in this book.

The second essay and translation of this book appeared as "'Tsuchigumo sōshi': The Emergence of a Shape-Shifting Killer Female Spider" in *Asian Ethnology* 72, no. 1 (2013). The fourth essay appeared as "Haseo soshi: A Medieval Scholar's Muse" in *Japanese Studies* 35, no. 2 (2015), and its short Japanese version appeared in *The Tradition and Creation of Yokai Culture: From the Viewpoint of Inside and Outside*, edited by Komatsu Kazuhiko, The 45th International Research Symposium (Kyoto: International Research Institute for Japanese Studies, 2015). The fifth essay has been published as "*The Tale of Amewakahiko*: A Japanese Medieval Story" in *Marvels & Tales: Journal of Fairy-Tale Studies* 29, no. 2 (2015), published by Wayne State University. The sixth essay and translation appeared as "'Hanayo no hime,' or 'Blossom Princess': A Late-Medieval Japanese Stepdaughter Story and Provincial

Customs" in *Asian Ethnology* 70, no. 1 (2011), and the seventh essay and translation was published as "Animating Objects: *Tsukumogami ki* and the Medieval Illustration of Shingon Truth," which appeared in *Japanese Journal of Religious Studies* 36, no. 2 (2009). I am grateful to the journals for permission to use the articles in the revised form.

Finally, but not least, the love and encouragement of my family—my husband Brent Reider, daughter MaryEllen, and son Warwick—are, as always, my driving engines.

Seven Demon Stories
from Medieval Japan

Introduction

Oɴɪ (ᴅᴇᴍᴏɴs, ᴏɢʀᴇs) ᴀʀᴇ ᴜʙɪǫᴜɪᴛᴏᴜs sᴜᴘᴇʀɴᴀᴛᴜʀᴀʟ ᴄʀᴇᴀᴛᴜʀᴇs ᴛʜᴀᴛ have played important roles in Japanese society and culture for centuries. In my previous book, *Japanese Demon Lore: Oni, from Ancient Times to the Present* (Utah State University Press, 2010), I situated the oni as the other and examined what oni have been and what they have meant throughout Japan's history, including their vicissitudes and transformations. While working on oni, I encountered a number of fantastic stories that have interesting cultural and societal perspectives and that would be of great value to scholars and students of Japanese culture. This book, comprising seven introductory research essays, each accompanied by a full translation, builds upon *Japanese Demon Lore* while focusing on the medieval time period for which oni were particularly important, as they were perceived to be living entities.

OTOGIZŌSHI AS A GENRE

Many of these fascinating tales are *otogizōshi* (Muromachi-period fiction, literally "companion tales"),[1] short stories written from the fourteenth to the seventeenth centuries for the purpose of both entertainment and moral or religious edification (Tokuda, *Otogi-zōshi hyakka ryōran* 2–9).

The term *otogizōshi* was coined in the eighteenth century when an Osaka publisher, Shibukawa Seiemon, published an anthology of twenty-three short medieval stories under the title *Goshūgen otogi bunko* (Auspicious Companion Library). Individual stories in this collection were called *otogizōshi* ("companion tales"); later, short stories written from the Muromachi period (1336–1573) to the early Edo period (1600–1867), of which there are well over 400 extant, came to be called *otogizōshi* as an umbrella term.

Otogizōshi fuse written text and illustrations, taking a variety of forms such as *emaki* (picture scrolls), *nara ehon* (illustrated woodblock-printed books of a certain size), and woodblock-printed books. According to Chieko Irie Mulhern, *otogizōshi* are literary works "distinguished from transcribed folk tales by their substantial length and scope; sophistication in plot structure, characterization, and style; gorgeous appearance in binding and illustration;

DOI: 10.7330/9781607324904.c000

and wide circulation. The origin, date, authorship, readership, means of circulation, and geographic distribution of the *otogizōshi* tales . . . remain largely nebulous" (Mulhern, "Analysis of Cinderella Motifs, Italian and Japanese" 1).[2] Nevertheless, *otogizōshi's* anonymous authorship, brevity, and context indicate an oral-derived literature (Steven 303–31). An "indicator of *otogizōshi's* origin in oral tradition is the emphasis on events and comparative lack of concern for details typical of auditory literature[3] . . . Standardized expressions and the mnemonic repetition of keywords and phrases often typify this oral-derived literature" (Steven 305).

There are a number of ways to categorize *otogizōshi*. According to Ichiko Teiji, the works are classified into six categories: the aristocracy, the priesthood and religion, the warriors, the common people, foreign countries and strange lands, and nonhuman beings (Ichiko, *Chūsei shōsetsu no kenkyū* 69–70).[4] The texts this book deals with touch upon almost all of these categories.

As Barbara Ruch, the author of "Nara ehon to kisen bungaku" (Nara-ehon and Literature of High and Low), states, *otogizōshi* tales capture essential elements of Japanese national traits. Oni in *otogizōshi* are portrayed vividly with emotional and physical intensity, and importantly these tales reflect the worldview of medieval Japan. While the stories are entertaining, they are also precautionary. The various messages of the texts inform the twenty-first century about the beliefs, customs, and mind-set of the medieval Japanese. Surprisingly, many of these beliefs and customs are still alive in contemporary Japan and are used in modern literature and visual media, including manga and anime.

ORGANIZATION OF THE BOOK

Without humans, oni do not exist. Oni are perceived as such through human senses. Hence, this book is organized according to the main characters who claim to have encountered oni. They are Samurai, Scholars, Women, and It (a personified object). The research essay preceding each translation addresses the text's significance, highlighting cultural, socio-political, and/or religious implications for the medieval Japanese psyche and society and, in its historical contribution, the text's appeal to contemporary audiences.

Part 1 discusses *Shuten Dōji* (Drunken Demon), Japan's most celebrated oni legend. The oni leader called Shuten Dōji kidnaps, enslaves, and eats young maidens if they displease him. The imperial court dispatches renowned courageous warriors to conquer the monstrous Shuten Dōji and his cohorts on Mt. Ōe. In the picture scroll *Ōeyama ekotoba* (Illustrations and Writing of

Mt. Ōe, ca. fourteenth century), the oldest extant text of the Shuten Dōji story, these warriors are two generals, Minamoto no Raikō (or Yorimitsu, 948–1021) and Fujiwara no Hōshō (or Yasumasa, 958–1036), accompanied by Raikō's *shitennō* (Four Guardian Kings) and Hōshō's retainer. Although Minamoto no Raikō and his *shitennō* are widely recognized as the preeminent supernatural warriors in Japanese culture, historical records are minimal. The introduction to the text examines who these oni-conquerors were and why they were chosen as the conquerors of oni. The translation is the oldest extant version, *Ōeyama ekotoba*.

Minamoto no Raikō and Watanabe no Tsuna (953–1025), the leader of the *shitennō*, are again the conquerors of a supernatural creature, *tsuchigumo* (earth spider), an oni variant. The picture scroll of *Tsuchigumo zōshi* (A Tale of an Earth Spider, ca. early fourteenth century) describes a parade of strange creatures in a haunted house whose owner, a beautiful woman, is a giant earth spider in disguise. The second essay discusses the emergence of the image of a *tsuchigumo* as a killer female shape-shifter in the medieval period through an association with oni. This killer image, incorporated into the Noh play *Tsuchigumo*, is firmly established in the ensuing period. The translation is the oldest extant picture scroll of *Tsuchigumo zōshi*.

Part 2 examines the representative tales of scholars who deal with oni. The third essay is a picture scroll of *Kibi daijin nittō emaki* (Illustrated Stories of Minister Kibi's Adventures in China, end of the twelfth century), a fictional story of a historical figure of the great scholar-bureaucrat Kibi no Makibi (695–775), one of only two scholars in Japanese history who was promoted to the position of minister of right. In this text a Japanese oni appears in China as a dead spirit and a helper for Kibi no Makibi to escape from his captivity there. It provides fascinating insights into medieval Japanese elites' strong desire to surpass the Chinese in skills and talents and a fundamental Japanese conception or attitude toward foreign powers. *Minister Kibi's Adventures in China* is also part of a series of the texts that situate Kibi no Makibi as a father of Onmyōdō, or the way of yin-yang. The translation is the picture scroll of *Kibi daijin nittō emaki*.

The fourth essay examines the picture scroll of *Haseo zōshi* (A Tale of Lord Haseo, early fourteenth century). An oni who lives on the Suzaku Gate appears as an avid player of the game of *sugoroku* (Japanese version of backgammon). He challenges Ki no Haseo (845–912), a famous scholar-poet, to play the game with a bet for the most beautiful woman in the world. When the oni loses, he offers Ki no Haseo a strikingly attractive woman, who turns out to be made from the parts of dead bodies. *A Tale of Lord Haseo* is captivating, with such characters as an oni that creates a human from corpses and a scholar who has fallen for sexual enticement. The introduction examines the relationship among oni, Ki no Haseo, Deified Sugawara no Michizane (845–903), the contemporary belief about an oni, or manmade human being, and gender roles. The translation is the picture scroll of *Haseo zōshi*.

Women play an important role in dealing with oni. Some sacrifice themselves to save their loved ones, and others undertake arduous journeys to unfamiliar lands to meet their husbands. In Part 3, the fifth essay discusses the picture scroll of *Amewakahiko sōshi* (Tale of Amewakahiko, fifteenth century), the Japanese version of *Cupid and Psyche*. The heroine journeys to the sky in search of her husband, a dragon king. In the sky she encounters her husband's father, an oni. Twenty-first-century readers may ask why an oni, usually a dweller in hell or mountains, lives in the sky and why he is the dragon king's father. The *Tale of Amewakahiko* helps us understand medieval Japanese perspectives on the living space of fantastic creatures and how medieval scholars' studies of ancient and classical Japanese literature influenced the story's formation. The translation is the oldest extant picture scroll of *Amewakahiko sōshi*.

The sixth essay introduces *Hanayo no hime* (Blossom Princess, ca. late sixteenth century or early seventeenth century), a Japanese Cinderella story in which a stepdaughter meets a *yamauba* (mountain witch, ogre, hag) or female oni on a remote mountain. The *yamauba* turns out to be the heroine's quintessential helper, who gives critical advice and gifts when they are most needed. The story of *Blossom Princess* has various folkloric elements, including the legends of "Obasute" (Deserted Old Women). It is also noteworthy for its description of contemporary provincial customs and embrace of monogamous unions. The translation is the oldest text of *Hanayo no hime*.

Not only human beings but also inanimate objects can deal with oni, and inanimate objects can become oni as well. An example is *tsukumogami* (animating objects or tools and utensils), the subject of the seventh essay, part 4. According to the picture scroll of *Tsukumogami ki* (Record of Tool Specters, the Muromachi period [1336–1573]), after a service life of nearly 100 years, tools and utensils receive souls and, like all things with individual souls, they develop an independent spirit. Resentful after having been abandoned by the human masters they so loyally served, the tools and utensils in *Tsukumogami ki* become vengeful and murderous specters. They want revenge on the humans who abandoned them but lack the malevolent impact Shuten Dōji and his cohort have exercised. I argue that the principal motivation of the author(s) was to spread the doctrines of Shingon esoteric Buddhism to a variety of audiences, ranging from the educated to the relatively unsophisticated, by capitalizing on preexisting folk beliefs in *tsuku-mogami*. The translation is the oldest extant picture scroll of *Tsukumogami ki*. The essays in *Seven Demon Stories from Medieval Japan* examine the texts' cultural and socio-political implications surrounding this astonishing creature.

Regarding the way Japanese names appear in this work, according to the Japanese custom they are written with the family name appearing first. For example, the family name of Komatsu Kazuhiko, a scholar of anthro-pology and folklorist, is Komatsu. The exception to this rule occurs when the names are well-known outside Japan in English circles. For example, the film director Akira Kurosawa remains Akira Kurosawa even though Kurosawa is his family name.

NOTES

1. The word *otogi* in *otogizōshi* is an honorific form of *togi* (*o-togi*). The Chinese character *togi* 伽 literally means "people join," that is, people gather and interact. According to Kuwata Tadachika, the *togi* is used with an honorific, *o-togi*, because the host or honoree of the gather-ing was a person of high social status. During the pre-modern period, the professional sto-rytellers (and advisers) called *otogishū* served their lords primarily by telling or reading stories (Kuwata 127–38).

2. For the study of *otogizōshi* in English, see Kimbrough, *Preachers, Poets, Women, and the Way*; Steven 303–31; Mulhern, "Otogi-zōshi" 180–98; Mulhern, "Cinderella and the Jesuits" 409–47; Mulhern, "Analysis of Cinderella Motifs" 1–37; Keene, *Seeds in the Heart* 1092–1128; Skord, *Tales of Tears and Laughter*; Childs, "Didacticism in Medieval Short Stories" 253–88; Childs, *Rethinking Sorrow* 14–22; James Araki, "Otogi-zōshi and Nara-ehon" 1–20; Ruch, "Medieval Jongleurs" 279–309; Putzar 286–97.

3. By "auditory literature," Steven means the work "typically heard by their audiences rather than read in silence" (Steven 304).

4. Matsumoto Ryūshin, coeditor of *MJMT*, considers Ichiko's classification most appropriate, and based on Ichiko's category he arranged his own as follows: the aristoc-racy, the warriors, religion, the warriors' legend, the common people, and nonhuman beings (*Otogizōshi-shū* 371–87).

Part I
Samurai

1

Drunken Demon (*Shuten Dōji: Ōeyama ekotoba*)
Imagining the Demon Conquerors

SHUTEN DŌJI (DRUNKEN DEMON) IS JAPAN'S MOST RENOWNED oni legend. The chief of the oni, Shuten Dōji, is a fantastic, demonic, and cannibalistic but charismatic creature. He and his cohorts kidnap, enslave, and cannibalize men and women.[1] Set against this imaginary character are the historical figures. According to the oldest extant text of the legend, the picture scrolls *Ōeyama ekotoba* (Illustrations and Writing of Mt. Ōe, ca. fourteenth century), whose translation follows this essay, two generals, Minamoto no Raikō (in the Sino-Japanese reading of the characters, or Yorimitsu 948–1021) and Fujiwara no Hōshō (or Yasumasa 958–1036), are charged by imperial command to rescue the captives of Shuten Dōji and eliminate him. Among a number of samurai who physically fight against oni, Raikō and his four lieutenants, called *shitennō* (Four Guardian Kings), are probably the most famous, since Hōshō's legendary status diminishes as time passes. While they are widely recognized as the brave warriors battling with the supernatural in legends, their historical records are minimal. This chapter examines who these samurai were and why they were chosen as the conquerors of oni. It also discusses some extra-literary events and the circumstances surrounding Shuten Dōji's statement that demons' power thrives when the king is wise.

SHUTEN DŌJI TEXTS

Although we know of the Shuten Dōji story through written texts, the evidence suggests that the story derives from a much older oral tradition. As is the case with popular stories with an oral origin, the story of Shuten Dōji has an array of textual versions. It is generally accepted that there are two versions of the Shuten Dōji texts: the Ōeyama (Mt. Ōe) version

DOI: 10.7330/9781607324904.c001

and that of Ibukiyama (Mt. Ibuki). The picture scrolls of *Ōeyama ekotoba* constitute the representative text of the Ōeyama version. Another picture scroll titled *Shuten Dōji emaki* (Picture Scrolls of Shuten Dōji, early sixteen century), owned by the Suntory Museum of Art in Tokyo (hereafter the Suntory version), represents the Ibukiyama version.[2] The major differences between them are twofold: one is the location of the oni's fortress. In the Ōeyama version, the fortress is located on Mt. Ōe, whereas the Ibukiyama version situates the oni's den at Mt. Ibuki. The second difference is that the Ibukiyama version includes a section of explanation of Shuten Dōji's *honji* (true nature or original form). Thus, in the Ibukiyama version we are told that Shuten Dōji is *dairokuten no maō* (the evil king of the Sixth Heaven in darkness) and the archenemy of Buddha. Likewise, the text tells us that Raikō's *honji* is Bishamonten (Vaiśravaṇa), Emperor Ichijō's *honji* is Miroku (Maitreya), and Abe no Seimei is Kannon-satta (Kannon Bodhisattva) ("Shuten Dōji-e jō, chū, ge" 176 [1904]: supplement 27). The Ōeyama version does not contain this *honji* section except for the *Ōeyama ekotoba*. Satake Akihiro assumes that the *honji* section of the Ōeyama versions may have been eliminated as exposure to the audience became more frequent (*Shuten Dōji ibun* 152). It is now generally accepted that the Ōeyama version came first. The Ibukiyama version was formed by incorporating a historical incident, the murder of a bandit named Kashiwabara Yasaburō at Mt. Ibuki in 1201, into the Ōeyama version (Satake, *Shuten Dōji ibun* 119).

Recently, Minobe Shigekatsu claimed that differentiating the texts as Mt. Ōe versus Mt. Ibuki is not fruitful because many Shuten Dōji texts can be taken as both versions. He suggests instead to classify the texts as those hued with the Tendai school of Buddhism vis-à-vis those without the Tendai color. For example, in the picture scrolls of *Ōeyama ekotoba*, Saichō (or Dengyō Daishi, d. 822), the founder of the Tendai sect of Buddhism who built Enryakuji on Mt. Hiei, expelled Shuten Dōji from his original abode, whereas in the Suntory version Saichō is replaced by Kūkai (or Kōbō Daishi 774–835), the founder of the Shingon sect of Buddhism.[3] Also, the deity of Hiyoshi Sannō Shrine who protects the Buddhist law of Enryakuji is missing in the Suntory version (Minobe and Minobe 129–32). The Minobes' classification seems appropriate.

There are a number of copies and versions of the story, but it was the early-eighteenth-century printed version of the Shuten Dōji story that reached the broadest audience, thanks to the bookseller Shibukawa Seiemon.[4] For all intents and purposes, the popularity of the Shibukawa edition put an end to further variations (Amano, "Shuten Dōji kō" 16). The location of the fortress in the Shibukawa edition is on Mt. Ōe, and it does not have the *honji* section; however, the detail of the story is that of the Ibuki version. Shibukawa published the "Shuten Dōji" story in an anthology of twenty-three short stories under the title *Goshūgen otogi bunko* (Auspicious Companion Library).

The *Ōeyama ekotoba* Picture Scrolls

The *Ōeyama ekotoba* is a set of two picture scrolls currently housed in the Itsuō Museum of Art in Osaka that date back to the second half of the fourteenth century. The scrolls are also referred to as *Katori-bon* because the set was formerly in the possession of a high priest of the Katori Shrine in Shimofusa Province.[5]

The scrolls consist of twenty sections of writings and illustrations.[6] The material has been damaged, and several sections of the scroll are missing. Further, a number of writing sections do not match the illustrations; in many cases, the sections are out of order because of an error or miscommunication in making a scroll, that is, in pasting the papers of illustrations and writings onto the scroll. The opening section of the first scroll is largely missing. Fortunately, this missing part can be supplemented by the *Shuten Dōji monogatari ekotoba* (Picture scroll of the Shuten Dōji story) housed in the Yōmei bunko (Yōmei Library, hereafter the text is referred to as *Yōmei bunko-bon* [Yōmei library edition]).[7]

The second scroll ends with the sixteenth illustration. The narrative after this spot, however, can also be supplemented by a different scroll that consists of four sections over nine pieces of paper. These sections, which are written text only, were perhaps copied in the mid-Muromachi period (*MJMT* 3: 122).

Regarding the calligrapher of the writing, some attribute it to Urabe Kenkō (or Yoshida Kenkō, 1283–1350), Keiun (?), or Nijō Tameyo (1250–1338), but there is no proof to back up this assertion. The painter is not known (Sakakibara, "*Ōeyama ekotoba* shōkai" 156).

Plot Summary of *Ōeyama ekotoba*

During the reign of Emperor Ichijō (986–1011), people begin to disappear mysteriously in and around Kyoto, the Heian capital of Japan. Abe no Seimei (921?–1005), a yin-yang master of the Heian Court, divines that it is the work of Shuten Dōji, the chieftain of the oni; Shuten Dōji and his cohorts abduct and devour people. The imperial court charges the two generals, Minamoto no Raikō (or Yorimitsu) and Fujiwara no Hōshō (or Yasumasa), to destroy Shuten Dōji and his evil minions.

Before Raikō and Hōshō set out on their quest with several loyal retainers, the troupe prays for success at four separate shrines. Their faith is rewarded, for while on their way to the oni's lair on Mt. Ōe, the group encounters four deities disguised as priests. The old priests advise Raikō's party to disguise themselves as *yamabushi* (mountain priests), providing the men with the necessary clothing. The warriors, now joined by the deity-priests, meet an old woman washing bloody clothes at a river on Mt. Ōe. She tells the heroes about the activities of Shuten Dōji and his band of oni. Arriving at the demon's mountaintop palace, the members of the royal troupe tell the oni guard that they are a band of lost *yamabushi* in need of lodging for the night. Shuten Dōji allows them into his palace and jovially regales the men with stories from his past.

After Shuten Dōji retires, a number of oni disguised as beautiful women visit Raikō and Hōshō in their quarters. Raikō gives the oni-women an intense glare, and the demons scurry off. Soon after, another group of oni disguised as a *dengaku* (field music) troupe emerges to entertain Raikō and his band. Again, Raikō's fierce stare wards the oni off. Raikō and Hōshō then scout out the palace compound. They discover a cage holding a kidnapped page of the Tendai sect's head priest and in another cage, Chinese captives. Raikō's and Hōshō's troupe then moves to Shuten Dōji's grand bedchamber. They find the entrance to his quarters blocked by an impenetrable iron door, but with the help of the deity-priests, the once impervious door magically melts away. Inside, Shuten Dōji in his true monstrous form lies in drunken repose. While the four deity-priests hold each of Shuten Dōji's limbs, the warriors behead him. As Shuten Dōji's head hurls through the air, his mouth tries to bite Raikō. Raikō quickly borrows Tsuna's and Kintoki's helmets, putting them over his own, and is thus saved from Shuten Dōji's final attack. Raikō's band then kills the rest of the oni and frees the surviving captives. Before parting with the warriors at Mt. Ōe, the four deities reveal their true identities and also show the heroes their own *honji* (true nature or original form).

After the troupe returns to the capital, Shuten Dōji's head is placed, by imperial command, in the Uji no hōzō (Treasure house of Uji). Both Raikō and Hōshō are generously rewarded for their heroic deeds.

DEMON CONQUERORS

The evil supernatural Shuten Dōji character is eliminated by the legendary historical figures Minamoto no Raikō, Fujiwara no Hōshō, Raikō's *shitennō*, and Hōshō's retainer. In a sense, they are legendary because they are known as courageous warriors mostly in legends—this is especially true of Raikō and Tsuna, Raikō's right-hand man and the first of Raikō's *shitennō*. They play an active role in the world of *setsuwa* (tale literature or narrative; myths, legends, anecdotes, and the like),[8] but historical records of them are sparse. An entertaining story is a great way of advertising or disseminating one's name or creating fame. In the process of story formation, extolling Raikō— an ancestor of the Minamoto clan—was a major issue for his descendants, and Tsuna was an important character to advance (or recover) the fame of his line of the Watanabe clan. In contrast, Hōshō, who produced few descendants, saw his status decline in the story as time passed.

Minamoto no Raikō (or Yorimitsu)

Minamoto no Raikō (948–1021) was the eldest son of Minamoto no Mitsunaka (or Manjū in the Sino-Japanese reading of the characters, 912?–97), one of the first chieftains of the Seiwa Genji line of *gunji kizoku*, or warrior-aristocrats. Mitsunaka accumulated wealth and influence by tying his fortunes to those of the Fujiwara Regency—the Fujiwara family's northern line monopolized the position of regent during the Heian period (794–1185).[9] According to Motoki Yasuo, Mitsunaka's greatest achievement was his role as an informer in the Anna Incident in 969 that politically ruined Minamoto no Takaakira (914–83); Mitsunaka thus played a role in helping establish the Fujiwara Regency under which he laid the foundation for his descendants to flourish.[10] Likewise, Oboroya Hisashi writes that Mitsunaka's significance lies in his moving to Tada in Settsu Province (the present-day eastern part of Hyōgo prefecture and the northern part of Osaka prefecture), developing his manor there, and forming an estate with his dependents; thus he laid the foundations for his descendants to flourish (Oboroya 66). Since Mitsunaka had his base in Tada, he is also known as Tada no Manjū. Raikō is said to have entered Tada, succeeding Mitsunaka.

Raikō: A Warrior-Aristocrat

Raikō first appears in the historical documents in the entry on the sixteenth day of the ninth month of 988 in *Nihon kiryaku* (Short History of Japan, ca. from the late eleventh century to the early twelfth century). Fujiwara no Kaneie (929–90) had a banquet for his newly built mansion on Second Avenue, and Raikō presented him with thirty horses (Kuroita, *Nihon kiryaku* 2: 165). Raikō was forty years old.

According to *Sonpi bunmyaku* (Genealogy of Noble and Humble),[11] the massive genealogical compendium compiled by Tōin Kinsada (1340–99), a high-ranking court noble, Raikō became the governor of Settsu, Iyo, Mino,

Owari, Bizen, Tajima, Sanuki, Hōki, and Awaji Provinces (Tōin 3: 107). Often, he did not go to the place of an appointment but stayed in the capital, sending someone else to work on his behalf while he received the tax revenue in the capital. Raikō was also appointed a member of the imperial palace guards, Military Guards, and the Household of Crown Prince, and he was a provisional captain of the Imperial Stables of the Left. In 1011, at age sixty-four, Raikō became senior fourth rank, lower grade, his final official rank. Importantly, while holding government positions, Raikō served the household of the Fujiwara Regent family. It was the time when the Fujiwara Regency was at its height, and the Fujiwara held the power of appointments and dismissals of the governorships. Ayusawa Hisashi, Raikō's biographer, writes that by serving the Fujiwara Regent family and having close connections with them, that is, currying favor with them, Raikō held the positions of various governorships and accumulated immense wealth—the same method his father, Mitsunaka, used (Ayusawa 22).

Indeed, Raikō served the Fujiwara family well. When Tsuchimikado Mansion, Fujiwara no Michinaga's (966–1027) residence, burned down in 1016 during a great fire in the capital, Raikō went to the capital from Mino Province, the place of his appointment, to express his sympathy after the fire (Oboroya 94–95). Michinaga's mansion was rebuilt with materials sent by various provincial governors and was completed in 1018. Among them, Raikō, at that time the governor of Iyo, was exceptional, as he supplied furnishings for the entire mansion. *Eiga monogatari* (A Tale of Flowering Fortunes, eleventh century) recounts:

> Minamoto Yorimitsu, the governor of Iyo, had provided the interior furnishings for the entire establishment, supplying everything that could possibly be needed by any of the three personages—to say nothing of blinds, mats, jugs, basins, and other furnishings for the ladies' apartments, and equipment for the offices occupied by retainers, chamberlains, and Escorts. In the whole house, there was nothing of which one could think or say, "Thus-and-so is lacking," Everything was so superbly planned that Michinaga, looking about, asked himself how Yorimitsu could possibly have done it all. The curtains, the workmanship of the screens and Chinese chests, even the gold and silver lacquered designs and trims—all showed a truly exceptional taste. Michinaga wondered about how Yorimitsu could have managed it, and the other lords were enthusiastic in their praise. (McCullough, *A Tale of Flowering Fortunes* 2: 485)

A *setsuwa*, *Jikkinshō* (A Miscellany of Ten Maxims 1252), describes Yorimitsu as a zealous retainer of the Fujiwara Regent family. When Raikō was fifty-eight years old, while Fujiwara no Tomoakira (?–?) was performing his duties for the Special Festival Party at the mansion of Fujiwara no Yorimichi (Michinaga's eldest son, 992–1074), "his fellow employee, Yorimitsu, joined him. Tomoakira chased him off saying that it was a breach of protocol for two men to perform the same duty. Although this may be an example of excessive zeal on the job, it is interesting that the famous hero Yorimitsu was driven away by a fellow retainer" (Geddes 1: 208; Asami 99). *Jikkinshō* was compiled two centuries after Raikō's death, and we are not sure how true this episode is, but it presents a different image of Raikō than do other *setsuwa* that usually praise his bravery and military prowess.

Raikō had three daughters; they all married high-ranking aristocrats—one of them Fujiwara no Michitsuna (955–1020), Michinaga's half-brother. *A Tale of Flowering Fortunes* recounts that when Michitsuna had taken Buddhist vows, Yorimitsu's daughter who was much younger than Michitsuna was "terribly upset, and Yorimitsu also felt a keen sense of loss. He had knowingly allowed his young daughter to marry an older man, he lamented, and now it was his fault that she had been hurt" (McCullough, *A Tale of Flowering Fortunes* 2: 524). As Ayukawa states, from historical records, Raikō's life appears to have been more like a middle-ranking aristocrat aspiring to succeed in the capital than that of an eminent warrior (Ayukawa 123).

Raikō as a Poet

Sonpi bunmyaku comments that Raikō was a poet (Tōin 3: 107), which went along well with an aristocratic life because composing poems was a requirement for gentlemen and gentlewomen. His wife was the mother of a famous poet, Lady Sagami (998–1061).[12] Raikō had three poems included in imperial anthologies of Japanese poems—one in *Shūi wakashū* (Collection of Gleanings 1005), one in *GoShūi wakashū* (Later Collection of Gleanings of Japanese Poems 1086), and one in *Kin'yō wakashū* (Collection of Golden Leaves 1127) (Motoki 124). This does not necessarily make him a poet in particular, but Raikō exchanged letters with Ōe no Masahira (952–1012), a famous poet and scholar, and the husband of Akazome Emon (956–1041), one of the thirty-six poetic sages, in 1001—around the time when Raikō was assigned to the governorship of Mino Province and Ōe to the governorship of Owari Province (Ayusawa 54–55).

Raikō as a Military Strategist

Sonpi bunmyaku also reports that Raikō excelled in military strategy. Interestingly, however, there is no historical record that endorses Raikō's image as an excellent military tactician. He had never participated in any military expedition, though he held military positions such as imperial palace guard, provisional captain of the Imperial Stables of the Left, and member of the Military Guards. It should be noted that *Sonpi bunmyaku* was compiled in the second half of the fourteenth century when the story of Shuten Dōji had already been formed.

Chapter 5 of *A Tale of Flowering Fortunes* mentions Raikō or Yorimitsu's name; when Fujiwara no Korechika (974–1010), Michitaka's eldest son and Michinaga's nephew, and his younger brother Takaie (979–1044) were to be banished in 996, Raikō was one of their guards: "Extraordinary precautions went into effect at the imperial palace. On duty in the guards' offices, where each commanded the services of innumerable warriors, were descendants of Mitsunaka and Sadamori—Former Michinoku Governor Korenobu, Lieutenant of the Left Gate Guards Koretoki, Former Bizen Provincial Official Yorimitsu, and Former Suō Provincial Official Yorichika" (McCullough, *A Tale of Flowering Fortunes* 1: 184; Yamanaka et al., 1: 238). The time of Raikō is the backdrop of Shuten Dōji, but in 994, the fifth year of Shōryaku, *Nihon kiryaku* records that the court "sent the men of prowess, Minamoto no Mansei, Taira no Koretoki, Minamoto no Yorichika [Yoshinaka or Manjū's second son], and Minamoto no Yorinobu [Manjū's third son] to the mountains to have them look for the bandits" (*Nihon kiryaku* 2: 177). Raikō's name is not there.

A century later, Ōe no Masafusa (1041–1111), scholar-poet-nobleman, listed in his *Zoku honchō ōjōden* (Records of Japanese Individuals Who Achieved Rebirth in the Pure Land, Continued, ca. 1101–11) the names Minamoto no Mitsunaka (or Manjū), Minamoto no Mitsumasa (or Mansei), Taira no Korehira (or Ikō), Taira no Muneyori (or Chirai), and Raikō as peerless warriors under Emperor Ichijō's reign (Hanawa, *Gunsho ruijū* 5: 412). Raikō, as the eldest son of Mitsunaka, must have been known as a strong warrior a century after his death. Indeed, a little later than *Zoku honcho ōjōden*, a story titled "Tōgū no daishin Minamoto no Yorimitsu no ason kitsune wo iru koto" (Raikō, Member of the Household of Crown Prince, Shoots a Fox)[13] appeared in *Konjaku monogatarishū* (Collection of Tales of Times Now Past, ca. 1120), the greatest *setsuwa* collection. As Raikō successfully shoots a fox in the distance with a whistling arrow, the impressed crown prince presents him with a horse. The story portrays Raikō as an excellent archer and a man with compassion—a warrior who does not wish to take the life of a fox and one who does not boast about his skill. In *Nichūreki* (Combination of Two History Books), thought to have been compiled during the thirteenth century, Raikō's name appears under *musha* (warriors) (*Nichūreki* 3: 107).

The story of Shuten Dōji gives an impression of Raikō as a mighty warrior, but as mentioned earlier, from the historical records alone, an image of the heroic subjugator of fantastic villains does not easily emerge. Raikō's younger brother, Minamoto no Yorinobu (or Raishin 968–1048), who was *Chinjufu shogun* (commander-in-chief of the Defense of the North) and the third son of Mitsunaka, is the most historically documented among Mitsunaka's sons.[14] The lack of historical documents allows the story of Raikō to be free from any factual records; he can soar in the writers', painters', and readers' imaginations.

Raikō Endowed with Supernatural Power, a Demon Conqueror

Alongside "poet" and "excels in military strategy," *Sonpi bunmyaku* also states that Raikō was endowed with supernatural power (Tōin 3: 107). This annotation may have influenced or been influenced by the legend of Shuten Dōji because, as mentioned, the story of Shuten Dōji had already been formed by the time of *Sonpi bunmyaku*'s compilation.

In the *Ōeyama ekotoba* picture scrolls, the narrator has a priest describe Raikō: "Although there are four strong generals, Chirai, Raishin, Ikō, and Hōshō, Raikō is held in awe by people inside and outside the capital, high and low, more than the sum of these four generals. Raikō is a manifestation of *Daiitoku* (Yamantaka, the Wisdom King of Great Awe-Inspiring Power). Therefore his subjugations of demons and bandits are superior to any human beings" (Yokoyama and Matsumoto 3: 137). Raikō was chosen to be a demon conqueror because he was essentially a divine Wisdom King.

Admiration for Raikō becomes more prominent in the Suntory version of the Shuten Dōji story, created in the early sixteenth century. The Suntory text describes Raikō as "a descendant of the Seiwa Genji and the leader of warriors. His power is superior to [that of] any human beings and his physical prowess is without equal—more that Hankai (Fan K'uai). He is *endowed with supernatural power*. His eyes are sharp, and he could see through things like things in his hand" ("Shuten Dōji-e jō, chū, ge" 176 [1904]: supplement 3; emphasis added). Here, Raikō is endowed with supernatural power, just as *Sonpi bunmyaku* states. The tales and historical records seem to feed each other.

According to the picture scrolls of *Ōeyama ekotoba*, not only Raikō but also his *shitennō* are manifestations of the Buddhist Four Guardian Kings—Tsuna is Tamonten (Vaisravana, the Guardian of the North), Kintoki is Jikokuten (Dhrtarasta, the Guardian of the East), Sadamitsu is Zōchōten (Virudhaka, the Guardian of the South), and Suetake is Kōmokuten (Virupaksa, the Guardian of the West); therefore, theoretically speaking, they should have supernatural power and be superior to other human

beings. But an important difference is that Raikō is a descendant of the
Seiwa Genji and the leader of warriors, whereas the rest are not.

Raikō as a Direct Descendant of the Seiwa Genji clan

The Seiwa Genji clan was the most powerful and successful military lineage
of Minamoto. The clan was founded by Minamoto no Tsunemoto (?–961,
commander-in-chief of the Defense of the North). As a son of Prince
Sadazumi (873?–916), the sixth prince of Emperor Seiwa (reign 858–76),
Tsunemoto was given the surname Minamoto. Minamoto no Mitsunaka,
Raikō's father, was the eldest son of Tsunemoto, and Raikō, the eldest son
of Mitsunaka, was a direct descendant of the Seiwa Genji clan.

Many famous warriors such as Minamoto no Yoritomo (1147–99),
the founder of Kamakura shogunate, and Ashikaga Takauji (1305–58), the
founder of Ashikaga shogunate, belong to the Seiwa Genji clan (Tōin 3:
252, 296). Also, Tokugawa Ieyasu (1542–1616), the founder of Tokugawa
shogunate, claimed to belong to this lineage (see Tōin 3: 248–49).

From the closing statement of the Shuten Dōji story praising Raikō,
Ayusawa Hisashi conjectures that the story was perhaps created primarily
to extol Raikō for the eldest son lineage of Minamoto warriors (*Genji no
chakuryū*) (Ayusawa 118–19).

Actually, Yoritomo and Ashikaga Takauji were directly descended
from Yorinobu, commander-in-chief of the Defense of the North and the
third son of Mitsunaka, rather than Raikō. As Raikō was the founder of
Settsu Genji within the Seiwa Genji clan, Yorinobu was the founder of the
Kawachi Genji branch of the Seiwa Genji. Yorinobu's activity base was in
the capital, but he extended his influence to the east. With internal discord
and as a result of the Heiji Disturbance in 1160, the Kawachi Genji was
eliminated from the center of politics in Kyoto by the late twelfth century.
When Minamoto no Yoritomo became the founder of the Kamakura shogunate, however, the Kawachi Genji branch became the major line of the
Seiwa Genji of Minamoto. While Raikō's line called Settsu Genji produced
Minamoto no Yorimasa (1104–80), a driving force in the rebellion against
Heike power and a great-great-grandson of Raikō, also known for slaying
the monstrous bird called *nue*,[15] Yorimasa did not have the military influence
or the base in the east that Yoritomo did.

Indeed, the major line of the military family of Minamoto was the
Kawachi Genji line. Later, when the Yoritomo line opened the shogunate
in Kamakura, Yoritomo foregrounded the concept of eldest son lineage
of Minamoto to strengthen his and his household's position among all
warriors. Yoritomo traced his ancestors, which began with Yorinobu, to

Yoriyoshi, Yoshiie, Tameyoshi, and Yoshitomo, his father. The high status of the main eldest son line of Minamoto on the military side was born out of Yoritomo's political maneuver.

Minamoto no Mitsunaka, Raikō and Yorinobu's father, who had built the base for the Minamoto power, was greatly worshipped as the ancestor of the Ashikaga shogunate during the Muromachi period. It was during that same period that the legend of Shuten Dōji was created (Motoki iv). In 1472 the title junior second rank was conferred posthumously on Mitsunaka. Motoki conjectures that among the ancestors of the Ashikaga clan, rather than the warriors with close connections to the eastern provinces such as Yorinobu, Yoriyoshi, and Yoshiie, Mitsunaka was considered more suitable as the founder of the Ashikaga clan and was a subject of worship because he guarded the court in the capital and had a distinct graveyard (temple) (Motoki 198). Also, Takahashi Masaaki offers an interesting interpretation as to why Raikō was chosen as the conqueror of the demons at Mt. Ōe. The name Raikō 頼光 is a homonym of Raikō 雷公, the thunder god; Raikō is associated with a thunder god, and the frightening effects of thunder and lightning were often required to eliminate similarly terrifying demons (Takahashi, *Shuten Dōji no tanjō* 34–35, 58–62).

At present, the Tokugawa shogunate's claim for the Seiwa Genji clan is considered highly doubtful, but during the Edo period (1600–1867) the creation of *Kan'ei shoke kakeizu-den* (Genealogy of the Lords of the Kan'ei, 1643), which linked the Tokugawa genealogy to that of the Minamoto clan, greatly helped heighten interest in the latter's ancestors (Itagaki 1: 439). Minamoto no Mitsunaka was so idealized that it is said that Tokugawa Yorinobu (1602–71), the founder of the Kii branch of the Tokugawa, ordered in his will that his tombstone be placed beside that of Mitsunaka in the inner sanctuary of Mt. Kōya (Itagaki 1: 422, 439). Further, in 1692, during the reign of the fifth shogun, Tokugawa Tsunayoshi (1646–1709), Mitsunaka received the highest rank, senior first rank.

Minobe Shigekatsu writes that the Shuten Dōji story was able to keep its status by legitimizing the Seiwa Genji clan's claim to have ruled Japan and exalting the Tokugawa shogunate for the Tokugawa family, which claimed to be descended from the Seiwa Genji. Therein lies the conceptual background for the thriving production of Shuten Dōji's folding screens and picture scrolls during the Edo period (Minobe and Minobe 148). The image of Raikō had been superimposed on that of the Tokugawa shogun, who claimed to be the head of the Minamoto clan. In other words, admiration for Raikō as a brave warrior and conqueror of supernatural creatures meant admiration for the Tokugawa shogunate. The theme of Shuten Dōji—that of courageous good conquering evil, reinforced by the image of the shogunate eliminating its enemies—was welcomed by all.[16]

Fujiwara no Hōshō (or Yasumasa)

In the picture scrolls of *Ōeyama ekotoba*, Fujiwara no Hōshō (958–1036) is paired with Raikō in the demon-conquering mission, though Raikō is clearly portrayed as the preeminent one.[17] It should be noted in the translation that the court first gives the task of conquering the demons to four warriors: Hōshō, Taira no Muneyori (or Chirai, ?–1011), Minamoto no Yorinobu (or Raishin, Raikō's younger brother), and Taira no Korehira (or Ikō, ?–?). They decline the court's request, saying that it is not possible to engage in a battle with demons, as they are invisible. Then the command goes to Raikō and—again—Hōshō. It is strange that Hōshō, who earlier declined the request, is summoned to the palace again and this time accepts it with Raikō. This could be an authorial (or narrator's) mistake, or Hōshō may have indeed been called again because he was so worthy. Hōshō had become part of a set of four superior warriors by the middle of the thirteenth century. The eleventh story of chapter 3 of *Jikkinshō* (Stories Selected to Illustrate the Ten Maxims, ca. 1252) states, "Yorinobu (Raishin), Yasumasa (Hōshō), Korehira (Ikō), and Muneyori (Chirai) are four superb warriors," and "if they fought each other, surely none would remain alive" (Asami 3: 136). Perhaps the writer of the picture scrolls used the four eminent warriors, wishing to reflect the reputation of the days of Emperor Ichijō's reign and also to contrast Raikō's loyalty to the emperor when he accepted the imperial command at once.

Hōshō was born to Fujiwara no Munetada (mid-Heian period, ?–?) and a daughter of Prince Genmei (mid-Heian period, ?–?). His wife was Izumi Shikibu (976?–1036?), a famous poet of the mid-Heian period[18] and the contemporary of Akazome Emon and Lady Murasaki, the author of *Genji monogatari* (The Tale of Genji); these ladies served Empress Shōshi (988–1074), the eldest daughter of Fujiwara no Michinaga.

Hōshō was of blue-blood aristocratic stock. He was a descendant of Fujiwara no Kosemaro (?–764), the Fujiwara family's southern line. His grandfather was Fujiwara no Motokata (888–953), whose daughter, Sukehime (926–67), was the mother of Emperor Murakami's (926–67) first son, Prince Hirohira (950–71). Prince Hirohira failed to become crown prince because Consort Anshi (927–64), the eldest daughter of Fujiwara no Morosuke (908–60)—Fujiwara's northern family and Motokata's rival—gave birth to Prince Norihira (950–1011), Emperor Murakami's second son and the future Emperor Reizei.[19] Motokata died in despair, as he failed to become the grandfather of the future emperor, and he was said to have become a vengeful spirit. Fujiwara no Morosuke was Michinaga's grandfather and Consort Anshi was Michinaga's aunt, just as Fujiwara no Motokata was Hōshō's grandfather and Sukehime was Hōshō's aunt. If Prince Hirohira had become crown prince, Hōshō might have flourished as Michinaga did.

According to *Sonpi bunmyaku*, Hōshō was a poet and a brave warrior, and he excelled in military strategy. Hōshō became the governor of Hizen, Yamato, Tango, and Settsu Provinces. His final official rank was senior fourth rank, lower grade (Tōin 2: 423). He was also appointed to the position of provisional captain of the Imperial Stables of the Right and served the household of Fujiwara no Michinaga and his eldest son, Yorimichi. Altogether, his résumé is very similar to Raikō's. As time passed, however, the status of Hōshō in combatting the oni steadily declined. In the Suntory version of the Shuten Dōji story, the court summons only Raikō, and Raikō asks Hōshō to join him. In the most circulated booklet versions of the early Edo period, Hōshō becomes one of Raikō's warriors. How could this be?

In short, Hōshō was not from a military household like Raikō was, nor did he have descendants who would advocate his lineage. A *setsuwa* story from *Konjaku monogatarishū* describes the courageous Hōshō subjugating a notorious robber named Hakamadare.[20] The narrative ends with a mixed comment. While praising Hōshō as a man of valor, it notes that his household did not prosper because he behaved like a warrior even though he was not from a military family:

> Yasumasa was not a warrior by family tradition because he was a son of Munetada. Yet he was not the least inferior to anyone who was a warrior by family tradition. He had a strong mind, was quick with his hands, and had tremendous strength. He was also subtle in thinking and plotting. So even the imperial court did not feel insecure in employing him in the way of the warrior. As a result, the whole world greatly feared him and felt intimidated by him. Some people said he didn't have any offspring because he behaved like a warrior though [he was] not from a military house. (Sato 33)

Sonpi bunmyaku lists Kaihan as Hōshō's son. Beside Kaihan's name is a comment that he had been honored with military skills and strategy, but there is no record of any descendants (Tōin 2: 423).

A *bushi*, or samurai, was socially distinguished by his professional military skills and his lineage; his family trade had always been martial arts. Those households were called *tsuwamono no ie* (household of samurai), *bugei no ie* (household of martial skills), or *buki no ie* (household of arms) (Takahashi, *Bushi no seiritsu bushizō no sōshutsu* 16). Those from a "household of samurai" were the descendants of persons such as Minamoto no Tsunemoto and Taira no Sadamori, who rendered meritorious service at the Revolts of Masakado and Sumitomo (Kimura 20–21).[21] Even though one excelled in military prowess as Hōshō did, one was not acknowledged as a martial expert or professional unless he was born to such a household; it was a hereditary profession.

The right pedigree was (and still is) essential; the Japanese generally take lineage seriously. This can be surmised when one recalls that until recently many Japanese considered themselves superior because the Japanese imperial household was *bansei ikkei* (one dynastic, unbroken imperial line). As Ben-Ami Shillony has written, "The belief that Japan is basically different from other countries because its royal house has never changed is almost as old as the dynasty itself. Throughout the ages this assertion has provided the Japanese with considerable pride" (Shillony 5). He continues, "There are families and institutions in the world which have enjoyed longer survival spans . . . but [they are] not hereditary" (Shillony 1–2).

During early medieval times, Jien (1155–1225), a Buddhist monk, poet, and Japanese historian, stated that "as a custom of Japan, it has been decided since the divine age the only person of imperial lineage is allowed to become an Emperor" (Jien, *Gukanshō* 328–29). Jien, who attempted to analyze the events of Japanese history (and his dreams), believed that the Seiwa Genji would bring peace to Japan and that it was the inevitable course of history for the military class to rule Japan. He wrote in his *Gukanshō* (Jottings of a Fool, 1220) that the loss of the Imperial Sword—one of the three Imperial Regalia of Japan[22]—when it sank to the bottom of the sea at the end of the Genpei War,[23] symbolized the emergence of military shoguns who protected Japan in place of the lost Imperial Sword (Jien, *Gukanshō* 265). For the influential warriors in the eastern provinces, Minamoto no Yoritomo's raising an army against the Heike meant a revival of noble birth. Yoritomo, the founder of the Kamakura shogunate, had the pedigree the warriors trusted (Kimura 23; Noguchi 173).

Hōshō did not have a military pedigree, though his ancestors had a chance. Hōshō's ancestors had a base on Kazusa (present-day Chiba prefecture), so when Masakado's Revolt occurred in 939, his grandfather, the aforementioned Fujiwara no Motokata, was actually first chosen to be the commander-in-chief. But because he made an unreasonable request to the court administration, according to *Gōdanshō* (The Ōe Conversations, ca. 1104–8),[24] the appointment was canceled (Noguchi 26). Had Motokata participated in the suppression of the revolt, his household would have become a military household. Equally important, Hōshō was not blessed with descendants who distinguished themselves in battles or with a storyteller who would raise his lineage high, as may have been the case for Watanabe no Tsuna (explained in the next section).

In the scrolls of *Ōeyama ekotoba*, Hōshō takes one retainer with him. He is Kiyohara no Munenobu (?–1017), who holds a position of *Dazai shōgen* (junior secretary of the Dazaifu office in Kyushu). This is also a historical fact. In the entry of the eleventh day of the third month of 1017 of *Midō kanpakuki* (Diary of Fujiwara no Michinaga), Michinaga recorded the death of Munenobu and noted that he was Hōshō's retainer. Munenobu was killed by a group of people who followed Minamoto no Yorichika (Yoshinaka, Manjū's second son, ?–?).[25] As Hōshō's status diminished in ensuing Shuten Dōji stories, Munenobu was entirely dropped from them.

Fortunately, Hōshō is still famous in the visual arts world with such prints as those by Tsukioka Yoshitoshi (1839–92) titled *Fujiwara no Hōshō gekka rōtekizu* (Fujiwara no Yasumasa Plays the Flute by Moonlight, 1883) and a Kabuki play that is based on this print.

Shitennō (Four Guardian Kings)

Shitennō, or Four Guardian Kings, are pre-Buddhist deities incorporated into the Buddhist pantheon to protect Buddha's Law, Buddhists, and Buddhist countries (specifically, Japan from the Japanese viewpoint). As mentioned earlier, they are Tamonten (Vaisravana, North), Jikokuten (Dhrtarasta, East), Zōchōten (Virudhaka, South), and Kōmokuten (Virupaksa, West). Each of them rules one of the cardinal points and a race of earthly devas. Later, the appellation *shitennō* also came to be used for four outstanding men of valor under a military commander. From medieval times on, Raikō's *shitennō* were Watanabe no Tsuna (953–1025), Sakata no Kintoki (?–1017), Taira no Sadamichi (also known as Usui no Sadamitsu, 954?–1021?), and Taira no Suetake (also known as Urabe no Suetake, 950?–1022?). In Raikō's time, however, there was no such thing as Raikō's *shitennō*; this was a later creation.

Konjaku monogatarishū, the largest *setsuwa* collection, compiled a century after Raikō's death, introduces Taira no Sadamichi, Taira no Suetake, and Kintoki as Raikō's retainers. The second episode of volume 28, titled "Yorimitsu no rōtōdomo Murasakino ni mono o miru koto" (Yorimitsu's Retainers Go Sightseeing at Murasakino), begins, "At a time now past, among Governor of Settsu Minamoto no Raikō's retainers were three outstanding warriors, Taira no Sadamichi, Taira no Suetake, and [. . .][26]

Kintoki." Watanabe no Tsuna's name does not appear here or in any Heian literature (794–1185) for that matter. The narrator continues, "They all look magnificent, excel in martial arts, [are] daring and thoughtful, and leave nothing to be desired. Further, they did a marvelous service in the East and people feared them, so Raikō favored these three, having them accompany him everywhere" (*SNKBZ* 38: 152).[27] Having started by admiring the three retainers, the story then tells how the three, who wanted to see a Kamo Festival's procession, miserably failed. Hoping to see the procession, the warriors decided to use an ox carriage, a transportation vehicle for aristocrats, and disguised themselves as women so no one would recognize them. However, not accustomed to riding in a carriage for the noble, they all had terrible motion sickness and could not see the procession at all. The story ends with a comment, "Brave and considerate warriors as they are, they have never been on an ox carriage before, so they had pathetic motion sickness. It is stupid or so it is handed down" (*SNKBZ* 38: 155). It is a comical story of a blunder by famous warriors. The narrator laughs at the warriors' heavy Eastern rural dialect and their hilarious manners. It is a typical view of Eastern warriors—bold but boorish—by people in the capital.

While this *setsuwa* tells us that Taira no Sadamichi, Taira no Suetake, and Kintoki were Raikō's famous men, in reality there is no historical evidence that Raikō had his own band of warriors, let alone *shitennō*. Again, this is where the imagination enters for creative writing.

Watanabe no Tsuna

When it comes to the supernatural episodes, Tsuna attracts oni as much as Raikō does. As discussed in chapter 2, according to the "Swords Chapter" of the *Heike monogatari* (Tale of the Heike, thirteenth century), for example, Tsuna encounters an oni and severs his hand. Tsuna also plays an important role in fighting another supernatural creature, an earth spider.

From medieval times on, Watanabe no Tsuna (953–1025) is known as Raikō's right-hand man and the leader of Raikō's *shitennō*. *Sonpi bunmyaku* also notes that Tsuna was the most eminent of Raikō's *shitennō* (Tōin 3: 14). Any relevant entry in a dictionary would make the same points. As mentioned earlier, however, Tsuna's name does not appear in any Heian literature. He is the newest member of the *shitennō* in both historical and fictional documents.

Tsuna's name emerges for the first time in *Kokon chomonjū* (A Collection of Ancient and Modern Tales That I've Heard, 1254), written by Tachibana no Narisue more than two centuries after Tsuana's death (Takahashi, *Shuten Dōji no tanjō* 199; Kobayashi, "Chūsei buyūdenshō to sono kisō" 961).[28] Included in volume 9, the story is titled "Minamoto no Raikō Kidōmaru o chūsuru koto" (Minamoto no Raikō Kills Demon Boy).[29] Tsuna appears there with Sadamichi, Suetake, and Kintoki, and they are identified as Raikō's *shitennō*. Kidōmaru literally means Demon Boy; there is no explanation about who this Demon Boy is and what he does. The story tells that Raikō stops by for warm *saké* at his brother's house one cold night when he sees Demon Boy tied up at the stable. Raikō warns his brother to tie Demon Boy more firmly. Insulted, Demon Boy attempts revenge on Raikō and escapes his bonds. The following day Demon Boy hides himself in a bull's belly and ambushes Raikō, who is on his way to Mt. Kurama. Tsuna sees through the situation and shoots an arrow into the bull in which Demon Boy is hidden. Demon Boy, pierced by Tsuna's arrow, jumps out of the bull and dashes off to kill Raikō. Undaunted, Raikō draws his sword and beheads Demon Boy with a single stroke; thereupon Demon Boy's head flies off and bites into the front rope decoration of the harness of Raikō's horse (Nishio and Kobayashi 409–13; Sato 62–64). The Demon Boy, his beheading by Raikō, and the flight of the Demon Boy's head targeting Raikō are similar to some core elements of the Shuten Dōji story.

According to *Sonpi bunmyaku*, Tsuna's father was Minamoto no Mitsuru (?–?) of the Saga Genji line. Minamoto no Mitsuru had his base in Mita, Musashi Province (present-day Tokyo, Saitama, and part of Kanagawa prefectures). Tsuna was adopted by Minamoto no Atsushi (?–?), who was of the Ninmyō Genji line (Tōin 3: 14). When one turns to the section on the Ninmyō Genji line, a comment is written that Minamoto no Atsushi was a son-in-law of Minamoto no Mitsunaka, Raikō's father, and that Tsuna was the founder of the Watanabe group (Tōin 3: 28). Tsuna was known as a Saga Genji warrior rather than as Ninmyō Genji. As Mitsunaka married the daughter of Minamoto no Suguru (?–?) of the Saga Genji line of the Minamoto and Tsuna's foster father married a daughter of Mitsunaka, perhaps it was more advantageous to identify Tsuna with the Saga Genji line.

Interestingly, some scholars such as Kobayashi Miwa and Takahashi Masaaki consider that the core of the oni legends surrounding Shuten Dōji was created by Watanabe. Kobayashi Miwa writes that many episodes in *Kokon chomonjū* are about the Watanabe family's history and that Watanabe is good at self-promotion. An extraordinary degree of Watanabe no Kakeru's (?–?) self-publicity described in the Jikōji edition of *Jōkyūki* (Records of the Jōkyū War, mid-thirteenth century) is, according to Kobayashi, the essence of the Watanabe group. She conjectures a connection between Kakeru fleeing to Mt. Ōe and legends of conquering oni on Mt. Ōe. It is possible to presume, Kobayashi writes, that an oni legend may have come from the Watanabe group, that is, Tsuna's spectacular reputation as an oni conqueror in the medieval period was created in the process of story transmission within that group (Kobayashi, "Chūsei buyūdenshō to sono kisō" 961–68).

Likewise, Takahashi Masaaki surmises that a faction of the Watanabe group created Tsuna and the oni stories to restore factional power within the Watanabe group. The group's vassalage relationship to the Settsu Genji is not confirmed until the time of Minamoto no Yorimasa (1104–80), a great-great-grandchild of Raikō (Takahashi, *Shuten Dōji no tanjō* 199). The Watanabe group, of which Tsuna is attributed to be the founder, was a band of warriors that had its main base at Watanabe around the mouth of the Yodo River in Settsu Province, controlling harbors in the vicinity. At the end of the Heian period the group was led by Minamoto no Yorimasa. A close relationship between Yorimasa, a driving force for the rebellion against Heike control, and the Watanabe group was detailed in volume 4 of the *Tale of the Heike*.[30]

Historically, the Watanabe group members had been appointed *Takiguchi*, or Palace Guards, and starting at the end of the eleventh century they received the position of *Ōe no mikuriya Watanabe sōkan* (controller of Watanabe in Ōe no mikuriya manor) to present seafood to the court. *Ōe no mikuriya* was a huge imperial compound located in Kawachi, present-day southeastern Osaka. The Watanabe group's base was an important location in the compound (Takahashi, *Shuten Dōji no tanjō* 196). Takahashi surmises that the people in the Saga Genji line created Tsuna to recover from an injured identity and resuscitate their political power by painting a striking image of their founder, Tsuna. There were two lines within the Watanabe group, Takahashi explains. One was the Saga Genji line and the other the Fujiwara Southern Family Endō line. The Saga Genji line of the Watanabe group initially had more power, occupying the position of *Ōe no mikuriya Watanabe sōkan*. In the early Kamakura period, however, the Endō line of the Watanabe group, which supported Minamoto no Yoritomo in the Genpei War, became more powerful than the Saga Genji line. The Saga Genji's declining status was exacerbated by the fact that the line supported the losing Retired Emperor GoToba (1180–1239) at the Jōkyū Disturbance in 1221, in which GoToba attempted to overthrow the Kamakura shogunate. The position of *Ōe no mikuriya Watanabe sōkan* was taken away from the Saga Genji line and moved to the Endō line (see Takahashi, *Shuten Dōji no tanjō* 193–220). In other words, Tsuna was concocted to achieve the political resurrection of the Saga Genji line.

A legend or story of Shuten Dōji, encompassing the advancement of the Sumiyoshi Shrine, the Yahata Shrine, and Mt. Hiei, saw its rough formation from the end of the Kamakura period to the beginning of the time of the Southern and Northern Courts, which corresponds to the first half of the fourteenth century. Making Raikō its protagonist was an important element to be added at the final stage. This is considered the final stage because Raikō's importance increased with the rise of the Ashikaga clan. So it has to have been after the establishment of the Ashikaga shogunate, Takahashi states. As noted earlier, the Ashikaga clan was Minamoto, and Ashikaga Takauji worshipped his ancestor Minamoto no Mitsunaka and his grave-shrine, the Tada Shrine, in Settsu. Raikō, who inherited the Tada manor from Mitsunaka, was the founder of Settsu Genji. Veneration toward Raikō increased during the Southern and Northern Courts and Muromachi periods. Tsuna's oni story became Raikō's under these circumstances (Takahashi, *Shuten Dōji no tanjō* 219). Since Suetake, Sadamichi, and Kintoki were already known as Raikō's favorite retainers by the early twelfth century, perhaps it was not difficult for some scribes of the Watanabe group to add Tsuna and make him *shitennō*.

Tanigawa Ken'ichi also suggests that the Ōeyama legend was born in Ōe, Watanabe's residence (Tanigawa 84). Behind an immensely popular story lurks the struggle of ambitious warriors who wanted to succeed and strengthen their power base. Needless to say, this was in addition to some influential religious institutions contributing their pitch for their deities' efficacy.

Sakata no Kintoki (or Shimotsuke no Kintoki)

In *Shuten Dōji* stories, Kintoki is second among Raikō's *shitennō*, after Watanabe no Tsuna.[31] In the picture scrolls of *Ōeyama ekotoba*, for example, Kintoki's name always appears immediately following Tsuna. When Shuten Dōji's severed head was going to attack Raikō, Raikō quickly borrowed Tsuna's and Kintoki's helmets. Raikō also ordered Tsuna and Kintoki to gouge out Dōji's eyes when the head bit into the helmets.

In the Suntory version of the Shuten Dōji story, Kintoki plays a more prominent role. At Shuten Dōji's banquet scene, an oni, commanded by the Dōji to entertain Raikō's troupe, sings a song and dances a couple of times: "People from the capital, how did they lose their way, to become *saké* and side dishes?" Understanding the meaning of this song, Tsuna becomes livid and is about to kill the oni, but Raikō calms him down. Kintoki, who is introduced as a renowned dancer in the capital, rises to dance and sings two to three times in response: "Spring has come to the old demon's cavern, wind will blow them out during the night." The narrator says Shuten Dōji is too intoxicated to pay attention to the meaning of Kintoki's song and enjoys "Kintoki's dance and singing voice" ("Shuten Dōji-e jō, chū, ge" 176 [1904]: supplement 16–17).[32]

Kintoki is without doubt the most familiar figure among Raikō's *shitennō*; this is not necessarily through the name Kintoki but rather as Kintarō, Kintoki's legendary childhood name. Kintarō is a boy with superhuman strength and is a popular character in folklore, Kabuki and puppet plays, children's books and songs, even as candies. In present-day Japan a Kintarō figure, wearing a red *harakake* (large bib that covers the chest and stomach) on which a big character *kin* (gold) is written, is customarily put up on Boys' Day (or Children's Day) in the hope that boys will become brave, strong, and healthy like Kintarō. By the end of the seventeenth century, a *yamauba* (mountain witch, ogress, hag) had come to be considered the mother of this Kintarō. Kintarō was raised in the mountains, wrestling with animals, and many legends say he was found by Raikō to become one of his *shitennō* (see Reider, *Japanese Demon Lore* chapter 4).

In my earlier work I wrote that there is virtually no record of the existence of Sakata no Kintoki except for an episode in *Konjaku monogatarishū* ("Yorimitsu's Retainers Go Sightseeing at Murasakino") and one in *Kokon chomonjū* ("Minamoto no Raikō kills Kidōmaru") (Reider, *Japanese Demon Lore* 73). Kintoki has often been considered an imaginary figure. But it turned out that there was a historical figure for Kintoki's model; he is Raikō's contemporary. His family name was not Sakata but Shimotsuke, that is, Shimotsuke no Kintoki (?–1017), a famous *Konoe toneri* (Attendant of the Left and Right Imperial Guards) (*Oyamachō-shi* 182). Kintoki's father, Shimotsuke no Kintomo (?–?), is also Konoe (*Oyamachō-shi* 204). Like Raikō and Hōshō, Kintoki served Fujiwara no Michinaga (966–1027).

Regarding the *Konoe toneri*, Helen Craig McCullough writes:

> In the eleventh century they enhanced the magnificence of state proces-
> sions, doubled as court-appointed Escorts for senior nobles, and partici-
> pated in archery contests and similar ceremonies, both at Court and at the
> private residences of great men, but their most important function was
> the provision of music and dancing at *kagura* performances. The *Shōgen*
> [lieutenants] and lower posts often went to professional and semiprofes-
> sional performers, and there is much evidence to indicate that at all lev-
> els the Bodyguards contained exceptionally skilled dancers and singers.
> (McCullough, *A Tale of Flowering Fortunes* 2: 814; see also Wada and Tokoro
> 136; Murasaki, *NKBT* 15: 210; *SNKBZ* 21: 421)

Toneri were expected to be remarkably skilled at music and dancing. Kintoki must have excelled at dancing and singing. In *Zoku honchō ōjōden*, Ōe no Masafusa (1041–1111) lists Kintoki—Shimotsuke no Kintoki—and Owari no Kanetoki (?–?) among peerless *Konoe* during Emperor Ichijō's reign (Hanawa, *Gunsho ruijū* 5: 412).[33] According to *Shimotsuke shi keizu* (Genealogy of the Shimotsuke Clan), Owari no Kanetoki was Kintoki's maternal grandfather. Kanetoki was an excellent dancer and horse rider—he was a dance teacher for Fujiwara no Norimichi (995–1065) and Fujiwara no Yoshinobu (996–1075), Michigana's sons (*Oyamachō-shi* 205; Fujiwara, *Midō kanpakuki zen chūshaku Kankō yonen* 37). Shimotsuke no Kintoki seemed to have a good reputation for his singing and dancing skills. On the entry for the sixteenth day of the ninth month of the second year of Chōwa (1013), Fujiwara no Sanesuke (957–1046) wrote in his diary, *Shōyūki*, that Kintoki served as a dancer after winning a horserace (Fujiwara no Sanesuke, *Shōyūki* 1: 356). That is why, in the Suntory version of Shuten Dōji, Kintoki is described as "a renowned dancer in the capital" whose voice and dancing captivated Shuten Dōji to the point that he paid no attention to the song's intent of killing oni.

Shimotsuke no Kintoki was also good at horse riding. On the thirteenth day of the ninth month of the same year, that is, in 1013, when Fujiwara no Michinaga privately held a horserace at his residence, Kintoki won the race (Fujiwara no Sanesuke, *Shōyūki* 1: 352–53). This must have been a famous topic in those days because Fujiwara no Tadazane (1078–1162) talked about this matter (and it was written down by Nakahara no Moromoto [1109–75] in *Chūgaishō* [Selection from What Tadazane Said, twelfth century] *Chūgaishō* 352–53). Similarly, Minamoto no Akikane (1160–1215) recounts this story in *Kojidan* (Tales of Olden Times, ca. 1212–15) (Minamoto, *Kojidan* 585).

On the first year of Kannin (1017), Fujiwara no Michinaga wrote in his diary that he learned of the death of Kintoki, a recruiter for sumo wrestlers, on the twenty-fourth day of the eighth month. As an annual court function, a sumo match was performed in the seventh month in the presence of the emperor, and it was one of the low-ranking *Konoes*' jobs to recruit sumo wrestlers in various provinces for this court event (Wada and Tokoro 198). Michinaga notes, "That man is my Escort, the best among the Left and Right Imperial Guards (*Konoe*), he is terribly missed by everyone" (Fujiwara, *Midō kanpakuki zen chūshaku Kannin gannen* 156). Kintoki's untimely death, missed by everyone as Michinaga put it, may have paved the way for the legendary figure of Kintoki.

While Kintoki was a contemporary of Raikō and Hōshō, working for Michinaga, there is no record or evidence that he was Raikō's subject.

So why is he known as Sakata no Kintoki? When one goes back to the original text of "Yorimitsu's Retainers Go Sightseeing at Murasakino" of *Konjaku monogatarishū*, where Raikō's three retainers are introduced, while

Sadamichi and Suetake are given their surnames, the part where Kintoki's surname is supposed to be written is missing. It is described as "Taira no Sadamichi, Taira no Suetake, and [. . .] Kintoki." The annotation to this lacuna in the various texts, however, states "this is Sakata no Kintoki."[34] Similarly, when one looks at "Minamoto no Raikō Kills Kidōmaru" of *Kokon chomonjū*, where Tsuna's name appears for the first time, Kintoki's name is written simply as Kintoki without a surname. The surname Sakata does not appear anywhere. But again his name is annotated in a headnote as Sakata no Kintoki (see Nishio and Kobayashi 410).

Torii Fumiko, the author of the book *Kintarō no tanjō* (Birth of Kintarō, 2002), writes that Kintoki's birth, life, and other information are not precisely known because no record of his birth and biography remains. His surname, Sakata, started to be used during the Edo period, and no one knows how he acquired it (Torii 7). Torii writes that the surname Sakata appears for the first time in the literature with *Genji no yurai* (Origin of the Genji clan, 1659), a *jōruri* (puppet theater) text; Kintoki is introduced as Sakata no Minbu Kintoki (Torii 26). *Zen-Taiheiki* (Chronicle of Pre-Grand Pacification, 1692?), a popular historical narrative widely read throughout the Edo period, describes Kintoki as Sakata no Kintoki (Itagaki 1: 328), and Chikamatsu Monzaemon's (1653–1725) popular play *Komochi Yamauba* (Mountain Ogress with a Child, first performed in 1712) also has Sakata no Kintoki.[35]

Kintoki must have been known as Shimotsuke no Kintoki during the medieval period. But because of the influence of Edo literature and performances, Kintoki in earlier works from *Konjaku monogatarishū* through *Shuten Dōji* is retrospectively called Sakata no Kintoki by modern audiences.

Taira no Sadamichi (Usui no Sadamitsu)

At the beginning of the twelfth century, when *Konjaku monogatarishū* was compiled, Taira no Sadamichi (Tadamichi, or Sadamitsu, also known as Usui no Sadamitsu) was probably the leader of Raikō's retainers because the aforementioned episode "Yorimitsu's Retainers Go Sightseeing at Murasakino" lists Taira no Sadamichi first, followed by Taira no Suetake, then [. . .] Kintoki. But as time passed, Sadamichi's position was replaced by Tsuna.

Sadamichi also appears in another story in *Konjaku monogatarishū* titled "Yorinobu no koto ni yorite Taira no Sadamichi hito no kashira o kiru koto" (Told by Yorinobu, Sadamichi Beheaded a Man).[36] In the story Yorinobu, Raikō's younger brother, publicly orders Sadamichi to get some insolent man's head for him. Sadamichi thinks the request is odd because he is serving

Raikō, not his brother, and it is unusual to hear such a personal request in public. Sadamichi is not going to pursue the matter, but the rude person boasts that Sadamichi is not strong enough to kill him. Angered, Sadamichi ends up killing him, realizing Yorinobu's wish. The narrator's major intent was perhaps to describe Sadamichi's swordsmanship and Yorinobu's boldness. But it is interesting to have Sadamichi specifically say he is Raikō's retainer while at the same time have him do a service for Raikō's brother, even though unintentionally.

Sadamichi was allegedly a son of Taira no Yoshifumi (mid-Heian period, ?–?). According to the *Sonpi bunmyaku*, Taira no Yoshifumi was a son of Takamochi-ō, or Taira no Takamochi (?–?), a founder of the Kanmu Heishi clan. Yoshifumi's final official rank was junior fifth rank, upper grade. The annotation to his name states he is also known as Muraoka no Gorō (Tōin 4: 12), and *Nichūreki* (Combination of Two History Books, early thirteenth century) lists Muraoka no Gorō under *musha* (warriors) (*Nichūreki* 3: 107). Recent scholarly studies indicate that Taira no Sadamichi was an ancestor of the Miura clan, a powerful military clique of the eastern province that was loyal to Minamoto no Yoritomo. While Yoshifumi was called Muraoka no Gorō, Sadamichi seemed to have been called Muraoka no Kogorō (Muraoka Gorō minor) or simply also Muraoka no Gorō (Noguchi 19).

Yoshifumi may have been an influential warrior in the east province. Number 3 of volume 25 of *Konjaku monogatarishū* tells a story of his duel with Minamoto no Mitsuru. Titled "Minamoto no Mitsuru to Taira no Yoshifumi no Kassen seru koto" (Minamoto no Mitsuru and Taira no Yoshifumi: The Duel),[37] the tale describes the like-mindedness of two great warriors, their recognition of each other's excellent archery skills, and how they fostered their friendship. Minamoto no Mitsuru was considered to have been Watanabe no Tsuna's father and Taira no Yoshifumi was Sadamichi's father; they were in the same generation, and according to *setsuwa*, both sons became Raikō's *shitennō*. It is ironic that Sadamichi, written as Raikō's retainer in a number of places in Heian literature and originally the first among Raikō's outstanding retainers, ceded his leading position to Tsuna, whose name does not appear in any Heian literature.

There is a famous *setsuwa* story of Sadamichi, nicknamed Muraoka no Gorō (Noguchi 19), in *Konjaku monogatarishū* titled "Hakamadare, Sekiyama ni shite sorajini o shite hito o korosu koto" (Hakamadare, Pretending to Be Dead, Kills People at Mt. Osaka).[38] In the story, Hakamadare (?–?) was pretending to be dead on Mt. Ōsaka in his attempt to kill and rob samurai of their belongings. When a fine-looking warrior accompanied by many of his retainers saw Hakamadare, the warrior warned his men to be cautious in passing by the man who appeared to be dead. Onlookers thought the war-rior's behavior unworthy of samurai, as the man was apparently dead. Later, another warrior came near Hakamadare and pitied him, believing he was dead, whereupon Hakamadare immediately killed the warrior and robbed him of his clothes and armor. People later learned the warrior who was cau-tious about Hakamadare was Muraoka no Gorō, officially named Taira no Sadamichi, and they admired his alert behavior.

This Hakamadare is the notorious robber who tried to rob Fujiwara no Hōshō and failed to do so. Hōshō in that episode instead gave Hakamadare some clothes and advised him not to steal, as he could get in trouble. Various characters in the Shuten Dōji story appear in earlier *setsuwa*; the scribes of the Shuten Dōji stories used these *setsuwa* well.

Taira no Suetake (Urabe no Suetake)

Taira no Suetake (also known as Urabe no Suetake, 950?–1022?) is also allegedly a descendant of the Kanmu Heishi clan, though it is not certain—his name does not appear in the *Sonpi bunmyaku*.

While Raikō and the rest of his *shitennō* were engaged in varying degrees with the supernatural in the world of *setsuwa* from the fourteenth century on, Suetake had already encountered a female ghost in the early twelfth century, *Konjaku monogatarishū*. The forty-third story of volume 27, titled "Yorimitsu no rōtō Taira no Suetake ubume ni au koto" (Taira no Suetake, Raikō's Retainer, Meets an *ubume*, SNKBZ 38: 134–38), describes a test of courage in which Suetake dares to meet an *ubume*, the ghost of a pregnant woman or a woman who died in childbirth. While Raikō is governor of Mino Province, his retainers gather at night talking about an *ubume* who appears at a river; the *ubume* tries to give her baby to anyone crossing the river. She is so frightening that no one can cross the river at night. Suetake then says that he can easily do it. The warriors wage their armor on Suetake not being able to make the crossing. Suetake leaves, and, as expected, an *ubume* appears while he is crossing the river. She hands him her baby. Suetake receives it, and now she wants the baby back. But Suetake ignores her plea and comes back to the gathering place with what he thinks is a baby. The baby turns out to be some leaves. The warriors are going to give their armor to Suetake, who declines it by saying the task was simple. The story ends with praise for Suetake for his bravery as well as his bigheartedness.

Again, there is no record that Suetake was serving Raikō, but he is cer-tainly described as worthy of his *shitennō*—brave, generous, and undaunted by ghastly supernatural creatures.

EXTRA-LITERARY SOURCES: RELATION BETWEEN
THE NARRATIVE AND HISTORICAL EVENTS

In the picture scrolls of *Ōeyama ekotoba*, Shuten Dōji makes an interesting statement that no other extant texts have: "When the king is wise, our power thrives too. The reason is that when the imperial authority declines, the power of his subjects also wanes; when divine protections become enfeebled, the land decays." At a glance, this statement may sound odd because when the imperial authority declines and divine protections are enfeebled, it seems logical that evil would take advantage of the situation and overwhelm the feeble forces. Shuten Dōji in this scroll brings calamities. According to the Buddhist scripture *Konkō myōkyō* (Golden Light Sutra), one of the three sutras for protecting the country, when the king does not rule with correct law and lets evil go unharmed, the deities will abandon the king and natural disasters such as famine and pandemics will occur (Mibu 267–76).[39] Similarly, according to the Chinese concept of the Mandate of Heaven, calamities are considered signs of the ruling emperor's unjustness and can be legitimate reasons for the ruler to be replaced. The Japanese emperors were well aware of the Mandate of Heaven, though they were exempt from such a concept because the lineage of the imperial family was what counted. Perhaps Shuten Dōji's logic is like that of a good competitor drawing strength from a worthy opponent. As Ii Haruki writes, his statement expresses admiration for the prosperity of Emperor Ichijō's court (Ii 86).

Emperor Ichijō's period was one of the ideal times for the nobility. Various medieval women's instructional texts such as the *jokunsho* "Menoto no sōshi" consider Empress Shōshi or Jōtōmon-in (988–1074) to be the exemplar of court ladies (Hanawa, *Gunsho ruijū* 27: 240). She was Emperor Ichijō's empress, the mother of Emperors GoIchijō (1008–36) and GoSuzaku (1009–45), and Fujiwara no Michinaga's daughter. Empress Shōshi's time was at the peak of the Fujiwara Regency, politically and economically the height of aristocratic power. Shuten Dōji's statement therefore constitutes a narrator's admiration for Emperor Ichijō rather than a defense of the Ichijō court. This narrator or narrators represent established noblemen and aspiring aristocrats. The narrator(s) may also be saluting the contemporary imperial court that wishes to exercise strong imperial authority. This could also be a reflection of the contemporary court's desire for managing political affairs directly—possibly during the time of the Southern and Northern Courts (1336–92), simultaneously hailing Raikō as an imperial subject.

While acknowledging that the *Ōeyama ekotoba* is a fictional story, Ii surmises that there must have been some frightening events and occurrences during the Shōryaku era (990–94), as the narrator specifically notes the dates (Ii 85). The text reads "From the early days of [. . .] through the Shōryaku era (990–995)." I surmise that the lacuna indicated by the square brackets is Eiso (989–90), the time immediately preceding the Shōryaku era, because disastrous events such as the disappearance of many people could not have been left unattended without taking swift measures. When one looks at the events of Eiso in *Nihon kiryaku*, in the eighth month of the first year of Eiso (989) a devastating typhoon caused a flood, killing people and animals and destroying paddy fields in the coastal areas of the provinces in the vicinity of the capital. *Nihon kiryaku* describes it as "unprecedented deaths and damages, devastating disaster" (2: 167). The event was so devastating that "Typhoon of Eiso" was used later as a simile for natural disasters.

In the eighth month of 990, the first year of the Shōryaku era, there were natural disasters, including typhoons and floods (Kuroita, *Nihon kiryaku* 2: 169). In 991, the second year of Shōryaku, there was famine in the sixth month (ibid. 171). In the sixth month of the third year of Shōryaku (992), thunder and lightning, earthquakes, and floods occurred (ibid. 173). In the sixth and seven months of 993, diseases spread widely, and thunder and lightning struck; in the eighth month there was a solar eclipse (ibid. 175–76). In the fifth year of Shōryaku (994), an epidemic wiped out more than half of Kyoto's population, including sixty-seven courtiers with the fifth rank and above, between the fourth and seventh months. In the twelfth month there was another solar eclipse (ibid. 178).

The Shōryaku era is followed by the Chōtoku era (995–99). In the first year of Chōtoku (995), a widespread epidemic that had started in the last year of Shōryaku killed Fujiwara no Michitaka (953–95), the chief adviser to the emperor, and his younger brother, Michikane (961–95). The atmosphere of the court became tense, primarily because of the power struggle between Fujiwara no Michinaga (Michitaka and Michikane's younger brother) and Fujiwara no Korechika, Michitaka's eldest son and Michinaga's nephew, for the chief adviser position. The conflict ended with Michinaga's victory. It is intriguing to postulate that there is some relationship between the backdrop of the story and historical events that led to Michinaga's prosperity. In the story, it is Michinaga who recommended that the emperor reward Raikō and Hōshō generously after the successful mission, as he did in history.

TRANSLATION OF *ŌEYAMA EKOTOBA*

This translation is based on *Muromachi jidai monogatari taisei* (Complete Works on Monogatari in the Muromachi Period; Yokoyama and Matsumoto 3:

122–40) and *Zoku Nihon emaki taisei* (Complete Works on the Picture Scrolls, Continued; Komatsu et al. 19: 75–103, 158–60, 171–78). *Muromachi jidai monogatari taisei* is the most standard work for *otogizōshi*[40] written texts, with the sections reorganized to be read as a coherent story. The missing opening section of the first scroll is supplemented by the Yōmei library edition printed in *Zoku Nihon emaki taisei*. The section from right after the end of the second scroll until the end of the story was supplemented by a scroll without illustration, perhaps copied in the mid-Muromachi period. *Zoku Nihon emaki taisei* provides full illustrations.

The Picture Scrolls of Mt. Ōe (Drunken Demon)
SCROLL ONE

When the emperor rules his country benevolently, Buddhas and Shinto deities protect his people, responding kindly to their wishes. When the emperor prays for the world in good faith, stars rejoice and shine their benevolent light on his reign. However, even in ancient times when the supernatural and emperors were honest and humble, evil demons and goblins stalked the land [. . .].[41] Even in the ancient times of the well-governed Three Dynasties and Two Hans[42] [. . .], it was easy to disobey [. . .].

In this country Emperor Jinmu[43] had great success in opening the land. More than 1,640 years had come and gone since Jinmu ruled the land when [Emperor Ichijō (reigned 986–1011)], the sixty-sixth emperor to guide his people, ascended the throne at age seven. He was already deeply engaged in poetry and writing at age nine. Early on he administered the state's affairs as earnestly and diligently as he studied literature. Emperor Ichijō was equally well versed in one hundred schools of profound thought. Later in life, he melted delusory thought into the ultimate truth, deeply respecting three treasures of Buddhism.[44] During his twenty-six-year reign, his gracious rule benefited his people; any unreasonable minds were straightened. The whole world looked upon him as a sacred beast personified. His virtues filled the country. [Emperor Sanjō (reigned 1011–16)] succeeded [Emperor Ichijō], and governing the state affairs again [. . .] whole world. The wise administration by the two emperors [. . .] like autumn dew, and their favors resembled [. . .].

As the prince of Emperor[45] [Enyū (969–91)], [Emperor Ichijō] ascended to the throne after [Emperor Kazan (968–1006)], and all the people rejoiced. At this time both exoteric and esoteric Buddhist sects revealed their signs, schools of various literary and martial arts competed in their skills, and medical and arithmetic studies advanced in their achievements. The fame of yin-yang masters' rendering their skills and services was unprecedented. Everyone, from lords and generals to simple men and women, was imbued with benevolence and received the favors of the natural and supernatural worlds. This was because four great wise men, Tadanobu,[46] Kintō,[47] Yukinari,[48] and Toshikata,[49] and all the officials of the empire performed their duties [in a devout and benevolent way].

However, when a mortar [. . .] many, even though there were ten of holy Emperor Shun and nine of virtuous Emperor Yao[50] [. . .], harmful evils gathered [. . .] guardian deities, and their wisdom could not completely protect the land.

From the early days of [Eiso (899–990)] through the Shōryaku era (990–95),[51] people of high and low estate, men and women inside and outside the capital, began mysteriously to disappear. Courtiers of the palace and rustic peasants of the countryside alike pined and grieved for their lost parents or siblings; people far and wide keened sadly for their lost wives, husbands, children, or [other] kin. In and around the city of Kyoto tears of sorrow flowed without end, and in every village the ceaseless sound of sobbing and weeping filled the air. Strange happenings occurred; tempests raged on in all their fury as thunder roared and lightning struck. Young courtiers on night duty, proper people's wives, princesses, and girl attendants in the service of court ladies continued to disappear. Those left behind felt all the more bitter, mourned, and feared to go out [. . .] for a long while. The emperor's ministers knew there could be no mortal cause to these events, that it must be the work of some demons.[52] The various and sundry Shinto shrines and Buddhist temples in and around the capital were ordered to [. . .], but it was hard for the high priests to reveal their [. . .]. The protection of miraculous Buddhas and Shinto deities was of no avail. It reminds us of the words of ancient times—"even in the most idle societies, seedlings are cut; even in the most well-administered society,[53] deer fight."

At this time there lived a great yin-yang master named Abe no Seimei.[54] When Seimei performed divination, his results were so exact it was as though he could see through a cataclysm. So the emperor's ministers immediately summoned Abe no Seimei to the capital so he might divine the cause of all the strange happenings. After much deliberation, Seimei reported, "These bizarre disappearances are surely the work of the demon king living on Mt. Ōe, northwest of the capital. If you fail to act soon, there won't be a living soul left in the palace or any province of the empire. The emperor is requested to be very careful as well, though his majesty has been hard at work, without rest, to restrain these evil doings. It is hard to enquire [. . .]." Hearing the report, beginning with the [. . .] in the palace, ministers [. . .], they were all overwhelmed with grief. Within [. . .] sorrow prevailed and became an outcry of [. . .]. The eight ministries of government and their various offices took great caution, surrounding [. . .] before the gods' authority. Great generals took matters in hand and stationed their armies to the north and south to repel the demons' wrath and to ease people's grief.

Court nobles and ministers gathered often to discuss the matter and after much discussion the [minister of] right proposed, "Our court has set the ways of the literary and martial arts; with literary art we administer state affairs, with martial art we subjugate rebellions in the provinces. Therefore, I suggest we immediately summon the warriors Chirai,[55] Raishin,[56] Ikō,[57] and Hōshō[58] and send them to conquer the demons."

The four warriors were thus summoned and given their instructions. But each warrior said, in turn, "Indeed it is true that the very purpose of bows and arrows is to subjugate imperial enemies. There is no reason to decline your command; one should always be devoted to loyalty and use his knowledge and skill to achieve the emperor's will. But these are demons, invisible and inaudible. Let us humbly say that it is beyond the reach of human hands and human weapons to engage them in battle."

Thereupon Lord Sanemi of Kan'in,[59] major captain of the left who at that time was middle counselor, said, "Even though they are shape-shifters, they live in the imperial land; how can they disobey the emperor's wish? We must send for Minamoto no Raikō (948–1021), governor of Settsu Province,[60] and Fujiwara no Hōshō (958–1036), governor of Tango Province."[61] Thus the nobles and ministers summoned the two great generals to the imperial palace, told them of this most alarming matter, and commanded the generals to subdue the evil creatures with their military prowess. The warriors left the palace with all due respect and no demur. Mist and smoke do not favor east or west but follow instead the direction of the prevailing wind; this is a virtue of submissiveness. Subjects may live near or far, but upon receiving an order, they run immediately to their lord; this is loyalty. Both generals returned to their homes, thinking it impossible to disobey the imperial order.

Raikō and Hōshō had wives and mistresses who were reluctant to be separated. Children and grandchildren were [. . .] each other. As they could only rely on the protection and the [. . .], patronage of their guardian deities at their shrines and temples, Raikō went to pray earnestly at Hachiman Shrine[62] and Hiyoshi Sannō Shrine;[63] Hōshō repeatedly prayed at Kumano Shrine[64] and Sumiyoshi Shrine.[65] They offered horses, various treasures, and prayer strips to the Shinto priests and stewards, as they wished to reunite with their loved ones after subjugating the enemy.

When the court heard that Raikō and Hōshō had already departed for the destination, they sent tens of thousands of warriors from neighboring provinces to aid the generals in their quest. Raikō, however, said, "Such a great number of warriors matters little in the face of such an enemy. Besides, I feel pity for their wives and children. When the imperial authority is effective, the imperial order should be strictly observed." So saying, the generals stopped the warriors from coming to their aid, and each warrior shed tears of joy and remained where he was.

Raikō [. . .] had four loyal retainers who pledged to live or die together, Tsuna, Kintoki, Sadamitsu, and Suetake [. . .]; with the lord and his four lieutenants, there were five horsemen. Hōshō's lone retainer was a junior secretary of the Dazaifu office.[66] [. . .] had visited the palace wearing *hitatare*[67] ceremonial clothes over which they put on armors of various colors, and they received a written proclamation from the emperor charging Raikō and Hōshō with the task of defeating the evil demons. [Raikō] wore the [. . .]-colored brocade robe with [. . .] threads and had [. . .] helmet. He placed a quiver containing twenty-four long, black [. . .] arrows on his back, used his famous rattan-wrapped bow as a staff, and wore a three-foot-five-inch sword decorated with gold. Hōshō wore a red brocade robe over which was a suit of armor with dark purple lacing. He carried a helmet with a hoe-shaped crest, carried a quiver of sharp arrows, and, like Raikō, used a rattan-wrapped bow as his walking staff. Carrying a sword with a hilt wrapped with white metal sheet in a sheath of tiger skin, Hōshō was a towering figure in the courtyard. Such was the loyalty people bore for the great warriors that the rest of their subjects felt impatient to accompany their generals, but again Raikō and Hōshō took pity on their subjects' wives and children and commanded them to stay; thus their subjects reluctantly remained and accompanied their lords no farther than the capital. From the nobles [. . .] in the palace to folks ranked high and low in the capital, people swarmed to see the expedition depart. Finally, the troupe left the capital on the first day of the eleventh month of the first year of [. . .] and set forth for Mt. Ōe where the king of [demons] was said to live.

After spending many days and nights in search of the demons of Mt. Ōe, going through peaks and valleys, rivers and clouds, mountains and gorges and mists, they still found nothing strange or mysterious. Pondering their long and fruitless search, Raikō said, "Without conquering the imperial enemy, we cannot return home," and Hōshō agreed. The warriors, being one in body and soul, continued to look for the enemy everywhere, walking sideways on narrow paths against rock cliffs, bowing their heads low under drooping branches. Thus, various and sundry places of trial and hardship faded behind them in the mist. [. . .] could be compared to a storm. The sky looked sooty and the landscape appeared somewhat [. . .]. There were dark clouds over the peaks, [. . .] looked light on the trees. Flying birds rarely chirped [. . .] in the clouds, and there was no sound other than [. . .] monkeys on the trees crying at the moon.

At last, they came to a place on Mt. Ōe that looked out over a small shrine in the mountain; it was then, as they gazed on the shrine, that their eyes beheld a strange thing. In the distance they saw four men: a white-haired old man, an elderly mountain ascetic, an old priest, and a young priest. Each appeared to have prepared food and drink on a Chinese chest and seemed to be waiting for someone. The warriors suspected that these strange men must indeed be shape-shifters, and they proceeded in the strangers' direction, unsheathing their swords and drawing their bows. As the warriors bore down on the strangers, the white-haired old man stepped forward, taking off his clothes to show he was unarmed and pressing his hands in prayer. Loudly he cried out to the warriors, "Pray let down your weapons and ease your suspicions, for we have awaited your coming many days. We have good reason for that. I have seven children but the demon king took them all from me. Yonder mountain ascetic has had many of his fellow ascetics taken as well, and this young priest has lost his master and disciples. Please think kindly on our grievances. We have heard that the two great generals have received the imperial command to seek the demon's castle, so we are delighted to accompany and lead you to your destination."

Raikō said to his warriors, "Although all they are saying speaks to their honesty, we must not let down our guard entirely. However, since we bear the written order of the emperor around our necks, no harm may befall us." The warriors sheathed their swords, relaxed their bows, and sat down together to the feast the odd strangers had prepared. As they discussed how best to look for the demons, the white-haired old man spoke again: "Your martial accoutrements won't do. Even with your own brothers, it will be hard for warriors so armed to receive a meeting. You must disguise your-selves as you seek the enemy." He then took from the Chinese chest items to accomplish the warriors' disguise, like rust-colored robes, monks' stoles, and round caps [*tokin*] of the same color. He produced as well nine ascetics' panniers in which to conceal the warriors' armor. Food and drink he gave as well. Nine people, [. . .] ascetic, elderly priest, young priest, Tsuna, Kintoki, [. . .], the warriors each carried a pannier on their back. The white-haired old man and Raikō both carried stout cypress staffs to guide their steps. Their horses were returned to their home by the servants.

Figure 1.1. Raikō's troupe meets the elders in the mountain. Courtesy of the Hankyu Culture Foundation, Itsuō Art Museum.

[As they sought the lair of the demon king, they came upon an ancient woman.] Her hair was all white, not a string of black. She was washing clothes stained with blood and drying them on tree branches and rocks. Looking at this site, the troupe thought she was a shape-shifter, but no sooner were they prepared to kill her than she pressed her hands together in prayer and begged for mercy. "I am no shape-shifter," she cried, "I was originally a lowly woman from Uta.[68] The demon king kidnapped me here, but because my bones are hard, my body sinewy, and my face ugly, I was abandoned and made to wash these clothes. I miss my hometown and family, but springs have gone and autumns passed; indeed, 200 wretched years have gone. Still, how did you come here?" she asked. "You should immediately return home. This is a place far away from human habitation. How interesting to see people, especially those in their prime."

"This mountain is the back of Mt. Ōe. What do you mean by 'far from human habitation?'" Raikō inquired. The old woman replied, "There is a rock cave on the way here. This side of the cave is a demon-hidden village."

"Tell us more about it. We are here by imperial command," said Hōshō.

"I will tell you all I know," replied the old woman. "The demon king's castle is up yonder from us. There is an eight-pillar gate; a framed board that says Shuten Dōji is hung over it, or so I hear. Often the demon king assumes a child-like appearance, and he loves *saké*. He abducts princesses and the wives of nobles and courtiers in the palace, high and low alike; he chops them with a knife and eats them. Now, because a man called Seimei in the capital worships *taizanfukun*,[69] serving gods[70] and divine boys[71] constantly surround the countryside to protect the emperor's people, so when the demon king comes back without human beings to eat, he gets fiercely upset, beats his chest, and clenches his teeth. He plays the flute idly and passes the time.

"There is a strange thing," the old crone continued. "The demon king took a very young disciple of Tendai Abbot Ryōgen (912–85),[72] a son of the priest of the Enshrinement Hall (Fujiwara no Michinaga [966–1027]),[73] and confined him in a cage made of iron and stone. This child does nothing but pray. His voice reciting Lotus Sutra can be heard here at dawn. I am receiving evil retributions like this while I am alive. I grieve over my sins. But when I hear his prayers, I feel like my sins are being extinguished. So I am most appreciative. Also, perhaps because Ryōgen himself performs services for the boy, various heavenly beings and benevolent deities gather like rain and clouds to protect him from early morning till late at night. The demon king knows not what to do with the boy."

Following the words of the old woman, they walked up the hill a little distance, and there indeed was a big gate with eight pillars. The pillars and doors were beautiful and admirably shining. The mountains in all directions looked like lapis lazuli, and the grounds were as if crystal sand were strewed all about. When they looked at the scenery carefully, deep frost grew in a stone hut as if one came to Kashō's[74] cave; small paths had light snow on them, as if one looked out on a confession yard.

Raikō summoned his retainer Tsuna and told him to enter the gate to seek an audience with the master of the house. Whereupon Tsuna, feeling like Hankai,[75] passed the gate alone. Reaching the place that looked like the main residence, Tsuna loudly announced, "Excuse me. Is anyone there?"

From within there came a grave voice, "Who is this?" and a man about ten feet tall appeared. Raising a bamboo blind with his hand holding a flute, Shuten Dōji had a human form, adorned in a quilted silk garment with a crimson *hakama*. There he stood looking serious and noble, with his sharp eyes.

Not a bit daunted, Tsuna replied, "We, more than ten of us, are mountain ascetics training through various provinces, but we have become lost and wandered here. Please give us lodging for the night."

"In that case," Shuten Dōji replied, "enter the veranda near the main gate," and he sent a maiden to guide the troupe.

The maiden, walking before Tsuna, pressed her face to her sleeve to wipe her tears. Tsuna asked why she was crying so bitterly. The young lady replied, "As I see it, you are an ascetic priest. After you come here you will not be able to go back to your hometown, and I am so sad and sorry for you. I am the third daughter of Lord Munenari, palace minister of Tsuchimikado. One night last autumn while I was viewing the moon, the demon took me away and brought me here. I am in such a miserable state. Shuten Dōji eats anyone whom he dislikes on the spot, calling them his snack. It's such a misery even to see him. I feel like a bird on snowy mountains, as I always worry that today will be my last. How terrible." Listening to her, Tsuna thought it a grave matter. But he pretended that it was not so serious and led his comrades onto the veranda.

After a short while, beautiful young ladies came onto the veranda with ten round straw mats for the troupe to sit on. They also brought *saké* in a large silver decanter and a golden bowl filled with unidentifiable meat. This encounter was perhaps comparable to that of Chōbunsei (Zhang Wencheng) in China, who met playful goddesses in an enchanted cave.

Raikō, in harmony with Hōshō, said compliantly, "It would be wonderful if the host could attend. Only we ourselves would be boring. Would you please ask for his presence?" After a while, Shuten Dōji came into the room. Ten feet tall and looking wise with his sharp eyes, he was adorned in clothing of various colors with a glossy silk garment over his upper body and a white *hakama*. Having made four or five beautiful maidens carry round straw mats or an armrest, he made the whole surrounding look radiant and solemn.

"Mountain priests," Shuten Dōji asked of Raikō, "where did you come from and where are you going?"

"We have been traveling in various provinces for training and sightseeing," replied Raikō, "but we lost our way in the mountains and arrived here."

Shuten Dōji then turned the conversation to himself. "I love *saké*, so my relatives and fellow men call me Drunken Demon," he said. "I lived on Mt. Hirano a long time ago because it had long been my property. But a strange priest named Saichō[76] took the mountain to build a temple on the peak and seven shrines at the foot. Because it had long been my place and I was reluctant to part with it, and to be honest I had nowhere else to live, I transformed myself into a camphor tree and tried to obstruct his project. But the priest cut down the tree, leveled the ground, and opened the area. So I changed myself into a bigger tree that night. But then the priest thought it strange and put a magical barrier over the area, chanting, "*Anokutara sanmyaku sanbodai no hotoketachi waga tatsu soma ni myōga arase tamae*" (I pray, the omniscient Buddhas, bless me and the temple I am about to build)."[77] I could hardly restrain myself, but as I was overpowered I revealed myself to the priest. 'Then please give a place to live,' I said. He gave me Mt. Kaga of Ōmi Province, since it was his property. So I moved to the new mountain.

"Then, Emperor Kanmu (737–806) sent an imperial envoy and had him read an imperial proclamation to leave the place. As I was living on sovereign land, it was hard not to obey the imperial command; besides, heavenly beings came to expel me. Powerless, I had to leave Mt. Kaga and had nowhere to go. Annoyed, I wandered around riding on wind and clouds for a long while. But sometimes, when I felt a grudge and an evil thought, I comforted myself by bringing disaster to the land of Japan, sometimes as a storm, sometimes as famine.

"During the reign of Emperor Ninmyō (reigned 833–50), around 849 perhaps," Dōji continued. "I started to live here. When the king is wise, our power thrives too. The reason is that when the imperial authority declines, the power of his subjects also wanes; when divine protections become enfeebled, the land decays. Under the reign of an ignorant one, my mind is of no use; during the reign of a wise king, I gain my supernatural power. I'll tell you more of my past. But first, have a cup of wine." So saying, he offered *saké*.

"You are the dōji," Raikō replied. "How can I have a cup before you? Please allow me to offer you one first."

"Your courteous words please me," Shuten Dōji smiled and drank three cups. Then, he offered one to Raikō. As Raikō raised the cup to drink it, it smelled extremely bloody and nauseating. Raikō, however, calmly drank it without so much as a disagreeable look. Raikō gave the cup to Hōshō, who pretended to drink it but discreetly threw it away. Then the old man and the mountain ascetic said, "Thank you for your *sake*. We too have prepared *sake*. If we don't take this out in front of you now, when should we do it?" So saying, they took a *sake* tube out of the pannier and offered it to Shuten Dōji. As the leader drank it up, they kept pouring it and all the participants followed. Soon the demon king lay slumped in a drunken stupor.

SCROLL TWO

[Led by the old man, Raikō and Hōshō set about the task of exploring the palace.] There, confined in room after room they found the young and old, from the cities and the countryside, to [. . .]. As the party moved on, they heard a whispering voice reciting a sutra. Wondering who it could be, they followed the sound of the chanting voice to the presence of a pure and clean-looking boy of fourteen or fifteen years old who, alongside four [. . .] maidens, was imprisoned in a copper cage. The child was wearing a silk garment with a white *hakama*. Having taken a small sutra from his charm, he was chanting tearfully. As Raikō and Hōsho looked to the left and right of this child, *Jūrasetsunyo* (Ten Female Rakshasis),[78] putting down various heavenly fruit, were guarding the boy, and so were *Jūnishinshō* (Twelve Divine Generals)[79] of Yakushi nyorai (the Healing Buddha),[80] who stood outside the bars. One monkey stood towering over the cage surrounded by roaring flames like Fudō myōō (Immovable Protector of Dharma).[81]

Looking on in amazement, Raikō asked the white-haired old man, "What is the meaning of all this?"

"Because of this child's virtue," the old man answered, "in reciting the Lotus Sutra, *Jūrasetsunyo* have descended to protect him. As for *Jūnishinshō*, this child's master performs the ritual of *shichibutsu yakushi* (the Seven Healing Buddhas),[82] so the Twelve Divine Generals, who protect and serve the Healing Buddha, descend to guard him. That very being who takes the form of yonder monkey is the deity enshrined in the Hayao Shrine[83] at Mt. Hiei. The original form of the deity is Fudō myōō, sworn protector, and a monkey is a messenger of the shrine; so both appearances are manifested as such."

Raikō thought to himself, "This old man is mysterious himself. It is true that without divine protection it would be hard to subdue the demon's heinous acts. This must be solely thanks to the benefits of the miraculous

Figure 1.2. Shuten Dōji entertains Raikō's troupe with unidentifiable meat and blood. Courtesy of the Hankyu Culture Foundation, Itsuō Art Museum.

deities we have always prayed for." Raikō was delighted and glanced secretly at Hōshō, who nodded to him in agreement. This child was the page about whom the old woman spoke—the disciple of Ryōgen and a son of Fujiwara no Michinaga, the priest of the Enshrinement Hall.

Leaving that place, they looked to the south. Near the eaves of the palace, the breeze wafted the scent of citrus *tachibana*, reminding them of the fragrance of sleeves in olden times; the underbrush of the woods grew wildly. Here and there, flowers of beloved star lilies looked on charmingly. It was then that they saw many large barrels placed in line, in which was human flesh pickled with vinegar. The smell coming from the barrels was foul, and the sight was too miserable to witness. Turning their eyes to the side, they saw mounds of carnage; moss grew on old corpses and bloodstains were on fresh dead bodies. When they look to the west, treetops were tinged with rain swishing; the color of paulownia and catalpa is red.[84] Dewdrops formed on a variety of fruit; bluebeards gave off fragrance. The sound of pine crickets was captivating. Then they saw a number of imprisoned Chinese people and realized that the demons abducted people not only from their own country but from India and China as well. It was indeed piteous.

In the direction of north, snow was heavy on the pine trees, pining for a storm;[85] autumn still lingered on the frosty chrysanthemums in the garden. It was appealing scenery.

The number of demons wasn't many, they thought. A little over ten. The rest were minor servants of various shapes, and they were numerous. Thinking it all mysterious beyond understanding, they returned to their quarters and reported their findings to their retainers.

About sunset, perhaps scheming to fool the troupe, five or six oni disguised as beautiful women adorned in multilayered ceremonial robes visited the group's quarters.

These oni, without saying much, tried to seduce them, like a heavenly maiden's love affair with Kaiō (King Huai, reign 329–299 BCE) of Sokoku (Chu guo) in ancient China.[86]

Hōshō said, "It is hard to believe that women come to the place of mountain priests. Leave immediately." But the women did not listen and remained there. Thereupon, Raikō gave the oni-women an intense glare. The demons, startled at the fierceness in Raikō's eyes, made a hasty retreat, murmuring, "This priest among them looks noble and important. His eyes are sharp and disturbing. We had better leave." Revealing their real appearances, the oni scurried off.

Shortly after that, black clouds shrouded the area and soon it became pitch black. The strong wind blew wildly, the earth was shaken, and thunder and lightning began to strike. "What's happening?" the warriors thought. While they were wondering, numerous shape-shifters, tall and horrendous-looking, emerged, dancing *dengaku* (field music and dance).

These goblins with different faces and shapes started to perform music. Some were funny, some were beautiful, and others were frightening. It was beyond description, beyond imagination. While the warriors were watching this, Raikō remained in his seat, unmoved, and stared fiercely at the shape-shifters for some time, whereupon five-colored lights began to emit from Raikō's eyes. The shape-shifters talked to themselves, "Have you seen that mountain priest? With his eyes and face, he is no ordinary person. I hear there is in the capital a man called Raikō of whom everyone is afraid. They say his eyes give out sparkles."

"Is that so? There is such a man, then. We won't be able to deceive such a person." So saying, they ran off in all directions, some stumbling over the rocks.

[. . .]

The warriors found Shuten Dōji asleep in a room strongly built of iron and stones. Four or five noblewomen were forced to massage his giant body. So strong and formidable did the room's fortifications appear that the warriors and their retainers found it impossible to enter. But then, the old and young priests made signs with their fingers underneath their stoles and earnestly prayed, "This is the time to reveal the merits of years of our training and prayers for the main Buddha. Exalted one, please do not break our vows!" Whereupon the iron and stones melted like morning dewdrops, and the sturdy-looking chamber was destroyed instantly.

Although the dōji had looked like a human being during the day, when the troupe entered the room he was revealed in his true monstrous form at night; his height was well over fifty feet, a five-colored giant; he had a red head and body, a yellow right arm, and a blue left arm. His left leg was black, and the right one was white. This oni with a five-horned head and fifteen eyes was sleeping peacefully, oblivious to the fate that awaited him. Looking at this giant, the warriors felt as though they were in a nightmare, but they calmed themselves and became anxious to attack the dōji. The young priest, however, warned that they would be uncertain of a quick victory if the warriors attacked Shuten Dōji on different places of his body with their swords. "If the dōji wakes up, it will be of great consequence indeed," the priest continued. "Therefore, we four priests will hold each of Shuten Dōji's limbs, and you the warriors must behead him in one accord."

Thus the four priests held on firmly to the Dōji's limbs; thereupon the demon king raised his head and cried, "Where is Kirinmugoku? Where is

Figure 1.3. The oni who played the *dengaku* performance run away from Raikō. Courtesy of the Hankyu Culture Foundation, Itsuō Art Museum.

Figure 1.4. Shuten Dōji's severed head lunges at Raikō. Courtesy of the Hankyu Culture Foundation, Itsuō Art Museum.

Jakengokudai?[87] Deceived by these men, I am now to be done with. Kill these enemies!" Hearing Shuten Dōji's voice, the decapitated oni rose from the ground and were running about without their heads.

No sooner had the demon cried out than the two generals and five warriors cut down Shuten Dōji's head in one combined stroke. His head hurled through the air, wildly roaring. Raikō quickly donned Tsuna's and Kintoki's helmets, putting them over his own. As people gazed on in frightened wonder, Shuten Dōji's head dashed to Raikō and bit him on his helmets.

"Gouge out his eyes!" Raikō yelled. Tsuna and Kintoki rushed to blind the dōji with their swords, and the demon king's head stopped moving. When Raikō removed his helmet and checked the other helmets, he found that Shuten Dōji's fangs had penetrated them all.

THE END OF THE SECOND SCROLL

Now, there were many still living who were abducted to this evil realm. Far from home, they missed their families while fearfully awaiting their demise in the oni's evil mouth. Trapped in a deep cave without knowing which direction was east or west, without seeing the sun or moon, the captives were comparable to flying birds without wings or fish in the water without scales. Thanks to the two generals, they now escaped from the demon king's evil lair. Their joy was more than that of a baby reunited with his mother or rice seedlings getting rain. They stumbled out with bittersweet feelings.

"If possible," the released Chinese captives asked, "please give us a blessing of neighboring friendship and allow us to return to our homeland. We wish to spread tidings of your wise emperor's majestic power and to spread word to foreign courts of the deeds these two brave generals have performed in these strange affairs." The two generals thought the request was reasonable, so they sent the Chinese to the Nine Provinces[88] and had them wait for a favorable wind at Hakata[89] of Tsukushi.[90] Thus, the Chinese were sent to the ferry landing on the Kanzaki River.[91]

Having calmed down from a state of rapture, that old woman who was washing the bloody clothes at the river was going to be on her way back home. But now that the demon king's supernatural power that had prolonged her life was gone, old age engulfed her and she laid down on the ground before leaving the mountain. The lines on her forehead were comparable to those on Ryoshō (Lu Shang), who went to the River I (Wei-shui River) to fish;[92] her hair was as white as the hair on the temples of En Shito (Yuan Situ), who left Mt. Shō (Mt. Shang) feeling cold. "Even though I return to my old town, I go without honor and triumph. It's been more than 200 years; how can I see the grandchildren seven generations after?" [she mused.] Still, she missed her hometown. She collapsed looking in the direction of the capital. The life of a mayfly is ephemeral, not waiting for evening; leaves of banana plants are fragile. The troupe felt great pity for her and pressed their sleeves onto their face.[93]

The four strangers who had joined the warriors' expedition and [. . .] return journey was without any difficulties. When they came to a certain place on Mt. Ōe, the four travelers said, "The whole event was unforgettable, and it is hard to part with you. But now it is time for us to leave. We wanted to help your grave imperial mission of subjugating the enemy, so we have accompanied you so far.

"Don't think the present emperor is an ordinary king. Since ancient times there have been many wise kings. This emperor is, though born as a king of a small country,[94] actually Miroku (Maitreya), who descended in this life and guides masses to enlightenment. His mortal appearance is an expedience to lead the masses on the path of enlightenment. Therefore, for the sake of all the officials and subjects, he prays and gives blessing on people, including guests from afar. Have no doubt of Shakyamuni Buddha's[95] precepts, and rely on the officiating priest's teachings. As for Seimei, he is an incarnation of Ryūju bosatsu (Nāgārjuna Bodhisattva), a master of *Shingon* (True Word) esoteric Buddhism. Long ago, he was manifested as Priest Hakudō,[96] and now he appears as Professor Seimei. As he attended to the secret skills of yin-yang with extreme earnestness, he appeared twice before and has now appeared in the reign of the wise king.

"Raikō, don't think lightly of yourself. Although there are four strong generals—Chirai, Raishin, Ikō, and Hōshō—Raikō is held in awe by people inside and outside the capital, high and low, more than the sum of these four generals. Raikō is a manifestation of Daiitoku (Yamantaka, the Wisdom King of Great Awe-Inspiring Power). Therefore, his subjugations of demons and bandits are superior to those of any human beings. People call Raikō's retainers *shitennō* (Four Guardian Kings)[97] for a good reason. Tsuna is Tamonten (Vaisravana, the Guardian of the North), Kintoki is Jikokuten (Dhrtarasta, the Guardian of the East), Sadamitsu is Zōchōten (Virudhaka, the Guardian of the South), and Suetake is Kōmokuten (Virupaksa, the Guardian of the West). They commiserate with the public and protect the court. Never doubt my words."

Hearing this, people—high and low—joined their hands in prayer. Indeed, people looked up to Emperor Ichijō as the authority, and Raikō was feared as a man with two lives.

Hōshō said, "The tryst of a previous life is easy to understand, and it is hard to forget, describe, or express the matters of this time. It would be such an honor if you would give me a memento for the memory of my later years and for my descendants to remember me by." The old man thought this quite reasonable, so he took off his white garment and gave it to Hōshō. Hōshō received it respectfully, and in return he offered his arrow. The mountain ascetic took off his reddish-brown robe and gave it to Hōshō, and he in turn offered his sword. The old monk said, "It is good to see the exchange of a keepsake. Lord Raikō, please come here. We shall exchange a memento." The old monk took out his crystal rosary and gave it to Raikō, who in return took off his helmet and offered it to the old monk. The young monk then gave his golden staff[98] to Raikō, who in return offered the young monk his sword.

"May I ask your names and where you live?" Raikō asked.

The old man replied, "I'm Kyūjin, Old Benevolent, and I live around Sumiyoshi," then he disappeared into thin air.

"I'm from Nachi of Mt. Kumano. My name is Unrō,[99] Clouds and Waterfall," the mountain ascetic said and likewise disappeared.

"I'm from the Hachiman area and came here because of Lord Raikō's earnest prayers," the old monk said.

The young priest followed, "I am a priest from the Enryakuji temples area," and he and the monk disappeared as well.

Thinking this matter over, the warriors thought, "Miraculous deities whom we have relied upon and prayed to for a long time have protected us because of their vows to look after the state and to benefit the masses." They were greatly appreciative and hopeful. Doesn't a revelation of divine authority result from men worshipping deities? Doesn't living to a ripe old age result from divine help? It is like an echo to a sound, the moon reflected on water. The divine response is the way of the world, but the event of this time was rare in ancient times and the future.

Thus, the original seven warriors accompanied by the demons' captives continued their journey home, and when they arrived at Ikuno at the foot of Mt. Ōe they built temporary huts. The generals sent Tadamichi[100] to the capital as a messenger to ask for horses and people to receive the released captives. As Tadamichi hurried and relayed the message to the families and relatives of the captured women and children in the capital, they were overjoyed and excited. They all shed tears of joy and rushed to Mt. Ōe with palanquins and horses. Before long they met their loved ones; some their wives, others their husbands. Some thought it was a dream. But there were those who looked for their parents or children but could not find any; their grief was beyond description. But as there was nothing they could do, they were soon on their way home.

The two generals made a triumphant return without changing their outer garments: they had their armor over the reddish-brown robe; Raikō had his round cap deep on his forehead with no helmet. Numerous people gathered to see them at the roadside, barriers, and mountain paths. The news arrived that the generals would enter the capital with the head of the demon king that day. The generals' subjects hurried to be at their side, making the generals' troop larger. The number of spectators exceeded tens of millions. It was so crowded that people had to stand on tiptoe; the carriages couldn't turn their shafts around.

"There are a number of people who were born to the military houses, trained in swordsmanship, and became famous for their valor; but it is a rare event to subjugate a demon king and oni, other than the achievement of Tamura Toshihito,"[101] people said loudly to each other.

As the evil demon was not allowed to enter the imperial compound, the emperor, retired emperor, regent, and everyone else went out in carriages to see the spectacle. What with the demon king's head and the generals'

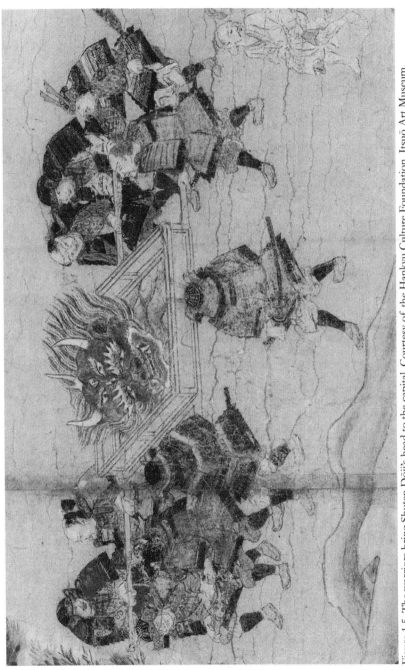

Figure 1.5. The warriors bring Shuten Dōji's head to the capital. Courtesy of the Hankyu Culture Foundation, Itsuō Art Museum.

awesome countenance, it was indeed a splendid sight. The generals made their report directly to the emperor, and it was decided by imperial decree that Shuten Dōji's head be placed in the Uji no hōzō (Treasure house of Uji).[102] Michinaga, the priest of the Enshrinement Hall and chancellor, then made a palace visit and advised the emperor, "Although there were many victories over the imperial enemies from ancient times, this is an unprecedented achievement. Rewards should be immediately given to the generals." So Hōshō, the governor of Tango, was appointed commander-in-chief to conquer Western barbarians and was given the Province of Chikuzen.[103] Raikō, the governor of Settsu, was appointed commander-in-chief to conquer Eastern barbarians and was given Mutsu Province.[104]

"As a rule, in a large country once one subjugates an imperial enemy, he is said to be awarded a half province and the prize lasts for seven generations. Our country is small to begin with, and governorship of one province is more than the prize of a half province. On top of it, the generals received an imperial proclamation to become the Eastern and Western commanders-in-chief. Those are tremendous rewards and prizes. But who is going to sustain them?" So people clamored at the court.

NOTES

1. For various theories about the origins of Shuten Dōji, see Reider, *Japanese Demon Lore* 46, 48–51.

2. For various Ibuki versions of texts, see *MJMT* 2: 357–426; *MJMT hoi* 1: 245–68, 335–59.

3. Kūkai founded Kongōbu-ji in Mt. Kōya in present-day Wakayama prefecture.

4. The Shibukawa edition is almost identical to a *tanroku-bon* (a picture booklet illustrated in green and orange), which was published during the Kan'ei era (1624–43). Matsumoto, "Otogi zōshi no honbun ni tsuite" 172. Regarding the text of the Shibukawa version, see *NKBT* 38: 361–84.

5. The writing in part of *Ōeyama ekotoba* is printed in *MJMT* 3: 122–40; both illustrations and writing are reproduced in Komatsu Shigemi, Ueno, Sakakibara, and Shimitani, *Tsuchigumo zōshi, Tengu zōshi,* and *Ōeyama ekotoba* 75–103, 158–60, 171–78.

6. Sakakibara, "*Ōeyama ekotoba* shōkai" 149–52. Also see *MJMT* 3: 122–40.

7. The remaining part of the language in *Ōeyama ekotoba* matches that of *Yōmei bunko-bon.* The *Yōmei bunko-bon* does not contain any illustrations. It is a written text only. Satake Akihiro considers that *Yōmei bunko-bon* was written by Konoe Sakihisa (1536–1612), chancellor, at the end of the Muromachi period and that it shows people were reading the *Ōeyama ekotoba* version of the story. Satake, *Shuten Dōji ibun* 142.

8. *Setsuwa,* a Japanese literary genre, broadly consists of myths, legends, folktales, and anecdotes. In the narrow sense of the term, they are "short Japanese tales that depict extraordinary events, illustrate basic Buddhist principles or, less frequently, other Asian religious and philosophical teachings, and transmit cultural and historical knowledge. These narratives were compiled from roughly the ninth through mid-fourteenth centuries in collections such

as *Konjaku monogatarishū (Tales of Times Now Past*, ca. 1120)" (Li, *Ambiguous Bodies* 1). When Haga Yaichi used the term *setsuwa* in modern times in the introduction to his *Kōshō Konjaku monogatarishū* (1913), he used it "in a general sense, to traditional stories passed down from one generation to another through many generations. This transmission can be oral or written" (Haga, *Kōshō Konjaku monogatarishū* I, quoted in Li, *Ambiguous Bodies* 19). However, *setsuwa* are now often considered to have an oral origin. *Setsuwa* are secondhand stories. They are presented as true, or at least as *possibly* true, and are short. Also see Eubanks 8–11, especially for an explanation about Buddhist *setsuwa* literature.

9. The family's strategy was to marry their daughters to emperors and have the daughters bear the next emperors. As a maternal grandfather, the Fujiwara exerted influence on the Japanese imperial court and politics.

10. Motoki also writes that Mitsunaka was nothing but a miniscule existence, as a cat's paw of those in power at the time of establishing the Fujiwara Regency government. Motoki i–ii.

11. Some information was added by Tōin family members after Kinsada's death.

12. *GoShūi wakashū*, the fourth imperial anthology of Japanese poems, includes the second-largest number of her poems. Izumi Shikibu, Hōshō's wife, has the largest number. See note 18, this chapter.

13. It is number 6 of volume 25. *SNKBZ* 37: 418–21; Sato, *Legends of the Samurai* 80–81.

14. According to *Sonpi bunmyaku*, Yorinobu's mother is Fujiwara no Hōshō's younger sister. Tōin 2: 423.

15. For the study of Yorimasa and the nue, see Oyler 1–32.

16. In "The Circular Letter" chapter of the *Heike monogatari* (Tale of the Heike), Raikō is mentioned as an excellent military man and Minamoto no Yoshinaka's ancestor; "Whether on horseback or on foot, [Yoshinaka] surely equals in every way Tamuramaro in days of old or Toshihito, Koremochi, Tomoyori, Yasumasa, or those forebears of his own, Yorimitsu or Lord Yoshiie" (Tyler, *Tale of the Heike* 322; *SNKBZ* 45: 442). Actually, Yoshinaka's forebears should be "Yorinobu or Lord Yoshiie" instead of "Yorimitsu or Lord Yoshiie." At the time of compilation of the *Tale of the Heike*, which is almost the same time as that of *Ōeyama ekotoba*, a move to exalt Raikō seems to have already been established. It is also of interest that Yasumasa or Hōshō is mentioned together with Raikō, as in the picture scrolls of *Ōeyama ekotoba*.

17. The fact that Hōshō is not as important as Raikō is known from the following: (1) When the priest reveals Raikō's *honji*, he says, "Although there are four strong generals, Chirai, Raishin, Ikō, and Hōshō, Raikō is awed by people inside and outside the capital, high and low, more than the sum of these four generals" (Yokoyama and Matsumoto 3: 137). Hōshō's *honji* is not narrated. (2) The shape-shifters disguised as ladies did not pay attention to Hōshō's words, but they feared Raikō's glare and ran off. (3) The shape-shifters performing *dengaku* ran away because of Raikō's eyes and reputation. (4) Shuten Dōji's head targeted Raikō. Raikō ordered that Dōji's eyes be taken out to put an end to him. (Hōshō was not the Dōji's target.)

18. *GoShūi wakashū* includes the largest number of her poems, followed by Lady Sagami, whose mother married Raikō. See note 12, this chapter.

19. Part of Takita Yōji's film *Onmyōji* treats the power struggle between Motokata/Sukehime and Morosuke/Anshi.

20. It is number 7 of volume 25, titled "Fujiwara no Yasumasa no ason nusubito no Hakamadare ni au koto" (Fujiwara no Yasumasa and Hakamadare: Presence of Mind). *SNKBZ* 37: 421–24; for an English translation, Sato, *Legends of the Samurai* 30–33.

21. They are the revolts led by Taira no Masakado (d. 940) and Fujiwara no Sumitomo (d. 941), which occurred separately in different locations but almost at the same time. Taira no Masakado, who had his base in eastern Japan, rebelled against the court in 939, calling himself the new emperor and controlling the major Kanto Provinces. He was killed by the imperial forces led by Taira no Sadamori and Fujiwara no Hidesato. Almost at the same time, in western Japan, Fujiwara no Sumitomo virtually controlled the Inland Sea. After Masakado was killed, the court could focus on suppressing Sumitomo's rebellion, and Sumitomo was finally suppressed in 941.

22. They are the Sword (*Kusanagi no tsurugi* or *Amenomurakumo no tsurugi*), Jewel (*Yasakani no magatama*), and Mirror (*Yata no kagami*).

23. A civil war and a conflict between the Minamoto clan (Genji) and the Taira clan (Heike) that lasted from 1180 to 1185. It ended with the fall of the Taira clan and the establishment of the Kamakura shogunate by Minamoto no Yoritomo in 1192.

24. The stories were written down by Fujiwara no Sanekane (1085–1112), who heard them from Ōe no Masafusa (1041–1111).

25. Michinaga comments, "Yorichika excels at murdering people" (Fujiwara, *Midō kanpakuki zen chūshaku Kannin gannen* 58). Incidentally, Kiyohara no Munenobu's younger sister is a famous poet and writer, Sei Shōnagon (966–1025), who served Empress Teishi (977–1001), Michinaga's daughter's rival.

26. There is a lacuna in the original text. A surname is supposed to be there.

27. This translation is mine. For an English translation of the whole story, see Sato, *Legends of the Samurai* 66–67.

28. Tsuna is also written as a newcomer in "Shibugaki" (Sour Persimmon, Never Doubt the Words of the Wise), an instructional text for warriors in the Kamakura period (1185–1333). As a newcomer to Raikō's *shitennno*, Tsuna asks Kintoki how to become mentally strong (Hanawa, Gunsho Ruijū 27: 157). The date of "Shibugaki" is unknown but is assumed to be the beginning of the fourteenth century.

29. See Nishio and Kobayashi 409–13; for an English translation, see Sato, *Legends of the Samurai* 62–64.

30. See "Kiō," *SNKBZ* 45: 291–300; Tyler, *Tale of the Heike* 211–17, 233–37, especially 235; "The Death of the Prince," *SNKBZ* 45: 322–28, especially 325–26.

31. This order seems to have been established by the time of *Kokon chomonjū* (A Collection of Ancient and Modern Tales That I've Heard, 1254). In the Kidōmaru episode of *Kokon chomonjū*, Kintoki is listed immediately after Tsuna, followed by Sadamichi and then Suetake. Raikō sent Kintoki off to his brother's house with a message asking whether he could stop by for *saké*.

32. A copy of the Suntory version called *Iwase-bon* (Iwase edition) has the same line. See *MJMT* 2: 392. This Kintoki dance scene is replaced by Tsuna in the Shibukawa version of the Edo period.

33. According to Fujiwara no Sanesuke (957–1046), Kintoki is *ukon'e* (Imperial Guard of the Right). In *Nichūreki* (Combination of Two History Books, early thirteenth century) Kintoki is also written as *Konoe Toneri* (*Nichūreki* 3: 113).

34. See, for example, the footnotes in *SNKBZ* 38: 152 and *NKBT* 26: 55. Modern Japanese translations of this episode spell out his name in their main texts as Sakata no Kintoki.

35. The play was first performed for *jōruri* in 1712. The first recorded Kabuki performance was in 1714. For the text of *Komochi Yamauba*, see Chikamatsu, *Chikamatsu jōruri shū* 177–226.

36. It is number 10 of volume 25, *SNKBZ* 37: 430–33.

37. *SNKBZ* 37: 395–98; Sato, *Legends of the Samurai* 19–21 for an English translation.

38. It is number 19 of volume 29, *SNKBZ* 38: 348–50; Sato, *Legends of the Samurai* 34–36.

39. It is well-known that Emperor Shōmu (701–56) copied the Golden Light Sutra himself and distributed it to the provinces. In 741 he called for the establishment of provincial temples called *konkōmyō-shitennō-gokoku no tera* (temples for the protection of the country by the four guardian deities of the golden light) throughout the country.

40. See the introduction for a brief explanation of *otogizōshi*.

41. There is a lacuna in the original text.

42. *sandai nikan.* The three dynasties are Xia Dynasty (2100–1600 BEC), Shang Dynasty (1600–1046 BCE), and Zhou Dynasty (1045–256 BCE). The two Hans are Western Han (206 BCE–9 CE) and Eastern Han (25–220 CE).

43. The first emperor of Japan who is, according to *Nihon shoki* (or *Nihongi*, Chronicles of Japan, 720 CE) and *Kojiki* (Ancient Matters, 712), purported to have been enthroned at Kashiwanomiya in Nara prefecture in 660 BCE.

44. *sanpō.* They are Buddha, sutras, and priesthood.

45. *jūzen* or ten good acts. It was believed that one became an emperor as a result of performing ten good acts in his previous lives. Ten good acts are not to (1) kill, (2) steal, (3) commit adultery, (4) lie, (5) use immoral language, (6) slander, (7) equivocate, (8) covet, (9) give way to anger, and (10) hold false views.

46. Fujiwara no Tadanobu (967–1035), courtier and an able official. As Fujiwara no Michinaga's right-hand man, he supported Emperor Ichijō. One of so-called Four Councilors of the Ichijō court.

47. Fujiwara no Kintō (966–1041), courtier, an able official, and one of the so-called Four Councilors of the Ichijō court.

48. Fujiwara no Yukinari (972–1028), courtier, an able official, and one of the so-called Four Councilors of the Ichijō court. He is known for his great calligraphy.

49. Minamoto no Toshikata (959–1027), courtier and one of the so-called Four Councilors of the Ichijō court.

50. Shun and Yao are legendary virtuous emperors of ancient China whose reigns were regarded as ideal.

51. Emperor Ichijō reigned during the Shōryaku era.

52. *tenma.* They are demons (the evil king and his relatives) of the sixth heaven in the realm of desire that try to prevent people from acquiring wisdom and doing good deeds.

53. *suikyō.* The *Shu Ching*, or *Book of History* states that in the era of Busei, or Wu Cheng, "the sleeves hang low and one folds his arms, the world is well governed in peace."

54. Abe no Seimei (921?–1005), a famed practitioner of Japanese Onmyōdō (the Way of yin-yang) during the mid-Heian period.

55. Taira no Muneyori (?–1011), a warrior of the mid-Heian period.

56. Minamoto no Yorinobu (968–1048), a warrior of the mid-Heian period. He was Minamoto no Mitsunaka's third son and Raikō's half-sibling (younger brother with a different mother).

57. Taira no Korehira (?–?), a warrior of the mid-Heian period.

58. Fujiwara no Yasumasa (957–1036).

59. This may be Fujiwara no Sanenari (975–1045), the eldest son of Fujiwara no Kinsue (956–1029), who started a Kan'in line of the northern branch of the Fujiwara family.

60. Present-day northwest Osaka through southeastern Hyōgo prefecture.

61. Present-day northern Kyoto. There seems to be a discrepancy here because Hōshō was summoned earlier and had declined the offer.

62. Hachiman sanjo, which is Iwashimizu Hachimangū. Located in present-day Kyoto, it enshrines the god of battle and the guardian deity for the Minamoto clan.

63. It enshrines a Shinto deity, Ōmononushi or Ōkuninushi. The shrine is a branch of Shinto formed within the Tendai school of Buddhism.

64. Kumano sansho. Located in present-day Wakayama prefecture, it is one of the strongholds of mountain asceticism (*shugendō*).

65. Sumiyoshi Myōjin, the god of navigation as well as the god of battle.

66. This is Kiyohara no Munenobu (?–1017).

67. The *hitatare* is a formal upper-body garment.

68. Or Ikuta. Located in present-day Kobe, Hyōgo prefecture.

69. A deity who is said to live on Mt. Taishan in China. In Taoism, he is in charge of life and death.

70. *shikigami* or *shikijin*. An agent—form of magic—that a practitioner of Onmyōdō, or yin-yang master, uses.

71. *gohō dōji*. A deity to protect Dharma. He has the appearance of a child.

72. The text has "Jikaku daishi" (i.e., Ennin [794–864]), but Yokoyama corrects it as "Jie daishi" (i.e., Ryōgen [912–85]). I am following Yokoyama's correction. Jikaku daishi, or Ennin, is the third Hiei abbot, and the date does not match the story's setting. Jie daishi, or Ryōgen, is the eighteenth Hiei abbot. Mt. Hiei refers to the Tendai institution at Mount Hiei.

73. The Fujiwara Regency reached its peak with Fujiwara no Michinaga. He took religious vows in 1019 and was the father-in-law of three emperors.

74. Mahā-ka-śyapa. One of the ten disciples of Gautama Buddha, famous for ascetic practices.

75. Fan K'uai (d. 189 BCE), a paragon of strength and courage. He was a retainer of General Liu Pan, the first emperor of the Han Dynasty in China.

76. Dengyō Daishi (d. 822), founder of the Tendai sect of Buddhism. He founded Enryakuji on Mt. Hiei in present-day Kyoto.

77. This poem is included in book 20 of *Shin kokin wakashū* (New Collection of Poems Ancient and New), the eighth imperial anthology (ca. 1205). The translation is by Honda, *Shin Kokinshū* 529. For the Japanese text, see Minemura 557.

78. Ten heavenly maidens who protect the Lotus Sutra.

79. They represent twelve vows of the Medicine Buddha.

80. Bhaiṣajyaguru Thathāgata.

81. *Ācala Vidyārāja*. Fudō myōō is a manifestation of Mahavairocana, the fundamental, universal Buddha of esoteric Buddhism, and he has a fearsome countenance as he destroys humans' delusions and material desires in exchange for the salvation of mankind. Fudō or Ācala, that is, immovability, refers to his ability to remain unmoved by carnal temptations.

82. An esoteric Buddhist ceremony that focuses on the Healing Buddha and his six manifestations. It was performed to pray for health, longevity, and safe delivery of a child.

83. One of the Hie shrines at Mt. Hiei.

84. *Goshū*. "Go" is an old name of *kisasage* or *Catalpa ovate*, and *shū* is *aogiri* or *firmiana simplex*. In the "Falling Leaves" section of volume 1 of *Wakan rōeishū* (Japanese and Chinese Poems to Sing, ca. 1018), compiled by Fujiwara no Kintō (966–1041), there is a poem by Minamoto no Shitagō (911–83): "In the shadows of paulownia and catalpa / a sound of rain swishing emptily / Above the back of the oriole / several bits of red still hanging on" (Rimer and Chaves 100; Sugano 168).

85. "Pining for (*matsu*) a storm" does not make sense here, but it sounds poetic with the previous word, pine trees, *matsu*.

86. The source of this simile appears in "Chu guo" of *Gao tang fu*, composed by Song Yu, a poet of the Warring period (403–221 BCE) in China.

87. Kirinmugoku and Jakengokudai are perhaps his oni's names.

88. Present-day Kyūshū.

89. Present-day Fukuoka city.

90. Present-day western and southern part of Fukuoka prefecture.

91. The river runs through present-day Osaka.

92. Lu Shang, known as Taigong Wang, is the adviser to King Wen (1152–1056 BCE) of the Zhou state. When Lu Shang was fishing at the Wei-shui River, waiting for someone to come and hire him to overthrow the king of Shang, the future king of the Zhou state came and asked Lu Shang to be his adviser. Lu Shang was eighty years old at that time.

93. To wipe tears.

94. This refers to Japan, compared to India and China.

95. Gotama Buddha (ca. 566–485 BCE), the founder of Buddhism. He was born to a noble family of the ruling class in Lumbini, present-day Nepal. He abandoned material life in pursuit of spiritual tranquility. When he was awakened to the truth about life, he became the Buddha, the enlightened one, and shared his teaching with others.

96. According to the preface of *Sangoku sōden onmyō kankatsu hokinaiden kin'u gyokuto-shū* (Transmitted through Three Countries, Collections of the Sun and Moon Yin-Yang Treatise Held in the Ritual Containers, ca. early fourteenth century), Hakudō became a disciple of Monju bosatsu (Manjusri). When he became enlightened he received a secret transmission called *Monju sesshū butsurekikyō* (Sutra of Buddha Calendar Assembled by Manjusri) from Manjusri. He brought the sutra to China and named the *Hokinaiden kin'u gyokuto shū* (Collections of the Sun and Moon Yin-Yang Treatise Held in the Ritual Containers), which became the sacred scripture for Japanese practitioners of yin and yang. Abe no Seimei is said to have received the scripture from Hakudō. The date, early fourteenth century, is given by Murayama, *Nihon onmyōdō* 323–24. For the text of *Hokinaiden*, see Nakamura, *Nihon onmyōdō-sho no kenkyū* 237–329.

97. The Four Guardian Kings are pre-Buddhist deities that were incorporated into the Buddhist pantheon to protect Buddhist teachings. Each of them rules one of the cardinal points and a race of earthly devas.

98. *Shakujō*, one of the eighteen possessions of a monk.

99. Nachi is famous for its waterfall, which emits mist like clouds.

100. This must be an official who lived in the Ikuno area.

101. Tamura is Sakanoue Tamuramaro (758–811), a famous general of the early Heian period who, having received an imperial command, conquered the native people of northern Japan. Toshihito is Fujiwara no Toshihito (?–?), a general of the middle Heian period who subjugated a number of thieves and bandits. Several legends hold that the military general Tamura Toshihito (Tamuramaro and Toshihito combined into one person) conquered oni.

102. Uji no hōzō was the treasure house built by Fujiwara no Yorimichi (992–1074), the eldest son of the regent Michinaga. Uji no Byōdōin buildings, which Uji no hōzō was part of, were built in 1052, thirty-two years after the death of Raikō.

103. Present-day northwestern Fukuoka prefecture.

104. Present-day Fukushima, Miyagi, Iwate, and Aomori prefectures.

2

A Tale of an Earth Spider (Tsuchigumo zōshi)
The Emergence of a Shape-Shifting Killer Female Spider

Mɪɴᴀᴍᴏᴛᴏ ɴᴏ Rᴀɪᴋō (ᴏʀ Yᴏʀɪᴍɪᴛsᴜ, 948–1021) ᴀɴᴅ Wᴀᴛᴀɴᴀʙᴇ ɴᴏ Tsuna (953–1025), leader of Raikō's *shitennō* (Four Guardian Kings), are again the conquerors of supernatural creatures, this time a giant earth spider. In *Tsuchigumo zōshi* (Picture Scroll of an Earth Spider, ca. early fourteenth century) the two warriors are lured into a dilapidated mansion whose owner, a beautiful woman, is a giant earth spider in disguise and tries to kill Raikō. Just like the Shuten Dōji story, *Tsuchigumo zōshi* extols the prowess of Minamoto no Raikō and Watanabe no Tsuna by recounting the murder of the monstrous spider. The work is well regarded, primarily because of its high-quality illustrations in the style of the orthodox *yamato-e* school (classical Japanese) decorative paintings (Nagasaka 18–19; Ueno 111). Unfortunately, the work tends to be neglected in the field of literature in spite (or perhaps because) of its entertaining content.

Although spiders appear in ancient Japanese texts, this picture scroll is the oldest extant work in which a spider is portrayed as a supernatural creature. During the early modern period, the earth spider was notorious in literature and theatrical performance as a shape-shifting killer. I speculate that this picture scroll plays a significant role in the emergence of *tsuchigumo* as a killer female shape-shifter, an image perhaps created through its association with oni. A medieval Noh play titled *Tsuchigumo* (An Earth Spider; ca. beginning of the fifteenth century)[1] greatly influenced subsequent works in literature and the performing arts featuring an evil, shape-shifting earth spider. The *Nihon shoki* or *Nihongi* (Chronicles of Japan) and "Tsurugi no maki" (Swords chapter) of *Heike monogatari* (Tale of the Heike) are the widely recognized sources for this famous Noh play. Perhaps *Tsuchigumo zōshi* should also be credited as a text that helped create an image of a female killer earth spider in Noh's *Tsuchigumo*. Acknowledging *Tsuchigumo zōshi* as a source for the Noh play leads

DOI: 10.7330/9781607324904.c002

to an interpretation of a maiden attendant named Kochō, who briefly appears at the opening of the play, as a shape-shifting killer spider, and this interpretation makes the Noh story more logical and coherent, giving depth to the play.

THE *TSUCHIGUMO ZŌSHI* PICTURE SCROLL

The *Tsuchigumo zōshi* picture scroll, currently housed in the Tokyo National Museum, dates back to the first half of the fourteenth century.[2] The scroll consists of nine sections of writing and illustrations. In the process of transmission from one family to another, the paper has been damaged, causing lacunae, and the order of the sections has been misarranged. Fortunately, the order of the story and illustrations was restored to the original from a copy of *Tsuchigumo zōshi* dated 1764. The writing on the box that contained the picture scroll and a certificate written by Tosa Mitsuyoshi (1700–1772), a chief court painter and head of the Tosa school, state that Priest Kenkō (1283–1350) wrote the text and Tosa Nagataka (late thirteenth century) made the illustrations, but there is no proof to back up this assertion (Nagasaka 18–19; Ueno 106–11).

Plot Summary of *Tsuchigumo zōshi*

One day the brave warriors Minamoto no Raikō and Watanabe no Tsuna saw a skull floating through the air. They followed the skull and it led them to an ancient, decaying mansion. Raikō entered the house alone and found it haunted with strange creatures, including a 290-year-old woman, a three-foot-tall woman with a remarkably large head, and animal-like objects. But among this supernatural melee was a singular gorgeous female figure. Raikō was dazzled by the woman's beauty, yet she threw cloud-like white balls at him. In response, Raikō unsheathed his sword and wielded it through her as she vanished into thin air. As Tsuna rushed to Raikō's side, they found a huge puddle of white blood on the floor. Following the trail of blood, they found themselves far off in the western mountains where they met a gigantic creature nearly 200 feet tall. The monster seemed to have no neck but had numerous legs. It said, "What has happened to my body, it's so painful." As the warriors approached the creature, the monster fiercely resisted their attack. But Raikō unsheathed his sword and decapitated it. When they cut open its flank, numerous small spiders about the size of seven- or eight-year-old children spilled out. In the creature's great belly, they found numerous skulls. The warriors dug a grave in the ground and buried the skulls, then set fire to the monster's den.

The Illustrations

With its skillful portrayal of architecture and figures using delicate lines, the artwork is often praised as a work produced by first-class orthodox *yamato-e* painters. The explanation of *Tsuchigumo zōshi* on the website of the Tokyo National Museum describes it as follows: "This scroll is considered to be one of the pioneering works leading to *otogizoshi emaki* (picture scrolls of popular short stories) that became prevalent in the Muromachi period. While most of the paintings in *otogizoshi emaki* were simple in style, the paintings in this picture scroll bear characteristics of the authentic painting styles of the Kamakura period and traditional *yamato-e* (classical Japanese painting style), making this valuable historical material."[3]

In contrast to the dignified Raikō, strange creatures such as a large-headed woman and animal-like beings are humorously depicted. Interestingly, the animal-like beings (see Figure 2.1) are portrayed like *tsukumogami*, or animating objects with features of animals, such as birds and cows. A cow-man has a tripod on his head, and a wicker basket has a smiling face on it holding a basin with handles (*tsunodarai*). This portrayal reminds me of an illustration in *Fudō riyaku engi* (The Benevolence of Fudō myōō; ca. fourteenth century). One illustration in *Fudō riyaku engi* portrays a scene of a yin-yang diviner praying and five unidentifiable creatures that represent illness (see Figure 7.2, this volume). Among the five creatures, two look like types of containers: one is a furry *tsunodarai*, and another looks like a large furry bowl. Such strange creatures seem to have been a popular subject to portray.

There is one noticeable mismatch between an illustration and the text. When Raikō and Tsuna follow the spider's blood trail and see the earth spider, the written text is rendered as "the monster seemed to have no neck but had numerous legs." But the illustration portrays two gigantic figures with necks and two legs (see Figure 2.3). This kind of mismatch is not uncommon in *otogizōshi* works.[4] In the case of *Tsuchigumo zōshi*, this mismatch seems to reflect the close relationship between an oni and *tsuchigumo* or even the fluid nature of *tsuchigumo*, as I explain later.

TSUCHIGUMO IN ANCIENT LITERATURE

What is *tsuchigumo*? Mark Hudson considers the *tsuchigumo* "an example of the Yamato language of political allegiance, whereby people who opposed the state were assigned the status of barbarian" (Hudson 201).[5] It is commonly accepted among scholars that *tsuchigumo* refers to the less-cultivated indigenous people of Japan who inhabited the islands after their creation by heavenly deities but before the arrival of the imperial family's ancestors,

Figure 2.1. Spirits and goblins visit Raikō. Courtesy of International Research Center for Japanese Studies.

who claimed authority to rule Japan and these indigenous people as descendants of heavenly beings. The term *tsuchigumo* is used derogatorily in ancient Japanese literature to refer to those who defied imperial (central) authority (Tsuda, *Nihon koten no kenkyū* 188–95). For instance, in *Kojiki* (Ancient Matters, 712; see Philippi), on his eastward expedition to claim his heavenly authority, Emperor Jinmu (reigned BCE 660?–BCE 585?) and his men smite a great number of indigenous pit-dwelling tribesmen described as earth spiders (Kurano and Takeda 157; Philippi 174–75). An overwhelming majority of earth spiders had fought and been eliminated in bloody battles, though a few survived by apologizing profusely for their resistance toward imperial authority and thus escaped capital punishment.[6]

As for the origin of the name, Urabe Kanekata, a Shinto priest of the thirteenth century, writes in his *Shaku Nihongi* (Annotated Edition of *Nihongi* or *Nihon shoki*), "According to *Settsu Fudoki* (Topography of Settu Province), in the reign of Emperor Jinmu, there was a villain called *tsuchigumo*—he was given the contemptuous name of 'earth spider' because this person always dwelled in a pit" (Urabe 132). William G. Aston also writes, "The 'short-bodies,' etc., of the 'Nihongi' description I take to be nothing more than a product of the popular imagination working on the hint contained in the name Tsuchi-gumo, which is literally 'earth spider' . . . In one of the passages above referred to, the Tsuchi-gumo are described as inhabiting a rock-cave, but in others they are said to live in muro or pit-dwellings, and this is obviously the origin of the name" (Aston 129). A *tsuchigumo* is thus depicted in ancient literature as a villainous human being whose living customs differ from mainstream conventions.

Tsuchigumo (Earth Spider) in *Nihon shoki*

One of the most important descriptions of *tsuchigumo* during the development of the *tsuchigumo* story appears in the *Nihon shoki*. During Emperor Jinmu's eastern expedition in Katsuraki (sometimes "Katsuragi"), "There were . . . *tsuchigumo* at the village of Taka-wohari, whose appearance was as follows: They had short bodies, and long arms and legs. They were of the same class as the pigmies. The imperial troops wove nets of dolichos, which they flung over them and then slew them. Wherefore the name of that village was changed to Katsuraki" (Aston 130; *NKBT* 67: 134; *SNKBZ* 1: 228–29).

Dolichos (*katsura*) is a general term for a creeper or vine, and Katsuraki literally means a dolichos castle. In the Noh play, the *tsuchigumo* introduces himself as the spirit of an earth spider who lived on Mt. Katsuraki in ancient times.

This episode of an earth spider in *Nihon shoki* has perhaps influenced *Tsuchigumo zōshi* in that a main character, a person or a spider, throws threads to capture its enemy, a spider or a person. In both cases the *tsuchigumo* is killed in the end, although the subject who throws the threads is either the imperial army or *tsuchigumo*, depending on the work. In *Nihon shoki*, the imperial army murders the defiant earth spiders by throwing the net of dolichos. In contrast, in *Tsuchigumo zōshi* (and other later literary and performing arts works) it is the earth spider that throws the strings to catch the prey. It is understandable to see a supernatural spider throwing silk threads when one considers the nature of a physical arthropod spider that catches its prey by extruding silk and making cobwebs.

The gender of Mt. Katsuraki's *tsuchigumo* is not known, but the spider of *Tsuchigumo zōshi* is presumed to be a female. When Raikō and Tsuna "cut open its flank, numerous small spiders about the size of seven- or eight-year-old children noisily trotted around." She is a large mother spider. This should not come as a surprise because, as many scholars point out, there are a number of female *tsuchigumo* in ancient literature (see, for example, Nagafuji, *Fudoki no sekai to Nihon no kodai* 175–96).

The physical description of *tsuchigumo* in *Nihon shoki* as "pigmies" or dwarfs (*shuju*) is interesting in that one of the strange creatures that appears to Raikō in the haunted house of *Tsuchigumo zōshi* is a three-foot-tall nun. Perhaps the author of *Tsuchigumo zōshi* has made the nun short to show his knowledge of the Tao-chou people who appear in Po Chu-i's (Bai Juyi's) poems,[7] but it is amusing to imagine that the author may also have alluded to the short height of the *tsuchigumo* killed in the battle at Katsuraki. For that matter, a floating skull that leads Raikō and Tsuna to a dilapidated mansion at the beginning of the *Tsuchigumo zōshi*, a decoy to entice Raikō into the house, may have been one of the skulls of *tsuchigumo* killed by the imperial army in ancient times.

KUMO (SPIDER) IN *NIHON SHOKI*

One noticeable element in regard to *Tsuchigumo zōshi* is that despite the title, the word *tsuchigumo* does not appear in the text. The spider is introduced as *yamagumo* (mountain spider).[8] Some scholars speculate that people may have given the title *Tsuchigumo zōshi* later (Ueno 106). Hence, strictly speaking, a spider in the text may not in fact be an earth spider. While the earth spider is a derogatory name for antiestablishment forces (or perhaps individuals), a physical spider in ancient literature is by and large considered a good sign in that it brings the person one waits for (*NKBT* 67: 334; *SNKBZ* 2: 119; Sudō 70–71).

The oldest extant example of such usage appears in *Nihon shoki* in the poem composed by Sotoori Iratsume on the second month of the eighth year in the reign of Emperor Ingyō (reigned 412?–53?) (Sudō 70). The poem is preceded by an explanatory note: "The emperor went to Fujiwara and secretly observed how matters were with Sotoori Iratsume. That night Sotoori Iratsume was sitting alone, thinking fondly of the emperor. Unaware of his approach, she made a song, saying:

Waga sekoga	This is the night
kubeki yoi nari	My husband will come
sasagane no	The little crab—
kumo no okonai	The spider's action
koyoi shirushi mo	Tonight is manifest."

(NKBT 67: 443; Aston 320)

Aston noted that "it was considered that when a spider clung to one's garments, it was a sign that an intimate friend would arrive. Little crab is another name for spider" (Aston 320). Consequently, scholars discussed how a spider, a good omen, became a shape-shifting supernatural creature of *tsuchigumo* in medieval Japan.

THE APPEARANCE OF SUPERNATURAL *TSUCHIGUMO* IN MEDIEVAL JAPAN

Sudō, who writes that the spider in the *Tsuchigumo zōshi* is the first appearance of a supernatural spider in Japanese literature, considers its shape-shifting ability to come from its venom, especially that of the *jorōgumo* (*nephila clavata*, literally a "prostitute spider") (Sudō). Although a *jorōgumo* as a supernatural creature starts to appear in Edo-period literature, she speculates that a prototypical image of *jorōgumo* must have already existed in the preceding period. She conjectures that the word *jorō* (prostitute) in *jorōgumo* is associated with the word *jōrō*, which refers to a lady-in-waiting, but in the Muromachi period it also referred to a prostitute. Thus, she suggests that the image of a prostitute may be behind the creation of the female shape-shifting spiders (Sudō 68–69).

Watase Junko speculates on the influence of Chinese literature primarily because the name *tsuchigumo*, or "supernatural spider," does not appear in any Japanese texts between ancient times and the *Tsuchigumo zōshi*, or "Swords chapter," of medieval times, and the *Shaku Nihongi* of the thirteenth century describes *tsuchigumo* as a human being, not a spider. Watase writes that the study of *Nihon shoki* during the medieval period focuses on the "Divine Age" book of the *Nihon shoki*, and readers probably did not read *Nihon shoki* in its entirety; consequently, it is hard to imagine from the annotations that the educated people of that time developed an image of *tsuchigumo* as a harmful supernatural being (Watase 78). Likewise, Sudō writes that she sees no ancient image of *tsuchigumo* as defiant people in *Tsuchigumo zōshi* (Sudō 67–68). It seems to me, however, that the image of defiance is present in Raikō's statement: "Our kingdom is a divine country. The gods protect our country, and the emperor rules the country with the help of his subjects. I am a subject and a grandson of a prince . . . Now when I look at this creature, it is a beast. Beasts . . . bring disaster to the country and are the foes of all humans. I am a warrior sworn to protect the emperor, and his compatriot, sworn to help him rule the country. How can you disobey?" (*MJMT* 9: 440).

Important poems such as the above-mentioned poem by Sotoori Iratsume—the poem cited in *Kokin wakashū*'s preface and the subject of serious studies in the medieval period—do appear later, that is, after the "Divine Age" book of the *Nihon shoki*, so it is hard to imagine that scholars overlooked the descriptions of the *tsuchigumo* of *Nihon shoki*. Perhaps with the notion of a creature injurious to the country, the scroll was titled *Tsuchigumo zōshi*. It does not mean, however, that I deny the influence of spider's venom and Chinese literature. But in my opinion, it is hard not to visualize the real spider from the name *tsuchigumo* of ancient literature such as *Nihon shoki*, "They have short bodies, and long arms and legs. They are of the same class as the pigmies." Indeed, as Nagasaka Kaneo notes, it is easy to replace a human being with a real spider later from such descriptions (Nagasaka 19–20).

Further, I speculate that the image of the killer female spider also came from the *tsuchigumo*'s association with oni—supernatural creatures known for shape-shifting and cannibalism exemplified in Shuten Dōji. I assume that *tsuchigumo*'s association with oni became tangible enough to be visualized in *Tsuchigumo zōshi*. The mysterious, beautiful woman in *Tsuchigumo zōshi* is a spider—a female earth spider—in disguise, and indications suggest that she is the first or one of the earliest portrayals of an earth spider as a female killer shape-shifter. In examining the image of the cannibalistic earth spider of *Tsuchigumo zōshi* and its relation to the "Swords chapter" of *Heike monogatari*, we can see the development of the image leading to its fruition in the Noh play *Tsuchigumo*.

Oni versus *Tsuchigumo*

Although oni and spiders are completely different creatures with different visual images, they have one major commonality—they both represent those who defied imperial (central) authority. A brief explanation of oni may be helpful here.

Ancient Japanese literature assigns a number of different written characters such as 鬼, 魑魅, and 鬼魅 to express oni (Tsuchihashi 95). Among them, the character used now is 鬼, which in Chinese means invisible soul or spirit of the dead, both ancestral and evil. The early examples of 鬼 appear in *Nihon shoki* and in *Izumo fudoki* (Topography of Izumo Province, 733), describing evil or antagonistic beings. In *Nihon shoki*, for example, when Takamimusuhi, the Deity of Heavenly Creation and an imperial ancestor, desires that his grandson rule the Central Land of Reed-Plains (Japan), he pronounces, "I desire to have the evil Gods of the Central Land of Reed-Plains expelled and subdued" (Aston 64; *NKBT* 67: 134).[9] He calls the inhabitants of the Central Land who are not subjugated *ashiki* 鬼, or evil gods. Another example is that when Emperor Keikō (reigned 71?–130?) tells Yamato Takeru (?–?) to conquer the rebels in the east, he says, "So by cunning words thou mayst moderate the violent Deities, and by a display of armed force sweep away malignant demons [*kadamashiki* 鬼]" (Aston 204; *NKBT* 67: 302). The corresponding phrase in *Kojiki* is "the un-submissive people" (*matsurowanu hitodomo*) (Philippi 81; *SNKBZ* 1: 223). In *Izumo fudoki*, a one-eyed 鬼 appears on reclaimed land in the community of Ayo in Izumo Province (present-day Shimane prefecture) and devours a man (*NKBT* 2: 238–39). Komatsu Kazuhiko writes, "People who had different customs or lived beyond the reach of the emperor's control" were considered some form of oni (Komatsu, "Supernatural Apparitions and Domestic Life in Japan" 3).

An earth spider defies central authority and has different physical features from those of mainstream culture. In this sense, the earth spider is considered one of the most ancient types of oni (Baba, *Oni no kenkyū* 170). One account that tells of an intertwined relationship between oni and *tsuchigumo* is the legend of Kugamimi no mikasa in the areas of Mt. Ōe and Ōemachi in present-day Kyoto. According to *Tango Fudoki zanketsu* (Account of the Topography of Settu Province), Hiko imasu no miko (?–?), a stepbrother of Emperor Sujin (reigned BCE 148?–BCE 29), led a force to smite the *tsuchigumo* named Kugamimi no mikasa (?–?) and Hikime (?–?). Hikime was killed, but Kugamimi no mikasa escaped. Hiko imasu no miko consulted a shaman to ascertain the whereabouts of Kugamimi no mikasa, and it was revealed that Kugamimi no mikasa had gone into hiding on Mt. Ōe of Tanba Province [the rest of the story is missing] (Minobe and Minobe 141). Mt. Ōe is famous for Shuten Dōji (Drunken Demon) as we saw in chapter 1, Japan's most renowned oni of the medieval period. Minobe Shigekatsu and Minobe Tomoko consider that the legend of Kugamimi no mikasa, that is, a *tsuchigumo*, is a source for the famous Shuten Dōji story (Minobe and Minobe 141–42). Also, Araki Hiroyuki reports the legend of Onihachi (lit. oni eight) in Miyazaki prefecture and concludes that Onihachi, who is believed to have rebelled against Emperor Jinmu's younger brother, is a *tsuchigumo* and an indigenous person of that area (Araki, "Onihachi denshō o megutte" 4–8). This report suggests a close relationship between oni—as it appears in the name Onihachi—and a *tsuchigumo*.

Another aspect of commonality between oni and *tsuchigumo* is their perceived power to cause illness in ancient and medieval times. For example, Takahashi Masaaki identifies an oni as a deity responsible for causing epidemics, in particular smallpox (Takahashi, *Shuten Dōji no tanjō* 4); a *mushi* (insect, bug, worm) was also believed to cause illness. Peter Knecht writes: "Under the influence of Chinese medical treatises, early medieval Japanese practitioners of medicine argued that the causes for human diseases are certain entities active inside the human body. These causes were conceived as oni, but at that time oni were not yet the terrifying figures they became later. However, in later interpretations it was thought that a kind of *mushi* (an imaginary 'insect') was active in the different parts of the body. Challenged by some outside being, these *mushi* were believed to cause a disease together with the intruder" (Knecht, Preface xiv).

Further, Knecht, Hasegawa, Minobe, and Tsujimoto report an interesting contagious disease called *denshi-byō* (illness caused by *denshi*), in which a person is emaciated by the time of death. The modern diagnosis of this illness is pulmonary tuberculosis, although this interpretation is open to debate. Fascinatingly, this *denshi* was considered both a *mushi* and an oni from the ancient through the early modern periods, and consequently a remedy was sought from both medicine and religion (Knecht et al., "Denshi 'oni' to 'mushi'"). As discussed later, Raikō's illness is caused by a spider's spirit in the earth spider story of the "Swords chapter" and the Noh play. I speculate that through the symbolic similarity as an enemy of imperial authority and perhaps some resemblance as a vector of illness, *tsuchigumo* came to adapt some of the characteristics of oni, namely transformational skills and cannibalism (Reider, *Japanese Demon Lore* 27–50).

Just as oni infamously eat humans in one gulp, the spider on its way out of the decayed mansion in *Tsuchigumo zōshi* eats "the old woman in one gulp." And as oni transform into men or women to get their targets, the spider shape-shifts to a beautiful woman and dazzles Raikō to capture him. The *Tsuchigumo zōshi* text seems to offer a close relationship between oni and *tsuchigumo* or perhaps a fluid intermingling of the two creatures.

As mentioned, there is a mismatch between the text and the figure when Raikō and Tsuna meet the spider after Raikō injured it. According to the text, "The monster seemed to have no neck but had numerous legs." But the accompanying figure portrays two creatures depicted more like gigantic *gozu* (ox-headed demons) and *mezu* (horse-headed demons), both types of oni. Minobe Shigekatsu and Minobe Tomoko believe hese creatures are the oni, although they understand the oni to be a relative of *tsuchigumo* (Minobe and Minobe 142) rather than the *tsuchigumo* itself. The *tsuchigumo*'s association with oni becomes clearer in the "Swords chapter," one of the sources for the Noh play.

Tsuchigumo zōshi and the "Swords Chapter"

The similarities between *Tsuchigumo zōshi* and the "Swords chapter" are remarkable, especially the sequence of the events and the relationship between the *tsuchigumo* and oni.

In the "Swords chapter," an episode of the earth spider (Asahara, Haruta, and Matsuo 522–23; Sadler 331–32) comes immediately after the oni episode (Asahara, Haruta, and Matsuo 518–22; Sadler 326–31), as the following summaries show. The oni episode is as follows:

> [Minamoto no Raikō inherited a pair of treasured swords, Higekiri (beard-cutting) and Hizamaru (knee-cutting), from his father.] During the time of Minamoto no Raikō, people begin disappearing in the capital. Raikō sends Watanabe no Tsuna to the capital on an errand. Thinking that the capital is dangerous given the many disappearances, Raikō lends his famous Higekiri sword to Tsuna to protect himself. At Modoribashi Bridge, which is in the capital, Tsuna encounters a beautiful woman of about twenty years of age who asks him to escort her to her home. Tsuna agrees and lifts the lady on his horse, just as she reveals her true identity—a monstrous oni. Grabbing Tsuna's topknot and flying in the air, the oni declares that s/he is going to take Tsuna to Mt. Atago. In rapid self-defense Tsuna manages to cut off one of the oni's arms, causing the oni to flee without Tsuna. Tsuna and the oni's severed arm fall on the southern corridor of Kitano Shrine. Later, the same oni, disguised as Tsuna's foster mother, attempts to enter his house. The foster mother–oni asks Tsuna to show her the famous oni's arm. Believing that the woman is actually his foster mother, Tsuna takes the disguised creature to the chest where he has placed the oni's arm. Seeing the severed arm, the creature reveals its true identity, grabs the limb, and flies away with it. In light of the incident with Tsuna, Raikō's renames his sword Onimaru (demon sword).

The oni episode is immediately followed by the *tsuchigumo* episode:

> In the summer of the same year, Raikō becomes ill. All the incantations and prayers by the monks and priests fail to cure his illness. Raikō's intermittent fevers continue for more than thirty days. One night a seven-foot-tall priest unfamiliar to everyone approaches Raikō's bed and tries to restrain him with ropes. Raikō takes up his Hizamaru sword and strikes the priest, who then vanishes. As his *shitennō* and others rush to Raikō's room they find a trail of blood that leads to a mound in Kitano where there is a giant spider. Raikō realizes that his illness has been caused by this spider. Raikō and his men impale the spider and transport it to the riverside as a warning. Raikō renames his Hizamaru sword Kumogiri (spider-cutting).

Raikō and his *shitennō*s' encounter with an oni and a spider is sequentially similar to Raikō and Tsuna's encounter with the oni (i.e., the spider illustrated as oni) and the spider in *Tsuchigumo zōshi*. The oni and spider in *Tsuchigumo zōshi* are effectively the same creature because the oni returns as a projectile aimed at Raikō—the sword tip Raikō lost in an earlier struggle with a spider, in the shape of an alluring woman. The oni and the spider in the "Swords chapter" could be related, too. One indication is that the oni's arm is dropped on the southern corridor of Kitano Shrine and the earth spider's mound is located in Kitano. Kitano Shrine is dedicated to the spirit of the famous scholar-statesman Sugawara no Michizane (845–903). Before he was worshipped as the deity of scholarship, he was an extraordinarily powerful vengeful spirit who posthumously fought imperial authority as the king of oni (Reider, *Japanese Demon Lore* 12–13). The oni that escapes Tsuna may have appeared as an earth spider to torment Raikō.

The events in the *tsuchigumo* episode of the "Swords chapter" and the *Tsuchigumo zōshi* are quite similar. Raikō in the *tsuchigumo* episode was alone and sick—not alert—when the strange priest attacked him with ropes. The gorgeous woman in *Tsuchigumo zōshi* attacks Raikō with white balls or strings when Raikō is alone and not alert—he is dazzled by the woman's beauty. The woman's action—throwing white balls or strings at Raikō—is the same as that of the strange priest who throws ropes at Raikō in the "Swords chapter." Kuroda Akira, who considers *Tsuchigumo zōshi* an important work in terms of the development of the *tsuchigumo* episode of the "Swords chapter," speculates that the beautiful woman in *Tsuchigumo zōshi* is an antecedent of a beautiful woman Tsuna meets at the Modoribashi Bridge in the "Swords chapter" (Kuroda, "Tsurugi no maki oboegaki" 325).[10] That is quite possible, although I am inclined to think the peerless beauty is a precursor of the eerie priest in the "Swords chapter." The rest of the plot of the *tsuchigumo* episode is the same as that of *Tsuchigumo zōshi*—Raikō unsheathes his sword and slashes his opponent, who vanishes, leaving a copious amount of blood behind; Raikō's loyal retainer(s) follow the blood trail, find a gigantic spider, and kill it.

Maiden and Spider in the *Noh* Play *Tsuchigumo*

The Noh play *Tsuchigumo* has had a great influence on later performing arts and literature, such as *Kanhasshū tsunagiuma* (Tethered Steed and the Eight Provinces of Kantō,[11] a Kabuki piece and puppet theater) written by Chikamatsu Monzaemon (1653–1725), *Tsuchigumo* (Earth Spider, 1881, a Kabuki dance piece)[12] by Kawatake Mokuami (1816–93), and *Shiranui monogatari* (The Tale of Shiranui; a *gesaku*, or popular literature of the late Edo period)[13] written by Ryūkatei Tanekazu (1807–58), just to name some notable examples. In all of these plays, an earth spider appears first as an attractive female figure.

According to the Noh text, Minamoto no Raikō is stricken by an unknown illness. His maid, Kochō, brings medicine but it does not help. One night, a strange priest appears at Raikō's bedside and begins casting silken threads across Raikō's body.[14] Surprised, Raikō strikes the creature with his renowned sword and the being disappears, dripping blood behind it. It turns out that Raikō's illness was caused by this strange creature, whose real identity is the spirit of the spider that had been killed by the emperor's army at Mt. Katsuraki. Raikō's vassal follows the trail of blood and kills the spirit of the spider.

A number of scholars consider Kochō to be a mere human maid and think the section on Kochō at the beginning of the play should be deleted as extraneous (Sanari 3: 2056). But I believe it is an important section, especially in foreshadowing the priest-spirit in the form of a female. It gives depth to the Noh play if we interpret that Raikō has been weakened slowly and steadily by Kochō, a spirit of the spider. As Ikenouchi Josui speculates, Kochō is not a mere human maid of Raikō's. Ikenouchi explains that the interpretation of Raikō's phrase *"iro wo tukushite yoru hiru no"* (Sanari 3: 2059; emphasis added) should be "exhausting love day and night" rather than the conventional "exhausting various [methods of healing] day and night" (my translation); that is, *iro* should be interpreted not as "various" (*iroiro*) but to mean the *iro* of "love, lust, sensuality" (Ikenouchi 14). Ikenouchi writes that even a great hero falls for a supernatural beauty in the transient world, and this concept of human weakness goes along with a Buddhist message of the Noh play, too (Ikenouchi 14–15). Ikenouchi's interpretation is insightful, and I agree that Raikō feels for Kochō, just as Raikō in *Tsuchigumo zōshi* let down his guard and was dazed when he saw the beautiful woman. But I believe Kochō is a spirit of the earth spider primarily because of the influence of *Tsuchigumo zōshi* as a female transformer who casts threads to trap the warrior and the poem the priest recites when he reveals his identity as the spirit of a spider.

The poem the priest recites is the aforementioned poem by Sotoori Iratsume, the version that appears in *Kokin wakashū* (A Collection of Poems Ancient and Modern, ca. 905, *SNKBZ* 11; McCullough, *Kokin wakashū*). In number 1110 of *Kokin wakashū*, Sotoori Iratsume's poem appears as "Waga seko ga, kubeki yoi nari, sasagani no, kumo no furumai, kanete shirushi mo" (This is the night, my husband will come, the little crab, the spider's action, it manifests in advance)—it is a love poem (*SNKBZ* 11: 28, 421).[15] As mentioned earlier, the spider in ancient literature is by and large considered a good omen, ushering in a person one pines for (Sudō 70–71; *NKBT* 67: 334; *SNKBZ* 2: 119). The poem in the Noh play reveals the priest's identity as a spider and the priest-spider's identity as Kochō. When the eerie priest appears to Raikō, Raikō asks who he is. The priest replies by reciting the first three lines of the poem: "Waga seko ga, kubeki yoi nari, sasagani no." While this poem discloses the priest's identity as a spider, it also carries an image of a female composer as a woman waiting—recall that Sotoori Iratsume was pining for the emperor. In other words, through the poem, the priest implies his true identity as a spider and, further, as Kochō, a woman who waits on (and awaits) Raikō. Perhaps what she gives Raikō is not medicine but venom to make him sick. This Kochō was once the stunningly beautiful woman who waited for Raikō in the haunted house. As the beauty turned out to be a gigantic female spider, Kochō in the Noh play is a spirit of the spider who also shape-shifted into the priest. But Raikō does not recognize the priest, so he continues the fourth line "kumo no furumahi" (the spider's action) but changes the last line to "kanete yori shiranu to iu ni nao chikazuku" (in advance I know not, but it still approaches) (Sanari 2060), as the spider's spirit Kochō is an important part of the play.

The Noh play *Tsuchigumo* is categorized as a demon play.[16] According to Terui Takeshi (Leaflet), a Noh performer and scholar, it is the most popular of the demon plays. The popularity does not necessarily stem from the plot but rather from the lead actor *tsuchigumo*'s spectacular performance of throwing numerous spider threads on the stage (see also Yokoyama, "Noh *Tsuchigumo*"). Kanze Kasetsu (1884–1959), a famous Noh performer of the Kanze school, says of *Tsuchigumo* that it is a small, light piece, and there is nothing special to learn and no secret transmission to perform (Kanze 33).

I believe that when one realizes the relationship between Kochō and the earth spider, it not only deepens the plot layers but, further, the play's level or status will rise, requiring better skills to perform Kochō, the priest, and the spider.

Tsuchigumo in ancient times were both men and women who defied sovereign authority. The imperial conquerors who claimed to rule Japan as descendants from High Heaven labeled them as such. *Tsuchigumo* in the medieval period also defied the imperial authorities, yet the conquerors were not emperors or princes but rather warriors who were the subjects of the emperor. The significant difference is that medieval *tsuchigumo* are not human beings but shape-shifting supernatural creatures. Minobe Shigekatsu and Minobe Tomoko write that Japanese medieval tales such as *Tsuchigumo zōshi* could have become a mythology of the warriors of the Seiwa Genji clan's regime to claim their legitimacy to rule Japan.[17] Instead, the tale turned into a monster-conquering story because the image of the spider as a monster was foregrounded while the symbolic meaning of "recalcitrant people" became weak (Minobe and Minobe 148).

The supernaturalness of *tsuchigumo*, which I believe is caused in part by the *tsuchigumo*'s association with oni, makes the story more entertaining and appealing, especially as it involves an attractive woman. Indeed, at a time when the power of the supernatural was still real and influential in everyday life, the subject of a striking beauty attacking a renowned warrior—whose descendants held influential and important positions in the shogunate at the time—or a loyal warrior conquering a humongous earth spider must have been excellent material for author(s), painter(s), and the audience.

Tsuchigumo zōshi may have some didactic messages for the reader, such as to be mindful of a beautiful woman whose allure is powerful enough to lull even the strongest man into a false sense of security, or warnings of the dangers of curiosity, just as Raikō was led by a strange floating skull. Didacticism or moral edification is expected of an *otogizōshi* story. With the illustrations of the orthodox *yamato-e* school and allusions to various classical Chinese poems and verses, *Tsuchigumo zōshi* is an entertaining work.

Importantly, it is a work in which *tsuchigumo*, oni, and a beautiful woman become one entity. The image of a female killer spider took shape in *Tsuchigumo zōshi*, influencing the Noh *Tsuchigumo*. Kochō, whose appearance was considered more like an appendix to the plot, is an important part of the play as a mysterious shape-shifting spider's spirit with vengeance. Later stories of the earth spider follow the role *tsuchigumo* in the Noh play, making the maiden figure more Machiavellian.

TRANSLATION OF *TSUCHIGUMO ZŌSHI*

This translation is based on *Muromachi jidai monogatari taisei* (*MJMT* 9: 436–41) and *Zoku Nihon emaki taisei* (*ZNET* 19: 161–64). *Muromachi jidai mono-gatari taisei* is the standard work for *otogizōshi* written texts, with the sections reorganized to be read as a coherent story. Some lacunae are supplemented in *Zoku Nihon emaki taisei*, which provides full illustrations.

A Tale of an Earth Spider

Minamoto no Raikō, descendant of the emperor [Seiwa],[18] was renowned as a courageous, daring, and resolute warrior. Around the twentieth [day] of the tenth month, he journeyed to Kitayama,[19] reaching as far as Rendaino.[20] He was [. . .][21] accompanied by his loyal retainer, Tsuna, a skilled, renowned, and courageous warrior in his own right. Raikō wore a three-foot sword, and Tsuna wore armor with a bow and arrows. During their journey, they saw a skull floating through the air. The skull rode upon the winds, soaring in and out of the clouds. Raikō and Tsuna pondered the strange matter for some time and then followed the skull all the way to Kaguraoka,[22] where it suddenly disappeared. There, before their eyes, was an ancient and decay-ing mansion. As they traipsed through . . . the wild and spacious yard, their sleeves became wet from the heavy dew on the tall, neglected grass. The gate was terribly decayed, with vines entangled all over. Even in its ruined state the warriors could clearly see that at one time this must have been the residence of an aristocrat. To the west of the ruined mansion stood a mountain, resplendent in autumn colors. A lapis-lazuli–colored pond lay to the south. Orchids and chrysanthemums bloomed in wild profusion in the untended garden, while the garden gate had become the nests of birds and small animals. When they reached this garden gate, Raikō ordered Tsuna to stay behind and then carefully proceeded alone through the gate to the ruins of the once stately mansion.

The kitchen was separated by *paper sliding door*, and upon reaching the threshold Raikō could feel the lurking presence of someone, an old woman, moving slowly behind the door. He knocked on the door and entered the house. "Who are you?" Raikō asked. "This house seems strange and I don't understand this." "I have been living here for a long time" the wretched old woman replied. "I am 290 years old and have served, in their turn, nine lords of this house." Her hair was ghostly white. She used a tool called a *kujiri*[23] to lift her eyelids, which were flipped over her head like a hat. She pushed her mouth open with what looked like a long hairpin, and her lips were [enlarged][24] and tied around her neck. Her breasts sagged to her lap as if they were [clothes].[25] "Spring comes and autumn goes," the old creature mournfully continued, "but my sad thoughts remain the same. Years begin and end, but my misery is eternal. This place is a demons' [den];[26] no human dares pass through our gates.[27] My sorrowful youth has gone, but my old self sadly remains. I lament that bush warblers depart and swallows on the beam fly off.[28] To meet you here is like a singing girl of Chang'an meeting Bai Juyi in the Yuanhe era.[29] People and places may be different, but the sentiment is the same. Over there, whenever the singing girl saw the moonlight reflected on the river, she wept tears.[30] I see that I have met a wise man at last. Please kill me. I wish to pray for Amida Buddha ten times and look for the coming of three Buddhas.[31] There could be no better favor than this."

Raikō soon realized the futility of questioning the old crone any further, so he left her to chatter as he went in search of his own answers. In the meantime, Tsuna made his way to the kitchen area to see what had detained his master for so long.

As dusk gathered and the sky turned an ominous gray, leaves whirled furiously off the trees. The fierce wind blew ever harder, and lightning flashed and thunder roared in the sky. Tsuna did not think he could survive and pondered what exactly he should do. "If I stay here, and if some monsters should swarm about us, my lord and I can surround them and kill them from various directions. But if we cannot surround them, so be it, it can't be helped. On the other hand," he thought, "it is folly to stay in one spot waiting for an attack to come, though to run away is a cowardly disgrace." He sighed to himself, "They say 'a loyal subject never serves two lords; a filial daughter does not have a husband.' How can I ever disobey my lord's order and forget his favors?" So the loyal Tsuna stayed there, beaten by heavy rain and wind. As he stood steadfastly at his lone watch, Raikō calmly continued his quest of the ruined house. As he listened carefully, he could hear the sound of footsteps resembling the sound of a hand drum (*tsuzumi*). Soon, numerous spirits and goblins of various shapes and sizes entered the room from the opposite side and stood in Raikō's path with only a pillar in the center of the room to hold them at bay. As he looked in the direction of a lamplight, his eyes shone brightly like the precious stones engraved in the middle of the forehead of a Buddha image. To Raikō's consternation, the creatures suddenly burst out laughing and left, closing the sliding door behind them.

Then a small creature dressed as a nun entered the door through which the goblins and spirits had just departed. She was small, like a person of Daoshou. She could not have been more than three feet tall.[32] Her face was two feet long and her body less than a foot in height; her legs, therefore, were extremely short. When she sidled up to the lamp and tried to put out the light,

Raikō glared at her, and she smiled. Her eyebrows were thick, and her parted deep red lips revealed her two blackened front teeth. She wore a purple hat poised precisely on her head and wore a red *hakama* (a long divided skirt worn over a kimono), but there was nothing on her body. Her arms were as thin as string, and her skin was as white as snow. [Stillness][33] filled the room. She then disappeared as if the snow and haze of her white body had simply melted.

It was almost the time when the "rooster man" cried out at dawn,[34] when the loyal subjects waited at court.[35] "What could happen now?" Raikō thought, when he heard strange footsteps and a sliding door facing Raikō [opened][36] slightly and through the small gap of the doors he saw something come into and out of sight—the being looked more tender than a spring willow swaying in a gentle breeze. It stood up feebly and opened the sliding door, and a woman leisurely entered the room. She looked distant and unapproachable, as she gracefully sat on a tatami mat. Indeed, her beauty was so superlative that Yang Guifei or Lady Li[37] would have envied her. Raikō held her in his gaze, thinking she must be the mistress of the house come to greet him. A cool breeze drifted through the room; outside was growing light. The woman calmly stood up and appeared to retire. Her hair was swaying to the front, and her eyes, staring at the light, shone brightly like a reflection of fire on black lacquer.

Raikō was dazzled by the woman's beauty, when she kicked up the hem of her *hakama* and threw at Raikō something resembling balls of white clouds, approximately ten in number. He was momentarily blinded by them but soon unsheathed his sword and in a single slash from draw to strike passed his sword through her as she vanished into thin air. Raikō's sword had cut through the wooden floor and cloved a foundation stone in half.

As the image of the beautiful woman faded from his sight, he heard the sound of a familiar voice. Tsuna had come to Raikō's aid. "You have done splendidly, my Lord," he said, "but I'm afraid the tip of your sword must have broken." As Raikō drew the sword out of the floor, indeed, it was broken. On the floor was a huge puddle of white blood, part of which had stained Raikō's broken sword.

The warriors followed the trail of blood and came to the place where Raikō had encountered the old woman the day before. Although there was white blood, not a soul was visible. "The creature must have eaten the old woman in one gulp," they thought. Following the blood trail out of the room, they reached the western mountain, far off. There, white blood flowed like a stream from a dark cave.

Tsuna said to Raikō, "The way the tip of your great sword broke brings to mind the story of filial Mikenjaku (Mei jian chi) of Sokoku (Chu guo),

Figure 2.2. Raikō strikes the beautiful woman. Courtesy of International Research Center for Japanese Studies.

who [broke][38] the tip of his treasured sword to avenge his father's death.[39] May I suggest we make an effigy from rattan and vines and adorn it with a court robe and an *eboshi* headdress[40] and carry the thing before us?"[41] So they prepared the effigy.

Thus armed, they proceeded into the dark cave, but after what seemed like only 400 or 500 yards, they had reached its farthest recess. There stood an old hut that looked like a storehouse. The tiled roof was [covered][42] with pine needles, and moss grew on hedges. It was a deserted and desolate place. There they found a gigantic creature nearly 200 feet tall that to all appearances wore brocade on its head. The monster seemed to have no neck but had numerous legs. Its eyes shone brightly, like the sun and the moon together. A heavy, thunderous voice resounded, "Damn! What has happened to my body, it's so painful." As the warriors expected, no sooner had the creature uttered these words than something shiny shot out from white clouds at the effigy and the effigy collapsed.

They examined the shiny object—it was the tip of Raikō's sword. "What Tsuna said is true. This is an extraordinary creature indeed," Raikō thought. The creature had ceased to make noise, so Raikō and Tsuna soon approached the creature and began to drag it out of the cave.

The monster was strong, however, and fiercely resisted the warriors' attack, attempting to destroy them. Indeed, the monster's force, it seemed to the warriors, could move a huge boulder. Raikō prayed to the Sun Goddess Amaterasu and Shō Hachimangū:[43]

> Our kingdom is a divine country. The gods protect our country, and the emperor rules the country with the help of his subjects. I am a subject and a grandson of a prince—I was fortunate enough to be born in the line of an Imperial family. Now when I look at this creature, it is a beast. Beasts are born to this world as such because of heinous, atrocious, and destructive actions in their previous lives; they bring disaster to the country and are the foes of all humans. I am a warrior sworn to protect the emperor and his compatriot sworn to help him rule the country. How can you disobey?

As the two warriors pulled the roaring creature, the monster first struggled to fight, but it soon succumbed and collapsed to the ground on its back. In a lightning flash, Raikō unsheathed his broken sword and decapitated it. As Tsuna moved to open the creature's great belly, he found a deep gash in the middle of [. . .]. It was the slash made by Raikō at the old house. They felt sure the monster was a *yamagumo* [mountain spider]. From the sword's incision, 1,990 heads poured out. When they cut open its flank, numerous

Figure 2.3. A gigantic creature with numerous legs (or two oni?) challenges Raikō and Tsuna to a fight. Courtesy of International Research Center for Japanese Studies.

Figure 2.4. Raikō and Tsuna kill the monstrous spider. Courtesy of International Research Center for Japanese Studies.

small spiders about the size of seven- or eight-year-old children noisily trotted about. When they looked further into its stomach, they found very small skulls numbering around twenty. The warriors dug a grave in the ground and buried the skulls, then set fire to the monster's den.

The emperor, when he heard the story, was impressed and grateful to his retainer for his valiant service. So he appointed Raikō the governor of Tsu Province[44] and bestowed upon him the court rank of senior fourth lower. Tsuna was given the Province of Tanba[45] and was given the rank of senior fifth lower.

NOTES

1. The date is given by Baba Kazuo (80). For the Noh text of *Tsuchigumo*, see Sanari 3: 2055–67. For an English translation, see Suzuki 87–92.

2. I have followed the date given by Komatsu Shigemi et al., *Tsuchigumo zōshi* in *ZNET* 19. For the printed text, see Komatsu Shigemi, *Tsuchigumo zōshi, ZNET* 19: 1–11 (pictures and writing) and 161–64 (writing); *MJMT* 19: 436–41 (writing); Nagasaka 31–38 (writing) and 54–66 (pictures).

3. See the Tokyo National Museum website, which gives the date of the scroll (*Tsuchigumo no sōshi emaki* [Narrative Picture Scroll of the Story of Earth Spider]) as the thirteenth century during the Kamakura period (1185–1333); http://www.emuseum.jp/detail /100257?x=&y=&s=&d_lang=en&s_lang=ja&word=%E5%9C%9F%E8%9C%98%E8% 9B%9B%E8%8D%89%E7%B4%99&class=&title=&c_e=&region=&era=&cptype=&o wner=&pos=1&num=1&mode=simple&century= (accessed January 12, 2013).

4. See the introduction for a brief explanation of *otogizōshi*.

5. Japanese scholars seriously and heatedly discussed *tsuchigumo* as part of the debate on indigenous Japanese before World War II, especially in the first two decades of the twentieth century (Okiura 37–39). For a summary of various theories on *tsuchigumo*, see Matsumoto, "Tsuchigumo ron."

6. For example, one *tsuchigumo* named Ōmimi in the district of Matsuura of Hizen Province promised to give the emperor food as a tribute (*SNKBZ* 5: 335–36). Another *tsuchigumo* called Utsuhiomaro in Sonoki district of the same province even saved an imperial ship (*SNKBZ* 5: 345).

7. Bai Juyi (772–846) was a gentleman poet and government official of the Tang Dynasty.

8. The spider in the "Swords chapter" is also called *yamagumo*.

9. In *Kojiki*, Amaterasu rather than Takamimusuhi makes this announcement. The corresponding section is written as "Kono kuni ni chihayaburu araburu kunitsu kami domo" (unruly earthly deities in this land). See *SNKBZ* 1: 99. For an English translation, see Philippi 121. The 鬼 character is not used in *Kojiki*.

10. Kuroda Akira uses the "Swords chapter" attached to *Taiheiki* (Chronicle of Grand Pacification, ca. fourteenth century) rather than to *Heike monogatari*. Their contents are very similar.

11. For the Japanese text, see Chikamatsu, "Kan hasshū tsunagi uma." For an English translation, see Chikamatsu, "Tethered Steed and the Eight Provinces of Kantō."

12. For the Japanese text, see Kawatake, "Tsuchigumo." For an English translation, see Kawatake, "Tsuchigumo," translated by Donald Richie.

13. For the Japanese text, see Ryūtei, *Shiranui monogatari*.

14. It appears to be fairly common that a strange-looking priest or physician was blamed for the demise of a nobleman. Prince Fushiminomiya Sadafusa writes in his diary *Kanmon nikki* that on the seventh day of the second month of the twenty-fourth year of Ōei (1417), a strange-looking doctor visits Prince Haruhito (Fushiminomiya Haruhito). The prince had seen him before and invited him into his room. The physician gave "good medicine" to the prince and left. Four days later the prince suddenly died (Yokoi 142–43; Hanawa, *Zoku gunsho ruijū*, 65).

15. The translation is mine, based on Aston's translation of the poem. Helen McCullough translates as "I know in advance / from the acts of this spider / like a tiny crab / tonight is surely a night / when my beloved will come (McCullough, *Kokin wakashū* 248).

16. There are five types of plays categorized according to the role of the lead actor (*shite*). Sequentially, these categories are plays that focus respectively on gods, warriors, women, mad people, and demons. The five categories of plays are presented in a single day's program, that is, plays about gods, then warriors, women, mad people, and finally demons. This categorization was established in the seventeenth century.

17. Regarding the Seiwa Genji clan, see the section "Raikō as a Direct Descendant of the Seiwa Genji clan" in chapter 1.

18. There is a lacuna in the original text.

19. Kitayama is the area located on the north side of the capital of Kyoto (present-day Kitaku in Kyoto).

20. Rendaino is a famous ancient cemetery located at the western foot of Mt. Funaoka, northwest of the capital of Kyoto. It houses the crematorium mounds for Emperor GoReizei (1025–68) and Emperor Konoe (1139–55). Rendaino generally means cemetery or graveyard. In many places, Rendaino is also a place name.

21. There is a lacuna in the original text.

22. This is another name for Mt. Yoshida, located northeast of the capital of Kyoto (present-day Sakyō-ku in Kyoto). Together with Mt. Funaoka, Kaguraoka was known as a cemetery in ancient times.

23. A *kujiri* is a tool that looks like an awl and is used to undo a knot.

24. There is a lacuna in the original text.

25. There is a lacuna in the original text.

26. There is a lacuna in the original text.

27. Kuroda Akira assumes that this old woman is the antecedent of Tsuna's foster mother-oni in the oni episode of the "Swords chapter." But I am inclined to connect this old woman, who is 290 years old, to the 200-year-old washing woman Raikō and his group first met at Mt. Ōe in Ōeyama ekotoba (Picture Scroll of Mt. Ōe, early fourteenth century). The old woman says to Raikō, "This place is a demons' den; no human comes," just as the old washing woman of Mt. Ōe describes Shuten Dōji's den. See the translation of the Shuten Dōji story in chapter 1.

28. According to Kuroda, the old woman's speech up to this point is based on Bai Juyi's New Yuehfu, no. 7, "White-Haired in the Shangyang Palace: Pitying the Unloved" (Kuroda, "Tsurugi no maki oboegaki" 321). For the original poem, see Takagi, *Haku Kyoi* 12: 41–47. For an English translation, see Watson, *Po Chü-i* 25–27.

29. The Yuanhe era was between 806 and 820 CE, during the Tang Dynasty.

30. The three sentences from "To meet you here is . . . " onward are based on "Song of the Lute" by Bai Juyi (Kuroda, "Tsurugi no maki oboegaki" 321). For the original poem of "Song of the Lute," see Takagi, *Haku Kyoi* 13: 116–32. For an English translation, see Watson, *Po Chü-i* 77–82.

31. The three Buddhas (Sanzon) are Amida Buddha, Kannon Boddhisattva, and Seishi Boddhisattva.

32. This sentence is based on Bai Juyi's New Yuehfu, number 15, titled "The People of Tao-chou." For the original poem, see Takagi, *Haku Kyoi* 12: 79–82. For an English translation, see Waley 168–69.

33. There is a lacuna in the original text.

34. This phrase refers to the first line of poem number 524, "The 'Rooster Man' Cries out at Dawn," in *Wakan rōeishū* (Japanese and Chinese Poems to Sing, early eleventh century). A rooster man is a type of night watchman who tells the time at court. For an English translation of the poem, see Rimer and Chaves 160. For the Japanese text, see *SNKBZ* 19: 278.

35. This phrase refers to the second line, "Ah! such the loyal minister paying court at dawn," of poem number 63, "The Cock Has Crowed," in *Wakan rōeishū*. For an English translation of the poem, see Rimer and Chaves 42. For the Japanese text, see *SNKBZ* 19: 50.

36. There is a lacuna in the original text.

37. Yang Guifei (719–56) was the favorite concubine of Chinese Emperor Xuanzong (685–762) of the Tang Dynasty, and Lady Li (?–?) was the favorite concubine of Chinese Emperor Wu (157–87 BCE) of the Han Dynasty. This sentence refers to Po Chu-i's famous poems titled "Lament Everlasting" and "The Lady Li." For the original poems, see Takagi, *Haku Kyoi* 13: 92–116 and 12: 165–70, respectively. For English translations of "Lament Everlasting" and "The Lady Li," see Levy 136–42.

38. There is a lacuna in the original text.

39. There are various versions of this story. The story told in volume 13 of *Taiheiki* is close to the episode in *Tsuchigumo zōshi* in that it includes an episode of the tip of the sword. According to *Taiheki*, the king of So (Chu) ordered Kanshō (Gan Jiang), a famous swordsmith, to craft two swords. It took the swordsmith three years to produce a pair of swords, which he named after himself, Kanshō, and Bakuya (Mo Ye). However, Kanshō presented only one sword, Bakuya, to the king who had commissioned the sword(s). When the king learned that two swords were manufactured but only one was given to him, he ordered Kanshō's death. Before his arrest, Kanshō hid his sword and asked his pregnant wife to avenge his execution by the king through the child she carried if it were a boy. The baby was a boy and was named Mikenjaku (lit. eyebrows a *shaku* [one foot] apart) because his eyebrows were noticeably far apart. Mikenjaku attempted to avenge his father's death with the sword Kanshō, but without success. After a number of failed attempts, Kanshō's old friend offered help to Mikenjaku. To avenge Kanshō's death, the old friend told Mikenjaku to cut the tip of the sword, hold it in his mouth, and then cut off his head. As the king stretched out his head to see Mikenjaku's head in the boiling water, Mikenjaku spat out the tip of the sword in the direction of the king, severing the king's head from his royal person. The king's head fell into the boiling water in the pot. See Yamashita 2: 288–97. For English translations of the Mikenjaku story, see Ury, *Tales of Times Now Past* 67–69; Li, *Ambiguous Bodies* 57–58. For a discussion of the story, see Li, *Ambiguous Bodies* 56–65.

40. An *eboshi* is a ceremonial black-lacquered hat, a type of headgear worn by court nobles.

41. The effigy is used as a shield.

42. There is a lacuna in the original text.

43. The Hachiman deity/Bodhisattva is the patron god of the Minamoto clan.

43. The area corresponds to present-day northwestern Osaka to southeastern Hyōgo prefecture.

44. The area corresponds to present-day Kyoto to eastern Hyōgo prefecture.

Part II
Scholars

3

The Illustrated Story of Minister Kibi's
Adventures in China (Kibi daijin nittō emaki)

Japanese Consciousness of Foreign Powers and a Secret Code

IN PART 1 WE SAW AN OUTSTANDING BAND of warriors, Raikō, Hōshō, and Raikō's *shitennō,* beat cannibalistic oni and a monstrous earth spider that went against imperial authority. But an oni can be a helper of imperial Japan, and so can a spider. In *Kibi daijin nittō emaki* (Illustrated Story of Minister Kibi's Adventures in China, end of the twelfth century), Minister Kibi escapes from captivity in China with the help of an oni, a spider, Japanese divinities, and his own magical skills. Kibi no Makibi (695–775) is a historical figure, famous for his depth and breadth of scholarship and administrative skills—he was one of only two scholars promoted to the position of minister of the right (Miyata, *Kibi no Makibi* 3). Scholars and priests take prominent roles in dealing with oni, especially before the rise of the samurai in the late twelfth century.

While using a historical figure as its protagonist, the *Illustrated Story of Minister Kibi's Adventures in China* (hereafter *Minister Kibi's Adventures*) is clearly fictional, like the previous two stories, *Shuten Dōji* and *Tsuchigumo zōshi* (Picture Scroll of an Earth Spider). Kibi's erudition and talents had given rise to various legends; by the beginning of the twelfth century he was considered a great magico-religious figure—the ancestor of Japanese Onmyōdō (the Way of yin-yang).[1] When this larger-than-life scholar is portrayed in *Minister Kibi's Adventures* against a fictional hostile Chinese court—a lone official envoy of small Japan against the powerhouse of imperial China that wants to kill him—Kibi no Makibi becomes a symbol of Japan. *Minister Kibi's Adventures* reveals a myth of Japanese diplomacy as well as augmenting the position of Kibi no Makibi as the Japanese ancestor of Onmyōdō.

DOI: 10.7330/9781607324904.c003

THE ILLUSTRATED STORY OF MINISTER
KIBI'S ADVENTURES IN CHINA

Minister Kibi's Adventures dates back to the end of the twelfth century. The scroll was created at the proposal of Cloistered Emperor GoShirakawa (1127–92, reigned 1155–58). The scroll was originally kept at Rengeō-in Temple, built in the Cloistered Emperor's residential compound called Hōjūji Palace, alongside *Ban dainagon ekotoba* (Illustrated Story of the Courtier Ban Dainagon, late twelfth century) and *Hikohohodemi no Mikoto emaki* (Illustrated Story of the God Hikohohodemi, late twelfth century), both commissioned by Cloistered Emperor GoShirakawa. Currently, the Museum of Fine Arts (MFA) in Boston owns *Minister Kibi's Adventures.*

Minister Kibi's Adventures had led a checkered life until it landed in Boston, Massachusetts, in 1932. According to the entry on the twenty-sixth day of the fourth month of 1441 in *Kanmon nikki*, Prince Fushiminomiya Sadafusa's (1372–1456) diary, Shin-Hachimangū Shrine of Matsunaga Manor in Wakasa Province (present-day southwestern Fukui prefecture) had this work, together with *Ban dainagon ekotoba* and *Hikohohodemi no Mikoto emaki*. The owners changed several times between 1441 and 1732, when the work is found in the possession of Kyoto merchant Miki Gondayū. Ownership changed a few more times after 1732, then an Osaka antique dealer, Toda Firm, made a successful bid to buy *Minister Kibi's Adventures* on June 14, 1923, at the price of 180,900 yen. No one in Japan was willing to buy this treasure from the dealer for a long time, possibly because of the aftermath of the Great Earthquake of Kanto in 1923. Finally, nine years later in 1932, Tomita Kōjirō (1890–1976), the MFA's curator of Oriental art, purchased the scroll through the intermediary of the Yamanaka Trading Company. Interestingly, the MFA's purchase of the scroll led directly to the strengthening of Japanese laws against exporting important cultural properties. When *Minister Kibi's Adventures* was sold to the MFA, it was on one scroll that measured 32.0 cm by 24.5 m. In 1964, however, the scroll was cut into four parts and sent to Japan for repair and maintenance. The Japanese specialists made the parts into the present form of four scrolls. As the year coincided with the Tokyo Olympics, in commemoration of the Olympics *Minister Kibi's Adventures* was made public for the first time in Japan at the Tokyo National Museum (see Komatsu Shigemi, *Kibi daijin nittō emaki* 3: 94–108, 166; Kanda 10–11; Kuroda, *Kibi Daijin nittō emaki no nazo* 38–52). The scrolls went back to Japan for exhibit four more times, in 1983, 2000, 2010, and 2012–13.

Regarding the painter(s), Tokiwa Mitsunaga (late Heian period) or someone close to him has long been considered the creater, but a recent postulation is that a number of painters familiar with Tokiwa Mitsunaga's style did the work (Kanda 11; *Bosuton Bijutsukan Nihon bijutsu no shihō* 243). The calligrapher is unknown.

PLOT SUMMARY OF *THE ILLUSTRATED STORY OF MINISTER KIBI'S ADVENTURES IN CHINA*

Minister Kibi no Makibi arrives in China as a Japanese envoy to Tang. Upon his arrival, however, he is taken by the Chinese court, which is jealous of Kibi's skills and intelligence, to a tower where prisoners frequently die over-night. Earlier, Abe no Nakamaro (698–770), who was also sent to China as a Japanese envoy to Tang, was starved to death in the same tower and turned into an oni. The oni, that is, Abe no Nakamaro's dead spirit, wants to hear news about his descendants in Japan but cannot get any informa-tion because whenever he approaches someone in the tower, the person dies of fear upon seeing him (oni). Makibi, undaunted, tells the oni about Nakamaro's descendants. In return, the grateful oni informs Kibi no Makibi about China. The following morning, Chinese officials are astonished to see Kibi alive. They give Kibi no Makibi four challenges: (1) understand-ing *Monzen* (*Wenxuan*, Selections of Refined Literature),[2] (2) learning *go* (*igo*), a board game,[3] (3) deciphering the poem "Yabatai" (see the section of Komine, *"Yabatai-shi" no mori*, about "Yabatai"), and (4) living life without food. After Kibi outsmarts all the challenges with the oni's help, his own skills, and the aid of Japanese divinities, he has the oni bring an old *sugoroku* set (board, dice, and a tube) and Kibi hides the sun and the moon in the tube. He threatens the Chinese court that unless it lets him return to Japan, China will remain dark. The Chinese let Kibi return to Japan.

CONDITION OF *THE ILLUSTRATED STORY OF MINISTER KIBI'S ADVENTURES IN CHINA*

Minister Kibi's Adventures lacks the opening written section and all the text after the first two challenges, that is, Kibi's understanding of *Monzen* and his winning a *go* game. Fortunately, the rest of the story is known from "Kibi nittō no kan no koto" (Kibi's Adventures While in China) of *Gōdanshō* (The Ōe Conversations, ca. 1104–8),[4] the source of *Minister Kibi's Adventures*. Many illustrations after the second challenge are also missing, except for such scenes as the Chinese scholars writing down the "Yabatai" poem, an urgent discussion about the disappearance of the sun and the moon, and the diviners arriving at the palace. These illustrations are, according to

Kuroda Hideo, pasted in the wrong locations, that is, illustrations are out of order plot-wise because of an error or miscommunication during the scroll making (or possibly repair). When the illustrations are correctly placed, the picture-story progresses more smoothly and rhythmically (see Kuroda, *Kibi Daijin nittō emaki no nazo*).[5]

THE HISTORICAL CHARACTERS
Kibi no Makibi, the Minister

According to *Shoku Nihongi* (Chronicles of Japan, Continued, 797), an imperially commissioned Japanese history text, Kibi no Makibi is one of only two students sent abroad who became famous in China (Aoki, *SNKBT* 15: 459).[6] He is also celebrated as one of only two scholars who reached the position of minister of the right in Japanese history (Miyata, *Kibi no Makibi* 3).[7] His father is Shimotsumichi no Kunikatsu (?–?), a minor official from Bitchū Province (present-day Okayama prefecture); his mother is from the Yagi family. Until he was awarded the name Kibi no Asome in 746, his name was Shimotsumichi no Makibi.

In 716, when he was twenty-two years old, Makibi was chosen to be part of the Japanese delegation to Tang China as a student, and the following year he traveled to China. Abe no Nakamaro was on the same mission, also as a student. After seventeen years in China, Makibi returned with an enormous number of books and goods that were presented to Emperor Shōmu (701–56, reign 724–49). He was awarded the senior sixth rank lower and became an assistant master for the university. While Makibi was in China, *Shoku Nihongi* records, he became fluent in thirteen areas of learning and arts, including three major ancient Chinese history books, the Five Classic Texts of Confucianism, yin-yang, calendars, astronomy, and divination (*SNKBT* 15: 459). In 743 Makibi was awarded the junior fourth rank lower and became the crown prince's household scholar.

Makibi was appointed a vice ambassador to Tang China in 751 as junior fourth rank upper, and he traveled to China the following spring. In China, Abe no Nakamaro was put in charge of receiving the Japanese delegation. After an arduous return voyage, Makibi arrived back in Japan in 754. (Priest Ganjin [Ch. Jianzhen, 688–763], an illustrious Chinese Buddhist monk, also came to Japan on this return trip, but on a different ship.) In the same year, he was appointed senior assistant governor-general of Dazaifu in Kyushu, where he prepared for a possible war with Silla. In 764 Kibi no Makibi was appointed to head an army to subjugate Emi no Oshikatsu's rebellion. With his victory, Kibi was awarded junior third rank. In 766 he became minister of the right and was awarded senior second rank in 769. When Empress Shōtoku (718–70, reigned 764–70 [reigned 749–58 as Empress Kōken]) became ill in 770, Kibi held several military offices in addition to minister of the right. After the death of the empress that year, Kibi lost the competition for his candidacy for the throne and submitted his resignation from all of the offices under the pretext of advanced age. The court accepted only his resignation from military office and retained him as minister of the right. He requested his resignation again in 771, and finally it was accepted. He was eighty-one years old when he died in 775.[8]

(The setting for the story of the scroll is derived from Kibi no Makibi's second visit to China, during which he was, in fact, given a warm reception.)

Abe no Nakamaro, an *Oni*

Abe no Nakamaro (698–770) is, according to *Shoku Nihongi,* the other student sent abroad who became famous in China. He is the most famous member of the Japanese envoys to Tang and the only known Japanese who passed the Chinese national civil service examination (Tōno 187). As a student Nakamaro left for China in 717 with the same Japanese delegation that took Kibi no Makibi to Tang. After passing the national civil service examination in 727, Nakamaro stayed in China and held promising court positions. In 733 he requested the emperor's permission to return home with an embassy departing for Japan, but his request was turned down. Finally, in 752 he received permission from Emperor Xuanzong (Jp. Gensō 685–762, reigned 712–56) to return home to Japan with the embassy for which Kibi no Makibi was a vice ambassador. Nakamaro's ship was crippled because of fierce storms at sea and reached the coast of the subject protectorate of Annam (present-day northern half of Vietnam). Nakamaro abandoned his hopes to return to Japan, and he went back to the Chinese capital. He served in high-level positions in the capital and as the governor-general of Annam. He was planning to return to his homeland in 770 but died without realizing his wish. Nakamaro stayed in China for fifty-three years. He interacted with some of the great poets of the Tang Dynasty, including Li Bai (701–62) and Wang Wei (699?–759) (Fogel 17–18; Murai 13–28; Wang 185–87).

His longing for Japan is well reflected in the poem in *Kokin wakashū* (A Collection of Poems Ancient and Modern, ca. 905), number 406:

Abe no Nakamaro. Composed on seeing the moon in China

> Ama no hara   When I gaze far out
> furisake mireba   across the plain of heaven
> kasuga naru   I see the same moon

| mikasa no yama ni | that came up over the hill |
| ideshi tsuki kamo | of Mikasa at Kasuga. |

The annotation to the poem reads "Long ago, Nakamaro was sent to study in China. After he had had to stay for many years, there was an opportunity for him to take passage home with a returning Japanese embassy. He set out, and a group of Chinese held a farewell party for him on the beach at a place called Mingzhou. This poem is said to have been composed after nightfall, when Nakamaro noticed that an extraordinarily beautiful moon had risen" (McCullough, *Kokin wakashū* 97; *SNKBZ* 11: 172).

(In *Minister Kibi's Adventures*, Nakamaro appears as an oni who introduces himself as Nakamaro's dead spirit. This is clearly fictional. He was alive when Kibi no Makibi visited China the second time as a vice ambassador. But Nakamaro being an oni as a dead spirit is true to the Chinese concept of *gui* 鬼. The letter 鬼 is a hieroglyph that presents the shape of a dead body at a burial during the Yin Dynasty [1500–770 BCE]; the fundamental meaning of 鬼 is therefore a dead body itself [see, for example, Li, "'Kiki' seiritsu ni okeru 'oni' to iu hyōgen oyobi sono hensen ni tsuite" 425].[9] Further, the fact that Nakamaro-oni's demonic appearance frightens to death anyone who sees him concurs with an ancient Japanese belief of an oni whose shapeless negative energy causes humans to fall ill or die [see Takahashi, *Shuten Dōji no tanjō* 3–4]. The oni's keen interest in his descendants' official rank is very Japanese as well.)

WHAT *THE ILLUSTRATED STORY* TELLS US

Minister Kibi's Adventures, with its skillful, humorous portrayal of human figures, is not only a remarkable hand scroll but also a multilayered text that issues three major signals. The most obvious one concerns medieval Japanese elites' attitude toward foreign powers in general and reflects their strong desire to be equal to or to surpass their Chinese counterparts in particular. The second is about domestic political affairs—the picture scroll is Cloistered Emperor GoShirakawa's clandestine code against Heike rule. The third is that this is part of the series of texts that give credentials to Kibi no Makibi as the founder of Japanese Onmyōdō.

Japanese Foreign Diplomacy toward Superpowers

Komine Kazuaki states that *Minister Kibi's Adventures in China* reveals the everlasting Japanese inferiority complex toward major powers and, as the reverse side of the coin, conscious superior pride in his own country

(Komine, "Kibi no daijin nittō emaki to sono shūhen" 3). The picture scrolls were not only prized objects of interest or hobbies to be stored in a treasure house, but they also existed as concrete objects to extol power (Komine, *"Yabatai-shi" no nazo* 69–70).

Similarly, Murai Shōsuke writes that *Minister Kibi's Adventures* had Nakamaro's birth one generation early and changed the Chinese imperial court's warm reception of Japanese embassies to that of persecution. The story boasts of the superiority of the Japanese intellectual's talents and of Japanese deities' miraculous efficacy over members of the Chinese court. Beneath the surface, however, one can readily see Japan's inferiority complex and xenophobia (Murai 26–27).[10] To understand this power game, we must first turn to pre-modern East Asian diplomacy.

Japanese Diplomacy with Tang China

Diplomacy in East Asia in pre-modern times took the form of the Sino-centric investiture and tribute system. This was based on the traditional Chinese worldview in which China edified foreigners-barbarians with Chinese culture. The most civilized and advanced country, China, was the center of the universe; and the rest, that is, external peripheral countries, were not yet civilized or were yet to be infused with Chinese culture. The Chinese emperor, the Son of Heaven, was the only emperor in the world, and anyone who wanted to trade with China accepted this investiture and tribute system in which the external countries offered tribute to the Chinese emperor in the form of a suzerain-vassal relationship and the Chinese emperor bestowed peerage such as a title of king. There are three major reasons Sino-centrism was accepted: (1) China was the most advanced civilization in East Asia, and (2) the tributary countries could make a profit. After offering tribute to China, the missions were presented with return bestowals that often surpassed their tribute. Further, once they entered China, the Chinese court paid their traveling and living expenses. (3) The Chinese Empire was willing to open its country to anyone, regardless of race or nationality, who was willing to learn its culture (Tōno 17–18).

As Tōno Haruyuki writes, the purpose of Japanese missions to Tang China was to have a friendly relationship with the strongest and most advanced country in East Asia and to adopt its superior culture (Tōno 15). Until the seventh century, the nature of these missions was mainly politi-cal—Japanese seeking acknowledgment in the international arena. But the purpose gradually evolved from political to cultural—Japanese absorption of the advanced Chinese culture—particularly in the eighth century and onward.

While sending missions to Tang China, however, Japan had its own Japano-centrism—a Japanese version of Sino-centrism in which Japan was the benevolent country to which the rest of the countries should pay trib-ute.[11] The famous letter written by Shōtoku Taishi (574–622), prince regent of Japan, to the emperor of China, "The Son of Heaven in the land where the sun rises addresses a letter to the Son of Heaven in the land where the sun sets. We hope you are well"—which so upset the Chinese emperor that he told "the official in charge of foreign affairs that this letter from the bar-barians was discourteous, and that such a letter should not again be brought to his attention" (Tsunoda 1: 10)—is often used as an example of Japanese diplomacy with China (attempting to be) on equal footing, as well as the origin of the name *Nihon*, "where the sun rises."[12] Murai Shōsuke explains:

> According to *Ryō no shūge* (Annotations for Laws and Regulation, mid-ninth century), the areas within the reach of [the] Japanese Emperor's rule were called *kenai*, other areas, outside of the Japanese imperial control, were *kegai*. *Kegai* had three categories: "*rinkoku*" (neighboring countries) which was Tang, "*bankoku*" (uncivilized countries) that included Silla, and "*iteki*" (barbarian countries) such as Emishi (indigenous Japanese who lived in the northeastern part of the mainland). Some regulations even regarded China as "*bankoku*," which was far from reality. The category, "*rinkoku*," was created to fill this gap. These ideal international relations, with Japan's position equal to China and a notch above the countries in the Korean Peninsula, became a firmly held concept among Japanese ruling elites from the eighth century over the medieval period. (Murai 31–32)

Thus, in the eighth century and onward, Japan used different political standards for home and for the Tang imperial court. While the domestic reg-ulations were written as if China were subservient to Japan, Japan's delega-tion seemed to take its state letter as addressing its superior; the state letters from Tang, inconvenient to the Japanese court, were quietly dismissed. Wang Zhenping writes that Japanese courtiers managed to pay only lip service to the regulations in regard to Tang state letters. The Japanese state letters, "while superficially recognizing China's superiority, not only offered a Tang emperor no real political submission, but also dignified the Japanese ruler. This seemingly unattainable goal was achieved by an ingenious manipulation of language" (Wang 3). It was actually more than manipulation of language because from the record of "Tōketsu" (Answers from Tang), we learn that Japan officially agreed to provide tribute once every twenty years (Tōno 27–33; Inamoto, "Kentōshi sono hikari to kage" 14). In the almost 300-year span of the Tang Dynasty (618–907), the number of Japanese diplomatic missions sent to China, including those that were planned but not carried out, totaled twenty (Inamoto, "Kentōshi sono hikari to kage" 6).[13]

Japanese Diplomacy with Song China

After the Japanese missions to Tang ceased in 894 according to the proposal of Sugawara no Michizane (845–903), no official missions were sent to Song China from Japan. Private citizens were not allowed to cross the ocean, though Song merchants came to such Japanese ports as Hakata in Kyushu and Tsuruga on the coast of the Sea of Japan. In the post-Tang period, as Joshua Fogel writes, "economic motives joined cultural ones, as well as vestiges of political ones from even earlier, as the fundament for continuing Sino-Japanese ties" (Fogel 20–21).

The Northern Song (960–1127), from the time of Shenzong's enthronement in 1068, frequently asked Japan for tribute. But after Kaikaku's group of Buddhist monks went to China in 1082 on a pilgrimage, which the Chinese court considered a semi-official mission, no Japanese monks traveled to China for eighty-five years. Then in 1167 Chōgen's (1121–1206) group entered the Southern Song with timber necessary to repair Ayuwang Temple in Qing yuan fu (present-day Ningbo); this was perhaps sponsored by Cloistered Emperor GoShirakawa. The Southern Song court (1127–1279) considered Chōgen an official Japanese envoy (Taniguchi, "Kibidaijin emaki" 272; Yokouchi, *Nihon chūsei no Bukkyō to Higashi Ajia* 427).

The commercial exchange between China—Southern Song—and Japan was thriving in the second half of the twelfth century, especially with Taira no Kiyomori's (1118–81) efforts. In 1172 Southern Song emperor Xiaozong (1127–94, reigned 1162–89) sent a delegation to Japan to present gifts and state letters to both Cloistered Emperor GoShirakawa and Taira no Kiyomori, addressing the former as "King of Japan." As mentioned earlier, accepting the title of king meant accepting a subservient position to China, which was against Japan's official stance. Kujō Kanezane (1149–1207), a nobleman well versed in court customs, comments on the seventeenth day of the ninth month of 1172 in his diary titled *Gyokuyō* that offering the title "king of Japan" was "extremely weird" (Taniguchi, "Kibidaijin emaki" 274). Apparently, Cloistered Emperor GoShirakawa was a person who was not concerned about tradition or who was liberated from the common mind-set (Kobayashi, *GoShirakawa Jōkō* 235). GoShirakawa and Kiyomori met the Chinese delegation, which was further criticized as unprecedented. The king of Japan and Kiyomori gave the Chinese delegation return gifts and a letter and thus opened direct trade with China. Although no official diplomatic relations were established, beneath the surface of *Minister Kibi's Adventures* were lively Song-Japan activities.

It is significant that in *Minister Kibi's Adventures*, Kibi no Makibi called himself "a messenger of the king of Japan." (The same appellation is used in *Gōdanshō*, the source story.) This title had traditionally been taboo. But Cloistered Emperor GoShiraka, who allegedly watched the scroll making attentively, accepted this title in the scroll. Taniguchi Kōsei conjectures that GoShirakawa must have superimposed himself on the character of Minister Kibi, who solved the Chinese court's challenges one after another, and that an audience of *Minister Kibi's Adventures* could perceive GoShirakawa's fear and inferiority complex mixed with the distorted sense of national superiority toward China that he must have felt in dealing with the Song delegation (Taniguchi, "Kibidaijin emaki" 274). GoShirakawa, who did not seem too concerned about the significance of receiving the title king of Japan, may have simply enjoyed Kibi's ingenuity against the Chinese court as if it were his own. This leads to the second issue, the text used for Cloistered Emperor GoShirakawa's political machinations in domestic arena.

Internal Political Affairs: Cloistered Emperor *GoShirakawa*

While Japanese attitudes toward foreign diplomacy are overtly manifest, Kuranishi Yūko surmises that *Minister Kibi's Adventures* is signaling Cloistered Emperor GoShirakawa's covert message regarding his domestic politics; GoShirakawa had *Minister Kibi's Adventures* made as a manifesto to launch an anti-Heike campaign (Kuranishi 215).

As a person who has been incarcerated several times, Kuranishi believes GoShirakawa was interested in Minister Kibi's story. In pictorializing the story, GoShirakawa compared himself to the protagonist, Minister Kibi, who outsmarted the Chinese court. Earlier, Kuroda Hideo observed that the image of the Tang palace is actually the throne *Seiryōden*, or the Japanese emperor's private residence in the Japanese palace. He asserts that the way the Chinese officials sat directly on the green floor suggests that the floor was understood as a tatami mat, and the way the Chinese put their train of clothes on the railing suggested the Japanese aristocrats' custom at *Seiryōden* (Kuroda, *Kibi Daijin nittō emaki no nazo* 112–14). Kuranishi takes up Kuroda Hideo's observation and considers that if the Tang palace is construed as *Seiryōden*, then Emperor Gensō (or Xuanzong) in *Minister Kibi's Adventures* is the Japanese emperor Takakura or Antoku, titular emperor of the Taira clan. The tower where Minister Kibi was confined is comparable to the Hōjūji Palace where GoShirakawa was often incarcerated by the Heike. The oni in formal attire corresponds to GoShiraka's supporters at the

Shishigatani Incident of 1177, a failed uprising against Taira no Kiyomori's rule (Kuranishi 171–228).

Just as GoShirakawa sent his anti-Heike manifesto to the Genji clan in the provinces, Kuranishi Yūko hypothesizes that *Minister Kibi's Adventures* perhaps had the intent to visually present GoShirakawa's own predicament and his resentment of the Heike. Also, by illustrating the "Yabatai" poem, GoShirakawa wanted to inform the audience of the Heike's scheme to bring about the fall of Japan.[14]

The "Yabatai" poem needs a little explanation. It is a text of *mirai-ki* (writings on the future), foretelling Japan's demise—after the 100th emperor, self-proclaimed warlords vied for hegemony, and Japan would eventually perish. The text comprises 120 characters altogether, but the characters are placed at random so the reader has to decipher in what order the characters should be read. When these characters are properly ordered, it becomes a poem consisting of twenty-four lines, each of five characters. During the medieval period the poem had great authority as the textual source for naming Japan "yamato." As an authoritative text that directly concerns Japan, the poem spawned many annotations and quotes. Although during the Edo period a Confucian scholar, Hayashi Gahō (1618–80), suspected that the prediction poem was written by a Japanese person during the Heian period, throughout the medieval period Dhyana Master Bao Zhi (418–514), a mysterious monk during the time of Emperor Wu of Liang (464–549, reigned 502–49), was firmly believed to have been the author of this poem (see Komine, *"Yaba taishi" no nazo*).

To read *Minister Kibi's Adventures in China* as code for an anti-Heike operation is an interesting hypothesis. According to Michelle Osterfeld Li, "Tales set in the past would have been shaped in part by the contemporary concerns of compilers whether the stories were newly created, recorded from an oral tradition, or appropriated from earlier texts. There would have been no impulse to repeat stories without meaning for the new writers and audiences within the context of their own lives" (Li 141). Kuranishi notes that picture scrolls were sometimes created to convey a didactic message; for example, the *Tale of Heike* describes Shinzei presenting a picture scroll of Bai Juyi's famous poem "Chōkonka" (Lament Everlasting), portraying the love between Emperor Xuanzong and Yang Guifei (719–56), his favorite concubine, to warn GoShirakawa against his uprising (Kuranishi 213). Worldwide, there are many examples of paintings and artwork used as an edification or warning.[15] *Minister Kibi's Adventures* works not only as a catharsis for GoShirakawa and Japanese elites who suffered from the inferiority complex toward China but perhaps also domestically as a political instrument to start a civil war.

Kibi's Position as the Ancestor of Japanese *Onmyōdō*

Minister Kibi's Adventures is part of a series of texts that make Kibi no Makibi the father of Onmyōdō. By the beginning of the twelfth century there were a number of stories placing Kibi no Makibi as the Japanese ancestor of Onmyōdō. For example, Fujiwara no Akihira (989–1066) writes in *Shin Sarugōki* (Account of the New Monkey Music, ca. mid-eleventh century) that the husband of the tenth daughter of a secretary at the Six Guards Headquarters is an *onmyōji*, and he practices the art of Onmyōdō, which has been handed down since Kibi no Makibi (Fujiwara, *Shin Sarugōki* 132–34).[16]

A famous *setsuwa* about Kibi no Makibi is number 6 of volume 11 of *Konjaku monogatarishū* (Tales of Times Now Past, ca. 1120) titled "Genbō sōjō Tō ni watarite Hossō o tsutaeru koto" (Priest Genbō Brought the Hossō Sect of Buddhism to Japan from China). It describes that Kibi no Makibi was a master of Onmyōdō and used his yin-yang skills to appease the vengeful spirit of Fujiwara no Hirotsugu, who had killed Priest Genbō (*SNKBZ* 35: 52–55).

"Kibi nittō no kan no koto" (Kibi's Adventures While in China) in *Gōdanshō*, the source of *Minister Kibi's Adventures*, states at the end of the episode, "Ōe no Masafusa says, 'I haven't seen this story in detail on writing, but it has been handed down through the line of [the] late Lord Takachika [Masafusa's maternal grandfather] . . . We owe Japan's high reputation to Minister Kibi. Thanks to him, we have *Monzen*, *go*, and "Yabatai" Poem.'" *Monzen*, *go*, and the "Yabatai" poem were all introduced to Japan before Kibi no Makibi's time, but Kibi no Makibi is credited for bringing them to Japan.[17]

According to *Gōdanshō*, when the oni told Kibi no Makibi that the Chinese court was going to test the minister on his knowledge of *Monzen*, Kibi no Makibi asked the oni to listen to *Monzen* and let him know about it. The oni said that would not be possible, but he could take the minister to the Chinese palace using the oni's art of flying. (The oni's knowledge of the art of flying is not surprising, but one wonders why the oni did not take Kibi to some Chinese port and send him back to Japan or, better yet, why they did not fly back to Japan together so the oni could see his own descendants.) In *Minister Kibi's Adventures*, in contrast, it is Kibi who knows how to fly or escape the tower. Kibi no Makibi asks the oni: "'Is it possible for you to listen to their reading and let me know?' 'I can't do that,' the oni replied, 'but I can take you over there while they are discussing it and have you listen to them. But the tower is shut. How can we escape?' The Minister replied, 'I know the art of flying.'"

It is rather strange that the oni, without knowing how to fly, tells Kibi he can take the latter to the palace. But in any case, it is Kibi who knows the art, and that makes one wonder why the minister stays in the tower to begin with. According to Komine Kazuaki, Kibi's (self-)confinement is an opportunity for him to face superpower China and exhibit his abilities. It was China that had been challenged. Makibi's magical image had already been established in the Heian period. So the theme was to bring Kibi's ability into full play with such arts as invisibility, flight, and hiding the sun and the moon. Kibi's mission was to accept all the challenges and overcome difficulties (Komine, "Kibi no daijin nittō emaki to sono shūhen" 7). Kibi no Makibi is already magical in *Gōdanshō*, but *Minister Kibi's Adventures* empowers him even further. He is an almighty magico-religious figure of whom later diviners claim to be descendants.

For instance, in the preface of *Sangoku sōden onmyō kankatsu hoki naiden kin'u gyokuto-shū* (Transmitted through Three Countries, Collections of the Sun and Moon Yin-Yang Treatise Held in the Ritual Containers, ca. early fourteenth century, hereafter *Hoki naiden*),[18] a great yin-yang master, Abe no Seimei (921?–1005), is written as Kibi no Makibi's scion. The preface attempts to uphold the prestige of Abe no Seimei's lineage of divination by connecting Seimei to Kibi no Makibi. The annotation book of *Hoki naiden* titled *Hoki shō* (The Ritual Containers, Annotated), which was obviously created later than *Hoki naiden*, describes how Kibi no Makibi handed the invaluable *Hoki naiden* to Abe no Seimei as his legitimate successor.

A story of an undisputed underdog winning over an unequivocal favorite is entertaining. But when the nation's names are assigned, with the audience's perception of the story as real, the tale becomes less fantastic and the characters more empathetic for the audience. In the case of the *Illustrated Story of Minister Kibi's Adventures in China*, it was not considered purely imaginary in the medieval period, and as such it had the potential to become a political tool. Komine Kazuaki believes it was no accident that the picture scrolls of *Minister Kibi's Adventures*, *Ban Dainagon ekotoba*, and *Hikohohodemi no Mikoto emaki* were all housed in the Shin-Hachimangū Shrine of Matsunaga Manor in Wakasa Province after they left GoShirakawa's Rengeō-in Temple. GoShirakawa commissioned them as a set to maintain his sovereignty. *Hikohohodemi no Mikoto emaki* is a myth of ancestral imperial authority,[19] and *Ban Dainagon ekotoba* was made to appease vengeful spirits that attack the capital.[20] *Minister Kibi's Adventures* is, as we have seen, a myth of foreign diplomacy (Komine, "Kibi no daijin nittō emaki to sono shūhen" 13).

A myth of Japanese foreign diplomacy is intricately related to fear of the unknown. China, with its advanced culture, was unfamiliar space, with people unfamiliar to the Japanese. *Minister Kibi's Adventures* thus becomes a political tool. Various messages in the text centripetally point to GoShirakawa's claim to power—to show Japan's superiority domestically to expel his opponents. At the same time, Minister Kibi, upon whom GoShirakawa superimposed his alter ego, becomes almighty; his magical power is enhanced, and he gains the prestige to be the founder of Onmyōdō.

TRANSLATION OF *KIBI DAIJIN NITTŌ EMAKI*

This translation is of the *Illustrated Story of Minister Kibi's Adventures in China* (Komatsu, *Kibi daijin nittō emaki* 3: 162–65). The missing parts are supplemented by "Kibi's Adventures While in China" of *Gōdanshō*, the source for the *Illustrated Story of Minister Kibi's Adventures in China*. I have also consulted *Kibi daijin monogatari* (*Tale of Minister Kibi*, twelfth century to the beginning of the thirteenth century).[21] For the illustrations, see also *Bosuton Bijutsukan Nihon bijutsu no shihō* 82–95.

Minister Kibi's Adventures in China

When Minister Kibi, renowned for his intelligence and the most erudite of his peers, made his first visit to China to study, he excelled in numerous forms of scholarship and performing arts. He was wise and quick of thought, and in the face of such sage knowledge and wit, the officials of the Chinese court felt extremely inadequate and ashamed of themselves. When it became known that Kibi would return once again to China as an envoy of Japan's official legation, they secretly plotted Kibi's demise.

"I feel uneasy about Kibi coming here. We cannot lose in an ordinary competition. He will make us all look like fools in comparison," one of them said.

"Simply putting him to death will cause great problems with the Japanese, as will making him return to Japan," said another.

"But if he stays here," said the first, "it will result in great shame for us. When the Japanese envoy comes to China, we will lock him high in the haunted tower. No one who goes there has ever survived. So we have but to take him there and wait. Let us keep silent about our plans." Thus, on his arrival, Minister Kibi was taken to the tower (*Gōdanshō* 63).

It was late at night, perhaps. The wind blew hard and rain poured down in torrents. It was a frightening scene that Kibi beheld when an oni, looking around the area, came into the tower from the direction of northwest.[22] The oni could not see Kibi, for upon seeing the oni, Kibi had made a charm to make himself invisible.

Figure 3.1. The oni visits Minister Kibi. Artist Unknown, Japanese Minister Kibi's Adventures in China, Scroll 2, Japanese, Heian period, 12th century, Handscroll; ink, color, and gold on paper 32 x 459.3 cm (12 5/8 x 180 13/16 in.), Museum of Fine Arts, Boston, William Sturgis Bigelow Collection, by exchange, 32.131.2.

"I am a messenger of the king of Japan," said Kibi to the oni's surprise. "Things concerning the king are unshakable and not to be opposed. Who are you and what do you seek?"

"I am most happy," the oni replied. "I, too, came to China as part of the Japanese delegation to Tang. I would very much like to have a talk with you."

"If you seek an audience with the king's ambassador," Kibi replied in a voice of commanding authority, "you must change your appearance and come back in the proper formal attire." The oni left and indeed returned in formal attire, and Kibi appeared before him as promised.

The oni spoke first. "I, too, was an envoy to Tang China," he said again. "Do my descendants, the Abe family, still exist in your mortal world?" he then asked. "I've wanted to know this for a long time but am unable to get an answer. I came here as a minister,[23] but the Chinese put me here without food, so I was starved to death and became an oni, living in this tower. I have not the slightest desire to harm people, but when people see me, they are so frightened by my appearance that they die anyway. I've also tried to inquire into the state of affairs in Japan, but neither have I learned about this. Today, fortunately, I have met with you. There is no joy beyond this. Do my descendants have any official rank?"

Minister Kibi answered the oni in detail about the comings and going of the Abe family, the affairs of court, much to the oni's great delight.

"To repay your kind news," said the oni, "I will tell you all about China."

"I am most grateful," Kibi replied, and they talked until dawn, when the oni left.

The following morning, a guard opened the tower and brought in food. Having learned that Kibi was still alive, the Chinese officials thought it most strange.

"This Japanese messenger's talent is extraordinary. Let us make him read some difficult and unfamiliar text, and we shall laugh at his mistakes." The oni, who was listening to their conversation, returned to the tower and informed Kibi about their plot.

"What is the nature of this text?" Kibi asked.

"An extremely difficult writing of this country called *Monzen* in Japanese and *Wenxuan* (Chinese Literary Anthology) in Chinese," the oni replied.

"Is it possible for you to listen to their reading and let me know?" Kibi asked.

"I cannot do that," the oni replied. "I could, however, take you to the place where the Chinese scholars are discussing the text and have you listen to them yourself," said the oni. "But you are locked high up in this tower so far away from the court. How can we escape and make such a journey?"

The minister simply replied, "I know the art of flying."[24]

Thus, they slipped out together through the gap between the door and the wall and reached the palace where the deliberation over *Monzen* was being held. Kibi and the oni listened to thirty scholars reading aloud and discussing *Monzen* throughout the night and then returned to the tower.

"Did you hear it well?" the oni asked.

"Yes, I did indeed," the minister answered. "Can you bring me ten or so scrolls of an old calendar that are not used anymore?" Kibi asked. The oni immediately brought the old calendar scrolls. Thus supplied, Kibi wrote down volume 1 of *Monzen* onto the margins of three or four scrolls and scattered them around the room.

After a day or two, a Chinese professor, as an imperial messenger, came to the tower with thirty volumes of *Wenxuan*. As the professor was going to try the minister's knowledge of the text, he saw the dispersed scrolls on which *Monzen* was written. The Chinese thought it strange and asked, "Where did you find these?" The minister replied, "They are from Japan. They are called *Monzen*, very popular among Japanese." The Chinese professor was so astonished that he was going to leave with his *Wenxuan*. But the minister stopped him by saying, "Let me compare your *Wenxuan* with *Monzen* in Japan," and he took the Chinese *Wenxuan* from the professor.

The Chinese officials again plotted, saying, "Kibi may be intelligent, but he won't have any strategic or tactical skill. Let us try him with the game of *go* (board game). The Japanese will take the white stones and we will take the black ones.[25] We will kill him with shame this time." The oni heard this and again told the minister.

"What is *go*?" Kibi asked.

"There are 361 stones and 9 principal points," the oni explained, looking at the crisscrossed ceiling and comparing it to the grid of black lines on a *go* board.

The minister thought about the strategy throughout the night. The following day, an excellent Chinese chess player was sent to the tower as expected. It was a well-matched game, and it was hard to tell who was going to win or lose when Kibi secretly stole a black stone from his opponent and swallowed it. The result of the game was thus in Kibi's favor. The Chinese player thought it strange and counted the number of his stones. One was missing. When the Chinese player had a diviner look for the stone, the diviner said Kibi had swallowed it. The minister vehemently denied the allegation, but the Chinese insisted that Kibi take a purgative. The minister, however, used his own secret arts to prevent the stone from passing. Thus, the minister won. The Chinese

Figure 3.2. The oni and Minister Kibi listen to the Chinese scholars discuss *Monzen*. Artist Unknown, Japanese Minister Kibi's Adventures in China, Scroll 3, Japanese, Heian period, 12th century, Handscroll; ink, color, and gold on paper 32 x 722.3 cm (12 5/8 x 284 3/8 in.), Museum of Fine Arts, Boston, William Sturgis Bigelow Collection, by exchange, 32.131.3.

bureaucrats were so infuriated that they stopped feeding the minister. But the oni brought food every night, and thus several months passed.

Then one day the oni told the minister about the next Chinese conspiracy. "This time I won't be able to help you," the oni said. "They are having Priest Bao Zhi,[26] a wise and virtuous performer of highly esoteric practice, make a barrier to prevent informers—spirits and people with supernatural powers—from entering a place where they will create a writing you have to read. It is beyond my powers."

The minister seemed to be at the end of his resources when, as the oni predicted, he was taken down from the tower and taken to the palace. In front of the emperor, Kibi was made to read. As he looked at the writing, he became dizzy and lost focus; he could not see or make sense of a single character on the paper. Then, drawing on his faith, Kibi turned to the direction of Japan and appealed to Japan's patron deity and Buddha—specifically, the deity of Sumiyoshi Shrine and Bodhisattva of Hase Temple—whereupon his eyes became clear and he could see the characters. Still, he could not figure out in what order they should be read when a spider came down from nowhere, leaving its thread on the paper to show Kibi how to read the text. Thus, the minister could finish reading. The emperor and the writer were all the more astounded and made him return to the tower.

They continued, to no effect, to try to starve Kibi and terminate his life. "From now on, do not open the tower," was the command. The oni heard this and duly told the minister.

"Alas! How sad," said Kibi who had grown quite tired of the whole situation. "If there is in this land an old *sugoroku*'s (Japanese version of backgammon) tube, dice, and board that have existed for more than 100 years, I want to have them."

The oni replied "they exist" and brought a tube made from jujube and a board made from a *katsura* tree.

As the minister placed a pair of dice on the board and covered them with the tube, the sun and the moon disappeared entirely from the sky. Every Chinese, from the emperor to common folks, was astonished, crying and screaming so loud that they seemed to move heaven and earth in their fear. Of course, the Chinese had this phenomenon divined, and the divination revealed that it was an esoteric practitioner's doing, pointing to the direction of the tower where Kibi was confined. The frightened Chinese officials questioned Kibi.

"I know nothing about it," he said. "However, it could be that as I have been falsely accused and wrongly put in the tower, I have prayed constantly to Japanese deities and Buddhas; perhaps they have responded to my prayers. If you send me back to Japan, I'm sure the sun and moon will appear again." Upon hearing this, the Chinese officials decided to lose no time in sending Kibi back to Japan.

"Open the tower immediately," they cried, and when they had done so Kibi lifted the tube from the dice, and the sun and moon reappeared. Kibi soon returned to his beloved Japan.

NOTES

1. Regarding the translation of Onmyōdō as "the Way of yin-yang" and the spelling of Onmyōdō without italics and with a capital O, I have followed Hayek and Hayashi 3. Onmyōdō is an eclectic practice whose roots are found in the theory of the cosmic duality of yin and yang and the five elements or phases (metal, wood, water, fire, and earth). With the theory of yin and yang and the five elements formed in ancient China at its core, Onmyōdō adapted elements from the Buddhist astrology of the *Xiuyaojing* (Jp. *Sukuyōkyō*) and indigenous Japanese kami worship. The appellation Onmyōdō was formed in Japan between the tenth and eleventh centuries. See Hayek and Hayashi 1–18.

2. *Monzen* or *Wenxuan* is one of the earliest anthologies of Chinese poetry and literature: a selection of the best poetry and literature before the Sui-Tang period. It was compiled by Crown Prince Zhaoming (501–31 CE) of the Liang Dynasty and was extremely popular during the Tang Dynasty. The book came to Japan in ancient times and was already required reading during the Nara period. While the popularity continued in the Heian period, it was considered an extremely difficult classic by the early eleventh century.

3. The game of *go* was diplomatically important. In *Kaifūsō* (Fond Recollections of Poetry 751) it is reported that in 702 Bensei, who participated in Japanese missions to Tang as a student, was so skilled at *go* that he was favorably treated by Prince Wu Longji (later Emperor Xuanzong). Also, Tomo no Okatsuo became a member of Japanese missions to Tang China in 804 because he was an excellent *go* player (*Gōdanshō* [*SNKBT* 32:] 66).

4. *Gōdanshō* was written by Fujiwara no Sanekane (1085–1112), who heard the stories from Ōe no Masafusa (1041–1111). "Kibi nittō no kan no koto" is included at the beginning of volume 3 of *Gōdanshō*. For the text of "Kibi nittō no kan no koto," see Ōe, *Gōdanshō* 63–69.

5. Kanai Hiroko of the Tokyo National Museum agrees with Kuroda's thesis; see Kanai, "Umi o watatta nidai emaki" 95.

6. Regarding the university students, Borgen writes, "The students were primarily sons of the locally recruited district officials who, in turn, were descendants of the virtually independent local magnates of an earlier age. The *ritsuryō* system had given such men secure but very minor positions in local governments, and few of them played significant roles on a national level. Those who did were often men who had first earned reputations for their scholarship. The best known examples are Kibi no Makibi (695–775) and Haruzumi no Yoshitada." Borgen 74.

7. The other scholar is Sugawara no Michizane (845–903). Regarding Sugawara no Michizane, see the section "Kitano Tenjin: Benevolent and Vengeful Spirit of Sugawara no Michizane" in chapter 4.

8. For Kibi no Makibi's biography, see Miyata, *Kibi no Makibi*; Komatsu, *Kibi daijin nittō emaki* 108–19; Murai 13–28.

9. Izushi Yoshihiko explains that the original character of 鬼 (without ム, which was added later) is made up of two parts: 甶 and 儿. 甶 presents a dead person, and 儿 is the hieroglyph for a person. So he surmises that the various changing appearances of dead people or a difference between a living person and a dead person was displayed by 甶 (Izushi 416–18. Also see Reider, *Japanese Demon Lore* 4–10).

10. The story was popularly adapted during the early modern and modern periods. For example, Koikawa Harumachi (1744–89), a popular fiction writer, wrote *Kibi no Nihon jie* (Japanese Kibi's Ingenuity), and Kawatake Mokuami (1816–93) made a kabuki play titled *Kibidaijin shina tan* (Story of Minister Kibi in China).

11. This is often called *Shō Chūka* (small middle kingdom) or *Shō teikoku* (small empire).

12. When the 702 Japanese delegation led by Awata no Mahito (d. 719) arrived in China, its members were initially referred to as emissaries of the "great Wo [small]." Joshua Fogel explains that the Japanese envoy asked the Chinese empress Wu Zetian (Jp. Busokuten reigned 685–704) if they would change the state name from "Wo" (Wa) to "Riben" (*Nihon*) because, having unified many small states, they believed Wa was no longer a small state, and "they wanted a state name with a more explicitly positive ring to it. The transformation from Wa to *Nihon*—and especially that recognition by the almighty Tang state—represented a recognition that Japan (actually, Yamato) was now a state unified by law and regulations imported from the mainland." Their request was apparently granted, and thereafter the subsequent Chinese dynastic histories have a treatise on "Riben," not "Wo" (Fogel 19).

13. Tōno writes that Japanese emperors could consider themselves equal to Chinese emperors only because of Japan's geographic location—Far East islands across the ocean. It would have been impossible if Japan were located in a place where China could exert its pressure directly (Tōno 35–36). For a discussion of Japanese embassies to Tang China and Japan's double-standard diplomacy with China, see Tōno.

14. With that postulation, Kuranishi suggests that the picture scroll was completed by 1180.

15. For instance, Tang Yin (1470–1523), a Chinese literati of the Ming Dynasty better known by his courtesy name Tang Bohu, "mocks life and worldly matters, lashes out at the hypocrisy of moralists, and expresses his sympathy for courtesans and prostitutes" through his paintings, such as *Tao Gu Presents a Poem* (Yang, "Ming Dynasty" 223).

16. Since the Heian period, there have been two major schools of Onmyōdō: the Abe school and the Kamo school. In this episode the husband's name is Kamo no Michiyo, implying that he belongs to the Kamo school (see Nakamura, *Nihon onmyōdō-sho no kenkyū* 3).

17. In *Fusō ryakki* (Brief History of Japan, twelfth century), the author Kōen (d. 1169), priest of the Tendai sect of Buddhism, follows suit and adds that because of his talent, the Tang court did not allow him to return to Japan. Kōen writes that according to a certain book, Kibi no Makibi hid the sun and moon in China for ten days, whereupon the amazed Tang court called for a diviner. When the diviner told them it was Kibi no Makibi's doing, the court permitted him to go back to Japan (Kōen 558). This "certain book" must be *Gōdanshō*.

18. The date, early fourteenth century, is given by Murayama, *Nihon onmyōdō* 323–24. For the text of *Hokinaiden*, see Nakamura, *Nihon onmyōdō-sho no kenkyū* 237–329. Matthias Hayek explains *Hokinaiden* as "an esoteric compilation of hemerological knowledge, including elements from both the curial and the monastic (Buddhist) mantic tradition[s] . . . As a whole, the *Hokinaiden* can be characterized as the greatest example of how divinatory knowledge has been transmitted through the medieval period in a mythological form." Hayek, "Eight Trigrams" 346. For the text of *Hoki shō*, see Mashimo and Yamashita, "Hoki shō" 3: 167–95.

19. *Hikohohodemi no Mikoto emaki* is an adaptation of a myth from *Nihon Shoki* in which the younger brother, Hikohohodemi no mikoto, establishes his sovereignty by subjugating his

elder brother. Hikohohodemi no mikoto's grandson is the first emperor of Japan, Emperor Jinmu. Nagai Kumiko postulates that GoShirakawa had *Hikohohodemi no Mikoto emaki* made to assert his position as the legitimate successor of the imperial authority, not his elder brother, Emperor Sutoku, or Sutoku's son, Prince Shigehito. See Nagai, "Ototo no oken." For the text of *Hikohohodemi no Mikoto emaki*, see *NET* 22. For the stories of Hikohohodemi no mikoto in *Nihon shoki*, see *SNKBZ* 2: 155–89.

20. Kuroda, "Ban Dainagon emaki kenkyū" 332. "Ban Dainagon emaki" depicts a historical incident called the Ōtenmon Incident, which happened in 866. Ban Dainagon, or Tomo no Yoshio (811–68), set Ōtenmon, a major gate of the capital, on fire and blamed his political rival Minamoto no Makoto, minister of the left, for this crime. By blaming Minamoto no Makoto as the culprit, Ban Dainagon hoped to take his post. But the truth was revealed through the children's fight, and the real culprit, Ban Dainagon, was caught. It is said that Ban Dainagon, who died at Izu, the banished place, became a vengeful spirit and caused various epidemics. Also see number 11 of volume 27 of *Konjaku monogatarishū* titled "Aru tokoro no zenbu Yoshio no Tomo no dainagon no ryō o mirukoto" (A Chef Meets Yomo no Yoshiko's Spirit), *SNKBZ* 38: 42–43. According to Inamoto Mariko, this scroll is a picturization of the imperial authority to express royal military power through the detailed depiction of *kebiishi* (the Imperial Police). See Inamoto, "*Ban Dainagon emaki* to GoShirakawa" 61.

21. *Kibi daijin monogatari* is currently housed in *Dai Tōkyū kinen bunko* in Tokyo.

22. *Ushitora* (lit. ox-tiger), or the direction northeast, is known to be an ominous direction called *kimon* 鬼門—oni's gate 門, where oni enter and exit. Intertwined with this direction is the portrayal of an oni—typically depicted with ox horns on its head and wearing a tiger-skin loincloth. But apparently it was a directional theory originally imported from China. In a Japanese indigenous belief, Mitani Eiichi writes, the direction northwest, *inui*, was more feared. For example, strong, cold northwest winds that blew along the Sea of Japan coast from October through February every year were called *tamakaze* (spirit winds) and were believed to be caused by evil spirits. While northwest was the direction from which spirits came and went, simultaneously these harsh winds were thought to bring happiness and fortune. In short, the northwest direction was both good and bad, amphibolous (Mitani, *Nihon bungaku no minzokugakuteki kenkyū* 63).

23. The scroll says "Kibi" instead of "minister," but that doesn't make sense. According to *Gōdanshō* it is "minister," so I followed *Gōdanshō*. Incidentally, historically this is not true. Abe no Nakamaro entered China in 717 as a student.

24. According to *Gōdanshō*, it is the oni who knows the art of flying and takes Kibi to the palace. The question is that if Kibi knew how to fly or escape, as the scroll dictates, why did the minister stay in the tower?

25. In those days, a man with higher status took the black stones.

26. Dhyana Master Bao Zhi (418–514), 250 years before Kibi no Makibi's time.

4

A Tale of Lord Haseo (Haseo zōshi)
Literati, Demons, and Creators of Human Life

Iɴ *Kɪʙɪ ᴅᴀɪᴊɪɴ ɴɪᴛᴛō ᴇᴍᴀᴋɪ* (Iʟʟᴜꜱᴛʀᴀᴛᴇᴅ Sᴛᴏʀʏ ᴏꜰ Minister Kibi's Adventures in China) in chapter 3, the oni was a helper to the eminent scholar-bureaucrat Minister Kibi. In fact, the oni himself was an eminent scholar-bureaucrat before he became an oni. In the picture scroll *Haseo zōshi* (A Tale of Lord Haseo, dated between the end of the thirteenth century and the early fourteenth century), the oni is a gambler. Importantly, this oni has an artistic sense in that he is a creator of the world's most beautiful woman. Since ancient times, there has been a fascination with the idea of taking matter and creating a human being from it. The ability to create a human in this way is often considered a divine power. Japanese deities have been seen as possessing such power, too. In pre-modern Japan, when a childless couple prayed to a certain god, a Buddha, or a Bodhisattva for a child, their prayers were believed to be answered with the wife's pregnancy, resulting in the safe birth of a baby. Oni and people with special access to information from oni, meanwhile, were believed to possess the skills to create humans out of bones or corpses or to resurrect them.

In the medieval picture scroll of *Haseo zōshi* (A Tale of Lord Haseo), an oni challenges Ki no Haseo (845–912), a famous scholar-poet, to a game of *sugoroku* (a board game played with dice). Haseo wins the game, and his prize is a strikingly attractive woman the oni has fashioned from the best-looking parts of various corpses. The tale recounts how the oni is later angered and attacks Haseo, who is rescued by the sudden appearance of Kitano Tenjin (Kitano Heavenly Deity, or the Deified Sugawara no Michizane [845–903]) (see Tokuda, "*Sumiyoshi monogatari* zakki" 392–93; Tokuda, "Kitano Shatō no geinō"). *A Tale of Lord Haseo* is an early example of the genre *otogizōshi* (literally, "companion tales"), short stories written from the fourteenth to the seventeenth centuries intended for both entertainment and moral or

DOI: 10.7330/9781607324904.c004

religious edification.[1] While this chapter offers some insights into medieval Japanese beliefs surrounding the relationship between scholars and oni, it also asks questions regarding the structure and content of these stories. It looks at the background and sources for *A Tale of Lord Haseo* and probes the characterization of the literary scholar and his relationship to supernatural beings as both muse and nemesis, as well as contemporary beliefs about oni, or manmade human beings.

A TALE OF THE LORD HASEO PICTURE SCROLL

This picture scroll, currently housed in Eiseibunko Museum in Tokyo, dates back to the early fourteenth century.[2] The scroll consists of five sections of writing and illustrations, and it has been fairly well preserved. Unfortunately, its illustrator and calligrapher are unknown. According to Komatsu Shigemi, the calligrapher worked in the style of Sesonji, the most influential calligraphy school among court aristocrats during the medieval period (Komatsu and Murashige 90–98). One major feature of the illustrations is their large design and close perspective; Murashige Yasushi writes that this is perhaps because the storyline is fairly simple and does not require a large number of figures and landscapes (Murashige 83–89). Another characteristic is the sensibility of the character's portrayal: Ki no Haseo's facial expressions at key points in the scroll are portrayed aptly but somewhat humorously.

Plot Summary of *A Tale of Lord Haseo*

The plot of the story is as follows: one day an oni disguises himself as a man and approaches Ki no Haseo, who is known for his mastery of the game of *sugoroku*, inviting him to a contest. Haseo agrees and goes to the oni's abode, a gate called Suzakumon. The oni proposes a wager: if Haseo loses, the oni receives all of Haseo's treasures. Conversely, if the oni loses, Haseo receives a strikingly beautiful woman from the oni. The oni loses and as promised brings a woman of ethereal beauty to Haseo. He warns Haseo, however, that he cannot touch the woman for 100 days. Haseo acknowledges the warning, but he cannot resist her. After 80 days he attempts to make love to the woman. No sooner does he touch her than the woman melts into water. Three months later, while Haseo is on his way to the palace, the angry oni appears to Haseo and tries to attack him. Frightened, Haseo prays to Kitano Tenjin for help, whereupon the voice of Tenjin comes from heaven and drives the oni away. The woman made by the oni, it is explained, was created from the best parts of various dead bodies, and it was not until 100 days had passed that she was to be invested with a soul.

THE SCROLL'S SOURCES AND PROTOTYPES

The source for *A Tale of Lord Haseo* had long been a mystery, but recent scholarly studies discovered that its prototype dates back to the Kamakura period (1185–1333) or perhaps the late thirteenth century. Umezu Jirō first found the Lord Haseo story in *Zoku kyōkunshō* (Precepts Continued), a musical treatise compiled after 1270 by a court musician named Koma no Tomokazu, or Asakatsu (1247–1331). A story similar to *A Tale of Lord Haseo* is described in the flute section of this treatise (Kuroda, *Chūsei setsuwa* 363; Umezu, "Kaisetsu" 7).[3]

Kuroda Akira has observed that within the story of *Zoku kyōkunshō* is an explanation of Haseo's verse:

Niwa kesoku maseba seisa midori nari,
Hayashi yōki wo henzureba shukusetsu kurenai nari.

The garden takes added beauty, sand in clear sky shades green,
The woods are charged with vibrancy, leftover snow glows red.[4]

According to an oral instruction (*kuden*) in the *Zoku kyōkunshō*, Haseo compares Tenjin to the grasses and trees and compares himself to sand and snow (Kuroda, *Chūsei setsuwa* 363). The couplet transcribed above is Ki no Haseo's Chinese poem that appears in the Early Spring section of volume 1 of the anthology *Wakan rōeishū* (Japanese and Chinese Poems to Sing). Compiled in 1018 by Fujiwara no Kintō (966–1041), *Wakan rōeishū* is a very influential literary work that since the early twelfth century has spawned a number of annotated editions, such as the *Wakan rōeishū chūshakusho* (Annotated Editions of Japanese and Chinese Poems to Sing) (Itō and Kuroda 1: 7–8).

According to Kuroda Akira, a group of annotated editions called *Kenbunkei rōeishū kochūshakubon* (Observation Versions of Old Annotated Editions of Japanese and Chinese Poems to Sing; hereafter "Observation Versions") all include Haseo's story with an explanation of the poem above (Kuroda, *Chūsei setsuwa* 365). For example, *Tenri toshokan wakan rōeishū kenbun* (Observation Version of Japanese and Chinese Poems to Sing from the Tenri Library, sixteenth century; hereafter "the Tenri version"), a representative book of the Observation Versions, contains a story very similar to *A Tale of Lord Haseo*. After providing the story of Haseo, the Tenri version annotator explains, "afterward, Haseo went to Kitano Shrine, joyfully composed this poem and dedicated it to the Shrine. In this poem Haseo, therefore, compared Tenjin to the grasses and trees and compared himself to sand and snow" (Kuroda, *Chūsei setsuwa* 365; also see Itō and Kuroda 2: 20–21). Kuroda Akira thus located the earlier source of the Haseo story and concluded that

A Tale of Lord Haseo is *sōshi-ka* (a translation of a piece from Chinese characters to the Japanese syllabary), from the annotation of Haseo's Chinese poem in the Observation Versions (Kuroda, *Chūsei setsuwa* 369).

Among these versions, the oldest is *Chion'in wakan rōeishū kenbun* (Observation Version of Japanese and Chinese Poems to Sing from Chion'in Temple, 1186), though this volume does not include Haseo's story. Calculating from the date of the *Chion'in* edition, Andō Tamiji considers that Haseo's story was established by the end of the twelfth century (Andō 27), but that date cannot be confirmed. Rather, it would be safer to consider that the prototype was already written by the late thirteenth century, because the story is quoted in the *Zoku kyōkunshō*. As mentioned, the picture scroll of *A Tale of Lord Haseo* was produced in the early fourteenth century, which is not much later than the genesis of its prototype. Apparently the prototype story of Haseo caught the attention and curiosity of intellectuals and was thus used again in later calligraphy and artwork.

LITERATI AS MAIN CHARACTERS
Seeing an *Oni*: Literati and Gates

In ancient times, acquaintance with an oni or supernatural being was a privilege of superior scholars. Ki no Haseo was an excellent *sugoroku* player, but he was most renowned for his literary status. Common places for an encounter with an oni were often gates, bridges, and crossroads; these locations were, in folklore studies, where two realms were considered to meet. Suzakumon, the oni's residence in *A Tale of Lord Haseo*, was the most important of the twelve gates that surrounded the wall of the Greater imperial Palace and a known place for supernatural beings with artistic tastes to appear.[5] Likewise, many mysterious creatures were said to reside in the Rashōmon, the large gate located at the southern end of Suzaku Great Avenue, which ran north-south in the capital.[6] While in the picture scroll and in some Observation Versions the oni lived in the Suzakumon, two Observation Versions of the Haseo story use Rashōmon as the backdrop (see Kuroda, *Chūsei setsuwa* 359–73).[7]

A good example of an intellectual encountering an oni at the gate is Miyako no Yoshika (834–79), a scholar-poet-bureaucrat who was also a professor of literature at the university. According to the *Wakan rōeishū shichū* (Private Annotations to Japanese and Chinese Poems to Sing, Tokyo University edition, original text written in 1161), Yoshika was reciting the first line of his Chinese couplet while passing by Rashōmon. An oni at this gate heard Yoshika's poem and was so impressed that he added the second line to the poem (Itō and Miki 1: 355).[8] The oni of the gate, a connoisseur of poetry, could not help but respond to Yoshika, who he considered a very talented scholar-poet. The same story appears almost ninety years later in the sixth story of volume 10 of *Jikkinshō* (Stories Selected to Illustrate the Ten Maxims, compiled around 1252). Here, too, the oni lives in the Rashōmon (Asami 394; Geddes 491–92). But according to the third story of volume 8 of *Senjūshō* (Buddhist Tales of Renunciation, ca. 1250), which is contemporaneous with *Jikkinshō*, the oni's residence is the Suzakumon (Nishio 316–17). Perhaps to the medieval Japanese, the Suzakumon and Rashōmon were equally known as an oni's residence; and the two may have been used interchangeably in rumors, gossip, and tales.

Hirota Tetsumichi reports that a story very similar to *A Tale of Haseo* appears in *Hokekyō jurin shūyōshō* (Commentary on Lotus Sutra, Collected from Vulture Woods, 1512), written by Sonshun (1451–1514), a Buddhist priest of the Tendai sect. In this story, however, the protagonist is Miyako no Yoshika, not Ki no Haseo. Hirota believes Sonshun wrote the tale based on a Haseo story prototype (Hirota 169).[9] I propose that the names of Yoshika and Haseo may have been mixed up in these two versions because of certain similarities: both stories involve an oni at the gate, and their poems are placed side by side in *Wakan rōeishū* (Haseo's poem is placed immediately after Yoshika's couplet). Both Haseo and Yoshika are famous scholars who have interacted with oni.

A story in *Konjaku monogatarishū* (Tales of Times Now Past, ca. 1120) titled "Genjō to iu biwa, oni ni toraruru koto" (A *Biwa* Called Genjō Is Stolen by an Oni) also recounts a story of an artistic oni through the disappearance of a prized *biwa* (Japanese lute) called Genjō from the imperial palace.[10] While the emperor deeply laments its loss, the enchanting melody of the Genjō is heard from the direction of Rashōmon. Minamoto no Hiromasa (918–80), a noted aristocratic musician, thinks in amazement, "That's no human being playing the instrument, it can only be an oni or some such being" (Ury, *Tales of Times Now Past* 147). He follows the tune and discovers an oni at the Rashōmon playing the missing *biwa*. Komatsu Kazuhiko calls these oni "*fūryū no sainō no aru* oni" (oni with a talent for refined pursuits; Komatsu, "Biwa o meguru kaii no monogatari" 223), and Michelle Li comments that these artistic oni are "a delightful and relatively gentle bunch: clownish figures who mimic aristocrats in some of their interests. With their fine appreciation of poetry, music, and dance, these creatures affirm aesthetic pursuits even while mocking them and hinting at the ugly and monstrous side of the refined Heian elite" (Li, *Ambiguous Bodies* 117).[11] Whether at the Suzakumon or Rashōmon, these oni appreciate music, poetry, and artwork. These artistic oni are usually harmless, and they sometimes present themselves to like-minded worthy scholars or musicians who understand their talent. The oni of *A Tale of Lord Haseo* belongs to this group of oni. He is a great artist because he created the world's most beautiful woman out of the body parts of the dead.

Various late ancient and early medieval literary works comment on Haseo's behavior and character, mostly admiring his scholarly knowledge and erudition. According to the first story of volume 24 of *Konjaku monogatarishū* titled "Kitanohe Minister and Ki no Haseo," Haseo is believed to have seen a spirit (*ryōnin*), wearing aristocratic headgear and garments, reciting a Chinese poem on the Suzakumon on a moonlit night. The story ends with the line "Long time ago, there were people who could see this kind of miraculous happening, so I have heard" (mukashi no hito wa kakaru kii no kotodomo wo miarawsu hitodomo namu arikeru to katari tsutaetaru to ya, *SNKBZ* 37: 245–55). The spirit at the Suzakumon revealed himself to Haseo possibly because he thought that as a scholar-poet, Haseo would understand his poetry, and the oni of *A Tale of Lord Haseo* appears to Haseo because he considers Haseo an excellent scholar and a worthy opponent in the *sugoroku* game.

Ki no Haseo, a Scholar-Poet-Bureaucrat

According to *Hasedera genki* (A Record of the Miracles of Hase Temple, written in the early to mid-thirteenth century),[12] Ki no Haseo was born as a result of his father's prayers for a child to Bodhisattva at Hase Temple, hence the name Haseo (a boy from Hase) (Nagai, *Hasedera genki* 27). Haseo was born the same year as Sugawara no Michizane, but Haseo began his studies of literature in 876 at age thirty-three, much later than Michizane did. Haseo studied with various teachers, including Sugawara no Michizane, who greatly favored Haseo while he showed dislike for Miyoshi no Kiyoyuki (847–918), another famed scholar outside his circle. Michizane served as the examiner for Haseo when the latter applied for a professorship of literature. Michizane failed Kiyoyuki on the civil service examination, but later he passed Haseo to be a professor. Kiyoyuki was jealous of the favorable treatment Haseo received in the examinations and came to despise Haseo. According to *Gōdanshō* (The Ōe Conversations) and *Konjaku monogatarishū*, both collections of *setsuwa*,[13] Kiyoyuki's enmity was expressed when he reportedly said to Haseo, "I have never heard of ignorant professors. Perhaps you are the first one ever" (Borgen 135–36).[14]

Both Sugawara no Michizane and Ki no Haseo were scholar-poet-bureaucrats who were promoted through their talents in scholarship rather than by their family lineage. Michizane was close to Haseo; when he was exiled to Dazaifu, he sent Haseo a collection of his Chinese poems of indignant lamentation and despair over his exile. This was the time when various factions in both schools and family lineages competed for government positions and imperial patronage. Haseo may have possessed superior political or interpersonal skills to rise above factional disputes. When Michizane was driven from power, in spite of Haseo's close relationship with him, Haseo managed to continue to rise in office, eventually reaching junior third rank, middle councilor.

A story in *Konjaku monogatarishū*, the twenty-ninth story of volume 28 titled "Chūnagon Ki no Haseo no ie ni arawaruru inu no koto" (The Harmless Haunt), contains a *setsuwa* that portrays Haseo in a somewhat unflattering manner.[15] It starts: "As a scholar, Ki no Haseo was so magnificently learned that he had no rival in all the world. However, he knew nothing of yin-yang lore" (Tyler, *Japanese Tales* 232). After his dog behaved in an unusual manner, he asked a yin-yang diviner (*onmyōji*) about the meaning of this event. The diviner warned Haseo that the dog's behavior foretold that on a certain date a harmless oni would appear, so Haseo should stay secluded. Haseo forgot the diviner's advice and invited his students for a Chinese poetry gathering. It turned out that what the diviner had called a harmless oni was a dog with a bucket on its head. The narrator concludes: "So it hadn't been a demon after all, but the diviner had seen it as a demon because that's what the people first thought it was. Everyone admired how the diviner had even specified that the demon wasn't going to do any harm or deliver any curses. What a masterly insight that had been! On the other hand, no one thought much of Ki no Haseo. No doubt he was very learned, but it hadn't been very clever of him to forget all about the diviner's advice" (Tyler, *Japanese Tales* 233).

Here the learned Haseo is compared unfavorably to the yin-yang practitioner.[16] The episode of Haseo's blunder focuses on his stolidity or insensitivity to the divination or warning, in spite of his reputation as an erudite man who has experience with artistic spirits at the Suzakumon. The story must have drawn a laugh from some readers. This weakness in personality as portrayed in *setsuwa* by the beginning of the twelfth century—intelligent yet missing something—works well for the protagonist of *A Tale of Lord Haseo*. He is smart, yet he tends to fail at a critical moment—he could not resist the ghost's sensuous beauty despite the oni's warning. While admiring or envying the intellectual Haseo, readers can empathize with him for his mind's inability to assert itself over the flesh. The fact that a scholar as reputable as Ki no Haseo, a man who could survive the many political storms of his time, succumbed to a woman serves as a reminder that powerful intellectuals could also make foolish mistakes. This could be a reason why Haseo was chosen from among many noted scholars to be featured on this scroll.

Kitano Tenjin: Benevolent and Vengeful Spirit of *Sugawara no Michizane*

As mentioned, *A Tale of Lord Haseo* is the miraculous story of Kitano Tenjin (see Tokuda, "*Sumiyoshi monogatari* zakki" 392–93; Tokuda "Kitano Shatō no Geinō"). To show Tenjin's efficacy, he has to rescue someone from a great predicament; that someone is Haseo, and the troublemaker is an oni. Thus, the supposedly harmless and artistic oni of Suzakumon was arbitrarily given the task of attacking Haseo. Three months after his stunning creation had been destroyed, the oni appears in front of Haseo again, this time to attack him. At that moment, "Lord Haseo closed his eyes and prayed for Kitano Tenjin's divine help with all his heart and soul, and no sooner had he done so than an angry voice roared out from the night sky. 'What a nuisance you are!' the voice bellowed to the oni. 'Be gone immediately!' At these words the demon vanished into thin air" (Komatsu and Murashige 119).

Considering Haseo's background—born as a result of his father's prayer at Hase Temple and awarded promotion later in his life after praying at the same temple[17]—one would assume that Haseo should have prayed to the Bodhisattva of Hase rather than Kitano Tenjin, for his life. But as some scholars point out, Kitano Tenjin's voice from heaven reflects his rising power compared with other deities (Andō; Yang, *Oni no iru kōkei*; Hijikata; Murashige; Wakimoto).

While Sugawara no Michizane was alive, he fell victim to Fujiwara no Tokihira's slanderous tongue and was demoted from minister of the right to chief administrator in Kyushu. After Michizane died at his place of exile there, a rumor arose that his angry spirit might retaliate against his enemies. His dead spirit became Daijō-itokuten (Heavenly Awesome Merits) whose families, 168,000 evil spirits, were said to cause various natural disasters. These attendants resembled *kongō rikishi* (guardian gods), thunder gods, oni kings, *yasha* (*yakṣa*), and *rasetsu* (*rākṣasa*).[18] Legend has it that Michizane, as Daijō-itokuten, had received permission from the deities Bonten (Brahman) and Taishakuten (Indra or Sakra) to cause thunder and lightning to strike the emperor's residence in 930.[19] Before Sugawara no Michizane was raised to divine status as a protector of the wrongfully treated and the literati, he was one of the most feared angry spirits of Japan. As such, Komatsu Kazuhiko states that Sugawara no Michizane might well have been regarded by the imperial family as an oni chief (Komatsu and Naitō 117). After later emperors bestowed high court rank and *kami* status on Michizane and built shrines in his honor—the Kitano Shrine was built in 947, and Emperor Ichijō conferred the title Kitano tenmangū tenjin (Kitano Tenmangū Heavenly Deity) in 987—Michizane's anger is said to have subsided.[20]

Yang Xiaojie notes that although Tenjin was pronounced divine as a result of perceived spiritual vengeance, the scholarly characteristics of the man Michizane as the god Tenjin were emphasized and foregrounded through organizational efforts by the "Tenjinkō" (the Tenjin Association), established around the start of the thirteenth century, and others. The groups advocated Tenjin's ability to protect literati and to grant their wishes if they worshipped him. So it was natural for Haseo, who was a successor of Tenjin as a litterateur, to pray for help from Tenjin, the literati progenitor (Yang, *Oni no iru kōkei* 226–27).

Tenjin Sugawara Michizane became the tutelary deity (protector) of Hase Temple and the Hase community in the thirteenth century, as well as a place for the Tenjinkō to meet. According to the eleventh tale of volume 1 of *Hasedera genki*, Tenjin Sugawara no Michizane appeared in front of the Hase Temple's gate in 946[21] and met Takikura Gongen, the tutelary deity of the Hase Temple at that time. Tenjin asked to become acquainted with Hase Kannon and to receive favor from Kannon. Tenjin explained that when he was exiled, he had been malicious and hurt many people. He was stricken with regret and wanted to escape the cycle of sin and suffering with Hase Kannon's help. The Takikura deity then ceded his position as master of the region to Tenjin (Nagai, *Hasedera genki* 46–50; Nojiri 5).

Behind the creation of this tale lies the rising power of the Kōfuku-ji, to which Hase Temple became subsidiary. Kōfuku-ji had had close connections with influential shrines such as Ise and Kasuga. Kōfuku-ji seemed to exert more power in the region by introducing and promoting faith in Tenjin, similar to practices at the Ise and Kasuga Shrines where associated gods were famous for their miracles (and drew many fee-paying supplicants) (Nojiri 7). At the same time, the expansion of the Tenjin miracle benefited Hase Temple (see Yokota, "Hasedera to Tenjin shinkō"). In any case, Tenjin was certainly famous as a miraculous (and lucrative) deity while at the same time still remembered as a figure of the antiestablishment faction and the leader of "168,000 evil spirits" who could cause various calamities, as attested above.

BELIEF IN *ONI'S* SECRET RECIPE TO CREATE HUMANS

A climax of *A Tale of Haseo* is undoubtedly the revelation that the stunning beauty in the story turned out to be made from body parts of the dead. Was the oni's ability to create humans out of inanimate material an authorial invention, or were there beliefs about this in wider Japanese folklore?

From *Senjūshō*

One of the early well-known narratives of the supernatural creation of human beings appears in *Senjūshō* (Buddhist Tales of Renunciation, ca. 1250), which until the modern period was believed to have been authored by Saigyō (1118–90), an itinerant Buddhist priest and a famous poet. The scholarship from the Meiji period onward clarifies that the author is not Saigyō but instead is unknown. Despite this shift, *Senjūshō* is an excellent source by which to view life in the early medieval period (Wakimoto 413).

In the fifteenth tale of volume five of *Senjūshō*, titled "Kōya san ni oite hitogata o tsukuru koto" (Making a Human Figure at Mt. Kōya),[22] the narrator writes that Saigyō "heard a man whose knowledge he respected describe how a demon [oni] can collect human bones and make them into a human being."[23] Seeking a companion, Saigyō attempted to make a human out of human bones. He went to a wild moor "where people left the dead, put bones together, and made a man himself." The resultant being, however, was far from satisfactory because of his procedural mistakes; the being had a voice but "had poor color and no heart or spark of life." Saigyō "considered breaking it up again, but that might be a murder . . . he [therefore] left it in a deserted spot" (Tyler, *Japanese Tales* 69; Nishio 199). What happened to this creature is unclear, but Saigyō must have felt uncomfortable about his failure because he did not attempt to make a human again, even after he learned the correct method. Saigyō was celebrated as a nature-loving poet after his death and perhaps had never again wanted to try to meddle with life and death.

Although Saigyō was not successful, there were other stories of characters who were able to create life, involving rites from the nether realm. Again, a *Senjūshō* episode gives an interesting account: "When Morofusa [Minamoto no Morofusa][24] made a human, an old man appeared in his dream and introduced himself as a supervisor of all the dead. He looked resentful and accused Morofusa that he took bones from him without asking permission. Morofusa immediately burned his diary in which the method of making humans was written because he thought that if he left his diary, his descendants would create humans and would be cursed by the spirits."[25]

This story shows that it was believed that a person had to ask the head of the nether realm's permission before attempting to create life; otherwise, the life of a human who made a human being would be threatened.

Furthermore, this story tells us about the secrecy of such projects in medieval Japan. In the story, the narrator relates that Minamoto no Moronaka (1116–72), poet and aristocrat, says, "I've made people by the Shijō major councilor's method. But I'm afraid I can't *tell* you the method because if I did, the people and other things I've made would all vanish" (Tyler, *Japanese Tales* 69; Nishio 201, original emphasis). This indicates that there were several ways to create life, and the knowledge of creation was extremely clandestine and well protected. Anyone who breached this rule would be cursed and risked death or banishment. Possession of such rare knowledge was invaluable, and it invariably enhanced the status of the possessor—whether as feared or awed.

From Yin-Yang Scriptures

A resurrection of the *yin-yang* master Abe no Seimei (921?–1005) using similar techniques is described in the preface of the book *Sangoku sōden onmyō kankatsu hoki naiden kin'u gyokuto-shū* (an abridged translation of this lengthy title would be *Yin-yang Treatise Held in the Ritual Containers*, compiled in the early fourteenth century),[26] an esoteric scripture that legitimizes Abe's power and lineage. The prefaces states that when Saint Hakudō, the Chinese teacher who expounded the esoteric scripture to Seimei, learned of Seimei's death, he traveled to Japan, collected Seimei's bones—12 big bones and 360 small bones altogether—performed the rite of resurrection, and restored him to life (Mashimo and Yamashita, "Hokinaiden" 106). The difference here is that Saint Hakudō brings a previously existing person back to life using his own remains rather than creating a new life from unrelated elements. The text of *Yin-yang Treatise Held in the Ritual Containers* does not say where Hakudō learned the art of resurrection, but he may have acquired the knowledge when the text of this treatise was transferred to him by the Majusri Bodhisattva. In that case, Hakudō would have used knowledge from a Buddhist deity rather than an oni. In any event, this art was performed by a special person who was engaged with the supernatural. *Yin-yang Treatise Held in the Ritual Containers* tells us that creating life out of death was a sacred art for the select few and always involved supernatural assistance. Importantly, it was firmly believed to be true and sacred, at least among those who followed Onmyōdō.

From Buddhist Writings

Other religious writings also reveal an established belief about oni creating humans. Although they were published much later than *A Tale of Lord*

Haseo, some commentaries on Buddhist sutras provide descriptions of oni creating a human from parts of the dead (see Hirota 159–69). According to Hirota, among a group of Buddhist writings called *jikidanmono* (writings of direct sermons) written by monks at regional temples,[27] a number of texts on the Lotus Sutra and the Sukhavati Sutra contain a section on Ribata (known as Revata-khadiravaniya in Sanskrit, Shariputra's younger brother and a disciple of Shakyamuni Buddha). Part of this section describes how Ribata's other name, Kewagō ("false unity"), came about. The explanation of the origin of his name refers to an episode of an oni (re)creating Ribata from some parts taken from the dead (Hirota 159).

An example appears in *Hokekyō jikidanshō* (Direct Sermon and Annotation about [the] Lotus Sutra) written by Eishin (1475–1546), a Tendai monk. When Ribata was meditating on a deserted pavilion late at night, a small oni brought a corpse to the pavilion and left. Then, a big oni entered the pavilion; just as he was about to eat the dead body, the small oni returned and claimed the corpse. The big oni asked Ribata, who had seen the entire situation, to be the judge of the ownership of the corpse. Ribata sided with the small oni, who then ate the corpse. The big oni, angered by this, pulled Ribata's limbs off one by one and ate them. Sympathizing with Ribata, the small oni took parts from other corpses and attached them to Ribata's limbless body. He then spat on their joints and made mystic incantations. Ribata was resurrected (Hirota 159–60; Eishin 135–36). This story is followed by a text that teaches readers the fundamental falseness and impermanence of the human body.

Kuroda Hideo notes that there is some Buddhist imagery of meditation, as seen, for example, in the *Kusō shi emaki* (Picture Scroll of Poems on Nine Stages of a Corpse), behind the creation of a beautiful woman from bones; that is, readers could vividly conjure up these nine stages (including the swelling, oozing filth, and exposure of the corpse's white bones) when they learned the beautiful woman was made from corpses. Contemplations on the nine stages of a body's putrefaction after death are supposed to lead one to relinquish the desire for a (beautiful) human body (Kuroda, *Rekishi to shite no otogi zōshi* 212–13). It is interesting to consider that the beauty in *A Tale of Lord Haseo* follows almost the reverse process of the nine stages of a corpse, in that the beauty in this story starts from the eighth stage, which features nothing but bare bones. Haseo is not released from sexual desire, however, because the woman disappears while Haseo is making love to her, and he is unaware of her origins as a corpse. On the contrary, his desire increases with his intense regrets. He is arguably a victim of his own desire.

ROLE OF THE BEAUTIFUL WOMAN

Interestingly, the woman Haseo was infatuated with does not utter a word throughout the tale. The oni described her as "a woman of unparalleled beauty, gracefulness and character" (Komatsu and Murashige 117). Haseo observed that she was "truly beautiful" and "doubted his own eyes that a woman of this exquisiteness had ever existed in the world" (Komatsu and Murashige 118). According to the narrator, Haseo "learned how gentle and graceful she was," and he "wanted her by his side all of the time; he could not leave her side even for a moment" (Komatsu and Murashige 118). All of the descriptions are from the perspective of someone other than the woman. Since the woman's state of mind is never described, there is little opportunity for the reader to feel empathy or sympathy for her when she disappears. This recalls Michelle Li's idea that "representations of women as victims in tales tend to direct our attention to men. Female characters are often constructed to make points about male characters and their challenges" (Li, *Ambiguous Bodies* 128–29). Indeed, the reader's attention is focused on Haseo's behavior. The oni's beautiful woman may be perceived as a victim of male desire, and her woman's body without a soul is used more like a conduit to shed light on the man's character and actions. This manmade beauty, like an art object, may remind one of Pygmalion's ivory statue, but unlike Pygmalion's woman, Haseo's beauty moves about with grace and feeling; she is animate.[28] If one sees her from Haseo's position, she represents living but untouchable sexual desire. One can sympathize with Haseo when one considers how difficult it must have been for him to control himself. It is hard for Haseo to be released from the cycle of reincarnations, but he may be called a victim of his own desire.[29]

Speaking of victims in the tale, the oni is perhaps the most pathetic being in the scroll, as he lost a valuable object that was destroyed. In fact, the narrator even says at the end of the story, "As Haseo very regrettably broke his promise and made love to her, she completely melted away. How much the oni must have regretted that (entrusting his creation to Haseo)!" Furthermore, at the end the oni is chased away by Kitano Tenjin. This pathetic oni is very much humanized; the descriptions of his actions and his state of mind seem to mirror the medieval Japanese psyche. Komatsu Kazuhiko writes that medieval tales even speak to contemporary humanity; that is, to study oni is to study humankind (Komatsu, *Yōkaigaku shinkō* 12).

What is the cause of the oni's regret? It is not only the loss of the beautiful woman but also the loss at the game of *sugoroku*. In the scroll, much space is spent on the oni gleefully taking Haseo to the Suzakumon to play *sugoroku*, and the scene of the two characters playing the game there is vividly illustrated. The risk associated with the game makes the oni emotional; during the game the enthusiastic oni reveals his true form.[30] If not for the excitement of the *sugoroku* game, the oni would not have bet (and lost) his handiwork. Haseo would not have known of the existence of the woman. *Sugoroku* was enormously popular from the Heian period through the Kamakura period, and the government often issued regulations to prohibit it (Yang, *Oni no iru kōkei* 107, 117–24). In this sense, while this is a story of the miracle of Kitano Tenjin, *A Tale of Lord Haseo* can also be taken as a cautionary story regarding the dangers of desiring women's bodies and of *sugoroku* gambling.

INFLUENCE ON MODERN LITERATURE AND MEDIA

A Tale of Lord Haseo reveals much about medieval Japanese attitudes regarding scholarship, literature, and human frailty. Superior scholars were believed to have special gifts that allowed them to encounter and interact with the oni. While the medieval Japanese held those superior scholars in awe, they were also amused by their blunders. The sudden appearance of Tenjin at the end of the story mirrors the rising power of Kitano Tenjin at the time of the story's production, a time when there were also firm beliefs that oni could create human beings from corpses. Such beliefs are not prevalent in present society, but the story of *A Tale of Lord Haseo*, in its whole or in parts, continues to impact various kinds of contemporary entertainment, ranging from manga and anime to fiction. For example, in the manga and anime titled *Inuyasha* (Dog-Demon),[31] Kikyō, one of the main characters, is the creation of an oni. According to *Inuyasha*, the original Kikyō dies, but a female oni magically summons her back from the netherland fifty years after Kikyō's death, using her bones and the earth from her grave. The resurrected Kikyō is a beauty made from bones and earth, created by an oni.

There are further contemporary fictional works based on *A Tale of Lord Haseo*. One is "Haseo no koi" (Haseo's Love, 1993)[32] by Umehara Takeshi (1925–), a philosopher and writer. The oni, friendly in this tale, lives in Rashōmon. The oni challenges Haseo to a *sugoroku* game because he wants to save his family member "Demon" Tarō. Umehara gives ample background information about Haseo and Sugawara no Michizane and has the oni say, "I ended up a devil. That's how I was able to learn the art of making a beautiful woman from a pile of corpses" (Umehara, trans. McCarthy, "Haseo's Love" 53). Further, Umehara's oni compliments Haseo for resisting the beauty for as long as eighty days (in other words, Haseo has extraordinary fortitude). As Umehara's oni does not attack Haseo, Kitano Tenjin does not appear. This new version is no longer a miraculous story of Kitano Tenjin but is instead a story of a medieval scholar's friendship with a mysterious oni.

The other is an adaptation of a short piece of fiction titled "Ki no Haseo Suzakumon ni te onna wo arasoi oni to sugoroku wo suru koto" (Ki no Haseo Plays Sugoroku with an Oni at Suzaku Gate with a Bet of a Woman, 2001), written by Yumemakura Baku[33] (1951–), a popular fiction writer.[34] Yumemakura's story, with illustrations by a popular illustrator, Amano Yoshitaka, is tailored to a mass audience, with graphic depictions of sexual encounters. Yumemakura describes the oni of Suzakumon as someone who appreciates Chinese poems and arts and is sympathetic to Haseo. Interestingly, the beautiful woman has a name, and not only does she talk, but she actively entices him to make love with her. The story ends with Haseo's lamentation on losing his woman, poetically expressed through Haseo's Chinese poem. The oni is more like Haseo's companion and again, Kitano Tenjin does not appear.

Perhaps both writers, despite borrowing the medieval story, thought the moral of the tale—Tenjin's voice and its religious message—was not relevant in the present age. But even in the absence of the medieval belief system of the supernatural, *A Tale of Lord Haseo* is still an entertaining story, telling the reader what excites us regardless of the period: the perception of striking beauty, the story of a famed scholar's gaffe and weakness for women, and the workings of the supernatural. In this age, one can easily make a virtual woman of one's liking using computer graphics, but in medieval Japan, one may have entrusted the creation of one's ideal woman to an oni. Be it Pygmalion or Haseo, fiction's focus on the desire for unparalleled beauty—and the folly associated with gambling—does not seem to have greatly changed.

TRANSLATION OF *HASEO ZŌSHI*

This translation is based on volume 11 of *Nihon emaki taisei* (see Komatsu and Murashige 117–19).

A Tale of Lord Haseo

Middle Councilor Lord Ki no Haseo's (845–912) erudition encompassed nine schools of great scholarship, and he was renowned for his hundreds of refined accomplishments. Indeed, people both high and low thought very highly of him.

One evening as he was about to visit the imperial palace, an unusual looking stranger with sharp eyes approached him. "I spend my idle time playing the game of *sugoroku*," the stranger said, "I came here because I believe that you, my lord, are perhaps my only worthy opponent."

Although Lord Haseo thought this encounter rather odd, he could neither resist the flattering challenge nor suppress his desire to try his hand at the game.

"Your challenge is very interesting," said Lord Haseo to the stranger. "Where shall we play?"

"You home here is rather . . . um . . . inconvenient," the stranger replied. "Would you be so kind as to come to my abode?"

"That would be fine," replied Lord Haseo.

And out he went, without a carriage or an attendant. Alone, he followed the strange man to the foot of Suzaku Gate.

"If you will please climb this gate, my lord," the man said. "At the top we will play."

The climb looked impossible, but with the stranger's help, Lord Haseo easily ascended to the top of the gate. When they had seated themselves on either side of the game board, they began to discuss stakes.

"If I lose," said the stranger with some arrogance, "I will present to you a woman of unparalleled beauty, gracefulness, and character. What will you stake, my lord?"

"If I lose I will give to you all the treasures I possess," replied Lord Haseo.

"So be it," said the man, and they began playing *sugoroku*.

Much to the stranger's regret, Lord Haseo won game after game. With each defeat the sharp-eyed stranger, who had looked quite human at first, shook the dice all the more violently, groaned, and finally revealed his true form—that of a frightening oni. But although the oni looked frightening indeed, Lord Haseo prayed in his mind.

"If only I win," thought the lord, "he will have to be as gentle as a mouse."

And so they played on until Lord Haseo had won at last. Instantly, the stranger regained his human form.

"What can I say now?" cried the man. "I was sure I was going to win, my lord. Well, regrettably, I have lost. I will bring the woman as I have promised on such and such date," and so saying, he descended Suzaku Gate with Lord Haseo.

Lord Haseo thought it rather unlikely that the stranger would keep his promise, but nevertheless, as the agreed-upon date drew near, he had his servants arrange a room in his house appropriately for the occasion and anxiously awaited the stranger's visit. Deep in the night, the sharp-eyed man arrived as he had said, bringing with him a young woman of shining beauty.

Figure 4.1. Haseo plays *sugoroku* with the oni. Courtesy of International Research Center for Japanese Studies.

"How remarkable!" cried the lord, enthralled by the woman. "Are you really going to give her to me?" he asked.

"You have no worry here, my lord," said the stranger quietly. "As I lost the game, you need not return her to me. She belongs to you. But just one thing—you can make love to her only after 100 days from tonight. If you take her to your bed before 100 days have passed, you will never realize your wish."

"Of course I will observe your words." And so saying, Lord Haseo kept the woman, and the man left. When dawn broke, Lord Haseo was astonished to rediscover how truly beautiful the woman was. He doubted his own eyes—that a woman of this exquisiteness had ever existed in the world. As days passed and he learned how gentle and graceful she was, Haseo wanted her by his side all the time; he could not leave her side even for a moment.

Thus 80 days passed at what seemed to Lord Haseo a snail's pace.

"Many days have passed already," Haseo thought. "Surely the man didn't mean exactly 100 days." Haseo could bear it no more and surrendered to his lust. No sooner had he embraced her, however, than she melted into

Figure 4.2. The woman melts into water. Courtesy of International Research Center for Japanese Studies.

clear water and disappeared. Haseo regretted and bemoaned his foolish lust a thousand times, but it was all in vain.

Three months had passed since the woman's disappearance when one night, on his way home from the palace, Lord Haseo saw the sharp-eyed man coming toward the front of his carriage and calling out to him. "You are insincere! How hateful you are!" the stranger cried as he quickly approached Lord Haseo's carriage.

The oni's countenance looked more frightening than it had on that fateful night when they played *sugoroku* atop Suzaku Gate. Lord Haseo closed his eyes and prayed for Kitano Tenjin's divine help with all his heart and soul, and no sooner had he done so than an angry voice roared out from the night sky. "What a nuisance you are!" the voice bellowed to the oni. "Be gone immediately!" At these words the demon vanished into the thin air.

The man was an oni who lived in Suzaku Gate. The woman was composed of the best parts collected from various dead bodies, and her soul was to enter the body after 100 days. As Haseo very regrettably broke his promise and made love to her, she completely melted away. How much the oni must have regretted entrusting his creation to Haseo.

NOTES

1. See the introduction for a brief explanation of *otogizōshi*.

2. Wakimoto Jūkurō surmises it was at the end of the Kamakura period (1185–1333) (Wakimoto 421), as does Kuwabara Hiroshi (*Otogizōshi* 243). Umezu Jirō conjectures that it was at the turn of the fourteenth century (Umezo 18: 8), and Murashige Yasushi considers the date to be around 1310–20s (Murashige 11: 89). For the text of *A Tale of Haseo*, see Komatsu and Murashige 1–39, 117–19.

3. Umezu did not think the written text of *A Tale of Lord Haseo* came directly from the *Zoku kyōkunshō* story, but he believed the latter is close to its prototype.

4. Translation by Rimer and Chaves 32. For the Japanese text of the Haseo's verse, see Sugano 19: 24–25.

5. The Suzakumon had been destroyed by the mid-thirteenth century, so it did not exist by the time the story of Haseo was first written. Andō 184.

6. The stone monument for Rashōmon stands in Karahashi Saiji Park near Ninth Avenue, south of Kyoto Station.

7. The Tenri version and the Kyōdai version take the Suzakumon as the backdrop, and the Tōdai version and the Kokkai version take the Rashōmon as the backdrop. Kuroda, *Chūsei setsuwa* 366.

8. Yoshika's Chinese poem is, "The weather clears, breezes comb / the hair of young willows; / the ice is melting, wavelets wash / the whiskers of old bog moss" (*Ki harete wa kaze shinryū no kami o kezuru, kōri kiete wa nami kyūtai no hige o arau*). Translation by Rimer and Chaves 31. For the original version, see Sugano 19: 24. This poem appears in the Early Spring section of volume 1 of *Wakan rōeishū*, immediately before the poem of Ki no Haseo.

9. For Yoshika's story in *Hokekyō jurin shūyō shō*, see Sonshun110–11.

10. For the text of "Genjō to iu biwa, oni ni toraruru koto," the twenty-fourth story of volume 24 of *Konjaku monogatarishū*, see *SNKBZ* 37: 308–11. For an English translation, see Ury, *Tales of Times Now Past* 146–49.

11. For the explanations of oni in English, see Li, *Ambiguous Bodies*, especially chapters 4 and 5; Kawashima, *Writing Margins*, especially chapter 5; Reider, *Japanese Demon Lore*, especially chapter 1.

12. The early thirteenth century is the most accepted time period for when the *Hasedera genki* was produced. Yokota Takashi, however, claims the work was completed around the middle of the thirteenth century. See Yokota, "*Hasedera genki* no seiritsu nendai" 7.

13. See note 8 of chapter 1 for a brief explanation of *setsuwa*.

14. For the text of *Gōdanshō*, see Ōe, "*Gōdanshō*" 81–82. For the text of *Konjaku monogatarishū*, see *SNKBZ* 37: 311–12.

15. For an English text, see Tyler, *Japanese Tales* 232–33. For the Japanese text, see *SNKBZ* 38: 228–30.

16. Some famous diviners such as Abe no Seimei (921?–1005), however, could not only foretell but could also use magic. Like superior scholars, those who excelled in the way of yin-yang or Onmyōdō were believed to be able to see or predict the behaviors of oni. For example, the sixteenth story of volume 24 of *Konjaku monogatarishū* tells that Abe no Seimei saw a parade of oni and hobgoblins his teacher could not see; *SNKBZ* 37: 283. *Onmyōji* can create human-looking creatures out of paper or wood, but such artificial humans are essentially nonhuman. They usually revert to their former substance, such as paper, after their usefulness is over, though some nonhuman creatures may embark on their own lives after the *onmyōji* discard them. Tanaka Takako surmises that those abandoned creatures are the hobgoblins that appear in *hyakki yagyō* (the night processions of 100 demons); Tanaka, *Hyakki yagyō* 141.

17. This episode appears in the twenty-fifth story of volume 25 of *Konjaku monogatarishū*, titled "Miyoshi no Kiyoyuki saishō to Haseo no kōron no koto" (An Argument between Councilor Miyoshi no Kiyoyuki and Ki no Haseo); *SNKBZ* 37: 311–12.

18. Both *yasha* and *rasetsu* are Buddhist guardian deities. They are said to devour human flesh.

19. For the texts of the *Illustrated Legends of Kitano Shrine*, see Komatsu, Nakano, and Matsubara 118–37; Sakurai, Hagiwara, and Miyata.

20. Michizane's story reveals the relationship between *kami* and oni proposed by Komatsu. That is, angry spirits turn into *kami* through people's worship; Komatsu, *Yōkaigaku shinkō* 193.

21. This is before Sugawara no Michizane was given the status of Tenjin.

22. For an English text, see Tyler, *Japanese Tales* 68–70. For the original Japanese text, see Nishio 198–202.

23. Translation is by Tyler unless noted otherwise. Tyler, *Japanese Tales* 69; Nishio 199.

24. Also known as Tsuchimikado Minister of Right (1008–77).

25. This translation is by the author, since Tyler did not provide one. For the Japanese text, see Nishio, 201–2.

26. This date is given by Murayama, *Nihon onmyōdō* 323–24.

27. *Jikidanmono* include many tales and poetry for easy understanding of Buddhist teachings.

28. Unlike the ivory statue transforming into a real human being because of Aphrodite's (divine) intervention, the oni's woman is extinguished because of Haseo's (human) intervention.

29. For the study of *setsuwa* and bodies, see Li, *Ambiguous Bodies*, especially chapter 4; Eubanks, especially chapter 3; Kawashima, *Writing Margins*, especially chapter 5.

30. Oni are customarily portrayed with one or more horns protruding from a disheveled scalp, with skin that varies in color, often red, and a wide mouth with large fangs.

31. Appearing first in Japan in 1997, the manga was so successful that it was made into a television anime series, and it inspired four feature-length films. For the Japanese manga texts, see Takahashi, *Inuyasha*. For the English manga texts, see Takahashi, *Inuyasha*.

32. The Japanese text is found in Umehara, "Haseo no koi"; an English translation is found in Umehara, trans. McCarthy, "Haseo's Love."

33. This is the pseudonym of Yoneyama Mineo.

34. For the text, see Yumemakura and Amano 61–161.

Part III
Women

5

Tale of Amewakahiko (*Amewakahiko sōshi*)
A Demon in the Sky, a Maiden in Search of Her Husband

In most cultures, demons and dragons reside at the heart of the supernatural, where their distinct status reflects their various cultural roles. This is also true of Japanese culture and folklore, where these creatures play prominent roles. For present-day Japanese, oni typically reside in Buddhist hell to punish mortal sinners or in deep mountains, but for their medieval counterparts the oni's role and the space oni occupied were much more flexible. Perhaps a prime example is *Amewakahiko sōshi* (Tale of Amewakahiko, fifteenth century), a fictional story that recounts one legendary origin of *Tanabata* (Festival of the Weaver; the Star Festival), the celebration of the annual meeting of the Weaver Maid and the Cowherd, who represent the stars Vega and Altair, respectively. In this version of the *Tanabata* story, that is, the *Tale of Amewakahiko*, an oni is standing in the beautiful serene sky. This oni turns out to be the father of a *kairyūō* (dragon king of the ocean), who also lives in the sky. This dragon king calls himself Amewakahiko (sometimes Amewaka*mi*ko)—hence the title. In search of her husband, the heroine, Amewakahiko's mortal wife, travels to the sky where she meets an intimidating father-in-law, the oni. The *Tale of Amewakahiko* reveals a medieval Japanese view of space boundaries (or lack thereof) of underground, earth, and heaven the characters travel; it also suggests that studies of ancient and classical Japanese literature (645–1185) by medieval Japanese scholars influenced the choice of the characters' names and their actions in this tale.

The plot of *Tale of Amewakahiko* is similar to that of *Cupid and Psyche* by Lucius Apuleius (second century CE). Some scholars in Japan recognize *Cupid and Psyche* as the *Tale of Amewakahiko*'s source, and others read the dragon king's tale as indigenous to Japan. While there is no finally persuasive evidence that the Japanese tale was influenced by *Cupid and Psyche*,

DOI: 10.7330/9781607324904.c005

it is worthwhile to examine the Apuleian tale's connection to the *Tale of Amewakahiko* and to share these different scholarly perspectives. This chapter thus discusses the various possible origins of the tale.

PLOT SUMMARY OF THE *TALE OF AMEWAKAHIKO* PICTURE SCROLLS

One day a huge serpent appears in front of a wealthy family's house. The serpent demands one of the family's three daughters for his wife, or he threatens to destroy the entire family. The two older daughters refuse to marry him, but the youngest daughter consents. A huge house is built near a pond as part of the wedding preparations requested by the serpent, and there, alone, she awaits her snake husband. When the gigantic serpent appears, he asks the girl to cut off his head. As she does so, a handsome young gentleman appears, and they live happily in their newly built house. After a while, the husband reveals his true identity as a dragon king of the ocean and tells the girl that he must go to the sky to do some business. He tells her how to find him in the sky if he does not come back. He orders her not to open a certain Chinese-style treasure chest—if the chest is opened, he warns her, he will not be able to return to earth. While he is away, her two older sisters visit her and become jealous of her wealth and happiness. They open the treasure chest, from which only smoke arises. When the girl learns that her husband cannot return, she goes to Kyoto as instructed by her husband before he left and buys a gourd whose vine grows to the sky in one night.

Climbing the vine up to the sky, the girl journeys in search of her husband, whose name, the reader has learned, is Amewaka*h*iko (or Amewaka*m*iko). With great difficulty, she finally finds him. While they are happy together, 0Amewakahiko expresses his concern that if his father, an oni, becomes aware of her, there could be trouble. So whenever his father visits him, the dragon king changes his wife into a pillow or a fan. But the secret is finally revealed one day, and the oni-father takes her away and imposes upon her four difficult tasks. The first task is to look after a thousand cattle in a field day and night. Amewakahiko helps her by giving her the sleeves of his robe, which are endowed with magical powers. As she waves the sleeves saying "Amewakahiko's sleeves," the cattle come under her power, and she succeeds in the task. The oni-father then tells her to move a million rice grains from one granary to another. Third, he orders her to stay in a warehouse full of gigantic centipedes and, fourth, to stay in a storehouse full of snakes. She successfully carries out these tasks, thanks to Amewakahiko's sleeves. Finally, the oni-father gives her his permission to live with his son—once a month. But the girl mishears the father's words as "once a year," and since then, the girl and Amewakahiko, as Vega and Altair, have seen each other only once a year.

THE *TALE OF AMEWAKAHIKO* PICTURE SCROLLS

The *Tale of Amewakahiko*, like many other works in this book, belongs to the *otogizōshi* genre.[1] The two picture scrolls of *Amewakahiko sōshi* date back to the fifteenth century: the first scroll is missing or no longer extant, although, fortunately, a reliable copy dating from the seventeenth century exists; the Museum of Asian Art in Dahlem, one of the Berlin State museums, has the second scroll.[2] At the end of this scroll it is written that the reigning emperor wrote the text and Tosa Hirochika (or Hirokane, ca. 1439–92), an early painter of the Tosa school, which held the leading position at the imperial court, produced the illustrations. Scholars generally agree that Tosa Hirochika executed the paintings. According to Akiyama Terukazu, the "reigning emperor" could be Emperor GoKomatsu (reigned 1382–1412), Emperor Shōkō (reigned 1412–28), or Emperor GoHanazono (reigned 1428–64); Emperor GoHanazono is the most likely, considering features of the calligraphy and the painter's active years (Akiyama 16–17).

The extant second scroll consists of seven sections of written text and illustrations. What caught my attention is that the oni, who is often associated with tormenting sinful mortals in hell, is standing with a serene, beautiful sky as his background. In religious paintings, oni as attendants of Buddhas, Bodhisattvas, and Devas often appear in a group that follows the divine beings. Tormenting sinful mortals in hell is one of the oni's jobs as attendants; they work as the wardens of hell. An oni can and does visit human beings, kidnapping them and eating human flesh in the mountains; but an oni standing on tranquil clouds with a lovely girl as in the *Tale of Amewakahiko*, away from the presence of a commanding deity and without an ominous background, strikes readers today as a little odd.

Certainly, there are many visual examples of an oni appearing by himself before a person(s). For example, a story in *Tales of Times Now Past* recounts an oni disguised as a woman on a bridge so the oni can assault a samurai (see Mabuchi, Kunisaki, and Inagaki 38: 46–52; for an English translation, see Tyler, *Japanese Tales* 19–22); a red oni is the spirit of murdered Abe no Nakamaro in the *Illustrated Story of Minister Kibi's Adventures in China* (see Komatsu, *Kibi daijin nittō emaki* 3: 28), and an oni plays *sugoroku* (traditional board game played with dice) in the *Tale of Haseo* (see Komatsu and Murashige 22, 35, 39). But oni appear on earthly ground. In *Kitano tenjin emaki* (Illustrated Legends of Kitano Tenjin Shrine, ca. early thirteenth century), Sugawara no Michizane (845–903), who became a horrendously vengeful spirit after his untimely death, is presented as a red-skinned oni who torments wicked mortals in hell (see Komatsu, Nakano, and Matsubara 25, 29, 31–35). As an angry spirit, he appears on dark, not serene, clouds. So why does an oni, most often known as a warden of hell, a human-eater, or a mountain-dwelling being, live in the sky? But it turns out that the father was originally Bontennō (Brahma), whose abode is located "1,290,000 *yojanas*[3] above the highest heaven of the realm of desire" (*Buddhist Cosmology* 63).

ORIGINS OF THE *TALE OF AMEWAKAHIKO*
The *Qian Luwei* Tale and *Kojiki*

Mitani Eiichi, a scholar of Japanese literature, found the tale's major source, an almost identical story to the *Tale of Amewakahiko*, in the annotations to a poem in *Kokinshū chū* (annotated text of *Kokinshū*, A Collection of Poems Ancient and Modern), written by Fujiwara Tameie (1198–1275) in the Kamakura period (1185–1333) (*Monogatari bungakushiron* 451 and 455, published in 1965).[4] The poem is about *Tanabata*, a festival that originated in China[5]—in which the love story of the Weaver Maid and the Cowherd had already taken shape by the late Han Dynasty (Kominami, *Seiōbo to Tanabata denshō* 29–30).[6] When the story was transmitted to Japan, the Weaver Maid was known in Japanese as *Tanabata* or Orihime and the Cowherd as Kengyū or Hikoboshi.

While the plot is almost identical—from the appearance of a huge serpent to a washing woman and the third daughter's marriage to the serpent, to the jealous sisters, the youngest sister's journey to the sky, and her reunion with her husband, with the ending of their meeting once a year because of her mishearing—the story in the *Kokinshū chū* annotation has different names for the characters. The wealthy household's master is called Qian Luwei (hereafter, this story is "Qian Luwei's Tale"), a Chinese name. The male protagonist introduces himself as Hikoboshi (Altair) who resides in *Shiōten* (Heaven of the Four Guardian Kings),[7] and his father is Bontennō, Brahma. As Bontennō resides in the sky, it is natural that Hikoboshi, a star, resides in the sky as well.

Hikoboshi tells Qian Luwei's youngest daughter that he has descended to the earth to marry her, and he stays there for three years. Hikoboshi is not an ocean dragon king, and the oni appears nowhere. It is Bontennō who imposes the difficult tasks when he finds out that Hikoboshi is living with the girl, and he gives tasks to both of them equally: the task for the girl is to weave a celestial robe, and the one for Hikoboshi is to herd 1,000 cows. She is referred to as a Weaver because she weaves the heavenly clothing; Hikoboshi (Altair) is called the Cowherd because he herds cows. This story is without doubt a variant of the story of the Cowherd and the Weaver Maid. In "Qian Luwei's Tale" the name Amewakahiko does not appear anywhere, and the miraculous power to help the girl weave the heavenly clothing comes from a Buddha who takes pity on her, not from the husband's supernatural sleeve (Mitani, *Monogatari bungakushiron* 454–56).

How, then, did the oni-father and Amewakahiko come to replace Bontennō and Hikoboshi in the *Tale of Amewakahiko*? Izumo Asako convincingly claims that the key lies in medieval Japanese studies of ancient and classical literature (Izumo).

Naming the Character: Amewakahiko or Amewakamiko?

Names are important. In many pre-modern traditions, naming a person, object, or supernatural being correctly has far-reaching consequences and implies more than simply being able to address someone or refer to something correctly; the very act of saying the name correctly provides total control over or summons a being whose name is usually withheld. Good examples of this can be found in the European folktale "Rumpelstiltskin" and the Japanese *Daiku to Oniroku* (Carpenter and Oniroku). In *Carpenter and Oniroku*, a carpenter has to build a bridge over a fast-moving river and is worried as to how to go about constructing it. A demon appears from the river and offers the carpenter a deal: he will build the bridge for him in exchange for the carpenter's eyes. The carpenter agrees, and the bridge is magically completed. Having fulfilled his side of the bargain, the demon intends to collect his prize, but the carpenter runs away from him. While running through the mountains, the carpenter hears a song that identifies the demon's name as Oniroku. The following day the demon demands his eyes again unless, he says, the carpenter says the demon's name correctly. The carpenter shouts "Oniroku," and the demon disappears.

When we turn to the *Tale of Amewakahiko*, as the title of this picture scroll dictates, the main male character's name is supposed to be Amewakahiko. However, instead of Amewakahiko, Amewakamiko frequently appears in the text. To be precise, Amewakahiko is used three times and Amewakamiko is used four times; they seem to alternate, as if the writer of the text, perhaps

Emperor GoHanazono, could not make up his mind as to which one he should adopt.

As many Japanese scholars point out, Amewaka*h*iko is a famous or perhaps infamous figure in the ancient works *Kojiki* and *Nihon shoki* (or *Nihongi,* Chronicles of Japan 720). He is a heavenly deity who acts against the decisions of the Heavenly Council; that is, he rebels against the central authority. According to the ancient accounts, Amewakahiko is sent from Takama ga hara (Plain of High Heaven—the realm of heavenly deities) to Ashiwara no naka-tsu-kuni (Central Land of Reed-Plains—Japan) in preparation for the descent of the Heavenly Grandchild of the Sun, Goddess Amaterasu Ōmikami (the progenitor of the imperial line), to pacify and take control of the Central Land. Earlier, another deity had been sent with the mission to negotiate with Ōkuninushi, an earth deity and lord of the Central Land, and arrange the transfer of power over the Central Land to the Heavenly Grandchild. But that deity failed to return, so Amewakahiko is given the same mission. Like his predecessor, Amewakahiko does not return to the Plain of High Heaven; instead, he marries Shitateru-hime, a daughter of Ōkuninushi, and plans to rule the Central Land himself. Takamimusuhi (the Deity of Heavenly Creation and an imperial ancestor) sends a pheasant to check on Amewakahiko's intentions, but Amewakahiko kills the bird. In return, Takamimusuhi dispatches an arrow that strikes the heart of Amewakahiko and kills him.

The name Amewaka*m*iko was instead widely known in Heian literature (794–1185) as a music deity who descends from heaven. For example, in *Utsuho monogatari* (Tale of the Hollow Tree, ca. tenth century), Amewakamiko descends from heaven and makes a *koto* (Japanese string instrument) for the male protagonist. In *Sagoromo monogatari* (Tale of Sagoromo, ca. eleventh century), impressed by the flute played by the tale's male protagonist, Sagoromo, Amewakamiko descends from heaven and attempts to take Sagoromo to heaven with him. According to Mitani, Amewakamiko, a deity who comes from heaven to interact with humans or other supernatural beings on earth, was never called Amewakahiko in the Heian period. In fact, *amewakamiko* was a term used more like a common noun, to refer to any heavenly deity. In this sense, Amewakahiko is an *amewakamiko* (as he, a heavenly deity, has descended from the Plain of High Heaven and married Shitateru-hime on earth), but the named Amewakamiko is not identical to Amewakahiko (Mitani, *Monogatari bungakushiron* 471).

The mixing up of Amewakahiko and Amewakamiko in the medieval tales seems to have occurred as a result of medieval Japanese scholars' studies of ancient and classical Japanese literature, as explained below.

Replacing the Names: The Influence of Medieval Approaches to Ancient and Classical Japanese Literature

During the medieval period (1185–1603), *Kokinshū* or *Kokin wakashū* (A Collection of Poems Ancient and Modern, 905) was required reading for the aristocracy. In particular, the *kana* preface to the *Kokinshū*, which laid the foundation for all subsequent poetics, was considered invaluable, tantamount to a sacred scripture. In this preface, a poem by Shitateru-hime is referred to as the oldest extant poem: "Our poetry appeared at the dawn of creation. But that which survives goes back to Shitateru-hime in the eternal heavens." This is followed by a note, added after the initial text was written, "Shitateru-hime was the wife of Amewakamiko." Here, Shitateru-hime's husband is written as Amewakamiko, not Amewakahiko. The comment in the note continues, "The reference is probably to the rustic songs in which she sang of hills and valleys lighted up by her divine elder brother's beauty" (McCullough, *Kokin Wakashū* 8; Ozawa and Matsuda 17). Shitateru-hime's poem, which is referred to as "the rustic song," appears in *Nihon shoki* (and slightly differently in *Kojiki*), "Ame naru ya / Ototanabata no / unagaseru / tama no misumaru no / anatama ha ya / mitani futawatarasu / Ajisukitakahikone" (Like the string of jewels / Worn on the neck / Of the Weaving-maiden, That dwells in Heaven—/ Oh! The luster of the jewels / Flung across two valleys / From Aji-suki-taka-hiko ne) (Kojima et al. 1: 127; Aston 75).

According to Katsumata Takashi, scholar of Japanese literature, the earliest example of the confusion of Amewakahiko and Amewakamiko appears in *Kokinshū kanajo kochū* (Old Annotations to the Kana Preface to A Collection of Poems Ancient and Modern, date unknown.)[8] *Kokinshū kanajo kochū* is also the earliest description of Amewaka*hi*ko in the literature of the Heian period. Katsumata assumes that when Amewakahiko was written in *hiragana* (a Japanese phonetic syllabary) as あめわかひこ, the "hi" ひ written in the cursive script was probably misread as "mi" み (Katsumata, "'Amewakamiko zō' no hensen ni kansuru ichi kōsatsu" 6).[9]

As a vital text, *Kokinshū* produced many commentaries. Likewise, during medieval times, many lecture notes and annotated writings on *Nihon shoki* were produced. According to intellectuals of the medieval period such as Ichijō Kanera (1402–81), a court noble with distinguished scholarly achievements, and Tōgen Zuisen (1430–89), a Buddhist monk, Shitateru-hime was often compared to and sometimes considered the Weaver, Oto-Tanabata. Ichijō Kanera writes in his *Kokinshū dōmōshō* (Secret Writings on *Kokinshū*) that Oto-Tanabata is Vegas (Hanawa, *Gunsho ruijū* 178; quoted in Izumo 52). Likewise, Tōgen Zuisen writes in his *Nihon shoki Tōgenkyō* that

Oto-Tanabata is the Weaver, and if the poem is interpreted as an expression of admiration by the people who gathered at Amewakahiko's funeral, Oto-Tanabata is compared to Shitateru-hime (quoted in Izumo 53). When the belief that Shitateru-hime equals Vega is applied to "Qian Luwei's Tale," Vega's husband's name becomes Amewakahiko, easily replacing Hikoboshi (Izumo 49–58). Thus, the replacement of Hikoboshi by Amewakahiko or Amewakamiko occurred in the process of producing various annotated editions of classical Japanese texts, especially *Kokinshū*. As Hikoboshi is a heavenly being who descends from the sky and marries someone on earth, he was easily replaced by Amewakahiko or Amewakamiko, who had a similar role.

Regarding Amewakamiko's status as an ocean dragon king and the change from Bontennō to an oni, Izumo notes that several annotated editions of *Kokinshū* consider Ōkuninushi to be a dragon deity. Some editions of *Nihon shoki*, such as *Nihon shoki tōgenshō* (Tōgen's Nihon shoki Commentaries, authored by Tōgen Zuisen), state that Amewakamiko is Ōkuninushi's son. This makes Amewakamiko a dragon king, too (Izumo 60–61).[10] In the same *Nihon shoki tōgenshō*, Ōkuninushi is considered an evil demon and a wicked deity (*akki jashin*). Izumo surmises that these various interpretations of ancient literary characters by medieval scholars may have caused the name change in the *Tale of Amewakahiko*'s characters. Presumably, the *Tale of Amewakahiko* was shaped by someone who had access to these various annotated writings and lectures on the Japanese classics.

Moreover, the name change may have possibly occurred because Bontennō, who frequently appears in esoteric Buddhism as a leading Deva among the Twelve Devas to give happiness and remove suffering, does not fit the role of a mean father who presents almost impossible challenges to a happy marriage. The role is more suitable for an oni considered evil by nature.

Cupid and Psyche

The plot of *Tale of Amewakahiko*, especially the difficult challenges the girl must endure, might remind readers familiar with Western literature and folklore of the tasks given to Psyche in *Cupid and Psyche* by Lucius Apuleius. In fact, the hypothesis that *Cupid and Psyche* is the origin of the *Tale of Amewakahiko* goes back to 1910, when Nonokuchi Seiichi published an article titled "The Origin of the Tale of Amewakamiko—Eros and Psyche," in which he wrote, "I do not doubt that the origin of the *Tale of Amewakamiko* is ancient Greek myth" (quoted in Inoue, *Nanban gensō* 290). While Nonokuchi does not mention the route of transmission, Tsuda Sōkichi, a Japanese historian, also suggested in 1916 that the origin of the

Tale of Amewakahiko is *Cupid and Psyche*, and the Greek story was perhaps transmitted through Buddhist scriptures. He surmises that stories of the Roman period were perhaps adopted into Buddhist scriptures, just as the Gandhāra style of Buddhist art was born, merging Greek, Syrian, Persian, and Indian artistic influences (Tsuda, *Bungaku ni arawaretaru waga kokumin shisō no kenkyū* 176–79; also see Inoue, *Nanban gensō* 290–91, 297–99). Tsuda repeated this suggestion in his monumental book *Bungaku ni arawaretaru waga kokumin shisō no kenkyū* (An Inquiry into the Japanese Mind as Mirrored in Literature), first published in 1917.

Indeed, the plots of the two tales are similar. In *Cupid and Psyche*, the youngest of three sisters becomes the wife of a divine being; the two older sisters cause the youngest sister to break her promise to Cupid; the girl travels in search of her husband, and she has to meet Venus's challenges to be finally reunited with her husband. In 1969 Doi Kōichi, a scholar of English comparative literature, identified further similarities: for example, Eros's apparatus is a bow and arrow, and these are Amewakamiko's tools as well. While Cupid is introduced as a dragon's son,[11] Doi writes that Amewakamiko calls himself Dragon King. Psyche goes to the underworld and nearly dies (falls into an "infernal" asleep), and a similar phenomenon may have happened to the girl when Amewakamiko tells her to wait for him to return for "seven, fourteen, or twenty-one days." This phrase, "seven, fourteen, or twenty-one days," suggests the Buddhist memorial days for the dead after one dies;[12] to join her husband in the sky, the girl's soul leaves her body and she becomes physically dead so she can travel to the heavenly realm. Moreover, the difficult challenges given to the girl are similar to the tasks given to Psyche (Doi 155–82). Doi further comments that the relationship between Cupid and Amewakamiko is like that of brothers. He reprinted his article in his book *Shinwa, densetsu no kenkyū* (Study of Mythology and Legends) in 1973.

Primarily based on Doi's scholarship, Katsumata Takashi lists their similarities ("Chūsei shōsetsu '*Tanabata*' to senkō bunken no kankei ni tsuite" 17–18). Katsumata, however, suggests that these similarities are not necessarily directly related to the two stories. I discuss Katsumata's similarities in the following paragraphs.

1. The youngest of the three sisters is the most beautiful in mind and appearance. Katsumata writes that it is not rare for the third daughter or youngest sister to be the most beautiful, as in the case of Cinderella stories or "Hachikazuki" (in this case, the youngest son's bride).[13]

2. Both heroines are left by themselves before their ominous marriages, and the monstrous husbands turn out to be the handsome, heavenly beings. In *Cupid and Psyche*, Psyche is left on the rock of a mountain peak because the oracle predicted she would become a monster's bride. The monster turns out to be Cupid, divine and immortal. In the *Tale of Amewakahiko*, the girl is left alone in a house by a pond because the letter from the huge serpent demanded that she wed the serpent. Amewakahiko is a good-looking dragon king who resides in the sky. Katsumata contends that there are many stories about a female being who is sacrificed to or marries a serpent. Good examples in ancient literature are the story of Yamata no Orochi (Eight-Headed Giant Serpent), who ate a female sacrifice every year, and the legend of Mt. Miwa, in which the deity (or messenger) of Mt. Miwa is a serpent who in the guise of a male human being marries a village girl.[14]

3. Before losing their husbands, both heroines live in gorgeous mansions with many servants. The elder sisters visit their younger sister and become jealous of her.

4. The younger sister's promise to her husband is broken because of her elder sisters. As their interdictions are violated, both husbands leave their brides. Psyche was urged to look at her husband, and unintentionally she hurts him by spilling a drop of oil from her lamp on his shoulder. Cupid leaves for his mother's residence on Mt. Olympus. In the *Tale of Amewakahiko*, the sisters open the forbidden Chinese chest from which white smoke emerges; thus, Amewakamiko is unable to come back to earth to be united with the girl. Katsumata writes, however, that there are numerous tales about a woman breaking her promise to her supernatural husband, resulting in separation from him. The "forbidden promise" or "taboo" that separates a couple is not particularly unique to *Cupid and Psyche* or the *Tale of Amewakahiko*.

5. Both Psyche and the girl set out on an arduous journey in search of their husbands, and both receive four difficult tasks from their in-laws. Psyche is tested by her mother-in-law, Venus; the girl by her father-in-law, an oni. The first difficult task for Psyche is to sort a random heap of seeds, which she achieves with the help of ants. In the *Tale of Amewakahiko*,

the second task for the girl is to carry a huge number of rice grains from one storage site to another; this task is also achieved with the help of ants. The second difficult task for Psyche is to obtain a tuft of fleece from a golden sheep. In the *Tale of Amewakahiko*, the first task for the girl is to take 1,000 cattle to pasture in the field during the day and bring them into the barn at night. However, Katsumata argues that a woman in search of her disappeared husband is common and that it is not unusual to see a parent impose difficult tasks on a son- or daughter-in-law and then bless the in-law's marriage once the difficult tasks are accomplished.

Further, as pointed out by Mitani Eiichi and others (see Mitani, *Monogatari bungakushiron* 457), the difficult tasks charged upon the girl in the *Tale of Amewakahiko* are closer to those that appear in the *Kojiki* (Ancient Matters, dated 712) (Katsumata, "Chūsei shōsetsu 'Tanabata' to senkō bunken no kankei ni tsuite" 18–20). Earlier in *Kojiki*, Ōkuninushi goes down to the underworld (*Ne no kuni*) to avoid being murdered by his older brothers. In the underworld he meets Suseribime, the daughter of Susanoo (the Storm God). Suseribime and Ōkuninushi marry without her father's consent. When Suseribime introduces Ōkuninushi to her father at his residence, Susanoo imposes four challenging tasks on Ōkuninushi. First, Ōkuninushi is confined to a chamber full of snakes. Suseribime gives Ōkuninushi her scarf and tells him to wave it as snakes approach. As he does so, no snakes come near him. On the next visit, Susanoo puts Ōkuninushi in a room full of centipedes and wasps. Suseribime again provides him with a scarf and gives the same instruction. He survives again. Ōkuninushi overcomes two more trials and finally escapes from Susanoo's residence with Suseribime. As the couple runs away, Susanoo grudgingly gives them his blessing (Yamaguchi and Kōnoshi 80–85; Philippi 98–102). Although the sex of the person who is challenged is changed, the tasks the heroine of the *Tale of Amewakahiko* has to undertake and their solutions are similar to those of Ōkuninushi. Indeed, the magical tool that saves the main character and the way she or he uses it are very much alike: in Ōkuninushi's case, he waves a scarf given to him by his lover; in the *Tale of Amewakahiko* the girl waves Amewakahiko's sleeve that was given to her.

Thus, the *Tale of Amewakahiko* seems to derive this section from the ancient literature.

6. When Psyche opens the casket, she finds nothing but "an infernal sleep, a sleep truly Stygian" (Apuleius, *Cupid and Psyche* 111), and she falls asleep; when the girl's sisters open the Chinese chest, they find nothing but a trail of white smoke. At the end, Cupid and Psyche get married with Zeus's permission. In the *Tale of Amewakahiko*, Amewakahiko's father gives permission for his son and the girl to live together. According to Katsumata, these similarities are not noteworthy and cannot be claimed as solid evidence of influence.

Katsumata and other scholars of Japanese literature in Japan[15] believe the possibility of Western literature having been transmitted to Japan in the early or middle Muromachi period and immediately influencing Japanese fiction is low, since it is recorded that westerners entered medieval Japan for the first time in the sixteenth century (Katsumata, "Chūsei shōsetsu 'Tanabata' to senkō bunken no kankei ni tsuite" 22). Because the methods and routes of the ways Greek myths were transmitted to Japan have not been documented in writing and, Katsumata writes, all the details of the components can be explained by examples from ancient and classical Japanese literature, it is safe to conclude that *Cupid and Psyche* had no direct influence on the *Tale of Amewakahiko*. As such, it is now generally accepted among Japanese scholars that the *Tale of Amewakahiko* is of Japanese origin, borrowing the framework from "Qian Luwei's Tale."

Similarities between the *Tale of Amewakahiko*'s plot and that of *Cupid and Psyche* for Katsumata were most likely based on humankind's similar thoughts rather than transmission ("'Amewakamiko zō' no hensen ni kan-suru ichi kōsatsu" 17). While Katsumata's argument is persuasive, perhaps the possibility of oral transmission should not be completely dismissed. Yamashita Tarō, a scholar of comparative thought and mythology, having observed similarities between Norse myth and Japanese myth, suggests that Norse myth was transmitted to Japan by the nomadic people of inland Asia (*Hokuō shinwa to Nihon shinwa* 86–113). The Silk Road is another possibility. It is also interesting that Japanese scholars of comparative studies support the theory of transmission from the West, whereas scholars of Japanese literature in Japan tend to consider the tale indigenous.

If we read the tale in the context of Japanese literature and history, it tells us something specific about medieval Japan's worldview. Jack Zipes states, "Though many ancient tales might seem magical, miraculous, fanciful, superstitious, or unreal to us, people believed them, and these people were and are not much different from people today who believe in religions, miracles, cults, nations, and notions such as 'free' democracies that have little basis in reality" (2). The medieval Japanese had an expansive worldview, and their understanding of space was broad and flexible. Originally, the oni-father was not an oni but Bontennō (Brahma). The change may have stemmed from medieval scholars' examinations and interpretations of earlier Japanese literature, or perhaps for them it may not have been significant to place an oni in the sky. The same is true in regard to the names and roles of the characters Amewakahiko and Amewakamiko—while this may have been a copying mistake, it reveals a flexible understanding of oni's space on the part of medieval Japanese as they readily accepted or created that space in the beautiful sky.

The tale may have also had gendered social functions in addition to being an etiological tale. The heroine of *Tale of Amewakahiko*, a daughter who sacrifices herself to marry a giant serpent to save her parents, has an arduous journey. Zipes writes, "Fairy tales begin with conflict because we all begin our lives with conflict. We are all misfit for the world, and somehow we must fit in, fit in with other people, and thus we must invent or find the means through communication to satisfy as well as resolve conflicting desires and instincts" (2). For medieval young women of good standing, who were highly restricted in their freedom to move about, the *Tale of Amewakahiko* was perhaps almost like a dream come true. A kind daughter obtains happiness after overcoming various challenges, including difficult tasks imposed by an oni father-in-law. Her dragon-husband loves her as his only wife. Because the *Tale of Amewakahiko* explains one origin of the Star Festival, it is inevitable that the happy couple's meeting time is restricted, and Amewakahiko-Altair and the girl-Vega can see each other only once a year.

If we read the *Tale of Amewakahiko* in a more comparative framework, the general plot and the ordeals the girl has to go through to be acknowledged by her father-in-law are similar to those of *Cupid and Psyche*, but, as we have seen, the framework is much closer to "Qian Luwei's Tale" written as the annotation of a poem in *Kokinshū chū*, and the difficult tasks the girl's father-in-law imposes on her are found in ancient Japanese literature. That said, I do not entirely reject the possibility that the writer of the *Tale of Amewakahiko* was inspired by *Cupid and Psyche* and looked for similar elements in Japanese literature. Only further discovery of textual evidence or oral transmission can determine whether the *Tale of Amewakahiko* is indigenous or indigenized. Regardless of its origin(s), it is a fascinating *otogizōshi* story of the medieval Japanese period that parallels the plot and motifs of a well-known European tale.

TRANSLATION OF *AMEWAKAHIKO SŌSHI*

This translation is based on *Otogizōshi-shū,* volume 36 of *Nihon koten bungaku taikei* (see Ōshima, *Otogizōshi-shū* 75–85). For the illustrations, see Shimada illustrations plates nos. 7–9, illustrations 9–13 and 37–41.

Tale of Amewakahiko

SCROLL ONE

Long ago, there was a maid washing clothes in front of her wealthy master's house. (As the maid was thus occupied, from out of nowhere) a huge serpent appeared in front of her.

"Listen to what I say," said the serpent, "or I will coil around your body and crush you."

"What could it be?" the maid replied. "I will do whatever I can."

The serpent then spat out a letter from his mouth and told the maid to show the letter to her wealthy master. The woman ran to her master with the letter, who immediately opened it and read: "Give me one of your three daughters or I shall kill you and your wife. In preparation for our union, build a house in front of a certain pond. Even a hundred-foot-frontage long house would be a little too small for me." Having read the letter, there was no end to the rich couple's sorrow and they cried infinitely.

Frightened beyond their wits, the couple summoned their eldest daughter and told her of the serpent's demand.

"Surely you must be joking," the eldest daughter replied. "Even in the face of so deadly a threat, I shall never marry a snake." Much to the frightened parents' chagrin, the answer was the same from their middle daughter. In tears, at last the parents called in the youngest and dearest daughter.

"I will do anything to spare the lives of my parents," the youngest daughter said. She was so piteous, and the parents tearfully prepared for the girl's departure.

The parents had the house built in front of the pond just as the serpent instructed, and the youngest daughter left for the new house with several attendants. Soon after the young girl arrived at the new house, her retinue departed, leaving the girl alone to face her fate. Around ten o'clock that night the wind suddenly picked up and rain began to pour as the roar of thunder and the flash of lightning filled the night sky. The girl saw monstrously high waves in the distance, and her soul nearly fled her body in fear. As she began to swoon, a snake as big as the house appeared before her.

"Don't be afraid," it said. "Do you have a knife? If so, cut my head off."

Although she was frightened of the snake, she felt oddly sad about his order, but, reluctantly, she did as she was asked and easily cut the snake with her fingernail-clipping shears. Much to her surprise, a beautiful young gentleman clad in aristocratic attire emerged from the snake's body. He wrapped the snakeskin around himself and went inside a small Chinese-style chest with the girl. They both laid down. The girl forgot about her previous fear, and the two slept tight in each other's embrace.

Thus they loved each other deeply and lived happily. As they had the Chinese-style chest that produced various things, they lacked nothing and led an extremely merry life. The man had many servants and relatives. One day he said, "I am actually an ocean dragon king, and sometimes I traverse the sky. Now that I have some business to attend to, I will ascend to the sky tomorrow or the day after tomorrow. I plan to come back after seven days. If things don't go smoothly and I don't come back, wait two weeks. If I still don't return, wait three weeks. If I still don't come back, then know that I will never return."

"Then what shall I do?" the girl asked.

"There is a woman in the western part of the capital," the dragon king replied. "She has something called a single-night-growing gourd. Buy that gourd from her, plant it, and climb up its (fast-growing) vine to the sky. This will be a huge undertaking and hard to achieve. But if you succeed and reach the sky, ask people you meet along the path where you might find the Amewakamiko's residence." Then he warned her, "Never open this Chinese-style chest. If you do, you will never be able to come back here." Having said this, he left for the sky.

Now her older sisters came to visit her to see her happy life. "We had a bad karma and thought the man was really frightening at that time," they said and started to open all the cabinets and chests in the house. When they saw the Chinese-style chest, which the man had strictly forbidden anyone to open, the sisters demanded the youngest sister open it: "Let's have a look! Let's see!" The girl refused, saying she had lost the key. But her sisters were persistent in their demand.

"Give us the key. Why do you want to hide it?" they shouted. As they began to tickle her, the key tied to the waist of her trouser-skirt hit the screen and made a sound. "Ah, here it is!" said the sisters and opened the chest. But alas, the chest was empty except for a wisp of smoke that drifted up to the sky. The sisters were disappointed and left the house.

The girl waited three weeks, but her husband never returned. So she went to the western part of capital as he had told her and bought the magic single-night-growing gourd from the woman. As she was leaving the home where she and her husband had been so happy, she deeply lamented how sad her parents would be when they learned of her disappearance. With painful reluctance, she started to climb up the vine.

"I will never be able to see my home again," she said to herself and recited a poem:

Au koto mo	I know not
isa shirakumo no	if I could ever meet my husband
nakazora ni	on the white clouds.
tadayoinubeki	My body drifts in mid-air,
mi o ika ni sen	what shall become of me?[16]

SCROLL TWO

The girl finally reached the sky and meandered around, when she saw a good-looking young man in an aristocrat's casual attire.

"Where is the residence of Amewakahiko?" she asked.

"I don't know," the man replied. "Ask the person you meet next."

When she asked who he was, he replied, "I am the Evening Star."

Then she encountered a man with a broom, so she asked just like before.

"I don't know. Ask someone you meet next. I am the Comet," and he moved swiftly onward. Next she met a group of people, so she asked them the same question. The reply was the same, and they introduced themselves as the Pleiades. As the reply was always like this, she wondered whether she would ever find her husband and felt extremely forlorn and disheartened. But as it was not in her nature to feel lonesome and do nothing, she pressed on. Before long she encountered a man in a splendid palanquin set with jewels. She asked the man the same question she had asked the others, with little hope of a different answer. This time, however, the man replied, "If you go just a little further, you will see a jeweled palace built upon lapis lazuli. Ask for Amewakamiko there." She immediately followed his direction.

Finally, she met Amewakahiko. As she told him how lonely she was, leaving home without knowing her destination, he pitied her immensely.

"Since I couldn't return to you on earth, I have been worried about you every day," he replied. "But I have comforted myself believing you would find me as you promised, and I have been waiting. I am so moved that you've felt the same way." So saying, the couple deepened their pledge to each other. Indeed, there must have been a strong bond between them from

Figure 5.1. The maiden asking the Comet where the residence is located. Courtesy of Senshū University Library.

the previous life. But then he said, "There is one more worrisome thing I must tell you. My father is an oni. I don't know what he will do to you if he finds you here. What shall we do?" She was surprised to hear this but thought, "It seems that I am destined to have many worries. This must be my fate. Even if this place is going to be hard to stay in, I have no home to which I can return, so I will just have to follow the course of fate."

Days passed, and one day his father visited his house. He immediately transformed the girl into an armrest to hide her from his father. But his father reclined on the armrest. He thought painfully about how his wife must feel. It was hard for him to watch as his father leaned on his wife. Finally, his father prepared to leave.

"It smells like a human," the oni said in passing. "It stinks."

After that, his father called on him frequently. But every time the oni-father came, he changed the girl into something like a fan or a pillow to protect her. But his father must have noticed it, for one day he came stealthily without making any sound. As he was taking a nap, he didn't have time to hide the girl.

"Who is this?" his father demanded to know. There was no point in hiding their secret anymore, so he told his father about the girl. "So she is our bride (daughter-in-law)," the father said, sneering all the while. "Since I don't have anyone who serves me, I will make her do some chores for me."

"As I feared," he lamented. But as he couldn't refuse his father, he handed the girl over.

The father said to the girl, "I have several thousands cows in the field. Keep them well. During the day, let them out in the field, and at night, bring them into the barn." As she didn't know what to do, she consulted with Amewakamiko, wherein he detached his sleeve and gave it to her. He explained that she should wave the sleeve while saying "Amewakamiko's sleeve, sleeve." When she went to the field and did as instructed, thousands of cows behaved as she wished—they went out to the field in the morning and went back to the barn at night.

"This is amazing!" the oni-father said after seeing how successfully the girl did her job. Then the oni-father imposed the next task.

"Move 1,000 *koku*[17] of rice in the granary to another granary now. Don't leave one single grain." The girl again waved the sleeve while saying "sleeve, sleeve." Thereupon, countless legions of ants came out and in only two hours transported the grains of rice. Seeing this, the oni-father calculated the rice with a device he had on hand.

"One grain is missing," he grumbled in a foul mood, "Find it!" The expression on his face did not bode well for the girl, and a sense of dread came over her.

"I will try to find it," the girl managed to reply and started to look for it, when she saw a back-bent ant tottering about with a grain. How happy she was. She joyfully carried that grain to the oni-father.

But the oni-father said, "Lock her up," and put her in the warehouse fortified with iron boards. These centipedes were no ordinary centipedes; they were one foot long and numbered 4,000 or 5,000. They gathered around her with their mouths wide open to devour her. The girl almost fainted with fear, but as she waved the sleeve saying "Amewakahiko's sleeve, sleeve," the centipedes receded to the corners and did not come

Figure 5.2. The ants carrying grains for the maiden. Courtesy of Senshū University Library.

near her. When the oni-father opened the door after seven days, the girl came out safely.

The girl was then locked in the snakes' den. But again as she waved the sleeve, no snake approached her. After seven days she came out from the den alive. The oni-father stood dumbfounded.

"You must indeed have been destined to become my son's bride," he said at last. "You may now see him once a month." But the girl misheard him.

"Did you say once a year?" she asked.

"As you wish, once a year it shall be," he replied throwing a melon to the ground. The melon hit the ground, smashed open, and became the Milky Way. The girl became Vega and he Altair. They now meet each other once a year on the seventh day of the seventh month.

NOTES

1. See the introduction for a brief explanation of *otogizōshi*.

2. The picture scroll housed in the Berlin museum is printed in Shimada illustrations plates no. 7–9, illustrations 9–13, 37–41, and 69–71 (written text). The annotated written text is included in Matsumoto, *Otogizōshi-shū* 75–85. There are several picture scrolls very similar to Berlin's picture scroll, such as those housed in the Suntory Museum in Tokyo titled *Amewakahiko monogatari emaki* (Picture Scroll of Tale of Amewakahiko, seventeenth century) and *Tanabata no sōshi* (Tale of Star Festival, seventeenth century) in Senshū University Library in Tokyo. Ōtsuki, "'Amewakahiko sōshi' kaigaka no tenkai katei" 70–71.

3. Ishida Mizumaro notes that "according to one theory, a *yojana* is 14.4 kilometers" (cited in Genshin 11).

4. The poem is *Kokinshū* or *Kokin wakashū* (A Collection of Poems Ancient and Modern, 905) 4: 175: "Amanogawa / momiji o hashi ni / wataseba ya / tanabatatsume no / aki wo shimo matsu" (It is for a bridge, of many-hued leaves to span, the heavenly stream, that the Weaver Maid awaits, the arrival of autumn?) (Ozawa and Matsuda 91; McCullough, *Kokin Wakashū* 48). While Izumo Asako, citing Katagiri Yōichi's research on *Kokinshūchū*, writes that this edition of *Kokinshū chū* was not written by Fujiwara Tameie and hence cannot be definitely dated to the early Kamakura period, she says the *Tale of Amewakahiko* was strongly influenced by "Qian Luwei's Tale" (Izumo 57). "Qian Luwei's Tale" is printed in Satake, *Kokinshū chū* 224–29, 455–57.

5. According to the legend, the Weaver, a daughter of the Emperor of Heaven, fell in love with a cowherd("'Amewakamiko zō' no hensen ni kansuru ichi kōsatsu" 17). and came to neglect her weaving duties. This angered the Emperor, who separated the lovers, placed them on different sides of the Milky Way (the "great river of heaven"), and allowed them to meet only once a year, on the night of the seventh day of the seventh month.

6. Michael Como writes that the cult of the Weaver and the Cowherd is known to have arrived in Japan by the reign of Emperor Tenmu (reigned 673–86) at the latest and that the Weaver Maiden and the Cowherd festival is the best-documented cult in Nara Japan, with clear roots in the Chinese festival calendar. Como 38–39, 110.

7. The Realm of the Four Guardian Kings (*Catur-maharaja-kayikah*) is located above the realm of humans but below the realm of Brahma. See Sadakata 56, 58.

8. Katsumata conjectures that the text that was written soon after the completion of *Kokinshū kanajo*. Katsumata, "'Amewakamiko zō' no hensen ni kansuru ichi kōsatsu" 16.

9. Roger Thomas of Illinois State University suggests insightfully that the confusion between "Amewakahiko" and "Amewakamiko" might have something to do with the fact that the phonemes hi/bi and mi often appear interchanged in many classical works (e.g., sabishi vs. samishi and the like).

10. Izumo Asako uses the name Amewakahiko rather than Amewakamiko in her article.

11. Doi writes, "In Apuleius's story, according to the oracle of Apollo at Miletus, he is a son of Draco, a monster with wings of wind and feared by all gods" (166). I could not find the words "a son of Draco" in *Cupid and Psyche*, but there is a description of Cupid as

> "something cruel and fierce and serpentine;
> That plagues the world as, borne aloft on wings,
> With fire and steel it persecutes all things." (Apuleius, *Cupid and Psyche* 47)

This description sounds like a dragon. In the notes, E. J. Kenney writes, "The allusive description of Cupid as the monster exploits his attributes to make him sound like a fire-breathing dragon; ambiguity was the stock-in-trade of oracles" (Apuleius, *Cupid and Psyche* 131).

12. On the forty-ninth day after one's death, it is believed that the soul of the deceased starts its new life on the other side of this life (or rebirth). Buddhist memorial services for the intermediate existence between one's death and rebirth are held every seven days until the forty-ninth day.

13. "Hachikazuki" is often considered a Japanese Cinderella story. For an English translation, see Steven 315–31.

14. Ikeda-AaTh 411C, "Snake Paramour." Also see Ikeda-AaTh 312B "Snake Husband Killed." See Ikeda, *A Type And Motif Index of Japanese Folk-Literature* 74–75, 103–4; Seki, "Types of Japanese Folktales" 69–70. For an example story, see Dorson 117–18. Dorson writes that "Thompson has the pertinent Motif T475.1, 'Unknown paramour discovered by string clue,' with solely Japanese references" (117).

15. See, for example, Tokuda, *Otogizōshi jiten* 142.

16. The poem pivots on the phrases *isa shira[zu]* (I know not) and *shirakumo* (white clouds).

17. One *koku* is approximately 180 liters. One thousand *koku* are therefore about 180,000 liters, or 40,863 US gallons.

6

Blossom Princess (Hanayo no hime)
Japanese Stepdaughter Story and Provincial Customs

LIKE MANY OTHER STORIES IN THIS BOOK, THE TALE *Hanayo no hime*, or *Blossom Princess* (ca. late sixteenth century or early seventeenth century), belongs to *otogizōshi*.[1] Among around 400 *otogizōshi*, three stories—*Blossom Princess*, *Hachikazuki* (The Bowl Girl), and Ubakawa (The Bark Gown)[2]—can be identified as Cinderella-type stories because they have suspected folklore origins and abundant fairytale motifs (Mulhern, "Cinderella and the Jesuits" 409). In these three *otogizōshi* stories, the stepdaughter receives from Kannon (Avalokiteśvara, Bodhisattva of Compassion) or *yamauba* (a mountain crone) clothes or a bowl that hide the girl's beauty until her true lover appears. The Cinderella-type stories, particularly *Blossom Princess*, are known for their strong association with folklore.[3] This chapter highlights some of the noteworthy folkloric elements, such as the legend of "Obasute" (Deserted Old Woman) reflected in the figure of a *yamauba*. While examining the relationship between the texts of *Blossom Princess* and three *mukashibanashi* (folktales), namely "Ubakawa," "Komebuku Awabuku" (The Komebuku and Awabuku Sisters), and "Obasute," I will also look at *Blossom Princess* as a text replete with contemporary customs and beliefs, especially in the area of Suruga Province (present-day central Shizuoka prefecture). Notable contemporary manners and customs, such as *shūto-iri* (literally, "entrance of the father-in-law") and female inheritance, are described well in *Blossom Princess*.

TEXTS OF *BLOSSOM PRINCESS*

The number of extant *Blossom Princess* texts is fairly small (Matsumoto, "Minkan setsuwa kei no Muromachi jidai monogatari" 8), and basically *Blossom Princess* exists in a single version (Mulhern, "Cinderella and the Jesuits" 447); four printed texts from woodblocks and two written copies

DOI: 10.7330/9781607324904.c006

exist (Inai 26–27). All four printed texts are from the same woodblocks, and the text consists of three books. They are in the possession of the Akagi Library (*MJMT* 10: 515–55), the Tōhoku University affiliated library (Shimazu, "Hanayo no hime"), the Tenri Library, and the Tōyō Library. One of the two written copies exists in the Hiroshima University Japanese literature research room, and its content is almost identical to the woodblock version (*MJMT* 10: 515). The whereabouts of the other copy, formerly in the possession of Takano Tatsuyuki, are not known (Inai 27).

Plot Summary of *Blossom Princess*

The heroine, Blossom Princess, is born in answer to her parents' prayers to Kannon. Her mother dies when she is nine years old. Moritaka, her father, dotes on her and continues to pray for his wife's happiness in the afterlife, but he remarries at the urging of his relatives. The stepmother hates Blossom Princess because Moritaka pays attention only to his daughter. While Blossom Princess's father is away from home, the stepmother has a samurai kidnap and abandon her on a remote mountain near Mt. Fuji. The Moritaka household grieves the loss of Blossom Princess, but unbeknown to the stepmother, Moritaka and the princess's nurses are consoled when a *miko* (diviner) predicts Blossom Princess's safety.

In the meantime, on the mountain the princess meets a *yamauba* who gives her a small bag of treasures and an *ubakinu*, or *yamauba*'s transforming clothes, to make the wearer look old. The *yamauba* also gives directions to a certain human habitation where she can work. While the princess works as a hearth maid at the mansion of a *chūnagon* (middle councilor), Saishō, the middle councilor's youngest son, falls in love with her. Saishō soon takes her to his nurse's house, where he can see her at his ease. Realizing that the son is visiting a woman, Saishō's mother holds a "bride's contest" so the son will be embarrassed and leave Blossom Princess. But on the day of the competition, the bag the *yamauba* has given to Blossom Princess produces fine clothes for her to wear and other valuable treasures. Blossom Princess's beauty and gifts impress everyone at the contest. She is happily married to Saishō and reunited with her father. In the meantime, the stepmother and her nurse clandestinely leave Moritaka's house for whereabouts unknown. Saishō moves to Blossom Princess's father's estate to inherit the lordship and manage the estate with Blossom Princess. The couple is blessed with many children, and Blossom Princess's father marries the middle councilor's niece and lives happily ever after.

Of the Cinderella-type stories, *Blossom Princess* is by far the longest. Unlike *Hachikazuki*, which includes many rhetorical descriptions of scenery and feelings, the elaborate plot of *Blossom Princess* makes the text long (Matsumoto, "Minkan setsuwa kei no Muromachi jidai monogatari" 26). The reader follows the story from two perspectives: one considers the heroine and the other Moritaka's household. The major plot tracks the events surrounding Blossom Princess, and the reader is informed on a regular and timely basis what is happening to Blossom Princess's family and nurses during her absence. It is "closest to the classical novel in its graceful fluid style, characteristically Japanese in its vocabulary and imagery" (Mulhern, "Cinderella and the Jesuits" 446).

YAMAUBA AND *KANNON*

One term requiring explanation that is "characteristically Japanese in its vocabulary and imagery" is *yamauba*. The medieval Noh text aptly titled *Yamamba*[4] describes *yamamba* (*yamauba*) as "a female oni living in the mountains."[5] Even now, to many contemporary Japanese the word *yamauba* conjures up images of an ugly old woman who lives in the mountains and devours humans. The witch in the Grimm Brothers' *Hansel and Gretel* and Baba Yaga of Russian folklore can be considered Western counterparts of the *yamauba* figure. The *Konjaku monogatarishū* (Tales of Times Now Past; ca. 1120) depicts one such *yamauba* in the story titled "Sanseru onna minamiya-mashina ni yuki oni ni aite nigetaru koto" (How a Woman with Child Went to South Yamashina, Encountered an Oni, and Escaped).[6] A young pregnant woman secretly gives birth in the mountain hut of a seemingly kind old woman, only to discover that she is actually an oni with plans to eat her newborn baby. In *Blossom Princess*, the heroine is extremely frightened about encountering the *yamauba* primarily because of the *yamauba*'s reputation for eating people.

The image of the *yamauba* is complex. In stark contrast to the *yamauba*'s representation in the woman-with-child story, some tales represent a *yamauba* as a nurturing character. Orikuchi Shinobu writes that a *yamauba* was originally a virgin offered to a mountain deity. The maiden nursed the deity to health and later became his wife (Orikuchi, "Okina no hassei" 363). The *yamauba*'s nurturing image is often associated with motherhood.[7] Hori Ichirō writes, "In the popular belief of rural areas, the mountain deity is believed to be a goddess who gives birth to twelve children every year. She is therefore called Mrs. Twelve (*Jūni-sama*), and her twelve children symbolize the twelve months of the year" (Hori 167). Indeed, in the fifteenth century, the Zen priest Zuikei Shūhō (1391–1473) recounts in his diary titled *Gaun nikkenroku* that a *yamauba* gave birth to four children: "The reason why the summer of that year had lots of rain was because the *yamauba* gave birth to four children, namely, Haruyoshi (Good Spring), Natsusame (Summer Rain), Akiyoshi (Good Autumn), and Fuyusame (Winter Rain)" (Tokyo Daigaku Shiryō Hensanjo 125). The year's abundant rainfall, the priest suggests, is the result of the *yamauba*'s multiple childbirths. The children's names seem to reflect an expression of reverence to a higher power and hope for good seasonal weather to come.

An interesting parallel appears in a folktale that describes a *yamauba* giving birth to a baby boy. In this story titled "Yamauba hōon" (*Yamauba*'s Gratitude), the *yamauba* comes to a married couple in a village and asks for shelter while giving birth, which the sympathetic couple gives her (Miyazaki 428–30). After the safe birth of her baby, the *yamauba* asks the couple to name the baby as well as her other nameless children. The couple feels honored and names the first child Natsuyoshikō (Good Summer), the second Akiyoshikō (Good Autumn), and the third one Fuyuyoshikō (Good Winter)—names very similar to those in the *Gaun nikkenroku*. The *yamauba* rewards the couple with two boxes—one that magically produces abundant gold and one filled with yarn.[8] Here, the *yamauba* as an oni-woman is clearly a bringer of wealth. As Yoshida Atsuhiko points out, the roots of the *yamauba* can be found in various female deities in Japanese myths, such as Ōgetsuhime in *Kojiki* (Ancient Matters, 712) and Ukemochinokami in *Nihon shoki* or *Nihongi* (Chronicles of Japan, 720), who produce food from different parts of their bodies (Yoshida, *Mukashibanashi no kōkogaku* iii, 108–12).

Thus, the *yamauba* may be identified as a dichotomous primordial goddess, the Great Mother, who brings fertility and wealth as well as death and destruction, similar to other mythico-religious figures such as Isis and Kali. In medieval Europe, the pagan archetype of the Great Mother who always possesses two aspects is no less complicated, as in fairy tales, which are mainly under the influence of Christian civilization: the light side is represented by the officially worshipped Virgin Mary, and the dark side, excluded from the image of Mary and maintaining much of its pagan influence, degenerates into a witch (Franz 105, 195).[9] Kawai Hayao regards Kannon as the positive image of the Great Mother in Japan and the *yamauba*, who appears in fairy tales as an all-devouring mountain witch, as the negative image (Kawai).

Compared with *yamauba*, Kannon is widely known in East Asia as the Bodhisattva of Compassion. A main purpose of *Blossom Princess* is to preach Kannon's blessing; the miracle associated with Shō Kannon (Aryavalokiteśvara, a manifestation of Avalokiteśvara) and Fuji Daibosatsu (Great Bodhisattva of Mt. Fuji) is given prominence in the text.

One of the most important and influential sutras of Mahayana Buddhism, the Lotus Sutra or Scripture of the Lotus Blossom of the Fine Dharma (*Myōhō renge kyō*), devotes an entire chapter to Kannon's salvific powers. Blossom Princess and her parents always recite the chapter titled "Kanzeon bosatsu fumonhon" (The Universal Gateway of the Bodhisattva Perceiver of the World's Sounds; see Watson, *Essential Lotus*), which is widely circulated separately as *Kannon kyō* (Kannon Sutra). According to the Lotus Sutra the Buddha declared: "Suppose there are immeasurable hundreds, thousands, ten thousands, millions of living beings who are undergoing various trials and suffering. If they hear of this Bodhisattva Perceiver of the World's Sounds and single-minded[ly] call his name, then at once he will perceive the sound of their voices and they will all gain deliverance from their trials" (Watson, *Essential Lotus* 119–20); "this Bodhisattva Perceiver of the World's Sounds has succeeded in acquiring benefits such as these and, taking on a variety of different forms, goes about among the lands saving living beings" (Watson, *Essential Lotus* 123). In other words, Kannon "will come to the rescue of anyone who appeals to him for his aid, whatever the nature of his or her distress. Moreover . . . [Kannon has] the ability to manifest himself in whatever shape, male or female, is best for accomplishing his salvific miracles" (Idema 6). As mentioned, Kannon's efficacy is explained throughout *Blossom Princess*. For example, Blossom Princess was born in response to the Moritaka couple's plea to Kannon. Moritaka believes he owes his reunion with his daughter to Kannon's protection; he says, "With your grateful vow to save Blossom Princess, I could see my daughter once again. I am very thankful. Please continue to protect her in the future" (*MJMT* 10: 556).

While Kannon worship is prevalent in the three *otogizōshi* stories, a *yamauba* appears only in *Blossom Princess*, and many scholars widely consider the *yamauba* of *Blossom Princess* to be an assistant to, or a manifestation of, Kannon (see Okada, "'Hanayo no hime' to minkan denshō" 70). This interpretation is reasonable because Kannon has the ability to transform into any shape and to save anyone who calls Kannon's name. Readers may have been expected to equate Kannon to the *yamauba* as a heroine's miraculous helper in time of need. But nowhere in the text does it say that Kannon gives the *ubakinu* (or *ubakawa*) clothes and a treasure bag to someone; it is the familiar *yamauba* in the *mukashibanashi* who gives the miraculous gifts to the heroine (Matsumoto, "Minkan setsuwa kei no Muromachi jidai monogatari" 27).

BLOSSOM PRINCESS AND MUKASHIBANASHI
"Ubakawa" and "Komebuku Awabuku"

The three *otogizōshi* stories are widely recognized as sharing similar plots to the "Ubakawa"-type stories and "Komebuku Awabuku"–type *mukashibanashi* grouped under the "stepchild stories" *(mamako-tan)*. Interestingly, though, Kannon does not appear in either the "Ubakawa"- or "Komebuku Awabuku"–type of *mukashibanashi* (Okada, "Otogi zōshi no bukkyō shisō to minkan denshō" 145–46). Again, it is a *yamauba* who gives the heroine wealth and assistance. In the "Ubakawa"-type stories the *yamauba* (or a frog) gives the stepdaughter *ubakawa*, or clothes that transform her appearance from a youthful heroine to an old crone. The summary of "Ubakawa" goes as follows:

A stepdaughter is driven away from her home. The girl, who is to be married to a serpent bridegroom, flees from him. The heroine meets with an old woman in the woods, or she stops at a solitary house in the woods where an old woman is present. The old woman (who is really the frog saved by the heroine's father) gives her an old woman's skin (or frog skin or hood, or a magic broom or towel), which makes the wearer dirty or old. She wears the old woman's skin and is employed in a rich man's house as an old kitchen maid or hearth maid. The rich man's son catches a glimpse of her in her natural form, when she is in her room alone. He becomes sick. A fortuneteller tells the rich man that his son's illness is caused by his love for a certain woman in his house. All the women in the house are taken before the son one by one to offer him tea or medicine. When he sees the heroine in the old woman's skin, he smiles at her and takes a drink from the cup she offered him. She takes off the old woman's skin and becomes the son's wife (Mayer 48–49; Seki, *Nihon mukashibanashi shūsei* 3: 899–911; Seki, "Types of Japanese Folktales" 114–15).

In the "Komebuku Awabuku"–type stories, the *yamauba* gives Komebuku a treasure box of fine clothes because she picks lice out of the *yamauba's* hair. A summary of "Komebuku Awabuku" is as follows:

A mother gives a broken bag to her stepdaughter named Komebuku and a good bag to her real daughter named Awabuku and sends them to the woods to fill their bags with chestnuts (or acorns). The two daughters stop at a *yamauba's* house in the woods. The stepdaughter takes lice off the *yamauba's* head, while the real daughter does not. When they leave the *yamauba's* house, she gives them each a basket. The stepdaughter's basket contains pretty dresses, and the real daughter's basket contains frogs or dirty things. The mother takes her real daughter to a play (or festival) and has the stepdaughter stay at home to perform tasks of carrying water and separating millet, rice, and other grains. The stepdaughter's friend (or a priest) and a sparrow help her perform the tasks, and then she goes to the play with her friend. While they are watching the play, (a) the stepdaughter is discovered by her stepsister, or (b) the stepdaughter throws something at her stepmother and stepsister. A young man who sees the stepdaughter at the play proposes marriage to her. Her mother tries to procure him for her real daughter, but the young man marries the stepdaughter. The real daughter wants to be married, and her mother goes to seek a suitor, carrying her in a mortar. They fall into a stream and turn into mud snails (Mayer 44–46; Seki, *Nihon mukashibanashi shūsei* 3: 822–44; Seki, "Types of Japanese Folktales" 111).

Legends of *"Obasute"* (Deserted Old Woman)

Another *mukashibanashi* that seems to have a strong relationship with *Blossom Princess* is "Obasute" or "Ubasute" (Abandoned Old Women) or "Ubasute-yama" (The Mountain Where Old Women Are Abandoned). Compared with the studies done on the two aforementioned *mukashibanashi*—the "Ubakawa" Type and the "Komebuku Awabuku" type—the amount of research on "Obasute" is very small in relation to that on *Blossom Princess*.[10]

The stories of "Obasute" vary in detail, but they all include as part of their plot structure the occurrence of an old man or woman being abandoned on a mountain.[11] It is the *yamauba*'s personal story that makes me believe in the "Obasute" influence. The *yamauba* of *Blossom Princess* tells Blossom Princess:

> Listen, I was human once. But I've outlived all my children. After that, my grandchildren and great-grandchildren were taking care of me, but they hated me so much and would not let me in their house. So I made the mountain my home, picking up nuts for food. One day an oni came and felt affection for me. He usually journeys from the peak of Mt. Fuji and sleeps in this cavern at night. During the day he cuts firewood and piles it at the cavern's entrance, and during the night I make a fire and warm myself by it. Even now when I have the mind of an ordinary human, I try to be compassionate. (*MJMT* 10: 530–31)

The extremely old woman lives on the mountain called "Ubagamine" (Old Women's Peak) because her kin abandoned her. Her voice is that of a lonely, deserted woman who wants someone to hear her story. The *yamauba* in the "Ubakawa"- or "Komebuku Awabuku"–type *mukashibanashi* do not offer any personal stories. As to why old folks are deserted on a mountain, *mukashibanashi* present various explanations, including: the old person is useless, superfluous, and consumes food; a law to abandon the old person is imposed by a regional lord; it is a custom of the village; an old person is unsightly; or a wife dislikes her mother- in-law and urges her husband to get rid of her.[12] In an attempt to understand the *yamauba*'s circumstances, let us examine the "Obasute" stories of these *mukashibanashi* more closely.

According to both Yanagita and Mihara, "Ubasute-yama" is a folk-tale in complete form that belongs to the "Cleverness at Work"–type of tale (Yanagita, *Nihon mukashibanashi meii* 173–75; Mihara, "Ubasute-yama"; for an English translation, see Mayer 168–71). "Ubasute-yama" stories are often divided into four types.[13]

The first type involves a middle-aged man with a son who nearly abandons one of his own parents by carrying him or her in a *mokko* (rope basket). The middle-aged man takes his son and his elderly parent to the mountain where he plans to abandon his parent. But just as he is about to do this, his son says he is going to bring the *mokko* back home to use the next time. Realizing that the next time will be his turn, the middle-aged man brings his elderly parent back to their home.

The second type concerns the wisdom of an old person in solving difficult problems. A lord imposes a law to abandon old folks, but a filial man is unable to do so and hides his parent in the cellar. One day, a neighboring country's king threatens to invade the lord's country unless the lord solves some difficult questions. The lord is unable to answer them and issues an order that anyone who can solve the problems will be rewarded. The man tells the questions to his hidden elderly parent, who easily solves the problems. The lord learns of the old parent's wisdom and rescinds the edict to abandon old people.

The third type is the breaking of branches to make marks on the mountain. On a journey to the place of abandonment, an old parent breaks branches of trees as a mark for the son to return home safely. Moved by his parent's love for him, he takes the parent back home. The fourth type is the attainment of wealth by a deserted old woman. An old woman abandoned by her son on the mountain becomes wealthy with help from an oni or mountain deity, and her son and his wife are punished.

In the last type, the attainment of wealth is particularly relevant to what I have described before and wish to focus on. An old woman is considered unproductive and is disliked to the point of being abandoned, but as if to compensate or redeem the negative treatment by the family members and villagers, after desertion she is endowed with the power to produce material wealth to make people, usually compassionate strangers, happy. An exemplar story transmitted in Iwate prefecture goes as follows:

A son has a wife, who initially is nice to her mother-in-law. As years go by, the wife increasingly treats her mother-in-law as a hindrance and speaks ill of her to her husband. Looking at her elderly mother-in-law chewing up lice from her hair, the wife slanders the mother-in-law to her husband that his mother steals and eats their precious rice. She then tells her husband to make a hut in the mountain, leave his mother there, and set fire to the hut. He does as instructed by his wife, but his mother escapes from the hut and warms herself by the fire with her legs wide open. Several oni children come there, see her genitals, and ask what they are. The old woman replies that they form a mouth that eats oni. Believing the old woman, the oni's children offer her their wish-granting mallet to save their lives. With the oni's mallet, the woman builds a town and becomes its lord. The wife learns the status of her mother-in-law and tries to do the same. But instead of getting rich, she burns to death in a hut in the mountain. (Sasaki, *Kikimimi no sōshi* 43–45)

Just as the old woman in *mukashibanashi* becomes wealthy, the abandoned woman as a *yamauba* in *Blossom Princess* is bestowed with miraculous power.[14]

Summary of Comparisons and Contrasts of Four Stories

First, as mentioned, the *yamauba* of the "Ubakawa"- or "Komebuku Awabuku"–type tales do not specify the reason they are on the mountain. In contrast, the *yamauba* of *Blossom Princess* and the old woman of "Obasute" are on the mountain because they are disliked and abandoned by their family members. There are few examples of an old woman going to the mountain by herself in *mukashibanashi* (Yoshikawa 123). In comparison, the *yamauba* in *Blossom Princess* probably walked to the mountain by herself to survive. In both cases, she is abandoned by her kin. The figure who is deserted on the mountain and expected to die is actually reflected in Blossom Princess. Blossom Princess is carried by a samurai on his back, as is often seen in other "Obasute" stories. Indeed, the samurai who kidnaps her from the veranda of her house "determinedly abandoned her there and returned without even looking back once" (*MJMT* 10: 525).[15]

Second, as for the *yamauba*'s task for the heroine, this part exists only in *Blossom Princess* and the "Komebuku Awabuku" type. The heroine of "Komebuku Awabuku" takes lice from the *yamauba*'s hair, whereas the *yamauba* in *Blossom Princess* makes her take snake-like worms from her head. Head lice are believed to be more of a day-to-day phenomenon than snake-like worms in the hair, but as the lice turn into more frightening snake-like worms in *Blossom Princess*, the reward for Blossom Princess is greater than those of the heroines in "Komebuku Awabuku"–type tales.[16] Head lice also appear in "Obasute"—the old "Obasute" woman eats lice from her hair. This becomes the major cause of her desertion in an "Obasute" story. Further, eating lice has a commonality with the *yamauba* in *Blossom Princess* eating the coiled worms in her head; after the *yamauba* made the heroine kill the coiled worms, "the *yamauba* picked them up and ate them saying, 'Ah, yummy'" (*MJMT* 10: 531). A mix of various *mukashibanashi* elements seems to appear in *Blossom Princess*, and some elements of *Blossom Princess* may have been influenced by these *mukashibanashi*.

Regarding the third and fourth points, a fire in the mountain and oni are involved in all the stories. The heroines of *Blossom Princess*, "Ubakawa," and "Komebuku Awabuku" are all lost in the woods or mountains and see a faint light in the distance. As the heroines walk in the direction of the light, they find a house or a cave in which a *yamauba* is making a fire. The place is also inhabited by (an) oni. In the "Obasute" story, the oni children are attracted by the fire and come to the fireplace. Okada Keisuke explains that the *yamauba* in *mukashibanashi* appears as a keeper of a sacred fire, which is a fire that casts away either evil or fire to welcome a mountain deity (Okada, "Otogi zōshi no bukkyō shisō to minkan denshō" 161). As mentioned earlier, according to Orikuchi Shinobu, a *yamauba* was originally a virgin consecrated to a mountain deity (Orikuchi, "Okina no hassei," 363). Okada notes that the relationship between an oni and a *yamauba* is based on this notion of a mountain deity and a maiden who serves the deity. In the text of *Blossom Princess*, when the heroine prays for the mountain deity, she encounters a *yamauba* and then the oni. As the narrator uses the word *kijin* (oni and deities), this oni himself suggests a mountain deity. The *yamauba* can be also considered a maiden who serves the mountain deity (Okada, "Otogi zōshi no bukkyō shisō to minkan denshō" 160–61; Okada, "'Hanayo no hime' to minkan denshō" 69–70).

Fifth, regarding the status of the *yamauba* of *Blossom Princess*, while the old woman of "Obasute" remains human after her encounter with an oni or deity, the *yamauba* in *Blossom Princess* became a supernatural being after she began living on the mountain. This is revealed when she says "I was a human before." The *yamauba* of the "Ubakawa" Type And the "Komebuku Awabuku" Type Are supernatural beings from the beginning. One may ask, what kind of supernatural being has the *yamauba* of *Blossom Princess* become? She could be an assistant to, or a manifestation of, Kannon, as many scholars believe. Or she could be a symbolic maiden who serves the mountain deity, as Okada interprets. Chieko Mulhern, who assumes *Blossom Princess* was written to proselytize Christianity, writes that the *yamauba* may represent a Japanese Jesuit brother (Mulhern, "Analysis of Cinderella Motifs" 15). Interestingly, Takahashi Mariko points out that the author of *Blossom*

TABLE 6.1. Comparative table of *Blossom Princess* and the *mukashibanashi* stories of the "Obasute" type, "Ubakawa" type, and "Komebuku Awabuku" Type Based on Matsumoto, "Chūsei ni okeru mamakotan no ichi kōsatsu."

		Blossom Princess	"*Obasute*" *type*	"*Ubakawa*" *type*	"*Komebuku Awabuku*" *type*
1	Reason(s) for being on the mountain	Lives long and is hated by grandchildren, so she comes to the mountain	Lives long and is hated by her daughter-in-law	Not specified	Not specified
2	*Yamauba's* task for the heroine	Makes the heroine take worms off the *yamauba's* head	No task. The old woman takes lice off her hair by herself	No task	Makes the heroine take lice off her head
3	What the *yamauba* does on the mountain.	Makes a fire in the cave and warms herself by the fire	Escapes from the hut that is on fire and warms herself by the fire	Makes a fire in the hut	Makes a fire in the hut
4	*Yamauba's* relation to oni	An oni is the *yamauba's* husband	An oni's children visit the old woman at the fireplace	The *yamauba's* hut is an oni's house	The *yamauba's* hut is an oni's house
5	*Yamauba's* status	Supernatural being, but formerly human (an assistant to or manifestation of Kannon, or an oni)	Human being	Supernatural being	Supernatural being
6	*Yamauba* and gifts	The *yamauba* gives a small bag with treasures, *ubakinu*, and *hanayone* (rice offering)	The *yamauba* receives a wish-granting mallet from the oni children	The *yamauba* gives *ubakawa*	The *yamauba* gives a treasure box with fine clothes in it

Princess seems to consider the *yamauba* to be an oni. After the happy marriage of Blossom Princess, the narrator notes, "Moritaka also revered the *yamauba's* wondrous clothes and had the priests hold a memorial service. The mound was built near the Kannon and a wooden grave tablet with a divine name and was erected for the clothes so the clothes, which were an intrinsic part of the oni's nature, might be transformed to a Buddha and rest in peace" (*MJMT* 10: 556). A popular belief dictates that a religious service should be held for the departed souls of one's ancestors so these ancestors will protect their descendants. In contrast, unattended souls are considered to roam this world to do harm to people as oni. Takahashi notes that the *yamauba* = oni, who does not have anyone who prays for her, can rest in peace for the first time after a memorial service is held for her (Takahashi, "Otogi zōshi 'Hanayo no hime' to minkan shinkō" 30). Earlier in the chapter I introduced a *yamauba* as a female oni. It is not unreasonable to surmise that the long-living *yamauba* of *Blossom Princess*, who roams in the mountains, has become an oni. Belief in the *yamauba*, portrayed as a female oni and a bringer of wealth in *mukashibanashi*, is reflected in the story of *Blossom Princess* along with popular Kannon worship.

As for the wondrous gifts the *yamauba* of *Blossom Princess* gives, they include the *ubakinu* of the "Ubakawa" type, the fine clothes of the "Komebuku Awabuku" type, and many more items such as swords, gold and silver, and other valuables. As the task the Blossom Princess did for the *yamauba* is more frightening or grotesque—taking snake-size worms off of her head—the reward could be substantial. Further, the *yamauba* of *Blossom Princess* gives the heroine *hanayone*,[17] rice grains offered to the Great Bodhisattva of Mt. Fuji. One grain of *hanayone* keeps Blossom Princess from starving for twenty days. The fact that the *yamauba* possesses the offering suggests that she is somehow related to the Great Bodhisattva of Mt. Fuji.

The Great Bodhisattva of Mt. Fuji

During the medieval period, the Great Bodhisattva of Mt. Fuji, another name for the Great Bodhisattva of Sengen, was largely considered to be the Senju Sengen Kannon (thousand-arms-and-eyes goddess of mercy) (Takeya, *Fujisan no saijinron* 131–41). Senju Sengen Kannon is one of the six Kannon, or six basic forms of Avalokiteśvara. Shō Kannon, to whom Blossom Princess's parents prayed for a child, is also one of the six Kannon.[18] After the happy reunion, the narrator continues, "[Moritaka] had a residence hall and pagoda built on a hill and employed twenty Buddhist priests to conduct religious services for Shō Kannon every morning and evening. Because of this miraculous Kannon, many people came to visit" (*MJMT* 10: 556). There may be a connection between Shō Kannon and the Great Bodhisattva of Mt. Fuji, though it may simply reflect the local worship of Mt. Fuji—the holy mountain of Suruga Province, the setting of the story.

The story of *Blossom Princess* ends with Kannon worship: "If you rely on the grateful Kannon single-mindedly, your desire will materialize in the end and your life in this world will be peaceful. Further, you will be born into a good place in your next life. Repeatedly think of compassion from morning till night" (*MJMT* 10: 559). As mentioned, Kannon's efficacy is advocated throughout the text. This may indicate some involvement of the Buddhist priest(s) in creating this text. Likewise, it is noticeable that the *miko*, or diviner, who happens to be in Suruga Province, plays a significant role in the story. Without her prediction, the father and princess's nurses would have believed the princess was dead, and the story would have ended quickly. The *miko*'s divination for the princess's survival and future happiness gives the father and caretakers of the princess hope and encouragement to live. The story ended happily because everyone believed in her divination. Moritaka "gave the diviner one hundred *koku* of rice and one hundred *kan* of currency, saying, 'You foretold well. I couldn't have known happiness or hardship without your divination'" (*MJMT* 10: 556). Likewise, "The princess also sent a gift of a quilted silk garment and one hundred gold coins to the diviner with a note that read, 'Because of your divination, I could see my father and nurse once again. How can I not be delighted?'" (*MJMT* 10: 556). The *miko*'s role is indeed crucial, and she is a focal point. The narrator then states that the princess becomes the diviner's long-term patron, as if soliciting the readers or audience to do the same. *Miko*, itinerant or temple-based preacher(s), may be involved in the formation of this *otogizōshi* text.[19]

CONTEMPORARY BELIEFS AND CUSTOMS REFLECTED IN *BLOSSOM PRINCESS*

Shūto-iri (The Bride's Father Enters His Son-in-Law's House for the First Time)

The text of *Blossom Princess* also reveals some interesting contemporary beliefs and customs. One such custom is *shūto-iri*, or the first time the bride's father enters his son-in-law's house. After the wedding, the bride's father goes to the bridegroom's house and there is a banquet; note that the *shūto-iri* customs vary according to region. According to Yanagita Kunio and Ōmachi Tokuzō, the term *shūto-iri* is widely used as one of the marriage rituals. For example, in Awa (present-day Tokushima prefecture), on the day after the wedding the bride's parents and the go-between make courtesy calls at the bridegroom's house and neighborhood. In the Shimoda area of Izu (Izu peninsula in present-day Shizuoka prefecture), *shūto-iri* means that the parents of both the bride and the bridegroom go to each other's houses to exchange expressions of gratitude (Yanagita and Ōmachi 200–201). The author of *Blossom Princess* spends several pages describing the custom, focusing on Moritaka's actions with a detailed list of the gifts Moritaka brings to the Saishō family. As Moritaka happily travels to see his long-lost daughter at Saishō's residence, the middle councilor (Saishō's father) brings his grown-up children with him to meet Moritaka, and the parents exchange greetings with *saké*. Moritaka gives each member of Saishō's family luxurious presents, such as scrolls of gold brocade, a fine horse with a gold saddle, and a gold sword. Saishō's family members are not the sole recipients of the gifts; those "from the ladies-in-waiting to lowly servants received numerous and diverse gifts. The clan's men and household retainers, without omission, from the old to the young, were given horses, saddles, armor, and swords," so much so that the narrator exclaims, "'What a splendid entry of the father-in-law!' said the people of the Middle Councilor's quarters" (*MJMT* 10: 553).

The very elaborate description of Moritaka's gift-giving to each member of the middle councilor's family is notable. The enumeration of the presents could simply indicate how wealthy Moritaka is—Moritaka is introduced at the beginning of the story as "an exceptionally wealthy man [who] lived in a mountain village near the foot of the famous Mt. Fuji in Suruga Province" and had "all the abundant treasures any man could desire." It could, however, also be interpreted as a record of the nuptial gifts or instructions for wealthy families in the countryside to emulate. In other words, the author or narrator may have intended to introduce a list of ideal gifts for *shūto-iri* for those who have the financial ability to provide such gifts but do not know the exact etiquette to follow. It could also be that the author or narrator simply wanted to exhibit his cultural knowledge. In either case, the author or narrator may have belonged to the cultural elite and been familiar with customs and manners.

Suruga Province, the setting of the story, was famous for its flourishing aristocratic Imagawa culture (*Imagawa bunka*), named after the Imagawa clan who ruled Suruga Province and created that culture. After the Ōnin War (1467–77), a number of aristocrats and cultural elites of the capital went to Suruga and Tōtōmi (present-day western Shizuoka prefecture) to avoid the chaos of Kyoto and brought their cultural heritage with them. Imagawa culture is called one of the "Three Great Cultures of the Warring Periods," the other two being the Ōuchi culture of Suō (present-day Yamaguchi prefecture) and the Asakura culture of Ichijōdani of Echizen (present-day Fukui prefecture). One of the similarities of the three cultures is that all three

warlords—Imagawa, Ōuchi, and Asakura—invited aristocrats from Kyoto
to pursue aristocratic customs and traditions (Owada 213).[20] Imagawa culture reached its peak with Imagawa Yoshimoto (1519–60), whose mother
was a Kyoto aristocrat, and he spent part of his childhood in a Zen temple
in Kyoto. Sunpu, the capital of Suruga Province, is called the "Kyoto of the
eastern provinces."

The middle councilor, who is "an aristocrat formerly attending the
imperial court in the capital" and who "moved to this [Suruga] province
because there was something unpleasant happening in the capital," could
be applicable to the situation of an aristocrat who went to Suruga (or heard
about things in Suruga) to avoid the inconvenience of Kyoto (*MJMT* 10:
537). Social gatherings held at the middle councilor's house also seem to
reflect the times. An example is the gathering for the incense-smelling ceremony—a fashionable pursuit among aristocrats in the late medieval period.
It is recorded that at Sunpu, Imagawa Yoshimoto's mother, Jukeini (?–1568),
and her ladies enjoyed the incense gatherings, particularly an activity called
Juchūkō in which participants would guess the correct name of a selected
incense (Owada 229–30).[21] In *Blossom Princess*, too, the middle councilor's
family, originally from Kyoto, often gathers to enjoy the incense-smelling
activity. Blossom Princess produces her own incense at the "bride's contest."

Blossom Princess's Right to Inheritance

Another custom is women's right to an inheritance. The inheritance of land
for the warrior class began to change to primogeniture around the fourteenth century, but if there was no male child, a female was permitted to
inherit the estate(s) as long as the property was not divided. Even after the
fourteenth century, the right to possess property was not totally denied to
a female of the warrior class (Nagahara, "Joseishi ni okeru Nanbokuchō ·
Muromachi ki" 152–56). This custom is reflected in *Blossom Princess* as well.
Moritaka has no children other than Blossom Princess, and she seems to
have been able to inherit Moritaka's land and properties just as her mother's
requested of Moritaka on her deathbed—that he marry Blossom Princess
to someone appropriate and have her succeed Moritaka. Blossom Princess,
however, is not the sole manager of her properties, as can be seen from her
nurse's comment: "It will be difficult for the princess to succeed you and
maintain this house all by herself. If you ask your former mother-in-law,
there may be some appropriate suitor in her clan to marry our princess
and succeed this house with her" (*MJMT* 10: 519–20). Obviously, Blossom
Princess is to manage the estate with her husband, and Saishō is adopted

into Moritaka's family to lead the clan. The narrator describes that "Moritaka makes Saishō succeed to his lordship, and hands over his fiefdom, his residence, and his many warehouses to both Blossom Princess and Saishō, who is renamed Tango no kami Moriie to succeed Moritaka" (*MJMT* 10: 557).

As Moriie succeeds the lordship and moves to Moritaka's land, the correct way of *shochi-iri* (the lord's first entry to his land after he receives his fief) is described as a serious concern: "The Middle Councilor came out with his two children to see the party off as a celebration of Moriie's first entry to his inherited fief. It was a serious matter. The Middle Councilor's party rode a long way with Moritaka's entourage. However, at last Moritaka urged them to return as the distance they had ridden together was already too far—thus being polite and respectful to each other, both entourages parted ways" (*MJMT* 10: 557). This, again, seems to show the author's knowledge of customs and manners.

Earlier I described a close relationship between *Blossom Princess*, one of the three Cinderella-type stories of the *otogizōshi* genre, and three *mukashibanashi* with similar plots or related situations. The association of *Blossom Princess* with *mukashibanashi* is close, especially in terms of the *yamauba* who has a dichotomous role of destruction as well as a bringer of wealth. The *yamauba* of *Blossom Princess* also represents an old woman who is abandoned in the mountain, as the story of "Obasute" portrays. The story of *Blossom Princess* also introduces some interesting contemporary customs at great length. The elaborate accounts of such customs as *shūto-iri* make one speculate that the author, be it aristocrat or preacher, wrote *Blossom Princess* not only for entertainment and religious or moral edification but also as an instruction for affluent provincial lords to emulate certain customs. *Blossom Princess*, a Cinderella-type story of the late medieval *otogizōshi*, is an entertaining and instructional tale.

TRANSLATION OF *HANAYO NO HIME*

This translation is based on a book print published in volume 10 of *Muromachi jidai monogatari taisei* (*MJMT*, 515–59). I also consulted Shimazu Hisamoto's edition of *Hanayo no hime* (Shimazu, "Hanayo no hime").

Blossom Princess
SCROLL ONE

When one meditates on human vanity, rapid shifts and fleeting moments in the rhythm of human life echo the way of the world. Sometimes good ebbs and evil flows. In this transitory world, icicles in the valley melt first in spring, and flowers begin to blossom. Yet, while flowers in the beautiful richness of full bloom enchant people, their moment is fleeting. Soon the deutzia flower and cuckoos start to sing their sweet songs in the mountains. The cicadas drone loudly in the trees. In the heat of summer it is delightful to be at the foot of spring water; but soon, the first autumn wind visits pine trees and the moon shines brightly in the clear sky. Almost imperceptibly, the crickets' chirpings dwindle in the evening at Sagano (a place of scenic beauty in Kyoto), and the sky of the Tenth Month is all a drizzling mist. It is hard to pass a long, cold night in only one's thin clothes, but life is difficult to abandon. Days and months go by while people lament an all too brief and wretched life.

Now, an exceptionally wealthy man lived in a mountain village near the foot of the famous Mt. Fuji in Suruga Province (present-day central Shizuoka prefecture). His name was Bungo no kami Moritaka[22] of the Wada clan. He had all the abundant treasures any man could desire; nothing was missing except for one thing—he did not have a child. The man and his wife lamented this fact, each thinking in his or her turn, "What is the use of building treasure houses in every direction if we have no child to whom we can leave this wealth and who will pray for our happiness in the next life?" Nevertheless, the couple was deeply religious and compassionate. They enshrined an image of Shō Kannon [Aryavalokiteśvara], the patron of those who suffer, in the hall of their great house. Every morning and evening when they burned incense, offered flowers, and chanted sutras for the Kannon, they prayed for a child, a boy or a girl, who would hold memorial services for them. But there was no sign thus far that Shō Kannon had heard their prayers.

One day while Moritaka's wife walked about Kannon Hall, she saw a sparrow lovingly playing with its baby birds on a plum tree in the garden and felt deeply envious of the birds with their babies. "What kind of retribution leaves us childless?" she said through her tears and went to Kannon Hall, prostrated herself before the image of Kannon, and grieved. That night, she had a dream that she was chanting a sutra as usual. Then a plum blossom in front of the Kannon was thrown onto her knees. When she picked up the plum blossom to look at it, the color and fragrance of it were unparalleled. The flower was at the height of its beauty. So enchanting, rare, and delightful was the blossom that she put it into her right sleeve. When she awoke from the dream, she thought it so extraordinary and unusual that she woke her husband, Moritaka, who was lying beside her, and told him all about the dream.

Moritaka said, "This is indeed an auspicious dream. The Kannon must have pitied us and given us a child. It must be a girl since you put the blossom into your right sleeve.[23] Regardless of the child's gender, this dream is indeed propitious." The couple was delighted by the dream. On the following day, Moritaka and his wife went to the hall and worshiped the Kannon all the more.

Soon, the lady started to feel unwell and her monthly courses stopped; indeed, it appeared that the lady had at long last conceived a child. Their attendants and servants, who had lamented their masters' childless state, were very happy to see the lady's symptoms. The months passed quickly, and in due course the lady safely gave birth to a beautiful, jewel-like baby girl. As this was what the couple had always wanted, their rapture was beyond description. Moritaka and the lady carefully selected appropriate nurses and assistants for their priceless princess.

Thus, they led a happy life and soon the princess became nine years old. That spring the lady started to feel unwell. "Could it be another auspicious sign?" people wondered, but that was not the case. The lady's body gradually weakened, and her chances of recovery looked less and less promising with each passing day. Moritaka was heartbroken—he prayed and had the priests in the temples and shrines pray for her recovery. But as days and months passed, her state only deteriorated.

The lady called her husband to her bedside and said, "It seems there is no sign your generous prayers will be answered. I don't care what becomes of me, but since you won't stay single after my death, my pity goes to our princess. Would you please raise her well, marry her to someone appropriate, and have her succeed you? That is the only concern I have." Moritaka looked helpless. She then called her princess.

Stroking her hair, the lady said, "Oh, how I regret to leave you behind. After I'm gone you can only rely on your father. Be mature and don't let people hate you. I have named you 'Blossom Princess' because when I conceived you I had a dream of a blossom given to me. As the prime of flowers is momentary, your well-being weighs heavily on my mind. My only joy among much grief is that I am leaving this world first. You must succeed your father. Nurses, do attend to her well, I beg you." So saying, she closed her eyes on thirty-three short years of life like a dewdrop in the morning.

The grief of Moritaka and the princess was indescribable. They agonized and wished to go to the other world with the lady, but that was all in vain. Since they could not hold on to her forever, her body was taken to the field for burial. Various memorial services were held for the lady, but there was no end to their tears.

While they toiled with their grief, three years passed and the princess became eleven years of age.[24] The New Year had come and gone, and when Moritaka's relatives gathered together they repeatedly recommended that Moritaka take a new wife and comfort himself, for being single forever could not make his late wife come back to this world. For a long time, Moritaka did not listen. The relatives did not give up, however. Saying that the princess would be lonely without a mother, the relatives made arrangements with a certain lady and urged Moritaka to marry her. Since Moritaka could not persist in his refusal of his relatives' decision, he grudgingly got married. However, Moritaka prayed morning and evening for his late wife's peace in the afterlife, just like his princess, and he rarely visited his new wife in her quarters.

Thus, years went by and the princess became fourteen years old. The older she grew, the more superior both her character and appearance became. Moritaka was pleased with the princess's fine growth and summoned her nurse: "Listen. My princess has already become fourteen years of age. I wish to have her marry an appropriate man. But that makes me miss her mother again, for with whom shall I consult about an appropriate husband for my princess?" So saying, he shed tears.

The nurse was of the same mind and cried, too. She then offered an idea: "It will be difficult for the princess to succeed you and maintain this house all by herself. If you ask your former mother-in-law, there may be some appropriate suitor in her clan to marry our princess and succeed this house with her." Moritaka agreed. So one day he summoned his adjunct, Isobe Saemon Tadafuyu, and told him to prepare for a journey because Moritaka was going to visit his former mother-in-law in the west for some business the following day. Tadafuyu immediately prepared a large oblong chest into which he put various gifts. On the following day, Moritaka summoned the princess's nurse named Akashi, her assistant Kojijū, and Kochōnomai— the princess's constant attendants—and said carefully, "As the princess has grown up, I am going to my mother-in-law to discuss the matter of her marriage. I will be back in two or three days. In the meantime, don't let the princess feel lonesome, as I will be home soon." He then left. As for the princess, who had never spent a day without her father, she was moved to tears in parting with him. Her tears could not have been more prophetic.

Among the people of Moritaka's household, Akashi, Kojijū, and Kochōnomai were particularly intimate with the princess. At the time of the princess's auspicious birth, Moritaka was exhilarated to find a nurse for his daughter and said, "Lady Akashi in the *Tale of Genji* had a most fortunate daughter with many august children.[25] I will call you Nurse Akashi." Usually, she is simply called Akashi. Kojijū was a little older and discreet; she was hired as Akashi's assistant to attend to the princess and raise the child carefully with the same mind as Akashi. Kochōnomai was Akashi's daughter. She was raised at her grandmother's home until she was five years old, when she was called to Moritaka's mansion to be the princess's playmate. Since then, she had always played with the princess and had never left her household.

In the meantime, the princess's stepmother was convinced that if the princess stayed in the house, her husband's neglect of her would only intensify. She consulted with her main nurse as to how to get rid of the princess while Moritaka was away. "My lady," said the nurse, "that is easy. I have a cousin who is a samurai. He is a smart fellow. I will ask him to come and take the princess away from this house and abandon her somewhere." Moritaka's new wife was delighted to hear this and thought up a plan to dupe the three people close to the princess. The new wife courteously invited the three servants to her chambers, saying, "Why don't you come to this quarter tomorrow to play, for the lord is away on business." Unfortunately, the princess's three servants were taken in by the new wife's ruse, and, considering her invitation to be genuine, they fell into her trap. Only one of them would later realize their mistake.

The following morning the stepmother feigned shock and told the princess and her three servants, "It sounds presumptuous, but I must tell you nonetheless. Last night I had a particularly ominous dream about the princess. Why don't you three make a wish to the gods and Buddhas for her safety? I would not say this if the dream were not so terrible."

Hearing this, Akashi had a vague apprehension and was moved to tears. "But I am not so sure because the lord is not here." Then she cried.

The stepmother said, "That's no problem. Just do as I say. I will entertain the princess here today, so you need not worry about her." As the stepmother threatened and coaxed the three to act as she schemed, they reluctantly took everyone who served the princess, from eight ladies-in-waiting to lowly maids, to a temple to pray for the princess's safety. The stepmother had her own nurse's younger sister accompany Akashi's party to mislead their way and trick them into spending a night away from the house. After they left, the stepmother pretended to entertain the princess, but the young girl was not amused. Quite the contrary—she was doleful and lonely. Since her birth, the princess had never been away from her three servants, so she was anxious about them and longed for their quick return.

In the meantime, the princess's grandmother was delighted at Moritaka's rare visit. Moritaka told her how beautiful the princess had grown and that he wanted to consult with her about the princess's future. While talking, both Moritaka and his mother-in-law could not help thinking about their beloved wife and daughter, and tears welled up.

The grandmother then said, "I understand that a middle councilor of the capital, who lives in the south of this house, is a splendid lord and has a number of lordly sons. Among them, the third son is seventeen or eighteen years of age and is still single. I hear that he excels in appearance, talent, and character. I was just thinking about sending a word about him to you. How timely is your visit." "Wonderful!" Moritaka replied, truly thrilled by the information. The grandmother entertained Moritaka for several days, and they did not have the slightest idea what was going on at home.

At Moritaka's house, while entertaining the princess, the stepmother pretended to look distracted, sometimes whispering to her nurse. Then she came to the princess's side and said, "I really don't want to tell you this but I have to, because this is not something we can hide forever. It's about your father. I don't know what devil enters his mind, but he has a mistress somewhere. Yesterday when he left he didn't go to your grandmother's house as he told you. Instead, he is visiting his mistress. His servant has just arrived to take you somewhere because your father has decided to bring his mistress here tomorrow and give your room to her."

Not knowing whether what her stepmother said was true, the princess wept bitterly nevertheless. She begged her stepmother to wait until her nurse returned. But the stepmother refused, saying her father's attendant would not wait that long, and she urged the princess to go meet the servant. The princess returned to her room for one last time, feeling as if she would drown in her despair. Again she broke down crying. "My father cannot possibly be doing this," she thought through her tears. The princess missed her nurse woefully as her stepmother kept remonstrating with her to leave immediately, saying, "The attendant is waiting impatiently." The princess put her valuables in a small embroidered bag: a charm of the Chinese brocade sutra her mother used every day, a gold jar, a small silver water dropper, and a lacquer comb—all mementos of her mother's. The princess was determined to carry them with her as long as she was alive. She tearfully put them into her sleeve and left the room.

The stepmother told the princess to be silent and led her to a backdoor at a veranda, where the man was waiting. The attendant quickly explained to the princess, as the stepmother had planned, that her father wanted her to leave. The stepmother turned to the princess, saying, "I will send your nurse to you as soon as she returns." The stepmother then ordered the samurai to accompany the princess until she met with the nurse. The princess was wearing a quilted glossy silk undergarment with layers of scarlet and purple garments and Chinese fabric over them. Over her head she wore a scarf of glossy silk. Though her eyes were swollen and red with tears, the princess looked beautiful as she left the home of her birth.

A greedy man of little imagination, this samurai neither thought nor cared much for the moral distinction between right and wrong. He lifted the princess onto his broad back, piggyback style, and ran through the alleys and mountain roads until he arrived at his house. "Listen," he said curtly to his wife, "this girl has incurred the lord's displeasure, and I was ordered to abandon her wherever convenient. Strip off her clothes. It's a pity to waste them." The princess was appalled to hear this.

"I am not to be blamed. What is happening? Is this a dream or reality? I wish my nurse were here. How hateful this world is." She felt as if she were about to faint.

Seeing the princess's utter despair, the man's wife felt pity for the girl; she approached the princess and tried to console her. "Don't grieve so much. If only you are alive, the end will be happy. They say a tortoise that completes its life goes to an enchanted land. I wish I could let you keep your clothes, but my husband strictly forbids it."

"Even if you kill me, please let me keep this undergarment. Please don't shame me until I die," the princess begged her. The samurai's wife was so moved to pity for the princess that she let her keep the undergarment in spite of her husband's orders. "Put my clothes over your under-things." So saying, the wife took off her light hemp garment and covered the princess's undergarment. She then trussed up the princess's beautiful long hair and hid her face with her hand towel. Finally, the wife put a sedge-woven hat on the young girl's head to hide her from people's eyes. The samurai's wife indeed felt deep pity for the princess. "I wish I could accompany you till your destination," she said, "but since this whole thing is to be carried out quietly, I cannot do that." So saying, the wife put her sleeves to her eyes to wipe her tears and begged her husband, "Leave her in a far field or on the other side of a mountain, but please save her life." She seemed to be a compassionate woman.

The princess did not know what to think and hoped this was a bad dream. The man again took the princess up on his back. He carried her through fields and over mountains until at last they entered a deep mountain valley into which nobody traveled. He stopped on a little hill where he dropped the princess. "You can go deeper into the valley than here," he said coldly, "but do not return. On the other side of this mountain, a samurai will be waiting. Don't blame me." Not knowing what to do, the princess prostrated herself and simply cried. The man's heart was like a stone. He abandoned her there and returned to his home without ever looking back. He went directly to the stepmother's place. She came out onto her veranda and met with him.

"Have you completed your task?" she asked. The man replied, "I went through mountains and entered a mountain called Ubagamine [Old Women's Peak] where nobody goes. I left her in the deep valley of the mountain. She will soon be the wild beasts' prey. She will not last the night."

"Well done!" The stepmother was delighted and sent him home with many gifts.

When the princess's nurse and her entourage returned home, the place was quiet. When they realized that the princess was nowhere to be found, the nurse became suspicious and asked the lady of the house what had happened. Through feigned tears the lady cried, "Just as I thought, a terrible thing happened while you were away. Around noon the day you left, the princess went out onto the veranda, then she disappeared. I looked everywhere, but nowhere could I find her." The nurse and the others were appalled to hear the news. "Why did we ever leave her?" they thought. They looked for her in her quarters again and again in vain. The nurse had never been away from the princess since her birth, not even for a moment. On that day, too, the nurse returned from the temple at a quick pace, worrying that her princess would be anxiously waiting. "Could this be real or is this a nightmare? What will become of my princess?" The nurse grieved, looking up to the sky and prostrating herself on the ground.

Moritaka, unaware of what was happening in his absence, took leave of his mother-in-law the following day. On his way home, he met an express messenger from his house and heard the news of the princess's disappearance. Moritaka did not believe it but hurried his horse homeward. Arriving at home, he did not see the princess. Instead, everyone in his household was crying in great confusion. When Moritaka inquired about the situation, the nurse tearfully reported what had happened. The lady of the house gave her version of affairs, all the while shedding crocodile tears. It is painful to imagine the father's heartache. Separation from an unsightly child among many children is sad, let alone this princess who was his only child, excellent in both appearance and character. Moritaka's fatherly love for her was unparalleled. Upon being told that the princess had vanished into thin air, he was so heartbroken that he wished to end his life.

"But then, who will pray for her in the afterlife?" he thought. He pulled himself together as best he could and started to look for his daughter. His search party went through the trees and grasses at the foot of Mt. Fuji, looking for her in every nook and cranny. Even if her body could be discovered, his servants thought that at least that could be presented to their lord—but nothing was found. Not a trace. The party dejectedly reported their failure, and, unable to come up with an alternative, Moritaka ordered that a funeral be held for his Blossom Princess. Various memorial services were held for her. Moritaka's pain deepened all the more as nothing of her remains existed. The nurse felt the same as her lord and said, "If I were with the princess even in the fire or at the bottom of the sea, I wouldn't be so distressed. Rather than surviving woefully in this fleeting world, I wish to drown myself and visit her." Seeing her so agonized, everyone wept.

At this moment, the wife of Isobe Saemon Tadahuyu, Moritaka's adjunct, pulled at the nurse's sleeve and took her to a place where no one could hear. She whispered, "How can you be sure to meet the princess even if you enter the water? I know a reliable diviner [*miko*].[26] I suggest you meet her and see whether the princess is still alive and then decide what you should do. I will take you to her myself, but tell no one." The nurse was heartened to hear this. She told the people around her that she was going to a temple to pray for the princess's happiness in the afterlife and quietly left the house with a set of the princess's quilted silk garments. Arriving at the house of Isobe's wife, the nurse met with the diviner. The diviner asked the nurse to tell her all about the princess, so the nurse told the diviner everything about the girl, from the princess's age to the dream the child's mother had at her conception to the girl being named Blossom Princess because of the plum blossom. The diviner listened carefully and consulted various fortune papers.

Finally she said, "This is a propitious fortune. I see a happy ending. First, having a dream of a plum blossom signifies the child was born with an auspicious omen. People use plum blossoms more than any other flowers because of their fragrance. It indicates prosperity because after the petals scatter, it bears fruit and doesn't waste anything. The princess's life is safe. Though she is suffering right now, she will find happiness next spring. So you have to be strong. You will be happy to meet your princess at the beginning of next autumn. The princess's character is currently buried underneath some dust, but spring wind will blow the dirt off and her real worth will be exposed. You have to be patient, though, and strong as well, because there will be no sign of her, not even a whisper, until early autumn. There is no mistake; if there were one, Myōō [*vidyaraja*, Buddhist deities who protect Dharma and eliminate evil and ignorance] would lose his credibility, so rest assured." The nurse was so delighted that she gave the diviner the princess's silk garment. The diviner declined it, saying she would take it after her fortune came true. But as the nurse insisted that the garment was an offering and that other gifts would be bestowed when the fortune came true, the diviner at last accepted the garment.

The nurse, happy and hopeful, returned to her master's house, went directly to Moritaka's room, and told her lord quietly and carefully what the diviner had told her about the princess's fortune. Moritaka's mind cleared a bit, but now knowing that she was alive, he was anxious about her hardships: "Why am I given a child with so many worries and cares? I feel like blaming even Kannon. If my daughter is really still alive, please let me see her just as she used to be once more." So he prayed and put down his head on a pillow. In his dream, Moritaka was praying before Kannon. There was a piece of paper in front of him. He picked it up and found a poem on it:

Tada tanome	Earnestly rely on [Kannon]
hana[27] *wa kuruma no*	a blossom is within the wheel
wa no uchi ni	meeting [her] in this world again
meguri au yo no	like on the turning wheel
mizu wa tsukiseji	water running endlessly.[28]

This was an auspicious and hopeful poem indeed. Moritaka prayed for his long-standing desire all the more strongly to Kannon, offering material gifts. People believed Moritaka was praying for the princess's afterlife. Moritaka had visited his present wife on occasion at the beginning, but the situation quickly changed. Now he would not even cast an eye on her. The lady lived only with her own grumblings.

While all this transpired, the abandoned princess was all alone in the unknown mountains. She was in a state of stupor first, but after awhile she came to herself and realized that the sun was about to set. Since the time was about the middle of the ninth month, fog was thick and the wind blew hard in the mountains. The princess felt all the more helpless: "What kind of crimes have I committed to be like this? How bitter this fleeting world is and oh, how I miss my father. There must be wild beasts in the mountains. Alas, I will be their prey." She was frightened to the point of despair. "If I am destined to die," she prayed, "please take my life without [my] being prey for wild beasts. Would my mother have known my fate? What a hateful ending to my life. God of this mountain, please take pity on me and save me. I am without sin." So saying, she composed a poem:

Chihayafuru	Please, the mighty god
kami mo aware o	of this mountain
kaketamae	Have mercy on me

| *shiranu yamaji ni* | On this strange mountain path |
| *madō wagami o* | I am so lost. |

Then she recited a sutra and prayed, "May Great Compassionate Kannon, if you please, help me and let me see my beloved people once again." When she opened her eyes and looked around, the moon shone on the mountain peak, but where the princess was, all was still dark. When she turned in the direction of the valley, she saw a hint of a bonfire in the distance. "There must be someone there, or there would be no bonfire. I'll go there." She got up tearfully and trod the mountain path with the bonfire as her guide. She reached a bamboo field, and as she pushed her way through it, her clothes became soaking wet. Through her tears and the fog the princess could barely see, and she nearly fainted. When she looked in the direction of the light, she discovered that it was not a house but a cave in which some fearful-looking creature was making a fire. This scary sight made her hair stand on end, and she was again frightened nearly out of her wits. But she had nowhere else to turn, so she simply stood there.

"Who is standing there? Come here," called a hoarse voice from inside the cave. The princess was petrified, but, resigning herself to the idea that there was no way out, she went in. There she found an extremely old woman—a *yamauba*—with a square face. Her eyes were sunk deep into her head, but her eyeballs still protruded. She had a big mouth, and the fangs from her lower jaw almost touched the edges of her nose. That nose resembled a bird's beak, and her forehead was wrinkled up; her hair looked as though she had recently worn a bowl on her head. The princess could not bear the sight of the woman and fell on the spot. The *yamauba* looked at the princess carefully and said, "You must be human. Come here and warm yourself by the fire. If you are wet, dry yourself. I'll tell you a story." Hearing the hideous woman's kind words, the princess pulled herself up and walked toward the fire. Though frightened, she dried her clothes. Then the *yamauba* began to talk. "How piteous," the old woman said. "You must be a fortunate person, and I'm sorry that you have unexpectedly lost your way." So saying, the *yamauba* began to cry.

"Ah," thought the princess, "as the old saying goes: even demons sometimes cry."

Then the old woman began the story of her past. "Listen, I was human once. But I've outlived all my children. After that, my grandchildren and great-grandchildren were taking care of me, but they hated me and would not let me in their house. So I made the mountain my home, picking up nuts for food. One day an oni came and felt affection for me. He usually journeys

Figure 6.1. Blossom Princes encounters the *yamauba*. Courtesy of Hroshima University Library.

from the peak of Mt. Fuji and sleeps in this cavern at night. During the day he cuts firewood and piles it at the cavern's entrance, and during the night I make a fire and warm myself by it. Even now when I have the mind of an ordinary human, I try to be compassionate."

"So, this is an oni's cave," the princess thought, and her fear increased all the more.

The *yamauba* then said, "My head is itchy. Would you kill the worms on my head?" The princess was stricken with terror, wondering what they were. The *yamauba* gave her iron tongs, red with fire, and said "pin down the worms with the tongs."

SCROLL TWO

When the princess looked at the old woman's head closely, her hair was as red as the fur of a yak's tail that is colored crimson,[29] and on her skull were fourteen or fifteen small horn-like bumps around which worms resembling small snakes had coiled. As the princess put the scorching tong on the worms, they fell from the woman's head one by one. Pleased, the *yamauba* picked them up and ate them, saying "ah, yummy." The princess was still scared but spent the night in the *yamauba*'s cave. Soon the dawn broke, and the *yamauba* thanked the princess for killing the worms on her head. "You are a fortunate person but [you] meet hardship like this because someone hates you," the *yamauba* said. "Still, in the end, you will be happy. Come here. I'll give you this small bag because you've done something for me. Open it when you marry a young man. I see you haven't eaten much recently. These are *hanayone*,[30] rice grains offered to the Great Bodhisattva of Mt. Fuji. One grain will keep you strong without food for twenty days." So saying, the old woman put three grains into the princess's mouth. "I want to let you go now," the *yamauba* continued, "but my oni-husband has come. If he sees you, you will be eaten. I'll hide you in a pit at the back of this cavern." The princess didn't feel like she was alive in the pit.

Soon, an oni came with a wild wind. When the oni peeked at the cavern, his eyes sparkled like lightning. "It smells fishy," the oni commented. The *yamauba* responded, "That's the smell of a head I threw away into the valley just a moment ago. The smell comes with the gust you brought." At this the oni laughed. There is nothing false in the words of demons, they say.[31] Laughing, the oni returned to his place on the peak of Mt. Fuji. After the demon had left, the woman pulled the princess from the pit. "If you go as you are, people will be suspicious," she said. "I'll let you wear my clothes that I put aside during summer because it's so hot. Here, wear this. This will make you look old. If you go over that peak, you'll see a river flowing from the south. Don't go downstream, but follow the river upstream instead. Then you'll see smoke in the distance. If you go in the direction of the smoke, you'll find a human habitation. When someone comes out and talks to you there, stay in that place." The *yamauba* accompanied the princess through the mountain and sent her in the right direction.

After the *yamauba* left, the princess pressed on as instructed. Indeed, she soon saw smoke in the distance. Relieved, she thought to herself, "How strange that I can finally reach a human habitation. It's a miracle that I'm alive, without becoming prey for oni." As she did not know exactly where to visit, she was a little apprehensive. But she trod on, step by step, and soon she reached a house. Remembering what the *yamauba* said, the princess followed the white water (*shiromizu*, water that has been used to wash rice) and arrived at the small back gate of the middle councilor's house. She could hear lively voices at the front gate of the house and wondered if anyone would come outside. Looking at the splendid house, she thought to herself, "My father's house is by no means inferior to this. What a hateful world this is." While the princess stood at the back gate and rested for a moment, a maid came out and looked carefully at the princess, who was disguised as an old woman. The maid asked kindly, "Old lady, where did you come from? Would you like to build up the fire each morning and night for this house?" The princess thought to herself, "How will I do this? I have never done such a thing before." As she had nowhere to go, tears started to well up in her eyes once again.

The maid, whose name was Akino, happened to be a compassionate woman, so she took pity on the princess and brought her to her house. That night the maid told the princess, "This is the house of the middle councilor, a splendid gentleman. My work is to make hot water, but I am so busy that I want you to make a fire for this pot, please." "How can I decline this woman's request?" the princess thought. "The maid is a kind person, and I believe I can rely on her." So, even though she had never made a fire before, she accepted the request.

"Oh, I'm happy you agree. Please put water in the pot and make the fire." Akino thought, "What kind of person could this old lady be? She looks a little feeble." Nevertheless, Akino tenderly taught the princess to build the fire and made her a sleeping place beside a cooking pot. The princess got up while it was still dark outside and made the fire for cooking. It was a pitiful sight, but as her job was only to make a fire at the back of the house where nobody came, she did not have to worry about people's eyes. Still, her tears came down constantly at the drudgery of such unfamiliar work.

The year passed and the New Year arrived. Various celebrations were held at the middle councilor's house, and people came and went in splendid clothes. "If I weren't in this state, I could be like them, too," thought the princess and wept without being noticed by anyone. Time passed quickly, and it was already the fifteenth of the first month. The middle councilor, the lady, and their four children gathered for an incense-smelling gathering, with various blends of fine incense and censers. *Saké* was offered. After the merrymaking was over, each gentleman went back to his quarters. But Saishō, the youngest son, feeling a little lonesome, did not return to his room. Instead, he played the flute, amusing himself by gazing at the hazy moon in the spring night's sky. When everyone had gone to bed and he was thinking about going to his room as well, he saw a faint light in the distance. He thought it strange and quietly stepped outside and walked in the direction of the light. He could dimly see an oil lamp that barely lit a small untidy area in the hedges. Curious, Saishō approached and peeped in. There he found a graceful maiden fourteen or fifteen years of age, combing her long hair with a lacquer comb. She had a lovely complexion with a sublime charm about her eyes—her beauty might be painted but could not possibly be described with words. There was no defect about her whatsoever. Her exquisiteness might be compared to a shining jewel. "As long as I live in this fleeting world," he thought, "I want to make love to a maiden like that just for the memory. How come such a beautiful young lady is in a place like this? So strange." Saishō wished to get a closer look at the young maiden, but on further consideration he thought, "What if the maiden is really a supernatural being out to trick me? I should go back now and return here tomorrow night to find out." Reluctantly and with a great deal of effort, Saishō returned to his room.

Saishō went to bed, but with the princess's stunning beauty remaining in his eyes, he could not sleep. "I have seen many people lately but never such a beauty," the young man thought. "I haven't had anyone that I have cared for, but since I saw her by chance, I can't help thinking of her. I won't be able to give her up. If only I can spend one night with her—even if she is a demon—I don't care if I die." On the following morning, he waited for the day to end. Before long, it was dark. Saishō called Matsuwaka-maru, his page, and said, "I want to tell you something. Don't tell anyone."

Matsuwaka-maru humbly replied, "Whatever it is, I will never reveal your secrets. I will swear to the gods."

"Good. Then I'll tell you," Saishō continued. "When night comes, I will go somewhere to visit someone. You will wait here as usual. I shall be fine," Saishō reassured his page, and he waited for people's voices to subside.

After the people of the house laid down to sleep and the house became quiet, Saishō silently left his room. Entering the princess's hut, he peered with the faint oil light. The princess was chanting the *Kannon Sutra* from her gold-painted scripture with a crystal rosary on her hands. After that, she went on to intone the "Devadatta Chapter" [*Daiba bon*].[32]

"Great Compassionate Kannon, please have mercy on me. With the merits of the *Kannon Sutra*, let me see my father once more. With the merits of the 'Devadatta Chapter,' may my mother in the netherland attain Buddhahood immediately." Thus she prayed for the repose of her mother's soul and wiped her tears with her sleeve. She then composed a poem:

Hito shirezu	Nobody knows
namida no kakaru	of my tears
waga sode wo	My sleeves
hosu hima mo naki	are ceaselessly wet—
haru ni au kana	Alas, this spring.

She closed her eyes and leaned on a nearby hedge. Thinking this a great opportunity, Saishō went quietly through the hedge and approached her. The princess noticed a sudden waft of a familiar scent. Thinking it strange, she opened her eyes. There, standing in front of her, was a good-looking young gentleman. Shocked by the sudden appearance of a man, she immediately put out the oil light.

Saishō whispered, "Please don't make a noise. We are destined to meet each other, so I came." He came closer and behaved affectionately. The princess felt ashamed and frightened at the same time. She cast her eyes down—her tears were brimming over. Her body was like a supple green willow in spring yielding to the wind. He pulled her toward him and spoke softly, "This must be our fate from a previous life. By accident I saw you last night and fell in love with you. Since then you've filled my heart. I waited until it got dark to come here and watched you intoning the sutra secretly from here. I heard your recitation—every word of your memorial service. You must be the daughter of a gentleman. I heard your poem. Please allow me to recite a poem in reply. Your sleeve may be wet, but I will dry it for you:

Sa nomi tada	Simply like that
namida ni nururu	wet from the tears
kimi ga sode	the sleeves of yours
haru no hikage ni	Let me dry them
hosazarame ya wa	in the spring sun.

Saishō talked lovingly to her, but she was too embarrassed to say anything and tears kept welling up her eyes.

Looking at the princess Saishō said, "You must be very cautious. I'll let you know who I am. Do you know the master of this house? He is an aristocrat formerly attending the imperial court in the capital. But there was something unpleasant happening in the capital, so he moved to this province where he had connections. He is Middle Councilor Tadafusa, and

I am his youngest son, Saishō. You can see I am not a demon or anything evil. Please yield to me," he begged. The princess thought it would be too unkind if she did not respond, so she murmured, "It must be so. But I am of humble origin and I don't know how you look at this. I am so embarrassed. If you don't forget me, please stop by again, but please leave now." She then looked down.

Saishō was determined. "How could I possibly forget you—whatever you say?" He pleaded, "How can you make me anxious forever?" He took off his silk garment and laid down with her on it. Although this took the princess completely by surprise, drowned in a current of sympathy and affection, she yielded to him. Saishō was in rapture. Although he wanted the night to last forever, the spring night was short and birds started to chirp. As Saishō wished to keep his love affair a secret, he very reluctantly parted with her. As for the princess, she started to make the fire. Then Akino came to get hot water. Although the princess knew Akino was unaware of anything that had transpired, she felt so embarrassed and sad that as soon as she finished making the fire, she went back to her place and laid down. Akino said sympathetically, "Are you all right, old lady? You must be feeling unwell. Please take care of yourself. I will make a fire tonight then."

The princess sat worrying about her situation. She said to herself, "There is nothing more bitter than a woman. I hear that a man swears his everlasting love just to have one night's passion. I don't think he will visit me again. What will happen to me if this incident is ever revealed? Should I throw myself from a cliff?"

The day came to an end, and again Saishō visited her. He continued to come for four or five days on end and promised their bond to the next life. Saishō then said, "People may start to suspect if I keep visiting here like this. I will move you to my nurse's house so I can visit you with ease." Thus, Saishō wrote to his nurse, "I have found someone in an unexpected place. Let her take lodging in your house. If it's all right with you, I will come to your place with her this evening. Please reply." Matsuwaka-maru carried the letter to Saishō's nurse. When the nurse received the letter, she wondered who it was—"This is indeed an unexpected thing." Although she asked Matsuwaka-maru who this person was, he had not the slightest idea. Since the master's request was to be obeyed by all means, she wrote a reply and had Matsuwaka-maru take it to Saishō. Saishō was delighted to see a positive response and went to the princess's place after dark.

"I have arranged for everything. Don't worry, come with me," said Saishō. The princess followed at his will and wrapped the *yamauba*'s clothes

carefully. "I must never be parted from these," said the princess and held
the bundle tightly. "I understand," Saishō said and took it from her and
carried it for her. Taking her hand, Saishō first went back to his room and
chose for her a superior silk garment. He then put one on himself to look
like a woman. Having Matsuwaka-maru carry his sword and letting him go
first, the two left his quarters for the nurse's house.

At the nurse's house, all day the nurse and her daughter, Chiyoi, had
been preparing for the princess's stay by dusting the tie beams and changing
the tatami mat on the floor. The nurse put the oil light on at night and had
been waiting. When she went out to welcome her master, Matsuwaka-maru
came to inform her of his master's arrival. She let Chiyoi show them directly
to the guest room and joined them a little later. Saishō, in good spirits, said
to his nurse, "I'm sorry to bother you, but please take good care of your
guest. And you, Chiyoi, serve this lady well."

Saishō and the princess looked harmonious together. "What will happen, I wonder," the nurse thought to herself. "He hasn't informed his parents of this matter." As the nurse looked carefully at the princess, she, too,
thought the young girl's beauty and elegance might be artistically portrayed
but could not be described in words. "No wonder my master has fallen in
love," was her thought. They celebrated the couple's happiness with *saké*.
After that, as Saishō visited the princess at the nurse's house every night
and his affection for her only increased, the nurse could not possibly treat
her badly. The princess felt at ease, but the welfare of her father and nurse,
Akashi, was constantly on her mind.

Back in the princess's old workplace, Akino came the morning following the princess's departure and found no fire in the stove. Thinking
it strange, Akino checked the girl's room, but the princess was nowhere
to be found. "I wonder where the old lady has gone—how piteous," she
sighed. A rice scooper said the old woman must have been a Buddha or
some supernatural being who came to help Akino during her busy winter
time. The scooper continued, "The rice never ran out in her utensil. I saw
her making a little hole in the rice. The old woman didn't even eat fish. She
is purifying herself by abstaining from eating meat. In fact, nobody saw her
eat at all. It is strange that the old woman vanished into thin air." The rice
scooper's observation was nearly correct, for the princess had put a small
amount of rice into an iron jar and had thus maintained her life.

One day the middle councilor's children gathered before their mother
and had a banquet. All the gentlemen showed their refined accomplishments, like poetry and music, but among them, Saishō looked particularly
superior. His mother felt proud and wished there were a suitable lady for

Saishō—a parent's fleeting compassion. Saishō, however, visited the princess sometimes even during the day, but since she was at his nurse's house, nobody suspected. One day when Saishō received a beautiful plum branch from an acquaintance, he thought it was so pretty that he wanted to show it to the princess. But as he could not share it openly, Saishō wrapped the branch in a thin paper and wrote a poem on it:

Koishisa o	Enveloping my love
tsutsumite zo yaru	I send to you
ume no hana	the plum blossoms
nioi o tome yo	hold their fragrance
kimi ga tamoto ni	in your sleeves, please.

Then he had Matsuwaka-maru carry it to the princess. At the nurse's house, Chiyoi received it and gave it to the princess, who looked at the gift and smiled shyly. Chiyoi also looked at the poem and said, "What a grateful heart." Chiyoi brought an ink stone and paper and urged the princess, "Please write a poem in reply." So the princess picked up the brush and after awhile she wrote:

Ume no hana	The plum blossoms
morite kokoro no	full of affection
iroka made	and fragrance—
nao hazukashiki	I humbly receive them
haru no kyō kana	this day in the spring.

Chiyoi took the poem, folded it, and gave it to Matsuwaka-maru. When Saishō received the princess's poem and looked at her exquisite handwriting, his affection for her deepened all the more.

At the end of the day, Saishō visited the nurse's house and complimented the princess on her poem of plum blossoms. He playfully told his nurse about it, too. The nurse said, "How auspicious; I will also add a poem." Then she recited:

Ume no hana	The plum blossoms
yae kōbai no	with added colors
iro soete	of double red-blossomed tree
kawaranu haru zo	May this spring
chiyo o henu beshi	last forever and ever.

When everyone felt comfortable, as *saké* went round, Saishō told Chiyoi, who was pouring wine for him, "You should add a poem, too. Come, do so." As Chiyoi blushed, she composed,

Ume no hana	The plum blossoms
iro sou haru no	deepening their colors in spring
kyō goto ni	today and everyday
chiyo yorozu yo no	Vestige of the lasting happiness
kage zo hisashiki	ever and forever.

The love between Saishō and the princess deepened increasingly, and Saishō's sole concern was that his parents know nothing about this. "What will happen later when this is revealed?" he thought. But as the nurse, Chiyoi, and Matsuwaka-maru were determined to keep it secret, nobody knew anything about the relationship.

Thus, Saishō came night after night and felt utterly comfortable, and nothing seemed to separate the couple. But because Saishō's mother had not the slightest idea about his affair, she pondered day and night about her son's future partner. One day after seeing Saishō off, the mother told his nurse, "You know, nurse, Saishō has grown up. He looks particularly mature recently. I have hesitated, but it's getting a little too late. I am considering a certain princess for his bride."

The nurse replied with a blush "I understand," worrying what her young master and the lady would think. The nurse went to Saishō and told him what his mother had said. Saishō was very upset and said, "You just cannot accept all of my parents' ideas." He cried. "This life is not worthwhile if I am to be separated from my lady and must marry a person I don't want to be with. If my parents force me to do this, I will leave the house and go wherever my feet take me. I will not abandon my lady. Tell this to my mother." Listening to him speak in this vein, the nurse was finally sure that her master's love for the princess was not simply a young man's fancy. She knew indeed that Saishō would never leave the lady. She also considered it cruel to separate the couple who were so much in love.

So the nurse later told Saishō's mother on an occasion of talking about something else, "Madam, recently I hear that the young master has someone he loves and visits. I doubt it, but . . ."

"What? How terrible," the mother interjected. "What kind of woman is she? Well, that is simply not to be. The parents should plan for their children. I wonder whether someone recommended her. Matsuwaka-maru must know about this, eh? Ask him."

The nurse replied, "I'm afraid, Madam, Matsuwaka-maru says he doesn't know. The young master has hidden this so deeply that nobody knows." The mother regretted waiting so long to find Saishō someone extraordinary.

A lady-in-waiting serving the mother, age about sixty, proposed an idea. "I suggest you order a 'bride's contest.' There are examples now and past. If she is unaccomplished, the young master will feel ashamed and will abandon her." The mother thought it was a great idea and sent her lady attendants to Saishō with a message: "The plum blossoms in the garden have passed their height, but please come and look at them one last time tomorrow. All my daughters-in-law are coming, so please have your lady [Blossom Princess] attend the gathering, too. We will have a 'bride's contest.'"

To this, Saishō replied without hesitation, "Although my lady is a woman of humble origin, your order is of the utmost importance. I will have her attend the party." After reporting his message back to the lady of the house [Saishō's mother] and leaving her presence, the lady's attendants whispered, "The young master's insolence is extraordinary. Has he no sense of shame? We didn't know he was such an unkind person." Hearing Saishō's message, his mother, too, became anxious.

When the sun had set, Saishō came to his nurse's house and told the story of the day. The princess said, "What a bitter request. I am prepared to leave for wherever. Please obey your parents' wishes."

Saishō responded, "If you are leaving, take me with you till the end of the earth. But how can we hide like this forever?" he pleaded, "After this, we can stay together openly. As for your dress for tomorrow, I will have my nurse request one from my little sister."

The nurse responded, "That's not necessary, young master. I have prepared a set of costumes for Chiyoi's marriage someday. Your lady can use the costumes for tomorrow's occasion. Please rest assured." The couple was extremely pleased and grateful. The nurse was happy as well, for she knew the princess was superior to any of the brides of Saishō's brothers.

The following morning, the princess took a bath in a washtub and applied her makeup beautifully. Then she remembered what the *yamauba* had told her to do when she met the man she was to marry. "I shall do it now," she said and went behind the screen. She opened the bag and found a jewel of variegated colors. Before her eyes, the jewel immediately changed into an abundance of gold and silver, twill and brocade fabrics, Chinese cloths and lady's costumes, hairpieces, sashes, beddings, and swords, piling upon each other. Bewildered, the princess called on the nurse, and the nurse was no less surprised to see the mountain of treasure. "What are these?" the nurse asked.

"This must be Kannon's promise," the princess replied.

"What a propitious promise indeed!" said the nurse. "So you are the Kannon-sent child then. Today's event is all the more auspicious." From the

Chinese brocade, Chinese cloths, to a scarlet *hakama* (divided skirt), there was nothing missing. A long hairpiece the princess put on her hair swayed gracefully. She looked like a blooming flower. The nurse was indeed pleased to see such a stunning sight, knowing no one could surpass her beauty.

Several messengers came from the parents' house and urged the princess to come forth without further delay. "In that case," the nurse said, "please bring a palanquin." The messengers whispered to each other, "That's funny. For whom is the nurse requesting a palanquin?" But considering the position of their young master, they sent a palanquin to the nurse's house. The princess quietly sat in the palanquin, followed by the nurse and Chiyoi. Soon they arrived at the middle councilor's house. Saishō's two elder brothers had been waiting for the princess's arrival—they had secretly planned to watch the princess as she came out of the palanquin and laugh at her. The princess came out of the palanquin with the assistance of the nurse and Chiyoi. Again, the princess's appearance might be portrayed but could not be described by words. Looking at her, the elder brothers forgot about laughing. They looked at each other and whispered, "Where does she come from?" Then they left.

In the banquet room the two wives and a younger sister were sitting with full confidence. There, the princess entered, as if a celestial being descending from the heavens. The middle councilor and his wife were so astounded and delighted to see her stunning beauty that his wife stood up and led the princess by the hand to the right side of her seat, looking at the princess thoroughly. The young lady looked about fourteen or fifteen years of age. Her face was like a shining jewel with sublime charm in her eyes. Her hair was softly hanging at both sides of her face, resembling a willow branch swaying in the spring wind. It was impossible to find a single flaw in her appearance.

Who could have known how beautiful and enchanting Saishō's lady would turn out to be? "Where could he possibly have found such a beauty?" The mother thought it so strange that she summoned Saishō's nurse and asked. But the nurse only replied, "I really do not know in the least. The young master simply says that he found her." "In that case," the mother mused, "she must be truly a celestial being descending on earth. She certainly does not look like an ordinary mortal."

Now the *saké* came. After three cups of *saké* and various entertainments, rare incense in a censer was brought in. The censer went around the party and was taken to the princess, for she was the guest of the day. After she gracefully put her hand around the censer and smelled the scent, she took out from her sleeve an exquisite gold incense box containing fine wooden incense and put it gently on the tray. Seeing the princess's gesture, the middle councilor asked for the tray with the princess's incense box. When he examined the incense, [he found that] it was *Ama no hagoromo* (Angel's Feathered Robe), so named because it was the angels' favorite and its fragrance went up to the sky.

"How rare it is!" So saying, the middle councilor broke some off and put it in the censer. The delicate scent was indeed superb, as if it erased human sins. People were sure that a heavenly being had indeed descended. "With what good fortune was Saishō born! Where did he find this angelic lady?" They were all curious.

The day was over, and so was the party. People went back to their own residences. The middle councilor and his wife felt the princess should not be allowed to live in a plain house, so they had her use a parlor designed as the middle councilor's entertainment room. Further, they attached a number of servants to the princess, from ladies-in-waiting to some humble maids to wait on her with utmost care.

Thus, Saishō and the princess stayed together as they pleased. Saishō's mother thought the princess was adorable and frequently visited the princess's quarters with her daughter and daughters-in-law. The ladies entertained the princess with various activities, including reading and writing and playing musical instruments, but the princess's skill surpassed anyone else's, as she even knew the secret music of *biwa*.

SCROLL THREE

In the meantime, the middle councilor and his wife had an auspicious day selected for building the residence for Saishō and his princess. A great number of carpenters were summoned, and the residence was soon completed. On the occasion of Saishō and the princess moving into the new house, the young couple received various congratulatory gifts. The middle councilor gave them two warehouses, one a treasury, the other a granary. People were envious of such a generous and propitious gift.

Thus, Saishō and the princess led a happy married life, pledging eternal marital vows to each other. There was nothing missing or lacking in their lives—except that the princess missed her father and nurse and wished her familiar servants were there at her side. With that weighing on her mind, she shed tears morning and evening. Time passed. In spring, they played with flowers—the late cherry blossoms flowered among green leaves, but sadly spring days were soon gone. With deutzia flowers, the summer came. A breeze from a fan was refreshing, and the fountain water comforted people. Quickly, though, the summer was gone and it was already autumn. It was the seventh day of the seventh month, the day of the Star Festival. Many offerings were given to the Weaver and Herd Boy in the sky. Saishō, too, composed a poem and offered it to the stars. While he was at it, he playfully wrote another poem and put it on the princess's lap. The princess read:

Aki machite	Long-awaited autumn
kyō Tanabata no	the joy of the Weaver and Altar tonight
yorokobi mo	is all the greater—
ware hatsuaki no	the first autumn
ureshisa zo masu	I spend with you.

She was amused by the poem. Saishō gave her his brush and asked her to compose as well. Finding it hard to resist, the princess wrote:

Tanabata no	Hearing it is
au hatsuaki to	the first autumn
kiku kara ni	when the Weaver and Altar meet,
itodo tsuyukeki	my sleeves are
waga tamoto kana	indeed wet.

She then put her sleeves on her face. Looking at her and her poem, Saishō asked, "Do you have, then, a secret lover whom you miss?"

"Oh no, never," she replied. "But my love for my father is no less great than my love for you." Listening to her, Saishō urged, "So you have a parent you miss terribly. Tell me who it is. Even if he is in a barbarian land, I will surely bring him back here. You are so cautious."

The princess realized that she should not hide her secret any longer, so she replied, "It shouldn't be concealed, but I had a great deal of scruples about saying it. My father is Bungo no kami Moritaka, who lives in a village at the foot of Mt. Fuji. I am his only child, and my parents have doted on me. But my mother died when I was nine years old, and my father grieved so much to the point of following her. Three years after my mother passed away, the relatives got together and through the good offices of someone close, my stepmother came to our house. My father would only think of praying for my mother's happiness in the next life from morning till night and hardly visited his new wife's quarters. She hated me because she thought my father did not frequent her quarters because of me. Although I pretended not to know her feelings, one day while my father was away from home, she schemed to have a samurai kidnap and abandon me in the deep mountains. Fortunately, perhaps by Kannon's power, I didn't become prey for the wild beasts, and instead a *yamauba* kindly gave me lodging for the night. This *yamauba* was compassionate. She gave me directions to a human habitation, accompanying me till midway. She then said that once I got there I should follow the white water. When I walked slowly along the white water, I arrived at the east gate of this house. While I was resting, Akino, a maid of this house, came out and took me to her home to take care of me. Later, she let me stay beside the cooking stove during the winter. I don't know what karma it was, but then you found me there. Nobody noticed me [during the day] because I was wearing a *yamauba*'s clothes that transformed me into an old woman. The treasure I found right before I came into your parents' house came from a small bag the *yamauba* gave me. I didn't wish to tell this story because I didn't want my stepmother's name to be revealed."

Listening to her story, Saishō also shed tears. "Indeed, you have steadfastly concealed this story. However, now that I know, please write a letter to your father. I will have it delivered to him."

"That I thank you, but please do it secretively," she said. Saishō understood. "Don't worry. I'll send a very trustworthy man. Rest assured, and do it quickly."

The princess happily wrote a detailed letter: "I miss you, Father, more and more recently. As I am a woman who caused you displeasure, I spend time lamenting. If you are so inclined, please come and see me soon, and let me see your unchanged appearance." Receiving her letter, Saishō summoned a man named Genta, who was wise and ran fast. Genta received detailed instructions and left Saishō's house the following morning while it was still dark outside.

Arriving at Moritaka's house before noon, Genta announced himself to an attendant. "I have brought a letter from the direction of the capital. I wish to see Lord Moritaka." The attendant conveyed Genta's message to Moritaka, who came out of his quarters and asked from whom the letter was sent. Genta unwrapped the paper and took out a letter on which was written, "A letter to Lord Moritaka from Blossom Princess."

"Is this a dream or reality?" Moritaka asked and immediately opened the letter and confirmed that it was indeed from his beloved Blossom Princess. Disregarding his surroundings, Moritaka pressed her letter to his face and wept, so happy was he to know his daughter was alive. Then he invited Genta to his quarters, clearing out the people, and he asked about his daughter in detail. Genta replied to Moritaka according to Saishō's instructions, and Moritaka was exuberant. "It is an auspicious sign to live," he said. "It was good that I did not commit suicide when my daughter disappeared." Moritaka summoned Saemon, his adjunct, and told him to keep this matter secret. He then ordered Saemon to send Genta home after entertaining him. Further, he asked Saemon whether there was someone who knew the way to the middle councilor's residence. Saemon replied that his wife was from the village of the middle councilor's house and therefore knew where he lived. Moritaka was delighted. While Saemon entertained Genta, Moritaka wrote a letter in reply to his daughter and gave it to Genta. Moritaka also gave Genta a quilted silk garment for a gift, which Genta received humbly and put on his shoulder. Further, Moritaka provide a fine horse with a saddle on it. "This horse runs fast. Please go quickly," said Moritaka's attendant, who accompanied Genta until he was outside the gate. Once outside, Genta got on the horse and whipped it to a gallop.

Genta took the matter as his own and hurried, so he arrived at Saishō's house before sunset. Immediately, Genta presented the letter to Saishō, who was delighted to see him back so soon. Genta showed the gifts of the quilted silk garment and horse and reported, "I have returned quickly riding on this horse. The lord lives in a magnificent house. He said that he would visit you tomorrow."

Saishō was pleased to give the princess the happy news. With the reports of her father's safety and anticipating their reunion, the princess shed tears of joy. She read his letter and impatiently awaited the following morning.

At Moritaka's house, immediately after Genta left, the lord commanded Saemon to prepare everything for an early departure the following day. "For this visit no treasure can be too good or wasteful," Moritaka said. "Open one whole warehouse. Prepare various gifts: gold, silver, gold-brocaded satin damask, Chinese twilled silk fabric, Chinese textiles, embroidered costumes, silk, and so forth. Into one oblong chest put golden armor, breast protectors, and swords. Another chest should include white cloths for all the expenses. Also, prepare thirteen fine horses with a golden saddle on each. Accompanying attendants should look fine, not unsightly: ten mounted retainers and twenty foot soldiers only. The visit should be secret; tell people that the entourage travels to pray at a shrine. Let them carry ample treasures." Lord Moritaka wanted to share his secret with Akashi. "But women are indiscreet. It will be regrettable if her face shows the joy and my wife notices the truth." So thinking, he went to his wife's quarters and summoned Akashi. In good humor, he told Akashi to stay home while he went to a shrine to pray for a long-standing desire the following day.

Moritaka was all smiles and left the quarters. His wife was happy to see him in such a good mood and vainly thought he would visit her upon his return.

On the following day, the party left while it was still dark outside. Though the entourage had been ordered to be small because of secrecy, one had to be cautious against bandits along the way. Thus, the accompanying number became large, with people equipped with spears and halberds.

A long line of people carrying the large oblong chests led the way. Looking at this sight, people whispered to each other, "That's strange. Which shrine is Lord Moritaka going to visit?" "Our lord is said to be secluded," was the common answer. None could make out the intentions of their lord.

Moritaka's party went quickly and soon arrived at Saishō's residence. Moritaka sent his man to report his arrival, and Genta came out immediately. As Genta had anticipated, Moritaka's entourage was quite large. He ushered Lord Moritaka and his immediate retainers in while having the rest of the party wait outside the gate. The princess scurried to the edge of the room, for she had been eagerly awaiting her father. She took her father's hand and ushered him into the room. She could not find words to express her joy. She stayed close to her father and wept. Moritaka also wept. "Blossom Princess," he said through his tears. "I am so happy to see you. After I lost you, I thought of killing myself. But I have survived until now, relying on the Buddha's oracle. It is indeed a miracle."

The princess looked up at her father and said, "I am sorry to see your emaciated face. My sin to make you worry so must be deep. While you were away, my stepmother, your wife, drove me out of the house, saying it was your wish to do so. The feigned messenger carried me on his back and, never stopping once, abandoned me on an unfamiliar mountain. But because of Kannon's help, I escaped the jaws of wild beasts and miraculously survived to see your unchanged appearance. How grateful I am," and she wept profusely. These were tears of joy; the nurse and attendants near the princess all shared their tears. The princess then asked after Akashi. Her father replied, "Akashi, Kojijū, and Kochōnomai are all well and waiting for your news. I haven't told them of this happy event yet. I will send for them tomorrow." Hearing this, the princess impatiently waited for the following day.

The middle councilor heard the news of Moritaka's arrival. "What an unexpected guest! It would be rude to send a messenger on my behalf while I am here." So saying, the middle councilor visited Saishō's residence with the rest of his children. Moritaka came out to meet the middle councilor in person. This was their first encounter. "Your arrival is indeed unanticipated. I regret that you didn't tell us earlier," said the middle councilor.

"You are quite right," Moritaka replied. "I am ashamed to visit so brazenly like this. However, I have only one child who disappeared the past autumn. By some miracle, I learned that she is staying at this house as the wife [of your youngest son], so I came here clandestinely without any regard to public gaze or shame—probably, I have lost control of myself for the love of my child. You are so fortunate to have so many fine, grown-up children. I am envious." Moritaka shed tears.

The middle councilor replied, "Thank you for your kind words. We are blessed with many children, and we love them all. Now that you are here, there is nothing more joyous than this. Please be kind to consider Saishō as your child after this."

The parents merrily exchanged *saké*, and then the middle councilor returned to his residence with two of his children. Saishō remained and entertained Moritaka with various stories. Moritaka's happiness was indescribable. Later, he made a return visit to the middle councilor's quarters and presented various gifts for celebration: to the middle councilor he gave ten scrolls of gold brocade, a fine horse with a gold saddle, and a gold sword; to the eldest son, a fine horse with a gold saddle and a gold sword; for the middle councilor's wife, three sets of Chinese textiles and gold dust; for Saishō's younger sister, one set of Chinese twill clothing and a shining decorative miniature citrus tree with three gold fruit. Everyone, from the ladies-in-waiting to lowly servants, received numerous and diverse gifts. The clan's men and household retainers, without omission, from the old to the young, were given horses, saddles, armor, and swords. "What a splendid entry from the father-in-law!" said the people of the middle councilor's quarters. All were delighted.

Moritaka then returned to Saishō's residence. He was thrilled to see his son-in-law and overjoyed to be with his beloved Blossom Princess again— the reunion might be compared to seeing the *udumbara* [or *udonge*] that is said to flower once every 3,000 years. The celebration gifts to Saishō were a six-year-old dappled gray horse with a fine saddle, three grooms for the horse, a gold sword, ten scrolls of gold brocade and a silk damask, and three packets of gold dust wrapped in paper—each worth 100 *ryō*. The wedding celebration gifts for the princess were three sets of Chinese red cloths, Chinese twill fabric and silk textiles, plus a scarlet *hakama*. For the nurse and Chiyoi and her female attendants, Moritaka gave gifts according to their rank. Moritaka told the nurse and Chiyoi, "Your kindness to my princess shall never be forgotten. The gifts here are only a token. Later, you shall receive more." Their joy was limitless.

After that, Moritaka sent a messenger to inform Akashi of the matter. Receiving the news, Akashi could not believe her ears. She was so ecstatic that she did not know what to think. As the messenger told the detailed story of the princess's adventures, joy began to settle in Akashi's heart. "How grateful. So it is really true. It is worth living this long." So saying, she wept for joy. Kojijū, Kochōnomai, the princess's eight ladies-in-waiting, and her maids were exuberant at the good news. The messenger said, "Of whom are you afraid now? Please depart immediately." Akashi sent a message to the lady of the house: "Our princess who disappeared the past autumn has been discovered. So please excuse us, we are going to see her," and she left for Saishō's house with her people. The stepmother was too appalled to speak. The lady's nurse came near her and said, "I heard that the princess had already been eaten by wolves. The person who has been found must be an imposter."

Whether it was happiness or hardship that brought them, tears flowed on the cheeks of the princess and her nurse. After a while, Akashi told the princess how terrible she felt after she had gone. Relying on Lord Moritaka's dream and the diviner's divination, however, she had been waiting for the first days of autumn. There was no end to her stories. As for the princess, she told how much she missed Akashi when the nurse left for the shrine the morning of her abduction, her worries when she was driven out of the house, the samurai's wife's kindness, her loneliness in the mountains, how scared she was at the *yamauba*'s cavern, and how relieved she was when the *yamauba* turned out to be kind and gave her miraculous clothes and led her to the middle councilor's gate. The princess told how Akino had found her and how she made the cooking fire at this house, how Saishō's nurse and Chiyoi were generous, and so on. They talked to each other from morning to night endlessly—interrupted only by frequent tears.

Moritaka had been staying at Saishō's residence for ten days, entertained by this person and that person. Since this was an event known widely in the province, people all over the province talked about it. The people close to the stepmother heard the rumor and thought, "How wretched! We shall lose face because of the lady's inhumane treatment of her stepdaughter. There is no need to write her a letter." So no one visited the stepmother. Everyone hated her. Since the woman could no longer live under Lord Moritaka's roof and there was nowhere else for her to go, she left the house with her nurse without any destination. It was a sad journey for her, to say the least.

Later, Lord Moritaka took leave of the middle councilor and said to the princess, "Now that I see your happiness, I have nothing to worry about. I will return home to offer my gratitude to the Kannon, and then I will come back here to discuss some matter with the middle councilor. Wait until then." He then bid farewell to Saishō and left.

When Moritaka returned home, his wife had gone. "They say 'when one is guilty, the world is small.' It cannot be helped." So thinking, Moritaka pursued the matter no further. He went immediately to Kannon Hall and prayed earnestly: "With your grateful vow to save Blossom Princess, I could see my daughter once again. I am very thankful. Please continue to protect her in the future." Soon he had a residence hall and pagoda built on a hill and employed twenty Buddhist priests to conduct religious services for Shō Kannon every morning and evening. Because of this miraculous Kannon, many people came to pay a visit. Moritaka also revered the *yamauba*'s wondrous clothes and had the priests hold a memorial service. The mound was built near the Kannon, and a wooden grave tablet with a divine name was erected for the clothes so the clothes, an intrinsic part of the oni's nature, might be transformed into a Buddha and rest in peace. After that, Moritaka gave the diviner 100 *koku* of rice and 100 *kan* of currency, saying, "You foretold well. I couldn't have known happiness or hardship without your divination."

The princess also sent a gift of a quilted silk garment and 100 gold coins to the diviner with a note that read, "Because of your divination, I could see my father and nurse once again. How can I not be delighted?" These were happy events. The princess presented the gifts with the intent to become the diviner's long-term patron. Further, Akashi and a number of lady attendants took off their quilted silk garments and offered them to the diviner, saying, "Because of this diviner, we found hope to live and wait for." The samurai who had kidnapped the princess was captured and sentenced to death by means of *surikubi*, beheading with a dull knife, for seven days and seven nights. The samurai's wife might have suffered a similar fate, but if she were killed immediately, she would not be able to atone for her sin; today's happiness existed because the princess's life was spared through the intervention of the samurai's wife. Still, because the woman had aided her husband, it was not possible to reward her. So, with a lecture she was sent home. As for Moritaka's evil wife, had her whereabouts been known, he would have sent her some form of stipend and "returned good for evil." But she was sinful and unaccounted for. It was indeed hard for the evil woman to avoid karma.

After Lord Moritaka had effected justice and directed events as he pleased, he quickly returned to the middle councilor's residence and requested that the middle councilor allow Saishō to become his successor. Moritaka wanted Saishō to succeed to his lordship and thus handed over his fiefdom, his residence, and his many warehouses to both Blossom Princess and Saishō, who was renamed Tango no kami Moriie. Further, Moritaka invited his mother-in-law to stay at his residence as a happy reminder of his late wife. As the middle councilor and his wife loved the princess without equal, they deeply regretted the young couple leaving. Moritaka consoled them by saying, "Please attend our various gatherings, including flower viewings in spring and those of maple leaves in autumn. Please come often to our house." Thus, Moritaka bid farewell to the middle councilor and his wife. As the princess got into a palanquin, Moritaka and Moriie rode on horses. The middle councilor came out with his two children to see the party off as a celebration of Moriie's first entry into his inherited fief. This was a serious matter. The middle councilor's party rode a long way with Moritaka's entourage. Moritaka at last urged them to return, as the distance they had ridden together was already too far—thus polite and respectful to each other, both entourages parted ways.

Meanwhile, in Moritaka's village, everyone from the most noble to the lowliest person came out to welcome the party home. "The princess is resurrected and returns with her husband," they cried. "There is nothing more auspicious than this." Moritaka's joy was without equal. Not only people in the household but also those outside came to visit with *saké* to celebrate. Moritaka continually held celebrations and banquets without comparison from morning to night. As Lord Moriie excelled in learning, martial arts, and various other accomplishments, people in Moritaka's clan considered Moriie their worthy leader.

Later the princess wondered, "Don't I owe my present prosperity solely to my mother? She revered Kannon so deeply that the Kannon's protection has been profound." So believing, she held memorial services for her late mother all the more frequently. She had a temple built and conducted services for the benefit of suffering spirits. On behalf of her mother, she gave treasures to needy people. As she was always compassionate, her family prospered all the more with Kannon's protection. Further, she summoned Akino and her husband, built a good house in which the couple could live, and sent rice and paid other expenses monthly so the couple became rich and lived luxuriously. The princess gave birth to a prince and a princess one after another. The appropriate wet nurses and nurses were chosen for each child. Akashi, the princess's nurse, and Saishō's nurse named Shii got along as if they were two halves of a whole, and everyone revered them. As Moritaka was too young to remain a widower, he married the middle councilor's twenty-year-old niece. There was a breach in the niece's previous engagement, and she had been single for three years. Moritaka considered her to be like his late wife, and they lived happily together. They both took to the moon and flowers and enjoyed dance performances and music.

If one is honest and compassionate and believes in Buddhas and gods, one's life in both this transitory world and the next will be good. For those who read this tale, be kind and compassionate to people. Akino and her husband prospered because she was compassionate and sympathetic to others. Further, if you rely on the grateful Kannon single-mindedly, your desire will materialize in the end and your life in this world will be peaceful. Further, you will be born into a good place in your next life. Repeatedly think of compassion from morning till night.

NOTES

1. See the introduction for a brief explanation of *otogizōshi*.

2. For an English translation of *Hachikazuki* and Ubakawa, see Steven 315–31; Mulhern, "Analysis of Cinderella Motifs" 31–36.

3. See, for example, Ichiko, *Chūsei shōsetsu no kenkyū*; Matsumoto, "Minkan setsuwa kei no Muromachi jidai monogatari"; Takahashi, "Otogi zōshi 'Hanayo no hime' to minkan shinkō"; Matsumoto, "Chūsei ni okeru mamakotan no ichi kōsatsu"; Ōchi, "Ubakawagata setsuwa to Muromachi jidai monogatari"; Okada, "Otogi zōshi no bukkyō shisō to minkan denshō"; Okada, "'Hanayo no hime' to minkan denshō." According to Toelken, "Folklore is made up of informal expressions passed around long enough to have become recurrent in form and content, but changeable in performance" (Toelken 37). Further, "Its primary characteristic is that its ingredients seem to come directly from dynamic interactions among human beings in vernacular performance contexts rather than through the more rigid channels and fossilized structures of technical instruction or bureaucratized education, or through the relatively stable channels of the formally taught classical traditions" (Toelken 32). In this chapter "folklore," as in "their strong association with 'folklore,'" a phrase frequently used when discussing Cinderella-type stories, specifically means *minkan* (folk) *setsuwa* (see Ichiko, *Chūsei shōsetsu no kenkyū*; Matsumoto, "Minkan setsuwa kei no Muromachi jidai monogatari"; Takahashi, "Otogi zōshi 'Hanayo no hime' to minkan shinkō"; Matsumoto, "Chūsei ni okeru mamakotan no ichi kōsatsu"; Ōchi, "Ubakawagata setsuwa to Muromachi jidai monogatari"; Okada, "Otogi zōshi no bukkyō shisō to minkan denshō"; Okada, "'Hanayo no hime' to minkan denshō"). For an explanation of *setsuwa*, see chapter 1, note 8.

4. Although the word has the same characters as *yamauba*, it is pronounced *yamamba*.

5. See *NKBT* 41: 279. For the Japanese text of the Noh play *Yamaba*, see *NKBT* 41: 275–87. An English translation is found in Bethe and Brazell 207–25. In Noh, there are five types of plays categorized according to the role of *shite* (the lead actor). These categories are plays that focus on gods, warriors, women, mad persons, and demons. The play *Yamamba* is categorized as a demon play. For the study of *yamauba* in English, see K awai; Reider (chapter 4 of *Japanese Demon Lore*).

6. This is the fifteenth story of volume 27. For the Japanese text, see *SNKBZ* 38: 54–58. An English translation is found in Ury, *Tales of Times Now Past* 161–63.

7. As Ōshima Tatehiko ("Yamauba to Kintarō" 51) writes, many legends and associated sites tell of *yamauba* giving birth to children and raising them.

8. Yanagita ("Yama no jinsei" 240) recounts a story of a family living on a mountain that finds a *yamauba*'s *tsukune* (a ball of hemp yarn [dialect word]), which produces infinite yarn. The *tsukune* makes the family rich, but soon thereafter the young wife gives birth to an oni's child with two horns.

9. Franz (104) interprets the witch in two of the Grimm fairy tales, *The Two Brothers* and *The Golden Children*, as an archetypal figure of the Great Mother and an archetype of the "unconscious." See also Jacoby, Kast, and Diedel 205–6.

10. I could find only one article (Takahashi, "Otogi zōshi 'Hanayo no hime' to minkan shinkō") that studies *Blossom Princess* in relation to the "Obasute" legends.

11. For the "Obasute" stories of *mukashibanashi* and legends, see Yanagita, *Nihon mukashibanashi meii* 173–75; for English translations, see Mayer 168–71 and Seki, *Folktales of Japan* 183–86; see also Seki, *Nihon mukashibanashi shūsei* 6: 530–49; Dorson 222–25. Regarding the legend of "Obasute," scholars conjecture that the elders were abandoned because in the village where food was scarce, people who consumed precious food without laboring were considered burdens and useless and redundant to the family and to village life

(Nishizawa 29, 65; Keene, "Songs of Oak Mountain" xii–xiii). Ōshima Tatehiko, however, writes that although scholars have long considered the lore and legends of "Obasute" as a reflection of some customs, including the abandoning of old parents/caretakers, there is no confirmation of the actual custom of abandoning elders in the mountains of Japan. The "Obasute" lore is grasped as a reflection of some customs of *yakudoshi* (an unlucky year), retirement, and funerals (Ōshima, "Obasute no denshō" 3–4; Seki, *Mukashibanashi to waraibanashi* 1–7). Similarly, Yoshikawa Yūko writes that "Obasute" stories are not tales of actually abandoning old people; rather, they are textualizations of the rituals of disposing of *taiyaku* (great misfortune) held at age sixty (*kanreki*, when one returns to the first year of the sexagenary cycle) and of the benefit of such rituals. In folktales, the age of old people is generally between sixty and sixty-two. Yoshikawa notes that the two commonalities of *mukashibanashi* about "Obasute" are the age at which old folks are deserted—either sixty or sixty-two—and the end of the custom of desertion at the story's conclusion. The age of sixty or sixty-two is one's *yakudoshi*, and a celebration or ritual of *kanreki* is held to exorcise or dispose of one's accumulated defilement and crimes. This celebration or ritual becomes both a commemoration of one's life and a prayer for longevity. She concludes that the folklore reflects the rituals and their benefit rather than the actual custom of abandoning the old (Yoshikawa). Indeed, after examining the population registers (*shūmon aratamechō*) of the early modern period, Laurel L. Cornell concludes that "female geronticide does not seem to have existed" (84). Cornell reasons that the "Obasute" stories "appear so prominently in the portrayal of the Japanese elderly in traditional times" because "given what ethnographers report about tension between mothers-in-law and daughters-in-law, the peasant husband and his wife must have wished, often, that they could abandon grandmother on the mountain" (87).

12. These reasons are very bleak, even if fictitious, but there are several advantages in being an old woman: "Ethnographic interviews with women in today's Japan find that many look forward to old age. What a relief to 'no longer keep a low profile and display feminine reserve.' Instead they can be bold, drink, and speak their mind, regardless of the company" (Walthall 156). From a viewpoint of gender studies, Mizuta Noriko considers *yamauba* as gender transcendent. She contrasts *yamauba* with the women of the village (*sato*). The *sato* was considered a safe place where people were protected and insulated from the various dangers of the mountains. According to Mizuta, the women of the *sato* are idealized and standardized—they are good mothers, good wives, chaste, humble, and obedient to their fathers and husbands (10–12). Conversely, a *yamauba* is someone who falls distinctly outside the norm. Although she often had excessive fertility, she lacked the feminine traits ascribed to the women of the *sato*, namely, chastity, obedience, and compassion. Mizuta notes that the norm for the *sato*'s women cannot be applied to *yamauba*, for her essential qualities are so nebulous and polysemous that she nullifies it. In other words, the *yamauba* exists outside the *sato*'s gender system (12–15). She refuses to be assigned a household role, such as mother or daughter, and will not be confined. Mizuta emphasizes that while the women of the *sato* stay in one place, *yamauba* are comparatively nomadic, moving constantly through the mountains, appearing in an array of locales, often outside or away from a town's territorial boundary (10).

13. Yanagita Kunio first made this division of four in his article "Oyasute-yama," published in 1945. In the article he notes that the first two types have foreign origins, whereas the third and fourth types are native Japanese stories. In Yanagita (*Nihon mukashibanashi meii*), however, he divides the stories into two categories: the first is about "a land of abandoned old people. The wisdom of an old person, hidden and cared for, helps solve problems and

they became happy . . . The second type is where children who take their parents to the mountains to abandon them are moved by the love of their parents and try to live with them again" (Mayer 168). Many scholars follow the division of four. Ōshima Tatehiko calls them four types independent of each other (Ōshima, "Ubasute-yama no mukashibanashi to densetsu" 513), and Mihara Yukihisa calls these four categories sub-types (Mihara, "Ubasute-yama" 110).

14. Yanagita Kunio writes that the *mukashibanashi* of this type is perhaps born out of similar stories like "Obasute-yama" of Sarashina in Shinano Province, best known as the 156th episode of *Yamato monogatari* (Tales of Yamato, ca. mid-tenth century) (Yanagita, "Oyasute-yama" 300–302).

15. It sounds fantastic to modern readers how easily Blossom Princess is snatched away from a veranda of her own house, but it was probably relatively common during the ancient and medieval periods. There are many examples in literature where a young lady is kidnapped from her house. Among them, an episode in *Konjaku monogatarishū* that immediately precedes the episode of "Obasute" is noteworthy. It is a story in which a daughter of the major councilor is kidnapped by a guard from the veranda of her house and carried away to a remote place, just like Blossom Princess (*SNKBZ* 38: 457–62). It is conceivable that the author(s) took the idea of kidnapping the princess from the veranda from this episode.

16. The task of taking something from the head is familiar from ancient times. For example, in *Kojiki* (712), Susanoo no mikoto commands Ōkuninushi no mikoto to take centipedes off his head.

17. *Hanayone* can mean two things: the first refers to rice grains wrapped in paper that is tied to a branch to be offered to a god. The second refers to sacred rice grains scattered before an altar to cast away evil.

18. Shō Kannon, who can be male or female, is the basic form of Kannon with one face and two arms and is in charge of the realm of hell.

19. Kimbrough describes in his insightful book the significant roles itinerant and temple-based preacher-entertainers played in the formation and dissemination of *otogizōshi* texts (Kimbrough, *Preachers, Poets, Women, and the Way*).

20. For example, a high-ranking aristocrat, Ōgimachisanjō Sanemochi (1463–1530), who married Imagawa Ujichika's sister, spent twenty-one years in Sunpu. His son, Ōgimachisanjō Kin'e (1494–1578), spent a little over twenty years, between 1521 and 1544, living there (Owada 215).

21. After carefully examining the history of Christian activities and Christian *daimyo* (Japanese feudal lords) of the sixteenth century, Mulhern suggests that Blossom Princess's model is Hosokawa Gracia Tama (1563–1600) and that the heroine's father is modeled after two samurai, Ōtomo Sōrin and Francisco Yoshishige, and the *yamauba* may represent a Japanese Jesuit brother (Mulhern, "Cinderella and the Jesuits" 416–17; Mulhern, "Analysis of Cinderella Motifs" 15). *Blossom Princess* thus reflects contemporary thoughts and customs.

22. "Bungo no kami" means a governor of Bungo Province, located in present-day Ōita prefecture.

23. According to yin-yang theory, "right" symbolizes female. Hence, the flower that is stored in the right sleeve represents a female child.

24. This should actually be twelve years old because three years had passed since Blossom Princess was nine.

25. *Genji monogatari* [Tale of Genji] (ca. 1010) was written by Lady Murasaki. Lady Akashi is one of Genji's mistresses who bore Genji his (and her) only daughter. Her daughter later becomes an empress (Empress Akashi) and has five children, including the crown prince.

26. *Miko* is generally translated as a priestess or shaman who is, "according to the *Kōjien* dictionary, a divinely inspired person who transmits the divine will while in a state of inspiration . . . the fact that they [Japanese *miko*] are generally used for persons who are able to contact spirits by incorporating them further suggests that here possession is thought to be the main form of contact" (Knecht, "Aspects of Shamanism" 4). *Miko* appears in such *otogizōshi* stories as *Kachō Fūgetsu* (Kachō and Fūgetsu, or Beauties of Nature). In this text, however, I translated a *miko* as a diviner rather than a priestess or shaman because the *miko* in the text is not possessed for divine inspiration; rather, she uses paper devices for predicting Blossom Princess's well-being. Interestingly, the picture of the diviner in *Blossom Princess* owned by the Hiroshima University Library is male. See Hiroshima University Library, http://opac.lib .hiroshima-u.ac.jp/portal/dc/kyodo/naraehon/research/01/.

27. In the Shimazu version, this is *haru* (spring) instead of *hana*.

28. The wheel, one of the most important symbols of Buddhism, represents the teachings of the Buddha and Dharma. The poem reveals the assurance of the Kannon; it suggests that a blossom, in other words, Blossom Princess, is protected by Kannon. Just as water running on the wheel is never exhausted—like Kannon's compassion—and goes around, Moritaka will meet his daughter again.

29. *Shaguma*, or fur of a yak's tail that is colored crimson, was used as a decoration for helmets, Buddhist priests' flappers, and wigs.

30. *Hanayone* can mean two things: one is rice grains wrapped in paper—the wrapped paper is tied to a branch to be offered to a god. The second refers to the sacred rice grains scattered before an altar to cast away evil.

31. The same expression appears in *otogizōshi*'s *Shuten Dōji* and the Noh play titled *Ōeyama*. The idea that demons are honest and not manipulative is not novel. For example, in the tale "Miyoshi no Kiyotsura no saishō no ie-watari no koto" (The Eviction) from *Konjaku monogatarishū*, Minister Miyoshi no Kiyotsura (847–918) says, "Real demons know right from wrong and are perfectly straight about it. That's what makes them frightening" (Tyler 123). The original Japanese text is found in *SNKBZ* 38: 97–101.

32. This is chapter 12 of the Lotus Sutra. The chapter includes a famous story of the Dragon Princess instantly transforming into a Buddha.

Part IV
It

7

The Record of Tool Specters (*Tsukumogami Ki*)
Vengeance of Animated Objects and the
Illustration of Shingon Truth

W<small>E HAVE SEEN HUMAN BEINGS INTERACT WITH ONI</small> in the previous chapters. Through human eyes, not only she or he but also it, an inanimate
object, can deal with oni. The "it" can become an oni as well. The recent
pop-culture boom in *yōkai* (monsters, spirits, goblins)[1] in Japan has brought
about renewed interest in various native supernatural creatures, among
which are *tsukumogami*, or "tool specters." Although animate tools appear
sporadically in the literature of the late Heian period (794–1185), the appli-
cation of the name *tsukumogami* to animate objects is largely a medieval
phenomenon, and portrayals and descriptions of *tsukumogami* increase notably in works of the medieval and Edo periods.[2] According to a text titled
Tsukumogami ki (Record of Tool Specters), dated to the Muromachi period
(1336–1573), after a span of 100 years *utsuwamono* or *kibutsu* (containers,
tools, and instruments) receive souls; and, like everything involving individual souls, they develop independent spirits and thus become prone to
tricking people. These spirits are called *tsukumogami*. Resentful after having
been abandoned by the human masters they so loyally served, the tools
and utensils in *Tsukumogami ki* become vengeful and murderous specters.
With imperial and Buddhist support, however, the wayward spirits learn to
repent their malevolent ways, enter lives of religious service, and, in the end,
attain Buddhahood through the Shingon sect of esoteric Buddhism. The
text emphasizes that the Shingon teachings enable even such non-sentient
beings as tools and containers to attain enlightenment.

While many references are made to this text as a major source for
the definition of *tsukumogami*, proper attention has not been paid to the
actual text of *Tsukumogami ki*. The *tsukumogami* story belongs to a genre
called *otogizōshi*.[3] Befitting the *otogizōshi* genre, the story, while amusing,

DOI: 10.7330/9781607324904.c007

is markedly religious in tone. The Shingon tradition developed a sophisticated materialist cosmology, but outside monastic institutions and the highly trained and educated few, the philosophy of objects was probably less easily accessible or understandable even to the elite, let alone the majority of the medieval population. Komatsu Kazuhiko (*Hyōrei shinkō ron* 338) writes that the text could have been employed to enhance Shingon Buddhist power. Indeed, I argue that the text was more than likely created to (re)claim Shingon's influence by highlighting the notion of *sokushin jōbutsu* (realizing Buddhahood in this very body), as exemplified in the case of Kūkai or Kōbō Daishi (774–835),[4] and asserting that the Shingon teachings enable even such non-sentient beings (*hijō, mujō*) as tools and containers to attain enlightenment.

TSUKUMOGAMI KI TEXTS AND PLOT SUMMARY

The *Tsukumogami ki*[5] story appears in a number of extant manuscripts with titles such as *Hijō jōbutsu emaki* (Illustrated Hand Scrolls on the Attainment of Buddhahood by Non-sentient Beings), *Tsukumogami ki* (Record of *Tsukumogami*), *Tsukumogami*, and *Tsukumogami emaki* (Illustrated Hand Scrolls of *Tsukumogami*). Essentially, there are two versions of the *Tsukumogami ki* story: Type A, represented by the *Hijō jōbutsu emaki*, which is written on two scrolls and owned by Sōfukuji in Gifu prefecture, and Type B, represented by all the other surviving manuscripts, which are written on either one or two scrolls.[6] The major difference between Types A and B is that A does not contain several narrative scenes; they are placed in square brackets in the following summary.

During the year-end *susuharai* (sweeping soot, housecleaning) events in the late-tenth-century capital of Heian,[7] old tools and objects are discarded in byways and alleys. The abandoned goods become angry at the humans who discarded them and plan, as specters, to torment their former owners. One discarded object, the rosary Ichiren Novice (Ichiren nyūdō), chides the others for their desire for revenge, but he is beaten up by the club of Rough John (Aratarō) and barely escapes with his "life." Another discarded object, Professor Classics (Kobun sensei), who in the picture is depicted as a scroll, proposes that they should all transform themselves into specters. With the help of a creation god (*zōkashin*), they do so on the day of *setsubun*, the lunar New Year's Eve.

As tool specters, the *tsukumogami* kidnap humans and animals for consumption, and they celebrate their new lives with such merrymaking as drinking, gambling, and poetry recitations. [In the Type B *Tsukumogami ki*, they then decide to worship their creation god, naming it the Great Shape-Shifting God (Henge daimyōjin). They propose to hold a Shinto festival in honor of their god, as other Shinto shrines do. In spring, while they are strolling through the capital for the Great Shape-Shifting God's festival procession, they encounter the Prince Regent's party. A *Sonshō Darani* (Skt. dhāraniī) charm the regent carries with him suddenly flares up and attacks the *tsukumogami*,[8] whereupon they scatter. The emperor hears of this incident, and, summoning the bishop who wrote the *Sonshō Darani* charm, he has him perform ceremonies in the imperial palace. In response to the prayers and rituals held by the bishop and other Buddhist priests, several Buddhist divine boys (*gohō dōji*)[9] appear above the palace, after which they fly off to the *tsukumogami*'s den.] The divine boys immediately subdue the *tsukumogami*, and the wayward spirits swear to convert to Buddhism. Repentant, the *tsukumogami* seek the guidance of Holy Ichiren (formerly Ichiren Novice) to help them embrace the Buddhist teachings and enter the priesthood. After some time as priests, the *tsukumogami* ask Ichiren how they might attain Buddhahood quickly, whereupon Ichiren describes the Shingon teaching of realizing Buddhahood in this very body. The *tsukumogami* thus become devotees of the Shingon sect, and after assiduous ascetic practices, they all become Buddhas. The story ends with the moral "if you wish to know the deep meaning of [the tale], it is that we should quickly escape from the net of exoteric Buddhism and enter Shingon esoteric Buddhism" (*MJMT* 9: 425).

I note three other points regarding differences between the Type A and Type B scrolls. First, some illustrations and textual passages are located in different places. For example, in the Type A text, the scenes of the objects' discussion of revenge and Ichiren Novice's beating by Rough John are inserted before Professor Classic's lecture on the art of yin-yang transformation, whereas in the Type B texts, the scenes are described after the professor's lecture. Second, the Type A narrative is generally more descriptive (i.e., it includes more poems and verses in its banquet scene). Third, the Type A text tends to be more specific. For example, it includes the explanation that "[*tsukumogami*] join a branch of Tōji and practice with the Yataku schools" (Okudaira 185).[10] This sentence is not seen in the Type B texts, which do not contain specific references to any particular sub-sect of the Shingon school. As often suggested, the author of the Type A text may have been a Tōji temple priest or someone otherwise associated with the temple. Type B texts, in contrast, could have been used for more general preaching on the Shingon teachings and been more easily modified to suit an individual priest's purpose.

The Date of the Texts

The issue of whether the aforementioned scenes were deleted from the Type A text or added to the Type B texts raises the question of which came first. Some scholars consider that the Type A Sōfukuji version predates the Type B texts and that the Type B texts are copies of the Sōfukuji text. For example, Shinbo Tōru argues that the format of the Type A scrolls follows that of early literary works that lack the additional *setsuwa* tale (in the preceding summary, the bracketed account of Prince Regent's encounter with the *tsukumogami*) (Shinbo 88). Likewise, Shibata Hōsei compares the language of the texts with that of *Kōbō daishi gyōjō ekotoba* (Illustrated History of Kūkai, ca. fourteenth century), a work predating *Tsukumogami ki*, and he reaches the same conclusion based on the similarity of Type A's language to that of *Kōbō daishi gyōjō ekotoba* (Shibata, "*Tsukumogami* kaidai" 395–99).[11] Scholars such as Kakehi take the opposite view because the Type B tale flows more smoothly, and the first and second scrolls are almost equally long.[12]

It is difficult to judge which came first. But in an entry for the tenth day of the ninth month of 1485 in *Sanetaka kōki*, the diary of Sanjōnishi Sanetaka (1455–1537), Sanetaka writes that he saw a set of *tsukumogami* scrolls (Parts One and Two) in the study hall of the imperial palace (Sanjōnishi 621). While it is not known which text Sanetaka saw, by 1485 at the latest, one set of *tsukumogami* scrolls had already been produced and was in circulation among aristocrats.

TSUKUMOGAMI KI: ENTERTAINMENT AND EDIFICATION
Word Play on *ki* 器

Without a doubt, the *Tsukumogami ki* author enjoyed writing the story, as we can see from the profusion of puns and parodies within the work. A prime example is the appellation of the protagonists, identified as *ki* or *utsuwa* 器. At the very beginning of *Tsukumogami ki*, the author defines *tsukumogami* as follows: "According to *Miscellaneous Records of Yin and Yang*, after a span of one hundred years, *utsuwamono* (*kibutsu*) receive souls and trick people. They are called *tsukumogami*" (*MJMT* 9: 417). Thus, *tsukumogami* are said to be the specters of *utsuwamono*: old containers, tools, and instruments. Yet in the very next paragraph the author explains that the custom of "renewing the hearth fire, drawing fresh water, and renewing everything from clothing to furniture at the New Year is . . . to avoid the calamity of *tsukumogami*" (*MJMT* 9: 418). The term *tsukumogami* is therefore apparently more inclusive than *utsuwamono*, embracing both clothing and furniture. Why, then, does the narrator use the word *ki* 器, as in "containers?"

Ki 器 *and Shingon Teachings*

I believe it is for the sake of metaphorical edification through wordplay. According to one metaphor used in *Kōbō daishi gyōjō ekotoba*, the master transmits the esoteric teachings to his disciple just as one fills an earthenware pot full of water and then transfers that water to another container without spilling a single drop.[13] The earthenware pot is, of course, a container, or *ki*. Hence the narrator says, "*Tsukumogami* are by nature big containers [to hold great knowledge] . . . so the Shingon esoteric teachings were transmitted to them completely" (*MJMT* 9: 424). This quoted sentence also contains another pun: "*tsukumogami* are by nature *taiki* 大器 (big containers)" precisely because they are *utsuwa*, or containers. *Taiki* signifies a person of great talent, in this case, "talented containers that can hold a great amount of knowledge" (Okudaira 185; *MJMT* 9: 424). The kanji compound 大器 further suggests another kanji compound 大機. *Ki* 機, a homonym of *ki* 器, is an important Shingon term meaning "sentient being(s)," and although 大機 is pronounced *daiki* rather than *taiki*, it, too, signifies a large *ki*. The author may have wished to express through 大器/大機 that the sentient protagonists (機), who are themselves quite literally "containers" (器), have exceptional capacities for understanding and exercising the Buddhist teachings.

Various Japanese Buddhist sects profess the possibility of *sōmoku jōbutsu* (the attainment of Buddhahood by plants), which means that not only animate sentient beings (*ujō*) but also non-sentient beings, represented by plants, can attain Buddhahood.[14]

This is related to *hongaku shisō*, or "original enlightenment thought," a vital concept in the medieval period according to which both sentient and non-sentient beings contain Buddhahood within them and could all attain enlightenment. The notion of *hongaku*, central to Tendai teachings and to the later sectarian developments of Kamakura Buddhism, is in fact influenced by the secret transmission of Shingon esoteric Buddhism in which *hongaku* is said to be privately transmitted from master to disciple.[15] As Jacqueline I. Stone writes, conceptions of Buddhahood for plants "originated not as responses to 'nature,' but in doctrinal debate over the implications of claims for universal Buddhahood, and developed as a specific example of a larger tendency" (Stone 30).[16] Indeed, Fabio Rambelli writes:

> In most premodern doctrinal tracts a term such as *sōmoku* usually did not refer literally to plants only but rather indicated the entire realm in the nonsentients; the latter comprises inanimate objects of any kind, including human artifacts. This synonymy was indeed strengthened by esoteric

ideas on the all-pervasiveness of the absolute body (Skt. dharmakāya,
Jp. *hosshin*) of the Buddha Mahāvairocana (Jp. Dainichi) . . . Therefore,
"plants" in the Buddhist theoretical vocabulary does not generally refer to
nature alone, and doctrines on the possibility for plants to attain salvation,
known as *sōmoku jōbutsu* (lit., "plants become buddhas") . . . refer rather
to the Buddhist philosophy of objects and the material world in general.
(Rambelli 12)

That is, the term *non-sentients* (*hijō, mujō*) includes the "realm of
objects" (*kikai*), "territory" (*kokudo*), and "plants" (*sōmoku*), the most
concrete and specific of the non-sentients (Rambelli 12). The protagonists of *Tsukumogami ki* who are in the realm of objects, *kikai* or *kisekai*,
are, according to esoteric Buddhist teachings, rightfully capable of being
awakened.[17] Kūkai (774–835) was the first person in Japan to mention the
possibility of the salvation of plants, and "on the basis of Kūkai's ground-
breaking conceptualization, the Shingon tradition developed a sophisticated materialist cosmology according to which . . . objects became the
legitimate subject of philosophical speculations precisely because of their
status as particular manifestations or embodiments of the Buddha-body"
(Rambelli 19–20).

Although the concept of non-sentients attaining enlightenment may
have been familiar to esoteric Buddhist practitioners, it was perhaps not
so for most medieval people, even though their belief in the supernatural tended to be much stronger than that of those in later periods. Also,
for many people outside monastic institutions, tools and utensils were
probably perceived as less sentient than plants. With the long-standing
tradition of ancient Shinto's nature worship, it is conceivable that people
outside monastic institutions could easily accept the notion of universal
Buddhahood in natural objects such as stones and mountains, where Shinto
deities traditionally manifest.[18] Material objects are, in contrast, day-to-day
implements that do not immediately inspire awesome feelings, let alone
achieve enlightenment of their own accord. But precisely because the idea
of an object realizing Buddhahood is extraordinary, Shingon's teaching in
the *Tsukumogami ki* scrolls is attractive and effective. Fortunately for their
author(s), there was an existing belief in *tsukumogami*, and thus the message
of *Tsukumogami ki* is that even lackluster material objects—or worse, vengeful ones—can realize enlightenment in their very bodies through the power
of Shingon esoteric Buddhism.

The fact that *tsukumogami* are initially evil and yet eventually able to
attain Buddhahood speaks all the more eloquently to the efficacy of the

Shingon teachings. The narrator of *Tsukumogami ki* says that "while other sects advocate only *sōmoku jōbutsu*, the Shingon sect alone goes so far as to say *sōmoku hijō hosshin shugyō jōbutsu* (plants and nonsentient beings become Buddhas by arousing the desire for enlightenment and performing ascetic and religious practices)" (*MJMT* 9: 425). These object-specters are considered demonic and are thus doubly challenged—they suffer from both artificiality and malevolence—but they still attain Buddhahood, thanks to the Shingon teachings. Thus, the message of the text is that if such trivial objects can achieve this ultimate state, then it is even easier for people like the viewer and reader to attain Buddhahood by means of Shingon esoteric Buddhism.

Ki 器 *and Hyakki Yagyō*

There is yet another pun on the character *ki* 器. From the Muromachi period, several picture scrolls titled *hyakki yagyō emaki* (Hand Scrolls of Night Processions of 100 Demons) were created, many of which are generally considered portrayals of a festival parade scene from *Tsukumogami ki*.[19] This *hyakki yagyō* (night procession of 100 demons)[20] could also be a play on the character *ki* 器. The author of *Tsukumogami ki* was conscious of *hyakki yagyō* when he wrote the story. For example, in the Sōfukuji text, the narrator says, "I thought that *hyakki yagyō* and the like were just fictions made up by ancient people. How terrible to see one before my very eyes" (Okudaira 182). Although the preceding line does not appear in the Type B texts, it is clear that the author made use of Heian literary works such as *Ōkagami* (The Great Mirror, ca. 1085–1125) and *Konjaku monogatarishū* (Tales of Times Now Past, ca. 1120) that describe *hyakki yagyō*.[21] Just as the Sino-Japanese reading of the character *utsuwa* 器 is *ki*, the Japanese reading of the character oni 鬼 (demon) is *ki*. In other words, *ki* 器 and *ki* 鬼 are homonyms. Thus, *hyakki yagyō* 百鬼夜行, "the night procession of 100 demons," could also be written or pronounced *hyakki yagyō* 百器夜行, "the night procession of 100 tools."

Parody on Shuten Dōji

The *Tsukumogami ki* illustrations are also parodic. For instance, some of the pictures in the Sōfukuji scrolls portray human tidbits—dismembered human flesh in a serving bowl and a human thigh on a plate—in the banquet scene. The thigh is similar to the one often depicted in picture scrolls of the demon Shuten Dōji, the infamous chief of a band of oni that lived on Mt. Ōe, as we saw in chapter 1. In fact, I believe parts of the *Tsukumogami ki* narrative (from the section in which the old tools

Figure 7.1. Detail of a *byakki yagyō* scroll. Courtesy of International Research Center for Japanese Studies.

become *tsukumogami* through the later banquet scene) constitute a parody of Shuten Dōji and his cohorts. Indeed, both the time and place setting are the same as those in the *otogizōshi Shuten Dōji*: late-tenth-century Japan, in the capital of Heian.

In *Shuten Dōji*, the oni have supernatural powers and can thus transform into anything they want. They enjoy drinking and dancing, and Shuten Dōji boasts, "I abduct ladies of my liking from the capital to use and enjoy as I wish," which includes eating their flesh and drinking their blood. He has a great palace in which all his pleasures are realized. Shuten Dōji brags, "How could any heavenly guardians surpass this?" Similarly, the *Tsukumogami ki* narrator claims that "*tsukumogami* went in and out of the capital to avenge their grudges. As they took all kinds of humans and animals for food, people mourned terribly. But since specters are invisible, there was nothing that people could do but pray to the Buddhas and gods. Unlike the mortals who had cast them aside, the vengeful specters were having a great time celebrating and feasting—building a castle out of flesh and creating a blood pond, dancing, drinking, and merrymaking. They even boasted that celestial pleasures could not surpass theirs" (*MJMT* 9: 419).

While Shuten Dōji and his cohorts are oni with demonic appearances, feared by maidservants and the imperial authority alike, the *tsukumogami* look more weird than frightening. For although *tsukumogami* are also man-eating oni, they are the oni of tools and instruments and thus lack the oni's usual stature.

The parody includes their residence, too. The *tsukumogami*'s den is located behind Mt. Funaoka, a famous graveyard during the Heian period. One might therefore say it is a convenient location for the *tsukumogami* who, after eating people, could easily dispose of the remains. But it is perhaps more likely that the *tsukumogami* selected Mt. Funaoka because of its proximity to the capital. The *tsukumogami* are said to have argued that if their home were "too far from human habitation, it would be inconvenient for obtaining food" (*MJMT* 9: 419). Mt. Funaoka is located northwest of the capital, and if one travels still farther northwest, one reaches Mt. Ōe in Tango Province, where Shuten Dōji is said to have lived. Shuten Dōji and his oni could fly through the air to get food from afar, but, sadly, the *tsukumogami* could not. Thus, Mt. Funaoka represents a kind of compromise location, where the *tsukumogami*, like miniature oni, seem happy drinking and reciting poems.

But why does the author parody Shuten Dōji? It seems to me that he may have wished to draw attention to the fact that while Shuten Dōji and his cohorts were ultimately destroyed by the emperor's warriors, the *tsukumogami* were given a chance by the Shingon "divine boys" (*gohō dōji*) to lead lives as priests and attain Buddhahood.

Ironically, the *tsukumogami* are proud to be animate: after receiving souls, they consider themselves socially superior to plants and stones. Realizing their failure to worship the creation god, they comment that they resemble "non-sentient beings like trees and rocks" (*MJMT* 9: 420). Furthermore, they opine that "Chinese poetry expresses one's heart. Without the talent for articulating the beauty of nature, we are no different from old tools without souls" (Okudaira 182). Mimicking humans, the *tsukumogami* compose delightfully playful poems, one of which (in the Sōfukuji text) is a parody of a famous verse in *Kokin wakashū* (A Collection of Poems Ancient and Modern, ca. 905, poem 53) and *Ise monogatari* (Tales of Ise, ca. late ninth century). The original *Kokin wakashū/Ise monogatari* poem reads:

Yononaka ni	If this were but a world
Taete sakura no	to which cherry blossoms
Nakariseba	were quite foreign,
Haru no kokoro wa	then perhaps in spring
Nodoka naramashi	our hearts would know peace.[22]

In contrast, a tsukumogami recites,

Yononaka ni	If this were but a world
Taete hito dani	to which humans
Nakariseba	were quite foreign,
Haru no kokoro wa	then perhaps in spring
Nodoke karashina	our hearts would know peace.

(Okudaira 182)

The *Tsukumogami ki* author was obviously familiar with such famous works of Heian literature as *Ise monogatari*, *Ōkagami*, and *Konjaku monogatarishū*. He seems to have expected his readers to appreciate his humor as well, although those without the requisite knowledge of classical literature could still enjoy the story.

Wordplay on the Title *Tsukumogami ki*

I believe there may also be wordplay within the title *Tsukumogami ki*. Tanaka Takako considers it possible that the author(s) of *Tsukumogami ki* drew upon Chinese sources—Chinese *Zhiguai* literature (Accounts of the Strange), such as Gan Bao's (fl. 317–22) *Sou shen ji* 搜神記 (In Search of Deities, ca. fourth century)[23] or Li Fang's (925–96) *Taiping guang ji* (Vast Records of the Taiping Era, 978)—for the idea of tool specters. For example, she points to the similarity between the quote from *Miscellaneous Records of Yin and Yang* at the opening of *Tsukumogami ki* and a story in volume 12 of *Sōshinki*: both works assert that things are formed through changes in the five *qi* of the celestial realm. Tanaka suggests that the Chinese yin-yang concept may have been adapted and Japan-ized to allow for the invention of *tsukumogami* (Tanaka, "*Tsukumogami* to chūgoku bunken" 210–13; Tanaka, *Hyakki yagyō no mieru toshi* 182–88). Considering the great influence of things Chinese in ancient and medieval Japan, it is certainly possible to imagine a Chinese origin for tool specters. After all, the text of *Tsukumogami ki* begins with a quote from the otherwise unknown *Miscellaneous Records of Yin and Yang*, supposedly a work of Chinese classical literature. However, as no one is sure of the existence of *Miscellaneous Records of Yin and Yang*, it is equally possible that the *Tsukumogami ki* author simply invented it to lend authenticity to preexisting Japanese *tsukumogami* beliefs.

Because of the author's predilection for enjoying his writing, I believe the title *Tsukumogami ki* 付喪神記 was in fact intended as a parody of the Chinese *Sou shen ji* 搜神記 (In Search of Deities).[24] In Japanese, *Sou shen ji* 搜神記 is pronounced *Sōshin ki* (or *Sōjin ki*). Likewise, the Sino-Japanese reading of *Tsukumogami ki* 付喪神記 is *Fusōshin ki* (or *Fusōjin ki*), which is homonymic with *Fu Sōshin ki* 付搜神記, "Addition to *Sōshin ki*." Moreover, the characters in *Fusōshin ki* mean something like "A Record (記) of Attaching to (付) and Parting with (喪) Deities (神)," which suggests the *tsukumogami*'s course of action—attaching themselves to their patron god—until they embrace the teachings of Shingon esoteric Buddhism. To better understand this second meaning, recall that *tsukumogami* 付喪神 were created from the combination of two elements: the tools' own merit of existing more than 100 years and the external power of the yin-yang creation god. Although this god, given its name, must be deeply related to yin-yang concepts, it is important that it is worshipped as a Shinto *kami* with the frivolous name Henge daimyōjin, or "Great Shape-Shifting God." As one *tsukumogami* says, "Japan is a divine country where everyone believes in Shinto. While we have already received our forms from the creation god, we have not worshipped him, and this is as if we were nonsentient beings like trees and rocks. I propose that we make the creation god our patron and worship him" (*MJMT* 9: 420). Accordingly, they construct a portable shrine to the Great Shape-Shifting God and hold a Shinto religious festival by parading along First Avenue.

This Shinto deity, the Great Shape-Shifting God, could be parodic of the emerging custom of professionals worshipping founding deities of their profession. Regarding this phenomenon, Rambelli writes that starting at least in the late Muromachi period, merchants and a number of professional households and guilds began to write narratives concerning their ancestors and the origins of their crafts and trades to draw connections between certain deities and professions (Rambelli 175–76). For example, the merchants' protector deity is Ebisu, a god of wealth. As a guild has its own protector deity, the *tsukumogami* have their own guardian deity, and thus the Great Shape-Shifting God's power is attached (付) to the *tsukumogami*. Then, during the procession the revelers meet the party of Prince Regent and are dispersed by the *Sonshō Darani*. Prompted by the Buddhist "divine boys," they eventually part with or mourn (喪) their *kami* (神), hence the term "parting with *kami* (喪神)."

Edification, Memorial Services, and Financial Profits

Finally, the lessons of *Tsukumogami ki* pertain not only to spiritual but to moral and financial issues as well. Interestingly, the narrator does not criticize the custom of throwing away old things and replacing them. The narrator explains that "this custom of renewing the hearth fire, drawing fresh water, and replacing everything from clothing to furniture at the New Year is thought to have started from the well-to-do's proud extravagance" because replacing old tools with new ones requires wealth (*MJMT* 9: 418). But the narrator observes that this is not in fact the case; the real reason is "to avoid the calamity of *tsukumogami*." As Hanada Kiyoteru (435–36) points out, the fact that tools and objects were casually thrown away indicates that replacements were rapidly produced, suggesting a significant development in productivity in the Muromachi period.[25] It may be wise to avoid using old tools and armor because they can break easily or fail, with disastrous consequences. Still, it is odd not to frown upon the act of discarding things that are still useful—otherwise, the custom would not have been considered to have "started from the well-to-do's proud extravagance."

The Sōfukuji variant contains an additional statement, to the effect that "if one puts away old things at the year-end and uses new things in the New Year, one will live for several thousand years without illness" (Okudaira 181). In essence, the Sōfukuji scrolls support a kind of proto-consumer culture by encouraging people to perform (or have a [Shingon] priest perform) memorial services for their discarded goods. Indeed, Rambelli has connected *Tsukumogami ki* with a particular kind of *kuyō*, or memorial service. According to Rambelli, *Tsukumogami ki* "tries to reduce the effects of commodification by introducing a ritual dimension in the disposal of used, exhausted objects. De-commodification of objects was carried out through the development of new religious services . . . In addition, by introducing a new ritual dimension, Buddhist institutions were able to expand their presence in society at the level of micropractices of consumption (and disposal) of objects" (Rambelli 246). By performing the memorial service, a priest would be able to exert influence on the client(s). For example, the priest bestows material benefits, such as peace in the household, to the clients. Equally important, a priest could earn income from his services. I imagine that financial factors as well as religious motivations may have been a great incentive for the creation of the text.

THE APPELLATION *"TSUKUMOGAMI"*

Etymology of *Tsukumogami*

I discussed earlier the author's playfulness in creating the text of *Tsukumogami ki*. But an explanation of the appellation *tsukumogami* and how it came to be used for vengeful specters of material objects may be required. *Tsukumogami* is written 付喪神 (lit. "joined mourning deity"), but it is generally believed that these characters are a phonetic equivalent of the syllabic *tsukumogami* つくもがみ (see Tanaka, "*Tsukumogami* to chūgoku bunken" 205). Usually, when Chinese characters are applied to the syllabic *tsukumogami*, the characters 九十九髪 (hair of 99 [years of age]) are employed. Written this way, the term signifies the hair of a 99-year-old person and is deeply associated with the following poem in the sixty-third episode of *Ise monogatari* (*SNKBZ* 12: 164–66):

Momotose ni	The lady with thinning hair—
Hitotose taranu	But a year short
Tsukumogami	Of a hundred—
Ware wo kourashi	Must be longing for me,
Omokage ni miyu	For I seem to see her face.

(translation by McCullough, *Tales of Ise* 110)

Ise monogatari includes the poem in an account about a love affair between a man (Narihira) and an old woman. The narrator does not specify that the woman is old, but she is known to be so from the man's reference to her hair in the poem. Her hair is described as "momotose ni hitotose taranu tsukumogami" (*tsukumogami* [hair of 99], but a year short of 100). The word *tsukumo* does not necessarily mean "99" years old; rather, it can signify "many" years. *Tsukumo* is said to derive from the resemblance between the woman's white hair and a plant called *tsukumo*, an old name for *futoi* (Sirpus tabernaemontani), whose inflorescence resembles an old person's white hair. It also plays on the character *momo* 百 (100). One hundred minus one equals 99, and minus its first, top stroke (the character for one 一), the character for 100 百 becomes "white" 白, signifying white hair. In both cases, the verse refers to an old person—that is, a person 99 years of age and/or with white hair. It is generally considered that the appellation *tsukumogami* for the tool specters came from an image conjured up from 九十九髪. Indeed, part of the preceding poem is used in an explanation of the Sweeping Soot event that appears in the opening section of *Tsukumogami ki*: "kore [Susuharai] sunawachi 'momotose ni hitotose taranu tsukumogami' no sainan ni awaji to nari" (Sweeping Soot is carried out so as not to meet with misfortune caused by *tsukumogami* tool specters but a year short of 100) (*MJMT* 9: 417).

Longevity and Special Power: From Aging Demonic Animals to Demonic Tool Specters

Komatsu Kazuhiko writes that the term *tsukumogami* signifies longevity (as explained above), and he furthermore suggests that it refers to someone or something that has acquired special powers as a result of its extreme longevity. He explains that the syllabic *tsukumogami* can also mean 九十九神 (ninety-nine deities; note: *kami* 髪, hair, and *kami* 神, deity, are homonyms), signifying spirits that are impregnated in extraordinarily long-lived persons or objects. When the spirit does something mysterious, it becomes a specter of an old person or object (Komatsu, *Hyōrei shinkō ron* 330).

Stories about aged beings turning demonic are contained in various narratives. Notably, *Konjaku monogatarishū* contains an account of a woman who becomes extremely old and transforms into an oni.[26] At the end of the story, the narrator explains that "when parents become extremely old they always turn into oni and try to eat even their own children" (translation in Ury, *Tales of Times Now Past* 165).

Demonic old animals are described in the *otogizōshi Tamamo no mae* (Lady Tamamo) and the Noh play *Sesshōseki* (Killing Stone), in which an extraordinarily old fox enchants a retired emperor.[27] Komatsu (*Hyōrei shinkō ron* 330) suggests that in addition to the *tsukumogami* of humans and animals, people in pre-modern times probably also believed in the *tsukumogami* of tools and utensils. I concur with Komatsu's suggestion, although unfortunately Komatsu does not provide any concrete examples of the old animals and objects to which he refers being called *tsukumogami*.

Tanaka, in contrast, contends that there is a major difference between the living creatures called *tsukumogami* and the *tsukumogami* of non-sentient beings. She suggests that some medieval *Ise monogatari* commentaries may help fill in the gap between the two. For example, according to the *Reizei-ke ryū Ise shō* (Ise episode 63), wolves, foxes, and *tanuki* that live for more than 100 years have both the power to change their shapes and the will to harm humans; those transformed animals are called *tsukumogami*. Tanaka writes that calling an aging, shape-shifting animal a *tsukumogami* is just one step away from calling the shape-shifting specters of non-sentient beings *tsukumogami* (Tanaka, "*Tsukumogami* to chūgoku bunken" 206–8).

That one step between the *tsukumogami* of aging demonic animals and *tsukumogami* tool specters seems to be bridged in part by an illustration in *Fudō riyaku engi* (The Benevolence of Fudō myōō, ca. fourteenth century).[28] In an illustration portraying a scene of praying by a yin-yang diviner or practitioner of Onmyōdō (the Way of yin-yang),[29] five unidentifiable creatures representing illness deities are depicted. Among the five, two look like some kind of container: one is a furry basin with handles (*tsunodarai*), and another one looks like a large furry bowl. They resemble containers made of animals. Indeed, all five deities have animal features—fur and paws. Earlier, I wrote "in part" because these creatures are considered deities of illness rather than spirits of tools. It could be the case that these illness deities possessed the tools (in the sense of "spirit possession" rather than "ownership") or were held in the containers, thus becoming vengeful tool spirits.

As mentioned in chapter 2, Peter Knecht, Hasegawa Masao, Minobe Shigekatsu, and Tsujimoto Hiroshige report an interesting contagious disease called *denshi-byō* (illness caused by *denshi*), in which a person is emaciated by the time of death ("Denshi 'oni' to 'mushi'"). The modern diagnosis of this illness is pulmonary tuberculosis, although this interpretation is open to debate. Fascinatingly, this *denshi* was considered both a *mushi* (worm) and an oni from the ancient through early modern periods, and consequently a remedy was sought from both medicine and religion. From the viewpoint of religious treatments, an esoteric Buddhist *denshi-byō* healing ritual is particularly interesting. According to an entry titled *Ji denshibyō hiden* (Secret Transmissions for Healing *Denshi-byō*) in the *Sho kaji hihō* (Various Secret Formulas of Incantation), the ritual includes leaving a picture of a *denshi-oni* underneath the victim's bed for three days, during which time a small amount of food is set aside from the patient's meals. After the ritual prayer is over, the priest strokes the victim's body with the picture to have the oni transfer to the picture, and he places the food set aside from each meal into designated utensils (*ki* 器). The priest then recites directly to the utensils: "attached spirits, eat this and leave this place" (Knecht et al., "Denshi 'oni' to 'mushi'" 60). That night, the picture is buried together with the food in the utensils.

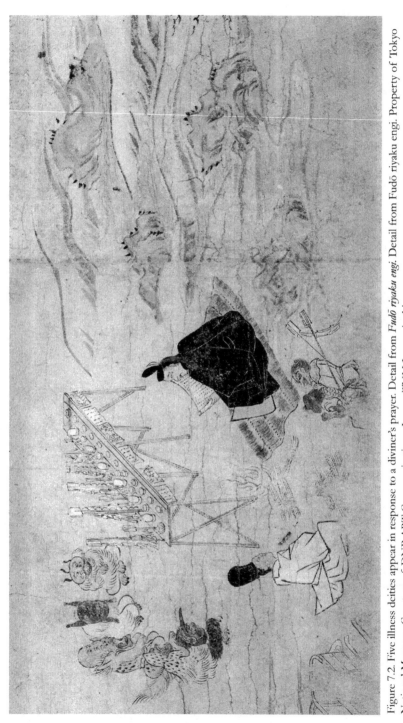

Figure 7.2. Five illness deities appear in response to a diviner's prayer. Detail from *Fudō riyaku engi*. Detail from *Fudō riyaku engi*. Property of Tokyo National Museum. Courtesy of DNP ART Communications. Image: TNM Image Archives.

What is noteworthy about the ritual is that the priest speaks directly to the utensil as if it were a living thing. Presumably, the oni is going to eat this meal, but (part of) the illness is already contained in the utensil through the victim's contaminated food. Practically speaking, the illness is already inside the utensil or inherently part of it. The illness deities that look like containers portrayed in the illustration in *Fudō riyaku engi* may have reflected that concept. That is, an oni or illness deity exists together with a utensil, and the utensil that was earlier associated with the oni becomes an oni itself. The oni-utensil that harms humans could be a precursor of *tsukumogami*. In any case, I assume that esoteric Buddhist monks as well as yin-yang diviners played a role in the spread, if not the birth, of *tsukumogami*, primarily through the use of objects in various rituals.

In fact, according to Tō Teikan (1732–97), the author of *Kōko shōroku* (A Minor Record of a Predilection for Things Old), the creatures portrayed in the *Fudō riyaku engi* illustration are *tsukumogami*. Quoting a line from *Sankaiki*, the diary of Fujiwara no Tadachika (1131–95), concerning a high Buddhist priest's ritual or magic for transferring a possessing evil spirit into a female medium and then depositing it into a thing, Tō comments that Buddhist priests and yin-yang diviners are good at ritual and magical techniques (quoted in Takasaki 52). It is unclear what this "thing" was. It could have been a *hitogata* (paper or straw representation of a human) or some other object. But the idea of objects into which evil spirits and defilements are transferred reminds me of a purification ceremony in which a jar is used. According to *Engishiki* (The Engi Codes, tenth century), the Ōharae (great purification ceremony) was held twice a year in the imperial palace when the emperor, empress, and crown prince transferred their impurities, as well as the accumulated impurities of the nation, into five bamboo scales, swords, and a pot into which they breathed (see *KT* 26: 26–28; Bock 83–85). These *agamono*, things into which pollution, defilement, and crimes are transferred for a purification ceremony, were then to be thrown away in the river or on riverbanks. The discarded *agamono*—paper dolls, jars, and whatever was used for the purification ceremony—were to be abandoned with people's breath and impurities. These abandoned objects may have been thought to contain evil spirits and to act vengefully. Again, tools and utensils used in rituals seem to have had a deep relationship with the formation of *tsukumogami* beliefs.

Belief in Animate Objects before and during the Medieval Period

As mentioned in the introduction to this chapter, animate utensils are not unique to the medieval period. A utensil transformation had already appeared in *Konjaku monogatarishū*, in which a copper decanter changed into a three-foot-tall man. According to a yin-yang diviner, this animate copper decanter was a harmless spirit (*mono no ke*). The narrator concludes the story by stating that "even from this, people come to know that the spirit of an object manifests itself through a human shape."[30] The comment indicates that the idea that objects are endowed with their own spirits existed by the end of the Heian period. It is interesting that this spirit of an object is simultaneously considered a harmless spirit and appears not as an animate decanter but as a human.

Stories of animate objects that hurt humans also exist. For instance, the same collection contains a tale about a small oil pot that kills a sick girl. In this story, however, the offending spirit is said to have possessed an oil pot rather than to have itself been the innate spirit of the pot (*SNKBZ* 38: 64–66). Again, these harmful utensils are not old material objects that receive souls and transform into vengeful spirits but rather evil spirits or oni that take control of the objects. One can assume from these stories that by the end of the Heian period there was a belief that when an object does not harm people, the spirit of the object may manifest as a human being, but when it does harm people, the appearance of the object remains unchanged while the harm is believed to have been caused by an oni or evil spirit possessing the object. When we turn to the Muromachi-period *Tsukumogami ki* and look at the illustration of Holy Ichiren, he does look like a human, and he transforms without the help of the creation god. In contrast, the other *tsukumogami* look like specters of tools or simply weird creatures. Apparently, Holy Ichiren's case represents a spirit manifestation in human form.

Interestingly, the idea that inanimate objects can be possessed by evil spirits or oni rather than possessing their own intrinsic spirits is expressed in *Tsukumogami ki* as well, but, importantly, the narrator condemns this view as an explanation by the preachers of exoteric Buddhism. The narrator explains, "Scholars of the exoteric Buddhist schools say that according to the *Agongyō*, oni and deities reside on the streets and in the houses, filling every inch of space. The exoteric Buddhists believe that the transformation of old tools into specters is due to the deities and oni possessing them. They ask, 'how could inanimate objects have souls?'" (*MJMT* 9: 425). Although this disagreement reflects the religious tone of the late tenth century, the differences between the esoteric and exoteric Buddhist schools of the Muromachi period were still distinct, and those schools maintained a fierce rivalry for predominance. So, the disagreement can also be interpreted as an aspect of an ongoing political and economic competition among the various schools of Buddhism during the Muromachi period. Indeed, R. Keller

Kimbrough writes that "it is important to keep in mind that competition among temples and sects tended to be fierce, and that doctrinal and institutional rivalries were often played out in the realm of seemingly innocuous tales" (*Preachers, Poets, Women, and the Way* 24).

Perhaps the notion of demons and evil spirits possessing objects was still popular while a belief in material objects receiving souls to do harm was simultaneously spreading. Buddhist priests and yin-yang diviners seem to have been at the center of *tsukumogami* thought, and, as we have seen, the author of *Tsukumogami ki* takes advantage of preexisting *tsukumogami* beliefs to emphasize the universal presence of souls in vegetation, tools, and other objects. Ironically, *Tsukumogami ki* then itself became a source for the definition of *tsukumogami*. According to the transcription of a *kyōka awase* (comic tanka contest) held in the first month of 1508, a poet composed a *kyōka* about old clothes that did not transform into new ones on New Year's Eve. The judge is said to have commented that "extremely old objects receive souls and turn into specters . . . Lord Fujiwara no Saneyori [himself] met various specters on his way to the imperial palace" (Hanawa, *Gunsho ruijū* 28: 615). As we can see from the judge's apparent allusion to *Tsukumogami ki* in his explanation of *tsukumogami*, the popular belief in tool specters both inspired and was itself later shaped by *Tsukumogami ki*.

As I have discussed in the body of this chapter, *Tsukumogami ki* is full of amusing wordplays and parodies, many of which are intertwined with Shingon Esoteric teachings. While entertainment plays an important role in the text, *Tsukumogami ki*'s principal purpose may have been to exert religious influence on a broad audience outside monastic institutions. Highly sophisticated Shingon Buddhist materialist cosmology may have been too complex for ordinary people, but through the vernacular *Tsukumogami ki*, which drew upon existing *tsukumogami* beliefs, the Shingon teachings could have been disseminated. Educated audiences would have understood the story's parodies and wordplays; although less educated readers might have missed most of these, they would still have been exposed to the esoteric teachings through the vernacular story with its many illustrations. *Tsukumogami ki* also encourages people to sponsor memorial services for their abandoned objects, lest the vengeful spirits harm their former owners. And through the act of performing ceremonies of propitiation, Shingon priests could influence the daily lives of medieval people. While those who requested services would receive material benefits, such as peace of mind, priests who performed the services would also benefit from material compensation. Thus, *Tsukumogami ki* seems to have played important religious and financial roles in wider Muromachi society.

TRANSLATION OF *TSUKUMOGAMI KI*

This is a translation of the single-scroll National Diet Library *emaki*, a Type B text, typeset in *MJMT* 9: 417–25. While translating it, I also consulted Kokumin tosho kabushiki gaisha's "Otogizōshi," 24–34, and Washio's "Tsukumogami," 15–25. The illustrations are from the Kyoto University Library's scrolls, also a Type B text. See Kyoto daigaku fuzoku toshokan, "Tsukumogami," http://edb.kulib.kyoto-u.ac.jp/exhibit/tsuroll/indexA.html and http://edb.kulib.kyoto-u.ac.jp/exhibit/tsuroll/indexB.html.

The Record of Tool Specters
SCROLL ONE

According to *Miscellaneous Records of Yin and Yang,*[31] after a span of 100 years, *utsuwamono* or *kibutsu* (containers, tools, and instruments) receive souls and trick people. They are called *tsukumogami*. In view of that, every year people bring out the old tools from their houses and discard them in the alleys before the New Year. This event, called *susuharai* (lit. "sweeping soot," year-end housecleaning), is carried out to avoid misfortune caused by *tsukumo-gami* tool specters but a year short of a hundred.

This custom of renewing the hearth fire, drawing fresh water, and renewing everything from clothing to furniture at the New Year is thought to have started from the proud extravagance of the well-to-do, but now we understand that the custom is meant to prevent the calamities caused by *tsukumogami*.

Around the era of Kōhō (964–67) perhaps, according to the usual custom of sweeping soot, old tools were thrown away from houses both inside the capital and in the surrounding area. Those abandoned instruments got together to discuss their fate: "We have faithfully served the houses as furniture and utensils for a long time. Instead of getting the reward that is our due, we are abandoned in the alleys to be kicked by oxen and horses. Insult has been added to injury, and this is the greatest insult of all! Whatever it takes, we should become specters and exact vengeance." In the middle of these heated discussions, a Buddhist rosary named Ichiren Novice (Ichiren nyūdō) cut into the debate: "Everyone, it must be our karma to be discarded like this. We should return hostility with benevolence." Hearing the Novice, a club named Rough John (Aratarō) became angry and yelled, "You meddling Novice! Generally speaking, it is half-baked Buddhist priests that people can't stand to look at. Go away!" Aratarō then beat Ichiren so badly that the Novice's rosary knot was nearly severed. Ichiren Novice was close to death, and only with the help of his disciples did he escape.

Thus, the discussion went on, and each was asked to voice an opinion. Professor Classics said: "The beginning of Creation is chaos, and there is no form for humans, grasses, or trees. But because of yin-yang energy and the heavenly furnace, things are given temporary shapes. If we chance upon the art of yin-yang and heavenly craft, we, inanimate beings, will surely be given souls. Aren't such stories as the old pebbles' talking[32] and Mr. Gu's turning into a carriage[33] testimony to the transformation of beings at the time of yin-yang change? So let us wait for the *setsubun* (lunar New Year's Eve), when yin and yang change their places and shapes are formed out of entities. At that time we must empty ourselves and leave our bodies to the hands of a creation god (*zōkashin*). Then we will surely become specters." Everyone wrote down what the professor said on pieces of cloth and left.

Meanwhile, although Ichiren Novice was a pious man, he could not help but feel bitter, and he insisted on going back to vent his anger. His disciples were able to restrain him, just barely, but he continued to seethe with resentment.

Hitosuji ni / omoi mo kiranu / tama no o no / musuboboretaru / waga kokoro kana

Like a string of rosary beads, my mind cannot be severed from angry thoughts.

Deshi to tada / ochite kienamu / michi no e no / kusaba no tsuyu no / inochi nariseba

I wish I could fall and disappear with my disciples, for my life is momentary, just like dew on the grass in an alley.

New Year's Eve arrived at last. The old tools emptied themselves as Professor Classics had told them and entered into the bosom of the creation god. Since the tools lived meritoriously for more than 100 years and the creation god had the power of transformation, no sooner did the two forces combine than the old tools became vengeful specters. Some tools became men or women, old or young; others took the shape of demons or goblins. Still others became beasts such as foxes and wolves. These various shapes were indeed fearful beyond description.

The *tsukumogami* discussed where they should live. "If it's too far from human habitation, it would be inconvenient for obtaining food." So they decided to move to the place behind Mt. Funaoka,[35] deep in Nagasaka.[36]

From there, *tsukumogami* went in and out of the capital[37] to avenge their grudges. As they took all kinds of humans and animals for food, people mourned terribly. But since specters are invisible, there was nothing people

Figure 7.3. The abandoned objects are transformed into *tsukumogami*. Courtesy of International Research Center for Japanese Studies. [The characters' remarks on the illustration:

1. "Hey, when that flute became an oni, I hear the oni was afraid of soybean vines. Don't you be afraid of soybean vines."
2. "Such a cowardly oni won't do at all. If someone throws soybeans at me,[34] I will pick them up and eat them as fine tea confections."]

could do but pray to the Buddhas and gods. Unlike the mortals who had cast them aside, the vengeful specters were having a great time celebrating and feasting—building a castle out of flesh and creating a blood fountain, dancing, drinking, and merrymaking. They even boasted that celestial pleasures could not surpass theirs.

Topic: Flowers

Haru tatsu to / iu sono hi yori / waga gotoku / sakura mo hana no / nasake tsukuramu

On the very first day of spring, perhaps the cherry blossoms have become sentient like me.

Ika ni shite / yōtaru hana zo / yamazakura / miru hito hoto ni / kokoro madowasu

How did mountain cherry blossoms get magical power? Their beauty enchants all who see them.

Chinese poetry expresses one's heart. Without talent for articulating the beauty of nature, we are no different from the old tools without souls we once were:

吾変明皇按楽来	I have changed myself into Minghuang[38] to play music
花驚褐鼓一時開	Startled by my drum,[39] [trees] simultaneously burst into bloom
今宵共奏春光好	This evening we play together "The Springtide Is Good"
永使茲身不可埃	This body will never be made into dust
珠簾影動落花春	Behind the jeweled screen move the falling spring petals
胡蝶成媒悩美人	A butterfly becomes a matchmaker and disturbs a beautiful woman
人似妖紅如一夢	A human is similar to a bewitching red flower—like a dream
須傾鸚鵡酒霑唇	Let us pour wine into parrot cups to wet our lips.

One day a *tsukumogami* said, "Japan is a divine country where everyone believes in Shinto. While we have already received our forms from the creation god, we have not worshipped him, and this is as if we were nonsentient beings like trees and rocks. I propose that we make the creation god our patron and worship him. That way we will be sure to have a long life with abundant posterity."

Thus, a shrine was built soon in the recess of Mt. Funaoka and was named the shrine of the Great Shape-Shifting God (Henge daimyōjin). They chose a Shinto priest's headgear for a priest, bells for shrine maidens, and wooden clappers for *kagura* performers,[40] and they offered prayers every morning and observed rituals every evening. Though they were evil and violent specters, they were pious. It is like that great thief Dao Zhi,[41] who followed the five cardinal Confucian virtues.[42]

They also proposed to have a religious festival as other shrines did, and they made a portable shrine. In the deep night of the fifth day of the fourth month, they made a procession eastward along First Avenue.[43] They made a festival float mounted with a decorative halberd and other elaborate decorations.

At that moment the prince regent's party[44] was proceeding westward along First Avenue to the imperial palace through Tatchimon Gate[45] for a special investiture. Here the regent's party encountered the *tsukumogami*'s procession.[46] Astounded, the escorts and outriders of the regent's party fell from their horses in a swoon of fright, while other attendants were stricken as well. The regent, alone of his party, was not agitated or frightened. From inside his carriage, he glared angrily at the specters. A flame suddenly spurted from an amulet the regent kept on himself, and in no time the flame spread and attacked the *tsukumogami*.[47] The specters fled for their lives before the flames.

The regent returned home, for the incident prevented him from visiting the imperial palace, but he reported this strange encounter to the emperor at dawn. The emperor was astonished and immediately had a diviner see to the matter. According to the diviner's report, restrained behavior was required, so the emperor ordered offerings to be made to various Shinto shrines and for Buddhist priests of the exoteric and esoteric schools to pray in their temples.

Inquiring about the miracle of the regent's amulet, the diviner discovered that a certain bishop had copied *Sonshō Darani*[48] and had prayed for the sake of his patron, the regent. The regent then kept the amulet on him everywhere he went. Hearing the story, the emperor issued an order to leave all future matter of prayers to the bishop. The bishop declined the request again and again, but an imperial order was hard to refuse. He finally agreed to carry out the Great Rite of *Sonshō Darani* at *Seiryōden*.[49] The attending priests were excellent and skilled in the Yogācāra teachings (yugakyō). Smoke from the ritual burning of mystic wooden sticks filled the court, and prayers resounded in the palace.

On the night of the sixth day, on his way to *Seiryōden* to listen to the service, the emperor saw a brilliant light just above the palace. Inside the light were seven or eight extraordinary-looking armed divine boys (*gohō dōji*). Some had swords and others had bejeweled staffs—they all flew northward. The emperor was moved to tears, understanding that the attendants of two Myōō (Vidyārāja)[50] had appeared to conquer the evil specters. The emperor then went to the place where the service was being held and worshipped the principal Buddha image. After the service ended and all the rituals were over, he summoned the bishop and said, "It's not that miracles of Shingon Buddhism have only begun now, but the miraculous appearance of the divine boys is due to your pious practice." The bishop was thankful for the imperial reverence for Buddhism and bowed out of the royal presence with tears of gratitude.

In the meantime, the divine boys flew to the *tsukumogami*'s den. Sacred Wheels of Dharma (*rinpō*) whirled around in the air; flames from them attacked the *tsukumogami* and with little effort, the divine boys conquered the specters. The divine boys did not destroy the *tsukumogami*, however. Full of mercy, they said, "If you forswear evil, promise not to harm humans, and revere the Three Treasures of Buddhism and seek Buddhahood, we will spare your lives. Otherwise, you shall all perish." The terrified specters forswore their vengeance and vowed to observe Buddhist doctrines.

Afterward, the *tsukumogami* gathered together shaken with fear, their close brush with doom fresh in their minds. One specter said, "We have incurred divine punishment because we took many lives and did much that was evil. But observing our penitence, they have generously spared our lives. We should abandon the quest for fleeting glory and follow the way of Buddha." The rest of the *tsukumogami* agreed and immediately sought spiritual awakening.

They discussed who would be their mentor in Buddhism. "That Ichiren whom we scorned is a revered master, known for his experience in the doctrine and practice of the various Buddhist schools. Let us ask him to guide us. What a shame that we humiliated him last winter. But if we show our repentance, he will perhaps benevolently forgive us." So saying, they visited Ichiren's dwelling.

As for Ichiren [who had become the most pious of the Buddhist priests and was now called Holy Ichiren],[51] he was deeply weary of this world since last winter's incident, so he became a recluse in the deep mountains. He made the wind through the pine trees his friend and thus awoke to the twelve links in the chain that binds us to suffering (*jūni innen*). He listened to the sound of water in the valley and thus cleansed 108 polluting thoughts from his mind.[52] One evening a faint sound of the evening bell in the distance made Holy Ichiren think "the day is almost over" when he heard a

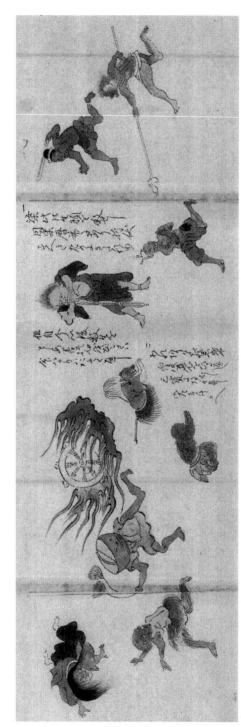

Figure 7.4. The divine boys attacking the *tsukumogami*. Courtesy of International Research Center for Japanese Studies.

[The remarks of the divine boys and *tsukumogami* on the illustration:

"All of you, we know what you've done. We've come to punish you. But if you stop killing people and decide to embrace Buddhism, we will spare your lives."

"Thank you, thank you! From now on we will not have any evil thought and we will convert to Buddhism. Please spare us."]

knock on the door. "Who could it be at such an hour?" he thought as he opened the door and was surprised to see specters of various extraordinary shapes gathered on his doorstep. Astonished, Holy Ichiren asked, "Who are you? Are you demons to shake my religious faith?" The *tsukumogami* replied that they were the specters of the familiar old tools and explained their situation—how the creation god had transformed them into specters and the Buddhist divine boys awakened their religious faith. To this, Holy Ichiren replied, "I was wondering what happened to you all since then. I'm so happy that not only you visit me but also that you have become religious." Among the old tools, the club that beat Holy Ichiren nearly to death was especially repentant for his behavior. The holy man, however, comforted him: "Don't say that. It was that very incident that led me to withdraw from the world. Thus, you should be called my mentor in the way of the Buddha."

Soon, Holy Ichiren shaved their heads and had them don Buddhist garb. Starting from the ten Buddhist precepts given to a novice, under the guidance of Holy Ichiren they progressed to receive more complex precepts.[53] One day the tool priests said to the holy man, "We understand that each and every Buddhist doctrine in the canon opens a passage to Buddhahood, but a pace of progress toward enlightenment depends upon the profundity of teachings. If possible, we would like to receive profound teachings and attain Buddhahood swiftly."

Ever modest, Ichiren replied, "Although I am a priest of limited ability, under the guidance of virtuous priests I have studied teachings of various sects that came to Japan. The profundity of Shakamuni Buddha's[54] teachings varies depending on the capacities of the sentient beings, but they all partake of the virtue of the Dharmadatu, and we cannot easily discuss their advantages and disadvantages. When it comes, however, to the immediate attainment of Buddhahood in this very body (*sokushin tongo*), it resides solely in the power of the Three Mystic Practices[55] of the Shingon esoteric sect. Long ago, when Kūkai preached the teaching of immediate attainment of Buddhahood, the master priests of various sects doubted it and did not follow his teaching. Consequently, important priests of various sects gathered at the imperial court and debated the doctrinal interpretations. The priests delivered powerful speeches, such as Kasen'en (Kātyāyana)[56] and Furuna (Purna),[57] but none surpassed Kūkai's eloquence, and his discourse on *sanmaji* or *samādhi* (meditative states) for enlightenment was as clear as glass. As he logically argued the teachings for the attainment of Buddhahood in this lifetime (*sokushin jōbutsu*), the scholarly priests of every school at the debate were rendered speechless.

"Then the emperor said, 'The excellence of your discourse is doubtless. But I still wish to see the proof of it.' Whereupon Kūkai sat facing south, and no sooner did he exercise the Three Mystic Practices than his body was fused with Mahāvairocana: on his head was the crown of Five Wisdoms,[58] emitting a halo of five colors from his back. The emperor bowed his head; his subjects and priests prostrated themselves and worshipped Kūkai, who had become Shana (Mahāvairocana). After a while, Kūkai returned to his human form and thus demonstrated to them the doctrine of *shōbutsu funi*, or the non-duality of a living human and Buddha. Any doubt about the immediate realization of Buddhahood was solved that day, and from then on Shingon esoteric Buddhism has prospered. Everyone, I urge you to pursue the teaching of the Shingon sect and attain enlightenment," and every one of the tool priests joyfully embraced the Shingon teachings.

As *tsukumogami* were all from birth great vessels (capable of holding vast knowledge), the reality and wisdom of the Two Mandalas as preached in the King of Sutras (Mahāvairocana Sutra) were transmitted to them completely, with nothing left out. Holy Ichiren said, "That Ryūchi Daishi (Nāgabodhi)[59] of old was waiting for Konchi (Vajrabodhi)[60] and Kōchi (Amoghavajra)[61] for 800 years, so he took an elixir to (extend his life and) transmit esoteric Buddhism. As for me, fortunately I am blessed with you disciples and can teach all doctrines of the Shingon sect. My wish is realized." So saying, at the age of 108, Ichiren entered the state of samadhi by reciting mantras and attained Buddhahood in the sitting posture, there, before his disciples. Immediately, the west gate of his hut opened, releasing a brilliant light, and the room transformed into the Paradise of Mahavairocana.

To witness a person attain enlightenment is unheard of even among the most advanced Bodhisattvas at the tenth stage on the path, let alone among ordinary and stupid mortals. However, because of the skillful means of miraculous grace, the practitioners of the Shingon sect are sometimes able to see it. After witnessing Holy Ichiren attain Buddhahood, the old tool monks applied themselves to the ascetic practices all the more.

After some time, one old tool monk declared, "While living together like this is good to teach one another and deepen our knowledge, we may become lenient toward each other, and this may disturb our practice. That's why the scripture says, 'Go deep into the mountains and seek the way of Buddha.' So we should go to the deep mountain valleys, severing any connection with the secular world, and devote ourselves to training." The rest of the tool monks agreed, and, though reluctant to part, they went their separate ways. One decided to live on the carpet of moss between rocks in deep mountains; another under a pine tree in a valley.

Thus, each tool monk matured in its ascetic practices and attained the state of Samadhi in their bodies. Depending on the principal Buddha or

Figure 7.5. The *tsukumogami* practice the teaching of Shingon esoteric Buddhism under the guidance of Holy Ichiren. Courtesy of International Research Center for Japanese Studies.

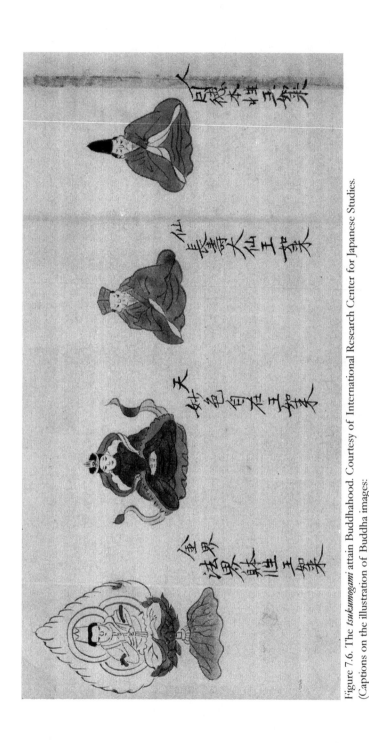

Figure 7.6. The *tsukumogami* attain Buddhahood. Courtesy of International Research Center for Japanese Studies. (Captions on the illustration of Buddha images:
Human, the Essential Cause of Virtue Buddha[63]
Hermit, the Immortal Adept Buddha[64]
Heaven, Longevity Immortal Buddha[65]
Golden realm, the Essence of the True Realm of Phenomena Buddha[66]

Bodhisattva each tool revered for his or her ascetic practices, the character of their attainments varies. Some master the mantra of Kudonsen[62] and attain the power of enlightenment associated with that Buddha and his mantra (*jimyō shicchi*); others attain the power of enlightenment of all the various Buddhas (*shobutsu shicchi*) by abiding in the central realm of the mandala [where Dainichi Buddha resides and from whence all other Buddhas emanate] and from whence one sees the true nature of all things (*chūdai hosshō*).

Regarding the teaching of non-sentient beings realizing Buddhahood, although both the Tendai and Kegon sects also preach this, their teachings are amorphous and they have not mastered all the subtleties. Therefore, while other sects advocate only *sōmoku jōbutsu* (the enlightenment of plants), the teaching of the Three Mysteries of the Shingon sect alone goes so far as to say that *sōmoku hijō hosshin shugyō jōbutsu* (plants and non-sentient beings can become Buddhas by arousing the desire for enlightenment and performing ascetic and religious practices). There is nothing in the *jikkai* (ten worlds)[67] that does not possess the virtue of the letter *A* 阿 [which is the substance of the universe, symbolizing the unity of the whole world, the origin of all elements of the world].[68] If attainment of Buddhahood by awakening and training is possible for animate beings, how much more so for non-sentient beings? Now, listening to the tale of how these old tools came to spiritual awakening, you must believe even more in the profundity of the yoga of the Three Mysteries.

Scholars of the exoteric Buddhist schools say that according to Agon,[69] oni and deities reside on the streets and in the houses, filling every inch of space. The exoteric Buddhists believe the transformation of old tools into specters is a result of the deities and oni possessing them. They ask, "How could inanimate objects have souls?"

Indeed, the difference between esoteric Buddhism and exoteric Buddhism is great. The self-nature of the letter *A* exists inherently in both the animate and inanimate, and the uncreated *A* does not disappear or become exhausted. How, then, could the tools—also inanimate objects—need to borrow the nature of others to become themselves?

If you wish to know the deepest meaning, quickly escape from the net of exoteric Buddhism and enter Shingon esoteric Buddhism.

NOTES

1. For the study of *yōkai*, see Foster, *Book of Yokai*; Foster, *Pandemonium and Parade*.

2. Kabat writes that tool specters thrive in eighteenth-century *kibyōshi* (yellow-backed comic books) of the early modern period. In many cases, these specters are little helpers to

humans and not the abandoned, aged objects that bear grudges against people. In that sense, as Kabat suggests, it might be better not to call them "tool specters *tsukumogami*" ("'Mono' no obake").

3. For a brief explanation of *otogizōshi*, see the introduction.

4. The founder of the Shingon sect of Buddhism. He founded Kongōbu-ji in Mt. Kōya in present-day Wakayama prefecture.

5. Following Tanaka Takako (*Hyakki yagyō no mieru toshi* 163), who views the variety of extant *Tsukumogami ki* texts as parodies of traditional Chinese *ki* 記 (descriptions, records), I use the title *Tsukumogami ki* to refer collectively to all *Tsukumogami ki* manuscripts discussed in this chapter.

6. I follow Kakehi's classification (5). There is only one Type A manuscript: the Sōfukuji scrolls, dated to the sixteenth century (Okudaira 180–87; Shinbo and Kaneko 121–29 [pictures] and 222–32 [text]; Gifushi rekishi hakubutsukan 67–73). The painter and calligrapher of the scrolls are not known. As for Type B texts, several Edo-period scrolls exist, including manuscripts in the possession of the National Diet Library (*MJMT* 9: 417–25); Kyoto University Library (Kyoto daigaku bungakubu kokugogaku kokubungaku kenkyūshitsu 337–47; Kyoto daigaku fuzoku toshokan; Iwase Bunko in Nishio City; Tokyo National Museum; Waseda University Library. Except for the Waseda University manuscript, in terms of illustrations and language, the Type B scrolls are all very similar. See Shibata, "*Tsukumogami kaidai*" 392–93.

7. *Susuharai* is not only a large annual housecleaning event but also a part of the preparation rituals for welcoming a Shinto god of the coming year or a harvest god. It is the day to remove the accumulated misfortunes of the year (*yaku*), as well as to expunge one's defilements and crimes. See Kagiwada 120. An entry for the sixth day of the twelfth month of 1236 in *Azuma kagami* (Mirror of the East, ca. thirteenth century) records the *susuharai* event at the Kamakura military court. It also recounts that *susuharai* activities were not carried out in a newly built residence for three years (*KT* 33: 185). Later, commoners are said to have followed this custom.

8. The *Sonshō Darani* is more properly known as the *Butchō Sonshō Darani* (Dhāranī of the victorious Buddha crown). It was widely used to prevent natural disasters, secure longevity, and ward off evil.

9. Guardian spirits who protect the Dharma from its enemies. Regarding *gohō dōji*, see Blacker.

10. Tōji is the head temple (*daihonzan*) and central training center (*konpon dōjō*) of the Shingon sect of esoteric Buddhism in Kyoto. "Yataku schools" refers to the Ono 小野 and Hirosawa 広沢 schools. Combining the second character from each school's name, that is, 野 and 沢, they are together called "Yataku" 野沢. They arose within the Shingon sect in the mid-Heian period. Each school was further broken down into six sub-schools.

11. Similar to the Sōfukuji text, *Kōbō daishi gyōjō ekotoba* (owned by Tōji) includes a paragraph describing the Tōji school's superiority. The paragraph explains that in response to a prince's command to summarize the teachings of the Shingon sect, Priest Seison (ca. early eleventh century) of the Ono school of the Shingon sect wrote that "there are various schools that teach esoteric Buddhism. But the Tōji school follows the teachings of Kūkai and possesses ten aspects that are superior to other schools" (*ZNET* 5: 114). *Kōbō daishi gyōjō ekotoba* also includes this explanation of Kūkai writing a waka poem at Muroto: "As a custom of Japan, [he] wrote the following waka" (*ZNET* 5: 109). The sentence is similar to a sentence in the Type B texts, to the effect that "[composing] waka is a traditional Japanese custom."

12. Kakehi surmises that the length of the original first and second scrolls would have been more or less the same. While the first scroll of the Type B texts is slightly shorter than the second scroll, the first scroll of the Type A text is considerably shorter than the second scroll (Kakehi 7). Tanaka follows Kakehi's assumption.

13. The transmission of Shingon teachings from Huiguo (746–806; the seventh patriarch in the lineage of Shingon esoteric Buddhism) to Kūkai is sometimes said to have resembled "[water] pouring into an earthenware pot" (*ZNET* 5: 114).

14. For a discussion of enlightenment for plants and trees, see LaFleur; chapter 1 of Rambelli.

15. See Stone, especially chapters 1 and 3. Also see Kushida 720–31.

16. The question of "universal Buddhahood" has been an important issue in Japanese Buddhism, eventually encompassing the idea of the attainment of Buddhahood by non-sentient beings. A major example of this debate is that between Saichō or Dengyō Daishi (d. 822), the founder of the Tendai sect of Buddhism, and Tokuitsu, Saichō's contemporary and a revered priest of the Hossō sect. The former contended that every person can attain Buddhahood, whereas the latter argued that the attainment of Buddhahood depends on the individual.

17. Furthermore, according to Buddhist cosmology, the natural world (*shizenkai*) is also called the material world or container world (*kisekai* or *kikai*), in accord with a view of the universe as a container. Thus, *ki* 器 encompasses not only the natural world but also the environment in which we live. By casting "containers" as the story's protagonists, the *Tsukumogami ki* author cleverly incorporates a Buddhist metaphor of the universe.

18. Shibusawa Tatsuhiko calls material objects *dai ni no shizen*, or Second Nature. He explains that as material civilization progresses, man becomes more skeptical and souls/ spirits become separated from the materials in which they were believed to reside. With technological progress, more complex tools are produced and the souls/spirits find their homes in those artifacts. Shibusawa writes that man's attitude toward the tools resembles the relationship between man and nature, and tools become substitutes for nature. The producers of the objects are excessively fond of what they create, and the objects easily become a fetish. See Shibusawa 89–92.

19. For a study of *hyakki yagyō emaki*, see Lillehoj.

20. For the definition of *hyakki yagyō*, see Foster, *Pandemonium and Parade* 8–9.

21. The *tsukumogami*'s encounter with the prince regent on his way to the imperial palace refers to the story of Fujiwara no Morosuke (908–60) in *Ōkagami* (*SNKBZ* 34: 166–67; McCullough, *Ōkagami* 136). Further, the *Sonshō Darani* charm on the regent that protects him from the demons is described in *Konjaku monogatarishū* 14: 47 ("Sonshō Darani no genriki ni yorite oni no nan o nogaruru koto") in *SNKBZ* 35: 508–12; Tyler, *Japanese Tales* 237–39). Komine ("Hyakki yagyō emaki and Parody" 12) asserts that the various *hyakki yagyō emaki* are parodies of Heian *hyakki yagyō*, while Tanaka considers them just variant representations of Heian *hyakki yagyō* (*Hyakki yagyō no mieru toshi* 160–61).

22. Translation by Helen Craig McCullough (*Tales of Ise* 125).

23. For the original text of *Sou shen ji*, see Gan, *Sou shen ji* 146–48. For a Japanese translation, see Gan, *Sōshinki* 232–35. A similar story of objects' transformations appears in an account of *yōkai* in volume 6 of *Sōshinki*. See Gan, *Sōshinki* 105; Gan, *Sou shen ji* 67.

24. Concerning the characters 付喪神, the commentary *Reizei-ke ryū Ise shō* (Reizei School Annotations to the Tales of Ise, ca. thirteenth century) explains that "[the woman who appears in the sixty-third story of *Ise monogatari*] is not exactly ninety-nine years old. However, she makes nocturnal strolls, peeks at Narihira, and creates wretched, painful misfortune 喪

[glossed *wazawai* (misfortune or calamity) in small katakana characters]" (Katagiri, *Ise monogatari no kenkyū* 358). Tanaka (*Hyakki yagyō no mieru toshi* 175) surmises that the characters 付喪神 (*tsukumogami*, lit. adding/joint mourning deities) was created from つくも髪 (*tsukumogami*, lit. hair of *tsukumo*) by applying phonetically equivalent characters that look monstrous.

25. Hanada (434) posits that the view of old tools as oni reflects a Muromachi-like materialistic interpretation of *hyakki yagyō*.

26. *Konjaku monogatarishū* 27: 23, "Ryōshi no haha oni to narite ko wo kurawamu to suru koto" (How the hunters' mother became an oni and tried to devour her children), in *SNKBZ* 38: 76–78; Ury, *Tales of Times Now Past* 163–65.

27. One day a mysterious young woman of peerless beauty and intelligence appears in the palace of the retired Emperor Toba (1103–56). The retired emperor falls in love with the woman, who is named Tamamo no mae, and he becomes seriously ill. A diviner attributes the retired emperor's illness to the mysterious woman, whose real identity is an 800-year-old fox with two tails. The fox had earlier disturbed India as the malicious consort Huayang, who asked for the head of the king; in China, the fox had become the wicked consort Taji. In the end, Tamamo no mae was killed and turned into a stone. The stone then killed the living creatures that came near it by emitting a toxic gas from within.

28. The *Fudō riyaku engi* story concerns a monk who sacrifices his life to save his master. A revered monk is afflicted by a serious illness, whereupon a diviner reveals that the monk will be saved if someone takes his place in death. An obscure monk, who regularly prays to Fudō, volunteers. Fudō is so moved by the obscure monk's sincerity and physical suffering that he deigns to save both men.

29. For Onmyōdō, see note 1 of chapter 3.

30. *Konjaku monogatarishū* 27: 6, "Higashi Sanjō no akagane no tama hito no katachi to narite horiidasaru koto (How the spirit of red copper on East Third Avenue took human form and was excavated)," in *SNKBZ* 38: 33–35.

31. *In'yōzakki*. The work is assumed to be in classical Chinese. However, nothing about this work is known; there is no known text with this title.

32. The story appears in *Zuo Zhuan* (Chronicle of Zuo, ca. fourth century BCE), the earliest Chinese narrative history. Quoted in the head note of Washio 16.

33. The reference is unknown.

34. Traditionally, on the night of *setsubun*, people scatter beans, one for each of their years alive, saying "oni wa soto, fuku wa uchi" (demons out, fortune in). In some rites, a male from the community goes to a house pretending to be an oni (wearing a paper oni mask) and is chased out while people scatter their beans.

35. Mt. Funaoka, which is more like a hill, is located northwest of the capital, Kyoto (present-day Kita-ku).

36. Nagasaka is a mountainous road that leads to Tanba Province (an area that straddles present-day eastern Hyōgo prefecture and the middle part of Kyoto). It is farther northwest of Mt. Funaoka.

37. Kyō-Shirakawa. City of Kyoto and Shirakawa, an area outside the capital, east of the Kamo River. Shirakawa is known as an important road with a checkpoint barrier as well as a place of scenic beauty.

38. Minghuang, Brilliant Emperor, is another title of Emperor Xuanzong (reigned 712–56) of the Tang Dynasty.

39. David Chen (professor, Ohio State University, personal communication) kindly pointed out that the character 褐, a commoner's clothes, is mistaken for 羯, an ancient barbarian tribe in northwest China. According to Dr. Chen, the 羯 tribesmen made a good

drum of a special design known as the Jie drum 羯鼓, which was adopted by early Chinese musicians, and this was the drum Minghuang liked to play. According to a legend about Minghuang, he was playing the drum in a garden pavilion in the first lunar month of spring, and his performance was so excellent that the trees were startled and all together burst into bloom before their natural flowering time. Upon this occasion, he improvised a song titled "The Springtide Is Good."

40. *Kagura* literally means "music of the gods"; it is the appellation for the most representative performing art of Japanese religious music. The etymology of *kagura* is *kami no kura*, the "seat of the kami"—the kami are seen as dwelling in the *kagura* performance. Averbuch 6.

41. A famous thief who was active during the time of Confucius (551–479 BCE).

42. *Gojō.* Benevolence, justice, politeness, wisdom, and fidelity.

43. The route of the *tsukumogami*'s procession going eastward along First Avenue corresponds to the route of *hyakki yagyō* (night procession of 100 demons) in "Ongyō no otoko Rokkakudō no Kannon no tasuke ni yorite mi o arawasu koto," the thirty-second tale of volume 16 of *Konjaku monogatarishū* (see Tyler, *Japanese Tales* 99–101; for the Japanese text, see *SNKBZ* 36: 271–76).

44. Kanpaku denka. Fujiwara Saneyori (900–970) becomes Kanpaku, or regent, in 967, which corresponds to the fourth year of the Kōhō era, the background for this story. According to *Ōkagami* (The Great Mirror, ca. 1085–1125), his younger brother, Fujiwara no Morosuke (908–960), encountered the *hyakki yagyō.*

45. One of the twelve external gates of the Greater Imperial Palace, or Daidairi. Tatchimon is located far east of the north side of the Greater Imperial Palace.

46. The prince regent's encounter with the *tsukumogami* on his way to the imperial palace refers to the story of Fujiwara no Morosuke in *Ōkagami* (*SNKBZ* 34: 166–67; for an English translation, see McCullough, *Ōkagam* 136).

47. The amulet (of *Sonshō Darani*) carried by the regent that protects him from the demons is described in "Sonshō Darani no genriki ni yorite oni no nan o nogaruru koto," forty-second tale of volume 14 of *Konjaku monogatarishū* (see Tyler, *Japanese Tales* 237–39; for the Japanese text, see *SNKBZ* 35: 508–12).

48. The full name is *Butchō Sonshō Dhāranī* (Dharani of the Victorious Buddha Crown). The Dharani was widely used to prevent natural disasters, secure longevity, and ward off evil.

49. The emperor's residence within the imperial palace compound.

50. *Nimyōō.* They are Fudō myōō (Acala Vidyārāja), the Immovable Protector of Dharma, and Gōzanze myōō (Trailokya-vijaya), Conqueror of the Three Worlds.

51. Ichiren's title changes from *nyūdō* (novice) to *shōnin* (holy priest) at this time.

52. *hyaku hachi no bonnō.* One hundred and eight kleśa, or afflictions. The number "108" signifies many.

53. *gusokukai* (upasampadā). Buddhist precepts for monks and nuns. There are 250 rules for the fully ordained Buddhist monk and 348 for the fully ordained Buddhist nun.

54. Gautama Buddha or Shakamuni (ca. 563–486 BCE). The founder of Buddhism.

55. *sanmitsu.* They are *shin-ku-i* (the action of body or mudra, speech or incantation of mantra, and mind or concentration on the Principal Buddha).

56. One of the ten great disciples of Gautama Buddha or Shakamuni. Kasen'en is famous for his debating skills.

57. One of the ten great disciples of Gautama Buddha or Shakamuni. Furuna is noted for preaching.

58. *gochi.* They are (1) the wisdom of knowing the quintessence of all existences; (2) mirror-like wisdom, which reflects all phenomenal things as they are; (3) the wisdom of

observing the equality of all things; (4) the wisdom of observing the distinctive features of all phenomena; and (5) the wisdom of accomplishing metamorphoses. Mahavairocana has a crown bearing five miniature figures of Five Wisdom Buddhas.

59. A Buddhist priest in south India and the fourth patriarch in the lineage of esoteric Buddhism. He had extraordinary supernatural power and is said to have lived several hundred years to transmit the esoteric teaching to Kongōchi.

60. Konchi signifies Kongōchi (?–741), the fifth patriarch in the lineage of Shingon esoteric Buddhism. After having a revelatory dream of Kannon Bodhisattva, he moved from India to China in 720 and taught esoteric Buddhism in China. He was revered by Emperor Xuanzong (Jp. Gensō, 685–762) and translated a number of esoteric scriptures in Chang-an and Lo-yang.

61. Kōchi signifies Fukū Sanzō (Amoghavajra, 705–74, also known as Fukū Kongō), the sixth patriarch in the lineage of Shingon esoteric Buddhism. He was a disciple of Kongōchi and translated a great number of scriptures he had brought from his trip to India and Sri Lanka.

62. An immortal mountain wizard who lived in ancient India.

63. *Intoku honshōō nyorai.*

64. *Chōju daisen'ō nyorai.*

65. *Myōshiki jizai'ō nyorai.*

66. *Hokkai taishōō nyorai.*

67. They are, in descending order, *bukkai* (realm of Buddhas), *bosatsu-kai* (realm of Bodhisattvas), *engaku-kai* (realm of Pratyekabuddhas), *shōmon-kai* (realm of srāvakas), *ten-kai* (heaven), *jin-kai* (world of men), *shura-kai* (world of aśura), *chikushō-kai* (world of animals), *gaki-kai* (world of hungry ghosts), and *jigoku-kai* (hell).

68. "A" is the first sound in the Sanskrit alphabet, and it embodies the mystic truth in esoteric Buddhist belief. According to esoteric Buddhism, all phenomena are originally "unproduced" or uncreated, and this principle is symbolized by the letter A. The one who meditates on A will attain Buddhahood.

69. A generic term for "hīnayāna" Buddhist sutras, as well as a specific group of sutras (the Āgama sutras).

Conclusion

LIFE IN MEDIEVAL JAPANESE SOCIETY UNDULATED and erupted with sweeping social changes and wars. The seven stories revolving around oni examined in this book reveal various customs and manners, socio-political and religious events, and folk beliefs of medieval Japan. As stories were transmitted orally or the text(s) copied, the authors and narrators would add or delete as they preferred, undoubtedly with changes to appeal to the intended audience. Certainly, audiences would understand the tales from their own perspective of their own time: "Tales set in the past would have been shaped in part by the contemporary concerns of compilers whether the stories were newly created, recorded from an oral tradition, or appropriated from earlier texts. There would have been no impulse to repeat stories without meaning for the new writers and audiences within the context of their own lives" (Li, *Ambiguous Bodies* 141).

With the rise of the warrior class, the imperial court of the central government was largely relegated to ceremonial duties and functions, although court aristocrats attempted to hold on to their waning political power. One hypothesis for the creation of *The Illustrated Story of Minister Kibi's Adventures in China* was that the work was one of many political tools employed by the Cloistered Emperor GoShirakawa to end the Heike hegemony. The Heike clan was eventually brought down by the rival clan, Genji—descendants of Raikō and his brothers—and by GoShirakawa's machinations with warriors and court nobles.

The production of *Minister Kibi's Adventures* was proposed by GoShirakawa possibly to beguile his audience with the allure of nationalism. The irony of this being the political paradigm of the time was that while the tale emphasized the intellectual superiority of the individual Japanese minister, the minister still needed the Chinese emperor's permission to return to Japan. The oni starved by Chinese officials was formerly a human being. He became an oni after his death, which is the Chinese concept of *gui*, 鬼 (Jp. oni). This oni, yearning for news of his descendants in Japan, is a touching creature. He may have represented wandering Japanese souls that had perished overseas, with nostalgic feelings for Japan.

With the fall of the Heike, Genji warriors gained political and military power—the social legitimacy of which was acquired through their lineage and titles. While *Drunken Demon (Shuten Dōji)* and *A Tale of An Earth Spider (Tsuchigumo zōshi)* are highly entertaining to present-day audiences because the hero conquers the monster(s), vanquishing a monster was effective propaganda to justify and solidify the Genji lineage. As one struggles for power, validating one's family name became a matter of life and death for every clan.

The warrior-aristocrat Raikō has been idolized in the world of *setsuwa* since the Kamakura period (1185–1333). These *setsuwa* also provided a propaganda vehicle for Watanabe clan members to make their lineage known and retrieve their diminished political power. For their aristocratic and political allies who created, described, or accepted the *setsuwa*, the Ichijō court was one of ideal times for the nobility (Motoki 199). People affiliated with the religious groups such as the four shrines and the Enryakuji temple that appears in the text should not be forgotten as supporters in the creation of such tales.

While Raikō was a historical figure, we do not know whether Kintoki, Sadamichi, Suetake, and Tsuna actually served Raikō. Nothing about Tsuna appears on record until the mid-thirteenth century. But when we look at the world of *setsuwa,* at least by the early twelfth century Kintoki, Sadamichi, and Suetake were considered Raikō's remarkable retainers, making way for Tsuna to join a century later. Hōshō's story suggests how important it was to be born in the right household or lineage and how critical it was to have descendants who would advocate for him or his pedigree. Even though Hōshō was as important as Raikō in the subjugation campaign against the mighty oni, the enemy of imperial Japan, he was eventually dropped from the story. Stories (and characters) cease to exist without scribes or tellers who hand down the tales, and those transmitters knew what audiences wanted to hear and accommodated them accordingly.

Tsuchigumo, a tale well-known in Japan since the medieval period, further emphasizes the rights and responsibility of the nobility because the miraculous sword that slayed an evil spider–oni should only be in the possession of a skilled leader with the authority of his illustrious lineage. But as the status of the sword waned, the story of *tsuchigumo* became more like a legend of famous warriors (Itō, "Ihon 'Tsuchigumo' emaki nit suite" 89). The oni and spider are symbolic of evil or "the other" that must be vanquished or subjugated for the good of society. That is, the conquerors are good, so the conquered must be evil.

From the point of view of the present study, *Tsuchigumo zōshi* is remarkable in that the *tsuchigumo,* oni, and a beautiful woman become one entity.

The scroll should be credited as an influential work that gave birth to the beautiful killer maiden or matron spider figure that appears in the Noh play, which exerted great influence on literary arts later in history.

As mentioned, enthusiastically advocating for one's name and exerting socio-political influence were important for religious institutions as well. Four helping Shinto deities seen in the Shuten Dōji story may, however, be less assertive than Kitano Tenjin in *A Tale of Lord Haseo* (*Haseo zōshi*). *Haseo zōshi* is a miraculous tale of Kitano Tenjin, behind the creation of which one can see the rising power of the Kitano Tenjin Shrine at that time. To save Ki no Haseo's life from danger and exhibit Kitano Tenjin's miraculous power, the oni who has an artistic sense in this story was given the role of an angry and violent attacker—an abrupt change from the honest creature.

Indeed, oni are fundamentally honest beings—perhaps sometimes even gullible. A number of ancient tales attribute honesty or loyalty as an oni trait. One of the earliest tales is the twenty-fifth tale of *Nihon ryōiki* (Miraculous Stories from the Japanese Buddhist Tradition, ca. 822) titled "On the Fiend [oni], Messenger of King Yama, Who Accepted the Hospitality of the One for Whom He Had Been Sent and Repaid It."[1] The oni, who is exhausted from searching for the human he is supposed to bring to King Yama, receives the sick person's banquet prepared for the oni—a bribe to save the man's life. The oni feels obligated to repay his debt. The oni says, "As I have accepted your hospitality, I will repay your kindness" (Nakada 194; Nakamura, *Miraculous Stories from the Japanese Buddhist Tradition* 195). Similarly, the preceding twenty-fourth story of *Nihon ryōiki* titled "On the Fiends [oni], Messengers of King Yama, Who Canceled Death in Exchange for a Bribe" (Nakada 189–93; Nakamura, *Miraculous Stories from the Japanese Buddhist Tradition* 192–94) tells of the oni repaying their debt. The three oni take an offering of a cow (bribe of food) from the man who is supposed to die, that is, to be taken to the netherland. The oni in return let the man go, that is, live, because they know they would be punished in the netherland for accepting the bribe. They ask the man to recite *Kongō hannyakyō* (the Vajracchedika Sutra, Diamond Sutra) to avoid being flogged. As the man prayed for the oni, they dutifully returned to thank him. It is interesting that the Kitano Tenjin section is completely omitted from the two contemporary adaptations of *Haseo zōshi*. In the modern stories, the oni who created the soulless beauty remains friendly to Ki no Haseo throughout—there is no sudden change of character.

Propagating divine worth is also one of the major purposes in *Blossom Princess*, a Japanese Cinderella story. The narrator strongly urges readers to pray to Kannon, perhaps to the Great Bodhisattva of Mt. Fuji, for their peace of mind and happiness. The backdrop of the story is not the capital but the countryside. As wars were fought in the capital area in the fifteenth and sixteenth centuries, a number of court aristocrats left Kyoto, taking refuge in various provinces. Their presence at the estates of provincial lords brought the courtly tastes and protocols of Kyoto to the provinces. An example of the spread of courtly tastes and protocols to the provinces is Suruga Province, the backdrop of *Blossom Princess* in which the middle councilor's family is said to be originally from Kyoto. The capital of Suruga Province was called the "Kyoto of the eastern provinces" because it enjoyed the disseminated aristocratic ambience. The *Blossom Princess* text elaborates on marriage rituals and beliefs of that era, which took an enormous amount of time and wealth as the occasion exhibited the party's power in the region. There the female oni, *yamauba*, appears as the heroine's helper who lived at the foot of Mt. Fuji. Although her appearance is brief, the *yamauba* is an integral part of the heroine achieving happiness, giving her an ample wedding dowry at the critical moment.

In a number of *otogizōshi* such as *Blossom Princess* and *Tale of Amewakahiko*, a husband loves one person only (at one time, at least) and marries one person only (at one time, at least). This one-to-one conjugal relationship seems to reflect the Muromachi period's (1333–1573) tendency to be a monogamous society. Wakita Haruko writes: "Because medieval society had the *ie* [corporal household] as its axis, it had to place importance on male-female conjugal relations. Of course, it cannot be said that sexual love was an equal relationship, for, although monogamous, the system allowed multiple concubines. However, in this system the status of the official wife was secure, unlike the *tsumadoi* [uxorilocal] or *mukotori* [son-in-law adopted by wife's family] marriages of the Heian period, where the wife's status was precarious" (Wakita, *Women in Medieval Japan* 38).

The Heian period (794–1185) was a polygamous society; although one wife was often recognized, albeit informally, as the first among equals in the stable of wives, that wife's status was not guaranteed. Frequently, when a husband stopped visiting, the marriage was dissolved. In contrast, the existence of the medieval household system rested on the principle of monogamy (Wakita, *Women in Medieval Japan* 21). As the patriarchal system became solidified, the marriage system changed, too. It shifted from *tsumadoi* (uxorilocal) or *mukotori* (son-in-law adopted by his wife's family) to yometori-kon, or patrilocal: "*Yometori* did not become the general practice until the medieval period" (Wakita, *Women in Medieval Japan* 128). In the *Tale of Amewakahiko*, the heroine leaves the familiarity of her parents' home to live in her husband's household. The story seems to reflect a matrimonial proclivity to a vililocal arrangement as the heroine moves from her parents' house eventually to her husband's house in the sky.

For medieval young women of high society who were restricted in many ways from moving about, the *Tale of Amewakahiko* was perhaps a thrilling adventure story, as the heroine travels into the unknown sky in search of her husband. The oni–father-in-law who resides in the sky, in a beautiful residence in serene surroundings, was originally Bontennō (Brahma). But to the medieval audience, whether the oni resided in the sky or underground did not seem to matter much, as discussed in chapter 5. *Tale of Amewakahiko* is a tale that explains an origin of *Tanabata*, now the firmly established customs in Japan.

Decentralized power during the Muromachi period forced traditional institutions, be it central government or religious establishments, to sustain their own political and economic viability alone. Clergymen affiliated with certain sects had to actively propagate the merit of their schools' survival. Another conspicuous promotion of a Buddhist school is *Tsukumogami ki* (The Record of Tool Specters). Incorporating the folk belief that when sentient beings become very old they turn into oni, the author of *Tsukumogami ki* makes insentient beings animated and mischievous when they become old. The discarded old tools then attack people out of vengeance. Making the most of puns and parodies, the narrator emphasizes the miraculous power of Shingon esoteric Buddhism in which even the tools that turned into oni can be enlightened, let alone ordinary human beings. "If you wish to know the deepest meaning, quickly escape from the net of exoteric Buddhism and enter Shingon esoteric Buddhism," the narrator says. This, incidentally, could have made people buy new tools.

An examination of oni stories from medieval Japan makes one wonder what oni are. Oni often seem to be used as a kind of political and economic tool—to highlight the heroes' prowess or religious efficacy. When one considers the nature of *otogizōshi*, short tales written for the purpose of both entertainment and moral or religious edification, one understands their overt and covert pedantic elements. To put someone or an entity in a positive light, it is easier to cast another (or oni) as a villain. This is perhaps a universal phenomenon, not necessarily limited to medieval Japan. In medieval Japan, the oni or disenfranchised entity was defined as real—a potential threat to allies. The impact on the audience, both oral and textual, of that time must have been somber indeed. While there are differences in perception and beliefs as environments have changed, present-day readers would find some commonalities in the behaviors and beliefs.

As Komatsu Kazuhiko writes, medieval tales even speak to contemporary humanity; that is, to study the oni in Japanese folklore is to study humankind (*Yōkaigaku shinkō* 12)

NOTE

1. For a Japanese text, see Nakada 194–96; for an English translation, see Nakamura, *Miraculous Stories from the Japanese Buddhist Tradition* 194–96.

Japanese and Chinese Names and Terms

A

A　阿
Abe no Nakamaro　阿倍仲麻呂
Abe no Seimei　安倍晴明
agamono　贖物
Agon　阿含
Akazome Emon　赤染衛門
Akiyoshi　秋好
Amaterasu　天照大神
Amenomurakumo no tsurugi　天叢雲
　　剣
Amewakahiko　天稚彦
Amewakahiko monogatari emaki　天稚彦
　　物語絵巻
Amewakahiko sōshi　天稚彦草子
Amewakamiko　天稚御子
Annam　安南
Anokutara sanmiyaku sannbodai no ho-
　　toketachi waga tatsu soma ni myōga
　　arase tamae　阿耨多羅三藐三菩
　　提の仏たちわが立つ杣に冥加あ
　　らせたまへ
Anshi　安子
Aratarō　荒太郎
Aru tokoro no zenbu Yoshio no Tomo
　　no dainagon no ryō o miruko-
　　to　或る所の膳部義雄の伴の大
　　納言の霊を見る語
Ashikaga Takauji　足利尊氏
Awata no Mahito　粟田真人
Ayuwang Temple　阿育王寺
Azuma kagami　吾妻鏡

B

Bai Juyi　白居易
Bao Zhi　宝誌

Bakuya　莫耶 (Ch. Mo Ye)
Ban dainagon ekotoba　伴大納言絵詞
bankoku　蕃国
bansei ikkei　万世一系
Bensei　弁正
Bishamonten　毘沙門天
biwa　琵琶
Bonten　梵天
Bontennō　梵天王
bosatsu-kai　菩薩界
*Bosuton Bijutsukan Nihon bijutsu no
　　shihō*　ボストン美術館日本美術
　　の至宝
bugei no ie　武芸の家
buki no ie　武器の家
bukkai　佛界
Busei (Ch. Wu Cheng)　武成
bushi　武士
Butchō Sonshō Dhāranī　佛頂尊勝陀
　　羅尼

C

Chang'an　長安
Chikamatsu Monzaemon　近松門左
　　衛門
chikushō-kai　畜生界
Chinjufu shogun　鎮守府将軍
Chion'in wakan rōeishū kenbun　知恩院本
　　和漢朗詠集見聞
Chōgen　重源
Chōju daisen'ō nyorai　長寿大仙王如
　　来
Chōtoku　長徳
chūdai hosshō　中台法性
Chūgaishō　中外抄
chūnagon　中納言

Chūnagon Ki no Haseo no ie ni arawaruru inu no koto　中納言紀長谷雄の家に顕るる狗の語
Cloistered Emperor GoShirakawa　後白河法皇

D

dai ni no shizen　第二の自然
Daiba bon　提婆品
Daidairi　大内裏
daihonzan　大本山
Daiitoku　大威徳
Daijō-itokuten　太政威徳天
Daiku to Oniroku　だいくとおにろく
dairokuten no maō　第六天の魔王
Daoshou　道州
Dazai shōgen　太宰少監
Dazaifu　太宰府
dengaku　田楽
Dengyō Daishi　伝教大師
denshi-byō　伝尸病

E

Eastern Han　東漢
Ebisu　恵比寿
eboshi　烏帽子
edo　穢土
Eiga monogatari　栄華物語
Eiseibunko　永青文庫
Eishin　栄心
Eiso　永祚
emaki　絵巻
Emperor Antoku　安徳天皇
Emperor GoHanazono　後花園天皇
Emperor GoIchijō　後一条天皇
Emperor GoKomatsu　後小松天皇
Emperor GoReizei　後冷泉天皇
Emperor GoSuzaku　後朱雀天皇
Emperor GoToba, Retired　後鳥羽院
Emperor Ichijō　一条天皇
Emperor Ingyō　允恭天皇
Emperor Jinmu　神武天皇
Emperor Keikō　景行天皇
Emperor Konoe　近衛天皇

Emperor Murakami　村上天皇
Emperor Reizei　冷泉天皇
Emperor Seiwa　清和天皇
Emperor Shenzong　神宗
Emperor Shōkō　称光天皇
Emperor Shōmu　v聖武天皇
Emperor Sujin　崇神天皇
Emperor Sutoku　崇徳天皇
Emperor Takakura　高倉天皇
Emperor Tenmu　天武天皇
Emperor Wu　武帝
Emperor Wu of Liang　梁武帝
Emperor Xiaozong　孝宗
Emperor Xuanzong (Jp. Gensō)　玄宗皇帝
Empress Shōshi　彰子 (中宮) (or Jōtōmon-in)
Empress Shōtoku　称徳天皇 (or Empress Kōken　孝謙天皇)
Empress Teishi　定子 (皇后)
Empress Wu Zetian (Jp. Busokuten)　武則天
En Shito　袁司徒 (Ch. Yuan Situ)
Endō, line　遠藤流
engaku-kai　縁覚界
Engishiki　延喜式
Enryakuji　延暦寺

F

Fu Sōshin ki　付捜神記
Fudō myōō　不動明王
Fudō riyaku engi　不動利益縁起
Fuji Daibosatsu　富士大菩薩
Fujiwara no Akihira　藤原明衡
Fujiwara no Hidesato　藤原秀郷
Fujiwara no Hōshō (or Yasumasa)　藤原保昌
Fujiwara no Hōshō gekka rōtekizu　藤原保昌月下弄笛図
Fujiwara no Kaneie　藤原兼家
Fujiwara no Kintō　藤原公任
Fujiwara no Korechika　藤原伊周
Fujiwara no Kosemaro　藤原巨勢麻呂
Fujiwara no Michikane　藤原道兼
Fujiwara no Michinaga　藤原道長

Fujiwara no Michitaka　藤原道隆
Fujiwara no Michitsuna　藤原道綱
Fujiwara no Morosuke　藤原師輔
Fujiwara no Motokata　藤原元方
Fujiwara no Munetada　藤原致忠
Fujiwara no Sanekane　藤原実兼
Fujiwara no Sanenari　藤原実成
Fujiwara no Sanesuke　藤原実資
Fujiwara no Sumitomo　藤原純友
Fujiwara no Tadachika　藤原忠親
Fujiwara no Tadazane　藤原忠実
Fujiwara no Takaie　藤原隆家
Fujiwara no Tameie　藤原為家
Fujiwara no Tokihira　藤原時平
Fujiwara no Tomoakira　藤原知章
Fujiwara no Yasumasa no ason nusubito no Hakamadare ni au koto　藤原保昌の朝臣盗人の袴垂に値ふ語
Fujiwara no Yorimichi　藤原頼通
Fukū Kongō　不空金剛
Fukū Sanzō　不空三蔵
Funaokayama　船岡山
Furuna　富留那
Fushiminomiya Haruhito　伏見宮治仁
Fushiminomiya Sadafusa　伏見宮貞成
Fusō ryakki　扶桑略記
Fuyusame　冬雨

G

gaki-kai　餓鬼界
Gan Bao　干宝
Gan Jiang　干将
Ganjin (Ch. Jianzhen)　鑑真
Gao tang fu　高唐賦
Gaun nikkenroku　臥雲日件録
Genbō sōjō Tō ni watarite Hossō o tsutaeru koto　玄昉僧正唐に亘りて法相を伝ふる語
Genji monogatari　源氏物語
Genji no chakuryū　源氏の嫡流
Genji no yurai　源氏のゆらひ
Genpei War　源平合戦
Genshin　源信
gesaku　戯作
go　碁

gochi　五智
Gōdanshō　江談抄
gohō dōji　護法童子
Gojō　五常
Goshū　梧楸
Goshūgen otogi bunko　御祝言御伽文庫
GoShūi wakashū　後拾遺和歌集
Gōzanze myōō　降三世明王
gozu　牛頭
Gukanshō　愚管抄
gunji kizoku　軍事貴族
gusokukai　具足戒
Gyokuyōshū　玉葉集

H

Hachikazuki　はちかづき
Hachiman sanjo　八幡三所
Hakamadare　袴垂
Hakamadare, Sekiyama ni shite sorajini o shite hito o korosu koto　袴垂関山に於て虚死をして人を殺す語
Hakudō　伯道
Hakui (Ch. Boyi)　伯夷
Hanayo no hime　花世の姫
hanayone　花米
Hankai (Ch. Fan K'uai)　樊噲
harakake　腹掛け
Haruyoshi　春好
Hase Kannon　長谷観音
Hase Temple　長谷寺
Hasedera genki　長谷寺験記
Haseo zōshi　長谷雄草紙
Heian　平安
Heiji Disturbance　平治の乱
Heike monogatari　平家物語
Henge daimyōjin　変化大明
Higekiri　鬚切
hijō　非情
Hijō jōbutsu emaki　非情成仏絵巻
Hikime　匹女
Hiko imasu no miko　日子坐王
Hikoboshi　彦星
Hikohohodemi no Mikoto emaki　彦火火出見尊絵巻
Hin River (Ch. Pin)　頻川

hiragana ひらがな

Hirohira, Prince 広平親王

hitogata 人形

Hiyoshi Sannō Shrine 日吉山王神社

Hizamaru 膝丸

Hizen 肥前

Hokekyō jikidanshō 法華経直談鈔

Hokekyō jurin shūyōshō 法華経鷲林拾葉鈔

Hoki naiden 簠簋内伝

Hoki shō 簠簋抄

Hokkai taishōō nyorai 法界体性王如来

Honchō shinsen den 本朝神仙伝

hongaku shisō 本覚思想

honji 本地

Hosokawa Gracia Tama 細川ガラシャたま

Hossō sect 法相宗

hyakki yagyō 百鬼夜行, 百器夜行

hyakki yagyō emaki 百鬼夜行絵巻

hyaku hachi no bonnō 百八煩悩

I

Ibukiyama 伊吹山

Ichijō Kanera 一条兼良

Ichiren nyūdō 一連入道

igo 囲碁

Imagawa bunka 今川文化

Imagawa Yoshimoto 今川義元

Intoku honshōō nyorai 因徳本性王如来

Inuyasha 犬夜叉

In'yōzakki 陰陽雑記

iro 色

Ise monogatari 伊勢物語

iteki 夷狄

Iwashimizu Hachimangū 岩清水八幡宮

Izumi Shikibu 和泉式部

Izumo fudoki 出雲風土記

J

Jakengokudai 邪見極大

Ji denshibyō biden 治伝屍病秘伝

Jie drum 羯鼓

Jien 慈円

jigoku-kai 地獄界

jikidanmono 直談物

jikkai 十界

Jikkinshō 十訓抄

Jikokuten 持国天

jimyō shicchi 持明悉地

jin-kai 人界

Jokunsho 女訓書

Jōkyū Disturbance 承久の乱

Jōkyūki 承久記

joro 女郎

jōrō 上﨟

jorōgumo 女郎蜘蛛

Jorōgumo no kotowari 絡新婦の理

jōruri 浄瑠璃

Jōtōmon-in 上東門院 (or Empress Shōshi)

Juchūkō 十炷香

Jukeini 寿桂尼

jūni innen 十二因縁

Jūni-sama 十二様

Jūnishinshō 十二神将

Jūrasetsunyo 十羅刹女

K

Kachō Fūgetsu 花鳥風月

kagura 神楽

Kaguraoka 神楽岡

Kaifūsō 懐風藻

Kaikaku 戒覚

Kaiō 懐王 (Ch. King Huai)

kairyūō 海龍王

kami (deity) 神

kami (hair) 髪

Kan'ei shoke kakeizu-den 寛永諸家家系図伝

Kanhasshū tsunagiuma 関八州繋馬

Kanmon nikki 看聞日記

Kannon 観音

Kannon kyō　観音経

Kanpaku denka　関白殿下

Kanshō (Ch. Gan Jiang)　干将

Kanzeon bosatsu fumonhon　観世音
　菩薩普門品

Kasen'en　迦梅延

Katori-bon　香取本

Katsuraki　葛城

Kawachi Genji　河内源氏

Kawatake Mokuami　河竹黙阿弥

kegai　化外

Kegon　華厳

Keiun　慶運

kenai　化内

Kenbunkei rōeishū kochūshakubon　見聞系
　朗詠集古注釈本

Kengyū　牽牛

Kenkō　兼好

Kenshō　顕昭

kewagō　仮和合

ki (or *utsuwa*)　器

Ki no Haseo　紀長谷雄

Ki no Haseo Suzakumon ni te onna wo
　arasoi oni to sugoroku wo suru
　koto　紀長谷雄朱雀門にて女を
　争い鬼と双六をする語

Kibi daijin monogatari　吉備大臣物語

Kibi daijin nittō emaki　吉備大臣入唐
　絵巻

"Kibi nittō no kan no koto"　吉備入唐
　の間の事

Kibi no Makibi　吉備真備

Kibi no Nihon jie　吉備能日本知恵

Kibidaijin shina tan　吉備大臣支那譚

kibyōshi　黄表紙

Kidōmaru　鬼同丸

kikai　器界

kimon　鬼門

kin　金

Kintarō　金太郎

Kintarō no tanjō　金太郎の誕生

Kinyō wakashū　金葉和歌集

Kirinmugoku　麒麟無極

kisekai　器世界

Kitano Shrine　北野ノ社

Kitano Tenjin　北野天神

Kitano tenmangū tenjin　北野天満宮
　天神

Kitayama　北山

Kiyohara no Munenobu　清原致信

Kōbō Daishi　弘法大師

Kōbō daishi gyōjō ekotoba　弘法大師行状
　絵詞

Kobun sensei　古文先生

Kōchi　広智

Kochō　胡蝶

Kōen　皇円

Kōfuku-ji　興福寺

Kōhō　康保

Koikawa Harumachi　恋川春町

Kojidan　古事談

Kojiki　古事記

Kokin wakashū (or *Kokinshū*)　古今和歌
　集 (or 古今集)

Kokinshū chū　古今集注

Kokinshū kanajo kochū　古今集仮名序
　古註

Kōko shōroku　好古小録

Kokon chomonjū　古今著聞集

kokudo　国土

Koma no Tomokazu (or Asakatsu)　狛
　朝葛

Komebuku Awabuku　米福粟福

Komochi yamauba　嫗山姥

Kōmokuten　広目天

Konchi　金智

Kongō hannyakyō　金剛般若経

kongō rikishi　金剛力士

Kongōbu-ji　金剛峰寺

Kongōchi　金剛智

Konjaku monogatarishū　今昔物語集

Konoe Sakihisa　近衛前久

Konoe toneri　近衛舎人

Konkō myōkyō　金光明経

konkōmyō-shitennō-gokoku no tera　金光明
　四天王護国の寺

konpon dōjō　根本道場

koto　琴

kuden　口伝

Kudonsen　瞿曇仙

Kugamimi no mikasa　陸耳御笠

Kujō Kanezane　九条兼実

Kūkai　空海

Kumano sansho　熊野三所

Kumo no ito azusa yumi　蜘蛛糸梓弓

Kumogiri　蜘切

Kusanagi no tsurugi　草薙剣

Kusō shi emaki　九相詩絵巻

kuyō　供養

Kyō-Shirakawa　京白河

kyōka awase　狂歌合

Kyūjin　旧仁

L

Lady Li　李夫人

Li Bai　李白

Li Fang　李昉

M

mamako-tan　継子譚

Matsuura　松浦

Menoto no sōshi　乳母の草子

mezu　馬頭

Midō kanpakuki　御堂関白記

Mikenjaku　眉間尺 (Ch. Mei jian chi)

Minamoto no Akikane　源顕兼

Minamoto no Hiromasa　源博雅

Minamoto no Mitsumasa (or Mansei)　源満正 or 満政

Minamoto no Mitsunaka (or Manjū)　源満仲

Minamoto no Mitsuru　源充

Minamoto no Mitsuru to Taira no Yoshifumi no kassen seru koto　源充と平良文と合戦する語

Minamoto no Moronaka　源師仲

Minamoto no Raikō (or Yorimitsu)　源頼光

Minamoto no Raikō Kidōmaru o chūsuru koto　源頼光 鬼同丸を誅する事

Minamoto no Shitagō　源順

Minamoto no Suguru　源俊

Minamoto no Takaakira　源高明

Minamoto no Tameyoshi　源為義

Minamoto no Tsunemoto　源経基

Minamoto no Yorichika　源頼親

Minamoto no Yorimasa　源頼政

Minamoto no Yorinobu (or Raishin)　源頼信

Minamoto no Yoritomo　源頼朝

Minamoto no Yoriyoshi　源頼義

Minamoto no Yoshiie　源義家

Minamoto no Yoshinaka　源義仲

Minamoto no Yoshitomo　源義朝

Minghuang　明皇

mirai-ki　未来記

Miroku　弥勒

Miyako no Yoshika　都良香

Miyoshi no Kiyoyuki (or Kiyotsura)　三善清行

Miyoshi no Kyotsura saishō to Haseo no kōron no koto　三善清行宰相紀長谷雄口論の語

Monju kesshū butsurekikyō　文殊結集仏暦経

mono no ke　物の怪

Monzen (or *Wenxuan*)　文選

Mt. Hiei　比叡山

Mt. Kōya　高野山

Mt. Ōe　大江山

Mt. Ōsaka　逢坂山

Mt. Shō　商山 (Ch. Mt. Shang)

mujō　無情

mukashibanashi　昔話

mukotori-kon　婿取婚

Muraoka no Gorō　村岡五郎

musha　武者

mushi　虫

Myōhō renge kyō　妙法蓮華経

Myōshiki jizai'ō nyorai　妙色自在王如来

N

Nagasaka　長坂

nara ehon　奈良絵本

Natsusame　夏雨

Ne no kuni　根の国

Nenchū gyōji emaki　年中行事絵巻

sanmaji 三摩地

sanmitsu 三密

Sanseru onna minamiyamashina ni yuki oni ni aite nigetaru koto 産女南山科に行き鬼に値ひて逃ぐる語

Sanzon 三尊

sato 里

Seiryōden 清涼殿

Sei Shōnagon 清少納言

Seiwa Genji 清和源氏

Sengoku otogizōshi 戦国御伽草子

Senju Sengen Kannon 千手千眼観音

Senjūshō 撰集抄

Sesonji 世尊寺

Sesshōseki 殺生石

setsubun 節分

setsuwa 説話

Settsu Fudoki 摂津風土記

Settsu Genji 摂津源氏

shaku 尺

Shaku Nihongi 釈日本紀

Shakujō 錫杖

Shang 商 (殷)

Shibugaki 渋柿

Shibukawa Seiemon 渋川清右衛門

shichibutsu yakushi 七仏薬師

shikigami or *shikijin* 式神

Shimotsuke no Kintoki 下(毛)野公時 (or Sakata no Kintoki)

Shimotsuke no Kintomo 下(毛)野公友

Shimotsuke-shi keizu 下毛野氏系図

Shimotsumichi no Kunikatsu 下道圀勝

Shin kokin wakashū 新古今和歌集

shin-ku-i 身口意

Shin Sarugakuki 新猿楽記

Shingon 真言

Shiōten 四王天

Shiranui tan 白縫譚

Shitateru-hime 下照姫

shitennō 四天王

shizenkai 自然界

Shō Chūka 小中華

Shō Hachimangū 正八幡宮

Sho kaji hihō 諸加持秘法

Shō Kannon 聖觀音, 正観音

Shō teikoku 小帝国

shōbutsu funi 生佛不二

shobutsu shicchi 諸仏悉地

shochi-iri 所知入り

Shoku Nihongi 続日本紀

shōmon-kai 声聞界

shōnin 上人

Shōtoku Taishi 聖徳太子

Shōyūki 小右記

Shu Ching 書経

Shūi wakashū 拾遺和歌集

shuju 侏儒

Shukusei (Ch. Shuqi) 叔齊

shūmon aratamechō 宗門改帳

shura-kai 修羅界

Shuten Dōji 酒顚童子, 酒呑童子

Shuten Dōji emaki 酒伝童子絵巻

Shuten Dōji monogatari ekotoba 酒呑童子物語絵詞

shūto-iri 舅入り

Sōfukuji 崇福寺

Sokoku 楚国 (Ch. Chu guo)

sokushin jōbutsu 即身成仏

sokushin tongo 即身頓悟

sōmoku hijō hosshin shugyō jōbutsu 草木非情発心修行成仏

sōmoku jōbutsu 草木成仏

Song 宋

Song Yu 宋玉

Sonoki 彼杵

Sonpi bunmyaku 尊卑分脈

Sonshō Darani no genriki ni yorite oni no nan o nogaruru koto 依尊勝陀羅尼験力遁鬼難語

Sonshō Dhāranī 尊勝陀羅尼

Sonshun 尊舜

sōshi-ka 草子化

Sotoori Iratsume 衣通郎姫

Sou shen ji 捜神記, 喪神記 (Jp. *Sōshinki*)

Sugawara Michizane 菅原道真

sugoroku 双六

Sui-Tang 隋唐

suikyō 垂拱

Sukehime 祐姫

Sumiyoshi Myōjin　住吉明神
Susanoo　スサノオ, 素戔男
Suseribime　須勢理毘売
susuharai　煤払
Suzaku Gate　朱雀門

T

Taigong Wang　太公望
Taiheiki　太平記
taiki　大器, 大機
Taiping guang ji　太平広記
Taira no Kiyomori　平清盛
Taira no Korehira (or Ikō)　平維衡
Taira no Koretoki　平維時
Taira no Masakado　平将門
Taira no Muneyori (or Chirai)　平致頼
Taira no Sadamichi (or Sadamitsu)　平
　　貞道(光) (or Usui no Sadamitsu)
Taira no Sadamori　平貞盛
Taira no Suetake (or Urabe no
　　Suetake)　平季武 (orト部季武)
Taira no Yoshifumi　平良文
Taishakuten　帝釈天
Takahashi Rumiko　高橋留美子
Takamimusuhi　高皇産霊
Takiguchi　滝口
Takikura gongen　滝蔵権現
Tamamo no mae　玉藻の前
Tamonten　多聞天
Tanabata　七夕
Tanabata no sōshi　七夕のさうし
Tang　唐 (Jp. Tō)
Tang Bohu　唐伯虎
Tang Yin　唐寅
Tango Fudoki zanketsu　丹後風土記残欠
tanroku-bon　丹緑本
Tao Gu　陶穀
Tatchimon　達智門
ten-kai　天界
Tendai　天台
Tenjinkō　天神講
Tenri toshokan wakan rōeishū kenbun　天理
　　図書館本和漢朗詠集見聞
Tenrō (Ch. Tian lao)　天老
Tō Teikan　藤貞幹

Tōgen Zuisen　桃源瑞仙
"Tōgū no daishin Minamoto no
　　Yorimitsu no ason kitsune wo iru
　　koto"　春宮の大進源頼光の朝臣
　　狐を射る語
Tōin Kinsada　洞院公定
Tōji　東寺
Tōketsu　唐決
tokin　頭巾
Tokiwa Mitsunaga　常磐光長
Tokugawa Ieyasu　徳川家康
Tokugawa Tsunayoshi　徳川綱吉
Tokugawa Yorinobu　徳川頼宣
Tokuitsu　徳一
Tomo no Okatsuo　伴少勝雄
Tosa Hirochika　土佐広周
Tosa Mitsuyoshi　土佐光芳
Tosa Nagataka　土佐長隆
tsuchigumo　土蜘蛛
Tsuchigumo zōshi　土蜘蛛草紙
Tsukioka Yoshitoshi　月岡芳年
tsukumogami　付喪神, つくもがみ, 九
　　十九髪, 九十九神
Tsukumogami emaki　付喪神絵巻
Tsukumogami ki　付喪神記
tsumadoi-kon　妻問婚
tsunodarai　角盥
Tsurugi no maki　剣巻
tsuwamono no ie　兵の家

U

Ubakawa　うばかわ
ubakinu　姥衣
Ubasute-yama (or Obasuteyama)　姥棄
　　て山
ubume　産女
Uji no hōzō　宇治の宝蔵
ujō　有情
Ukemochinokami　保食神
ukon'e　右近衛
Umehara Takeshi　梅原武
Unrō　雲滝
Urabe Kanekata　卜部兼方
Urabe Kenkō　卜部兼好 (or *Yoshida
　　Kenkō*)

Bibliography

ABBREVIATIONS

KT	*Kokushi taikei*
MJMT	*Muromachi jidai monogatari taisei.* 13 vols. Yokoyama Shigeru and Matsumoto Ryūshin, eds. Tokyo: Kadokawa Shoten, 1973–85. Also 2 *hoi*, supp. vols., Matsumoto Ryūshin, ed. 1987–88.
MN	*Monumenta Nipponica*
NET	*Nihon emaki taisei*
NKBT	*Nihon koten bungaku taikei*
NKBZ	*Nihon koten bungaku zenshū*
NST	*Nihon shisō taikei*
SNKBT	*Shin nihon koten bungaku taikei.* 100 vols., plus five *bekkan* and index. Tokyo: Iwanami Shoten, 1989–2005.
SNKBZ	*Shinpen Nihon koten bungaku zenshū.* 88 vols. Tokyo: Shōgakukan, 1994–2002.
ZNET	*Zoku Nihon emaki taisei*

Abe Tsuyoshi. *Mononofudomo: Konjaku monogatari no bushitachi.* Tokyo: Tokyo Tosho Shuppankai, 2010.

Akimoto Kichirō, ed. *Fudoki.* Vol. 2 of *NKBT.* Tokyo: Iwanami Shoten, 1958.

Akiyama Terukazu. "Amewakahiko zōshi emaki o meguru shomondai." *Kokka* 985.12 (1975): 3–25.

Amano Fumio. "Shuten Dōji: nihon kaanibarizumu no keifu no nakade." *Kokubungaku kaishaku to kanshō* 22.16 (1977): 104–5.

Amano Fumio. "Shuten Dōji kō." *Nōkenkyū to hyōron* 8 (1979): 16–27.

Amino Yoshihiko. *Igyō no ōken.* Tokyo: Heibonsha, 1986.

Andō Tamiji. *Shōmetsu to saisei no yūgi: Haseo zōshi no eizō to jikan.* Tokyo: Kinjudō Shuppan, 2006.

Andrews, Allan E. *The Teachings Essential for Rebirth: A Study of Genshin's Ōjōyōshū.* Tokyo: Sophia University, 1973.

Aoki Kazuo, Inaoka Kōji, Sasayama Haruo, and Shirafuji Noriyuki, eds. *Shoku Nihongi,* vol. 4. Vol. 15 of *SNKBT.* Tokyo: Iwanami Shoten, 1995.

Apuleius. *Cupid & Psyche.* Ed. E.J. Kenney. Cambridge: Cambridge University Press, 1990.

Araki Hiroyuki. "Onihachi denshō o megutte—tsuchigumo to yamauba." *Shizen to bunka* 60.3 (1999): 4–9.

Araki, James T. "Bunshō Zōshi: The Tale of Bunsho, the Saltmaker." *MN* 38.3 (Autumn 1983): 221–49.

Araki, James T. "Otogi-zōshi and Nara-ehon." *MN* 36.1 (1981): 1–20.

Arntzen, Sonja, trans. *The Kagerō Diary: A Woman's Autobiographical Text from Tenth-Century Japan.* Ann Arbor: Center for Japanese Studies, University of Michigan, 1997.

DOI: 10.7330/9781607324904.c009

Asahara Yoshiko, Haruta Akira, and Matsuo Ashie, eds. *Yashiro-bon kōya-bon taishō Heike monogatari*, vol. 3. Tokyo: Shinten-sha, 1990.

Asami Kazuhiko, ed. *Jikkinshō*. Vol. 51 of *SNKBZ*. Tokyo: Shōgakukan, 1997.

Aston, William G., trans. *Nihongi: Chronicles of Japan from the Earliest Times to AD 697.* London: Kegan Paul, Trench, Trubner, 1896. Rpt. London: George Allen and Unwin, 1956.

Averbuch, Irit. *The Gods Come Dancing: A Study of The Japanese Ritual Dance of Yamabushi Kagura.* New York: Cornell University East Asian Program, 1995.

Ayusawa Hisashi. *Minamoto no Raikō*. Tokyo: Yoshikawa Kōbunkan, 1968.

Baba Akiko. *Oni no kenkyū*. Tokyo: Chikuma Shobō, 1988. Rpt. of Tokyo: San'ichi Shobō, 1971.

Baba Kazuo. "'Tsuchigumo' no kenkyū—jō, chū, ge." *Kikan hōgaku* 59.06 (1989): 88–93; 60.09 (1989): 88–93; 62.03 (1990): 78–81.

Baird, Merrily C. *Symbols of Japan: Thematic Motifs in Art and Design.* New York: Rizzoli International Publications, 2001.

Bakhtin, Mikhail M. *The Dialogic Imagination.* Trans. Caryl Emerson and Michael Holquist. Austin: University of Texas Press, 1981.

Bender, Mark. *Plum and Bamboo: China's Suzhou Chantefable Tradition.* Urbana: University of Illinois Press, 2003.

Bethe, Monica, and Karen Brazell, trans. "Yamamba." In *Traditional Japanese Theater: An Anthology of Plays,* ed. Karen Brazell, 207–25. New York: Columbia University Press, 1998.

Blacker, Carmen. "The Divine Boy in Japanese Buddhism." *Asian Folklore Studies* 22 (1963): 77–88.

Bock, Felicia Gressitt, trans. *Engi-Shiki: Procedures of The Engi Era.* Tokyo: Sophia University, 1970.

Bodiford, William M. *Sōtō Zen in Medieval Japan.* Honolulu: University of Hawaii Press, 1993.

Borgen, Robert. *Sugawara no Michizane and the Early Heian Court.* Honolulu: University of Hawaii Press, 1994. Rpt. of Cambridge, MA: Council on East Asian Studies, Harvard University, distributed by Harvard University Press, 1986.

Bosuton Bijutsukan Nihon bijutsu no shihō. Ed. Tokyo kokuritsu hakubutsukan, Nagoya Boston Bijubutsukan, Kyūshū kokuritsu hakubutsukan, Osaka shiritsu hakubutsukan, and NHK Puromōshon. Tokyo: NHK Puromōshon, 2012.

Carter, Steven D. *Regent Redux: A Life of The Statesman-Scholar Ichijō Kaneyoshi.* Ann Arbor: Center for Japanese Studies, University of Michigan, 1996.

Chigiri Kōsai. *Oni no kenkyū*. Tokyo: Tairiku Shobō, 1977.

Chikamatsu Monzaemon. *Chikamatsu jōrurishū.* Ed. Shuzui Kenji and Ōkubo Tadakuni. Vol. 50 of *NKBT*. Tokyo: Iwanami Shoten, 1959.

Chikamatsu Monzaemon. "Kako no Kyōshin nanahaka meguri." Vol. 9 of *Chikamatsu zenshū,* 225–338. Tokyo: Iwanami Shoten, 1988.

Chikamatsu Monzaemon. *Chikamatsu jōrurishū.* Ed. Matsuzaki Hitoshi, Hara Michio, Iguchi Hiroshi, and Ōhashi Tadayoshi. *Chikamatsu jōrurishū.* 2 vols. Vols. 91 and 92 of *SNKBT*. Tokyo: Iwanami Shoten, 1995.

Chikamatsu Monzaemon. "Kan hasshū tsunagi uma." Vol. 2 of *Chikamatsu jōruri shū.* Vol. 92 of *SNKBT*, 355–462. Tokyo: Iwanami Shoten, 1995.

Chikamatsu Monzaemon. "Tethered Steed and the Eight Provinces of Kantō." In *Chikamatsu 5 Late Plays,* trans. and annotated by C. Andrew Gerstle, 325–427. New York: Columbia University Press, 2001.

Childs, Margaret H. "Chigo Monogatari: Love Stories or Buddhist Sermons?" *MN* 35 (1980): 127–51.

Childs, Margaret H. "Didacticism in Medieval Short Stories: Hatsuse Monogatari and Akimichi." *MN* 42.3 (Autumn 1987): 253–88.

Chō Yōichi. "Toyokuni no tsuchigumo." *Kōbe jogakuin daigaku ronshū* 22.3 (1976): 99–118.

Como, Michael. *Weaving and Binding: Immigrant Gods and Female Immortals in Ancient Japan.* Honolulu: University of Hawaii Press, 2009.

Copeland, Rebecca L., and Esperanza Ramirez-Christensen, eds. *The Father-Daughter Plot: Japanese Literary Women and the Law of The Father.* Honolulu: University of Hawaii Press, 2001.

Cornell, Laurel L. "The Deaths of Old Women: Folklore and Differential Mortality in Nineteenth-Century Japan." In *Recreating Japanese Women, 1600–1945,* ed. Gail Lee Bernstein, 71–88. Berkeley: University of California Press, 1991.

Daniels, F. J. *Selections from Japanese Literature.* London: Lund Humphries, 1958.

Dix, Monika. "Hachikazuki: Revealing Kannon's Crowning Compassion in Muromachi Fiction." *Japanese Journal of Religious Studies* 36.2 (2009): 279–93.

Doi Kōchi. *Shinwa • densetsu no kenkyū.* Tokyo: Iwanami Shoten, 1973.

Dorson, Richard M. *Folk Legends of Japan.* Rutland, VT: Charles Tuttle, 1962.

Dykstra Yoshiko and Yoko Kurata, trans. "The Yokube-Soshi: Conflicts between Social Convention, Human Love, and Religious Renunciation." *Japanese Religions* 26.2 (July 2001): 117–29.

Earhart, H. Byron. "Introduction." In *Shugendō: Essays on the Structure of Japanese Folk Religion,* by Miyake Hitoshi, 1–7. Ann Arbor: Center for Japanese Studies, University of Michigan, 2001.

Eiseibunko Museum. *Haseo sōshi.* Accessed November 13, 2013. http://www.eiseibunko .com/collection/chusei1.html.

Eishin. *Hokekyō jikidanshō: Kindaiin zōhon,* vol. 1. Kyoto: Rinsen Shoten, 1979.

Engi-shiki: Procedures of The Engi Era. Trans. with intro and notes by Felicia Gressitt Bock. Tokyo: Sophia University, 1970.

Eubanks, Charlotte. *Miracles of Book and Body: Buddhist Textual Culture and Medieval Japan.* Berkeley: University of California Press, 2011.

Fairchild, William P. "Shamanism in Japan." *Folklore Studies* 21 (1962): 1–122.

Farris, William Wayne. *Sacred Texts and Buried Treasures: Issues in the Historical Archaeology of Ancient Japan.* Honolulu: University of Hawaii Press, 1998.

Fogel, Joshua A. *Articulating the Sinosphere: Sino-Japanese Relations in Space and Time.* Cambridge, MA: Harvard University Press, 2009.

Foster, Michael Dylan. *The Book of Yokai: Mysterious Creatures of Japanese Folklore.* Berkeley: University of California Press, 2015.

Foster, Michael Dylan. *Pandemonium and Parade: Japanese Monsters and the Culture of Yōkai.* Berkeley: University of California Press, 2009.

Franz, Marie-Louise von. *Shadow and Evil in Fairy Tales.* Zurich: Spring Publications, 1974.

Fróis, Luís. "Nichiō bunka hikaku." Trans. Okada Akio. In *Nihon ōkokuki, Nichiō bunka hikaku.* Vol. 11 of *Daikōkai jidai sōsho,* 495–636. Tokyo: Iwanami Shoten, 1965.

Fujii Takashi, ed. *Muromachi jidai monogatari shū.* Vol. 9 of *Otogi zōshi kenkyū sōsho.* Tokyo: Kuresu Shuppan, 2003.

Fujioka Tadaharu, Inukai Kiyoshi, Nakano Kōichi, and Ishii Fumio, eds. *Izumi Shikibu nikki, Murasaki Shikibu nikki, Sarashina nikki, Sanuki no suke no nikki.* Vol. 26 of *SNKBZ.* Tokyo: Shōgakukan, 1994.

Fujishiro Tsuguo. "Kongetsu no ono 'Kochō.'" *Kadan* 12.2 (1998): 122–25.

Fujiwara Akihira. *Shin Sarugōki.* Ed. Kawaguchi Hisao. Tokyo: Heibonsha, 1983.

Fujiwara Kintō. *Hokuzanshō.* Ed. Shintō taikei hensankai. Tokyo: Shintō taikei hensankai, 1992.

Fujiwara Michinaga. *Midō kanpakuki zen chūshaku Kankō yonen.* Ed. Yamanaka Yutaka. Kyoto: Shibunkaku Shuppan, 2006.

Fujiwara Michinaga. *Midō kanpakuki zen chūshaku Kannin gannen.* Ed. Yamanaka Yutaka. Takashina Shoten, 1985.

Fujiwara no Sanesuke. *Shōyūki: Zōho shiryō taisei bekkan*. 3 vols. Ed. Zōho shiryō taisei kankōkai. Kyoto: Rinsen Shoten, 1965.

Fujiwara Tadazane and Nakahara no Moromoto. *Chūgaishō*. Ed. Yamane Taisuke and Ikegami Jun'ichi. In *Gōdanshō, Chūgaishō, Fukego* Vol. 32 of *SNKBT*, ed. Gotō Akio, Ikegami Jun'ichi, and Yamane Taisuke, 255–359. Tokyo: Iwanami Shoten, 1997.

Fukagawa Tōru, ed. *Heihō hijutsu ikkansho, Hokinaiden kin'u gyokutoshū, Shokunin yuraisho*. Vol. 3 of *Nihon koten isho sōkan*. Tokyo: Gendai Shichō Shinsha, 2004.

Fukasawa Shichirō. "Narayamabushi kō." In *Narayamabushikō, Fuefukigawa*, 245–77. Tokyo: Shinchōsha, 1981.

Fukuda Akira, ed. "Mukashibanashi no keitai." Vol. 4 of *Nihon mukashibanashi kenkyū shūsei*. Tokyo: Meicho Shuppan, 1984.

Fukui Teisuke, annotated. *Ise monogatari*. In *Taketori monogatari, Ise monogatari, Yamato monogatari, Heichū monogatari*. Vol. 12 of *SNKBT*. Tokyo: Shogakukan, 1994.

Fukushima Yoshikazu. "Tsuchigumo densetsu no seiritsu ni tsuite." *Jinbun ronkyū* 21.2 (1971): 47–74.

Gan, Bao. *Sōshinki*. Trans. Takeda Akira. Tokyo: Heibonsha, 1964.

Gan, Bao. *Sou shen ji*. Ed. Wang Shaoying. Beijing: Zhonghua shu ju, 1979.

Geddes, John Van Ward. "A Partial Translation and Study of the *Jikkinshō*." 2 vols. PhD dissertation, Washington University, St. Louis, MO, 1976.

Genshin. *Ōjōyōshū*. Ed. Ishida Mizumaro. Vol. 6 of *NST*. Tokyo: Iwanami Shoten, 1970.

Gerstle, Andrew, trans. *Chikamatsu 5 Late Plays*. New York: Columbia University Press, 2001.

Gerstle, Andrew. "Gidayū botsugo no Chikamatsu: Kokusen'ya kassen, Kanhasshū tsunagiuma." In *Chikamatsu no jidai*. Vol. 8 of *Iwanami Kōza Kabuki Bunraku*, ed. Torigoi Benzō, Uchiyama Mikiko, and Watanabe Tantoisu, 165–86. Tokyo: Iwanami Shoten, 1998.

Gifushi rekishi hakubutsukan, ed. *Kijin to majinai*. Gifu: Gifushi rekishi hakubutsukan, 1989.

Glassman, Hank. *The Face of Jizō: Image and Cult in Medieval Japanese Buddhism*. Honolulu: University of Hawaii Press, 2012.

Goodich, Michael. *Other Middle Ages: Witnesses at the Margins of Medieval Society*. Philadelphia: University of Pennsylvania Press, 1998.

Gorai Shigeru. *Oni mukashi*. Tokyo: Kadokawa Shoten, 1984.

Gosukō-in. *Kanmon nikki*. 3 vols. Tokyo: Kunaichō Shoryōbu, 2002–6.

Hamanaka Osamu. "Otogi zōshi 'Izumi shikibu' 'Koshikibu' ron." *Kokubungaku: kaishaku to kanshō* 60.8 (1995): 119–24.

Hanada Kiyoteru. "Gajinden (shō)." In *Muromachi shōsetsu shū*. Vol. 15 of *Hanada Kiyoteru zenshū*, 418–69. Tokyo: Kōdansha, 1978.

Hanawa Hokiichi, ed. *Gunsho ruijū*. Vols. 5, 27, and 28. Tokyo: Zoku gunsho ruijū kanseikai, 1986–87.

Hanawa Hokiichi, ed. "Jinkyōron." Vol. 32 of *Zoku Gunsho ruijū*, 223–48. Tokyo: Zoku gunsho ruijū kanseikai, 1958.

Hanawa Hokiichi, ed. *Zoku gunsho ruijū*. Parts 1 and 2 of vol. 32. Tokyo: Zoku gunsho ruijū kanseikai, 1958 and 1977.

Hanawa Hokiichi, ed. *Zoku gunsho ruijū*. Part 1 of *Hoi 2*. Tokyo: Zoku gunsho ruijū kanseikai, 1985.

Hara Yukie. "Heianchō ni okeru 'obasute' no denshō to tenkai." *Nihon bungaku fūdo gakkai kiji* 22 (1997): 18–28.

Hara Yukie. "'Obasute' kō—yōkyoku to kago no aida." *Geinō* 10 (2004): 23–34.

Hasegawa Tadashi, ed. *Taiheiki*. Vol. 54 of *SNKBZ*. Tokyo: Shogakukan, 1994.

Hayami Tasuku. *Jigoku to gokuraku: Ōjōyōshū to kizoku shakai*. Tokyo: Yoshikawa Kōbunkan, 1998.

Hayashiya Tatsusaburō. "Gōsonsei seiritsuki ni okeru machishū bunka." In *Chūsei bunka no kichō*, 215–35. Tokyo: Tokyo daigaku shuppan, 1953.

Hayek, Matthias. "The Eight Trigrams and Their Changes: An Inquiry into Japanese Early Modern Divination." *Japanese Journal of Religious Studies* 38.2 (2011): 329–68.

Hayek, Matthias, and Hayashi Makoto, eds. "Editors' Introduction: Onmyōdō in Japanese History." *Japanese Journal of Religious Studies* 40.1 (2013): 1–18.

Higo Kazuo. "Yamata no orochi (shō)." In *Ijin • ikenie*. Vol. 7 of *Kaii no minzokugaku*, ed. Komatsu Kazuhiko, 28–77. Tokyo: Kawade Shobō, 2001.

Hijikata Yōichi. "Haseo kyō sōshi." Vol. 5 of *Taikei monogatari bungaku shi*, ed. Mitani Eiichi, 80–89. Tokyo: Yūseidō, 1991.

Hiroshima University Library. "Hanayo no hime." In *Hiroshima daigaku toshokan Hiroshima daigaku shozō Nara ehon Muromachi jidai monogatari*, ed. Itō Kunio. Accessed January 2009. http://opac.lib.hiroshima-u.ac.jp/portal/dc/kyodo/naraehon/research/01/.

Hirota Tetsumichi. "Jinzō ningen no setsuwa to ronri." In *Eizan no waka to setsuwa*, ed. Arai Eizō, 155–73. Kyoto: Sekai Shisōsha, 1991.

Hisamatsu Sen'ichi and Nishio Minoru, eds. *Karon-shū, Noh gakuron-shū*. Vol. 65 of *NKBT*. Tokyo: Iwanami Shoten, 1961.

Honda, H. H., trans. *The Shin Kokinshu: The 13th-Century Anthology Edited by Imperial Edict.* Tokyo: Hokuseido, 1970.

Honda Yasuji. "Dengaku." Vol. 21 of *Sekai daihyakka jiten*. Tokyo: Heibonsha, 1972.

Hori Ichirō. *Folk Religion in Japan: Continuity and Change.* Chicago: University of Chicago Press, 1968.

Hsüan Hua. *The Wonderful Dharma Lotus Flower Sutra*, vol. 2. Trans. Buddhist Text Translation Society. San Francisco: Sino American Buddhist Association, 1977. (10 vols., 1976–82.)

Hudson, Mark J. *Ruins of Identity: Ethnogenesis in the Japanese Islands.* Honolulu: University of Hawaii Press, 1999.

Ichiko Teiji. *Chūsei shōsetsu no kenkyū.* Tokyo: Tokyo daigaku shuppan, 1955.

Ichiko Teiji. *Mikan chūsei shōsetsu.* Vol. 18 of *Koten bunko.* Tokyo: Koten Bunko, 1948.

Ichiko Teiji, ed. *Heike monogatari.* 2 vols. Vols. 45 and 46 of *SNKBZ.* Tokyo: Shōgakukan, 1994.

Ichiko Teiji, ed. *Otogi zōshi.* Vol. 13 of *Zusetsu Nihon no koten.* Tokyo: Shūeisha, 1980.

Ichiko Teiji, ed. *Otogi zōshi.* Vol. 38 of *NKBZ.* Tokyo: Iwanami Shoten, 1958.

Ichiko Teiji, Akiya Osamu, Sawai Taizō, Tajima Kazuo, and Tokuda Kazuo. *Muromachi jidai monogatari shū.* Vols. 54 and 55 of *SNKBT.* Tokyo: Iwanami Shoten, 1989 and 1992.

Ichiko Teiji and Noma Kōshin. *Otogi zōshi, Kana zōsh.* Vol. 16 of *Nihon koten kanshō kōza.* Tokyo: Kadokawa Shoten, 1963.

Idema, Wilt L. *Personal Salvation and Filial Piety: Two Precious Scroll Narratives of Guanyin and Her Acolytes.* Honolulu: University of Hawaii Press, 2008.

Igeta Ryōji, Tabata Yasuko, and Fukawa Kiyoshi, eds. *Ie to kyōiku.* Tokyo: Waseda daigaku shuppanbu, 2006.

Ii Haruki. *Emaki Ōeyama Shuten Dōji, ashibikie no sekai.* Ed. Itsuō Bijutsukan. Kyōto: Shibunkaku Shuppan, 2011.

Ikeda Hiroko. *A Type and Motif Index of Japanese Folk-Literature.* Helsinki: Suomalainen Tiedeakatemia, 1971.

Ikeda Hiroshi, ed. *Chūsei, kinsei dōkashū.* Vol. 180 of *Koten bunko.* Tokyo: Koten Bunko, 1962.

Ikenouchi Josui. "Tsuchigumo no Kochō ni tsuite." *Nōgaku* 1.11 (1903): 13–15.

Imahori Taitsu. *Gonja no kegen—Tenjin, Kūya, Hōnen.* Tokyo: Shibunkaku Shuppan, 2006.

Imamura Shōhei, dir. *Narayamabushi kō.* VHS. Public Media Home Vision, 1983.

Inaba Kikuo. "Nihon kankyō bunkashi ni kansuru kenkyū: Obasute to yamauba no kankeisei." *Osaka keidai ronshū* 54.5 (2004): 33–46.

Inada Kōji, Ōshima Tatehiko, Kawabata Toyohiko, Fukuda Akira, and Mihara Yukihisa, eds. *Nihon mukashibanashi jiten*. Tokyo: Kōbundō, 1977.

Inagaki Hisao. *A Dictionary of Japanese Buddhist Terms: Based on References in Japanese Literature*. Union City, CA: Heian International, 1988.

Inai Hitomi. "'Hanayo no hime' ni tsuite no ichi kōsatsu." *Aibun* 22 (September 1986): 26–28.

Inamoto Mariko. "*Ban dainagon emaki* to GoShirakawa." In *Imēji to patoron: bijutsushi o manage tame no 23 shō*, ed. Inamoto Mariko and Ikegami Hidehiro, 53–68. Tokyo: Seiunsha, 2009.

Inamoto Yasuo. "Kentōshi sono hikari to kage—Nara jidai o chūshin ni." In *Dai Kentōshiten: Heijō sento 1300-nen kinen*, ed. Nara Kokuritsu hakubutsukan, 6–16. Nara: Nara Kokuritsu hakubutsukan, 2010.

Inoue Katsushi. "'Kako no Kyōshin nanahaka meguri' no jōen nendai." *Kinsei bungei* 85.01 (2007): 1–13.

Inoue Shōichi. *Nanban gensō: Yurishīzu densetsu to Azuchi jō*. Tokyo: Bungei Shunjū, 1998.

Inoue Yasushi. "Obasute." Vol. 11 of *Inoue Yasushi shōsetsu shū*, 7–20. Tokyo: Shinchōsha, 1974.

Inoue Yasushi. "Obasute." In *The Counterfeiter and Other Stories*, trans. Leon Picon, 73–96. Boston: Tuttle, 2000.

Inukai Yasushi, ed. *Sarashina nikki*. In *Izumi Shikibu nikki, Murasaki Shikibu nikki, Sarashina nikki, Sanuki no suke no nikki*, ed. Fujioka Tadaharu, Inukai Kiyoshi, Nakano Kōichi, and Ishii Fumio, 273–384. Vol. 26 of *SNKBZ*. Tokyo: Shōgakukan, 1994.

Ishiguro Kichijirō and Shimura Arihir, eds. *Ōeyama emaki: Chester Bītī Raiburari shozō*. Tokyo: Benseisha, 2006.

Ishii Susumu. "Kakun, okibumi, ikki keijō." In *Chūsei seiji shakai shisō*, ed. Ishii Susumu, 309–67. Tokyo: Iwanami Shoten, 1972.

Ishikawa Matsutarō and Koizumi Yoshinaga. *Onna daigaku shiryō shūsei bekkan*. Tokyo: Ōzorasha, 2006.

Ishikawa Tōru. "Otogi zōshi ni egakareta josei to bukkyō." *Kokubungaku: kaishaku to kanshō* 69 (June 2004): 66–72.

Itagaki Shun'ichi, ed. *Zen-Taiheiki*. 2 vols. Vol. 3 of *Sōsho Edo bunko*. Tokyo: Tosho Kankōkai, 1988–89.

Itō Masayoshi and Kuroda Akira. *Wakan rōeishū kochūshaku shūsei*. Books 1 and 2 of Vol. 2. Kyoto: Daigakudō Shoten, 1994.

Itō Masayoshi and Kuroda Akira. *Wakan rōeishū kochūshaku shūsei*. Vol. 3. Kyoto: Daigakudō Shoten, 1989.

Itō Masayoshi and Miki Masahiro. *Wakan rōeishū kochūshaku shūsei*. Vol. 1. Kyoto: Daigakudō Shoten, 1997.

Itō Shingo. "Ihon 'Tsuchigumo' emaki nit suite." In *Ikai mangekyō: anoyo · yōkai · uranai*, ed. Kokuritsu rekishi minzoku hakubutsukan, 89–93. Sakura-shi: Kokuritsu rekishi minzoku hakubutsukan, 2001.

Itō Takashi. "'Kana kyōkun' kō." *Chūsei bungaku* 16 (1971): 6–11.

Itō Yūko. "'Amewakahiko sōshi' no nikeitō no honbun wo megutte—emaki kei kara sasshi kei e." *Kokugo to kokubungaku* 81.3 (2004): 28–42.

Iwasaki Kae, ed. *Shichijūichiban shokunin utaawase, Shinsen kyōkashū, Kokon ikyokushū*. Vol. 61 of *Shin nihon koten bungaku taikei*. Tokyo: Iwanami Shoten, 1993.

Iwasaki Masahiko. "Hyakki yagyō emaki." In *Otogizōshi jiten*, ed. Tokuda Kazuo, 414–16. Tokyo: Tokyodō Shuppan, 2002.

Iwasaka Michiko and Barre Toelken. *Ghosts and the Japanese: Cultural Experience in Japanese Death Legend*. Logan: Utah State University Press, 1994.

Iwase Hiroshi. *Denshō bungei no kenkyū: kuchi gatari to katarimono*. Tokyo: Miyai Shoten, 1990.

Izumo Asako. "'Amewakahiko monogatari' to tanabata Nisei." *Aoyama gakuin joshi tanki daigaku kiyō* 42 (November 1988): 45–64.

Izushi Yoshihiko. *Shina shinwa densetsu no kenkyū*. Rpt. and expanded ed. Tokyo: Chūō Kōronsha, 1973 [1943].

Jacoby, Mario, Verena Kast, and Ingrid Diedel. *Witches, Ogres, and the Devil's Daughter: Encounters with Evil in Fairy Tales.* Trans. Michael H. Kohn. Boston: Shambhala, 1992.

Japanese Architecture and Art Net Users System. "Juuniten." http://www.aisf.or.jp /~jaanus/deta/j/juuniten.htm.

Japanese Architecture and Art Net Users System. "Shitennou." http://www.aisf.or.jp /~jaanus/deta/s/shitennou.htm.

Jien. *The Future and the Past: A Translation and Study of The Gukanshō, an Interpretative History of Japan Written in 1219.* Trans. Delmer M. Brown and Ichirō Ishida. Berkeley: University of California Press, 1979.

Jien. *Gukanshō.* Ed. Okami Masao and Akamatsu Toshihide. Vol. 85 of *NKBT.* Tokyo: Iwanami Shoten, 1967.

Jones, Stanleigh H., trans. "The Deserted Crone." In *Twenty Plays of The Nō Theatre,* ed. Donald Keene, 115–28. New York: Columbia University Press, 1970.

Joseishi sōgō kenkyūkai. *Nihon josei seikatsushi: Kinsei,* vol. 3. Tokyo: Tokyo daigaku Shuppankai, 1990.

Joseishi sōgō kenkyūkai, ed. *Nihon joseishi kenkyū bunken mokuroku.* 4 vols. Tokyo: Tokyo daigaku Shuppankai, 1983–94.

Kabat, Adam. "'Mono' no obake—kinsei no tsukumogami sekai." *IS* 84 (2000): 10–14.

Kabat, Adam. "'Sōsaku' to shite no yōkai." In *Nihon yōkai taizen,* ed. Komatsu Kazuhiko, 145–78. Tokyo: Shōgakukan, 2003.

Kadoya Atsushi. "Ryōbu shintō." *Kokubungaku kaishaku to kanshō* 60.12 (1995): 61–66.

Kagiwada Yūko. "Matsuri—susuharai." *Haiku* 30.12 (1981): 120–23.

Kakehi Mariko. "*Tsukumogami emaki* no shohon ni tsuite." *Hakubutsukan dayori* 15 (Gifushi rekishi hakubutsukan, 1989): 5–7.

Kakei Yasuhiko. *Chūsei buke kakun no kenkyū.* Tokyo: Kazama Shobō, 1967.

Kakubayashi Fumio. "Tsuchigumo to Tateana jūkyo to shinden." *Kodaigaku kenkū* 165.6 (2004): 25–33.

Kanai Hiroko. "Umi o watatta nidai emaki." In *Bosuton Bijutsukan Nihon bijutsu no shihō,* ed. Tokyo kokuritsu hakubutsukan, Nagoya Boston bijubutsukan, Kyūshū kokuritsu hakubutsukan, Osaka shiritsu hakubutsukan, Boston bijutsukan, NHK, NHK Puromōshon, 92–95. Tokyo: NHK Puromōshon, 2012.

Kanai Sanshō. *Kumo no ito azusa no yumihari.* 2 vols. Yokohama: no pub., 1882–83.

Kanda Fusae. "*Kibi no daijin nittō emaki* saikō—sono dokujisei kara no tenbō." *Bukkyō geijutsu* 311.7 (2010): 6, 9–39.

Kanda Tatsumi and Nishizawa Masashi. *Chūsei ōchō monogatari, otogi zōshi jiten.* Tokyo: Benseisha Shuppan, 2002.

Kaneko Eriko. "Arasu shiritsu bijutsukan zō 'Tamura no sōshi' honkoku to kaidai." *Senshū kokubun Senshū daigaku nihongo nihonbungaku bunka gakkai* 84.1 (2009): 83–129.

Kanze Kasetsu. "Utaikata kōza—Tsuchigumo." *Kanze* 19.7 (1952): 33–35.

Kashiwagi Yasuko. "Ishi to kashite aru koto—yōkyoku 'Obasute' no ichi dokkai." *Yamaguchi daigaku tetsugaku kenkyū* 14 (2007): 1–22.

Katagiri Yōichi. *Ise monogatari no kenkyū: shiryō-hen.* Tokyo: Meiji Shoin, 1969.

Katagiri Yōichi, Takahashi Shōji, Fukui Teisuke, and Shimizu Yoshiko, eds. *Taketori monogatari, Ise monogatari, Yamato monogatari, Heichū monogatari.* Vol. 12 of *SNKBZ.* Tokyo: Shogakukan, 1994.

Katsumata Takashi. "'Amewakamiko zō' no hensen ni kansuru ichi kōsatsu." *Nagasaki daigaku kyōikugakubu jinbunkagaku kenkyū hōkoku* 55 (1997): 1–17.

Katsumata Takashi. "Chūsei shōsetsu 'Tanabata' to senkō bunken no kankei ni tsuite."
    Nagasaki daigaku kyōikugakubu jinbunkagaku kenkyū hōkoku 54 (1997): 17–22.
Katsumata Takashi. "Otogi zōshi 'Tanabata (Amewakahiko monogatari)' no shomondai."
    Nara ehon · emaki kenkyū 4.9 (2006): 1–15.
Kavanagh, Frederick G. "An Errant Priest: Sasayaki Take." *MN* 51.2 (Summer 1996): 219–44.
Kawai Hayao. *The Japanese Psyche.* Dallas, TX: Spring Publications, 1988.
Kawajiri Akio. *Taira no Masakado no ran.* Vol. 4 of *Sensō no nihonshi.* Tokyo: Yoshikawa
    Kōbunkan, 2007.
Kawamura Teruo, ed. *Shūchūshō.* Vol. 5 of *Karon kagaku shūsei.* Tokyo: Miyai Shoten, 2000.
Kawashima Shigehiro. "Shimotsuke no Kintoki to Kintarō densetsu no seiritsu." *Kokuritsu
    rekishi minzoku hakubutsukan kenkyū hōkoku* 45.12 (1992): 79–97.
Kawashima, Terry. *Writing Margins: The Textual Construction of Gender in Heian and Kamakura
    Japan.* Cambridge, MA: Harvard University Asia Center, distributed by Harvard Uni-
    versity Press, 2001.
Kawatake Mokuami. "Tsuchigumo." In *Kawatake Mokuami-shū,* ed. Kawatake Shigetoshi,
    697–711. Vol. 30 of *Nihon gikyoku zenshū.* Tokyo: Shun'yōdō, 1928.
Kawatake Mokuami. "Tsuchigumo." Trans. Donald Richie. N.p.: no pub., 1949.
Keene, Donald, trans. "Sannin Hōshi: The Three Priests." In *Anthology of Japanese Literature,*
    ed. Donald Keene, 322–31. New York: Grove, 1955.
Keene, Donald. *Seeds in the Heart: Japanese Literature from Earliest Times to the Late Sixteenth
    Century.* New York: Henry Holt, 1993.
Keene, Donald. "The Songs of Oak Mountain." In *The Old Woman, the Wife and the Archer:
    Three Modern Japanese Short Novels,* trans. Donald Keene, xii–xiii, 3–50. New York:
    Viking, 1961.
Keizai Zasshisha, ed. "Engi shiki." Vol. 13 of *KT,* 85–1163. Tokyo: Keizai Zasshisha, 1900.
Keown, Damien, ed. *A Dictionary of Buddhism.* Oxford: Oxford University Press, 2003.
"Kibi daijin monogatari." In *Daitōkyū kinen bunko zenpon sōkan chūko chūsei hen,* vol. 1, ed.
    Inoue Muneo, 401–15. Tokyo: Kyūko Shoin, 2007.
Kikuchi Yasuhiko, Kimura Masanori, and Imuta Tsunehisa, eds. *Tosa nikki, Kagerō nikki.*
    Tokyo: Shogakkan, 1995.
Kimbrough, R. Keller, trans. "The Demon Shuten Dōji." In *Traditional Japanese Literature:
    An Anthology, Beginnings to 1600,* ed. Haruo Shirane, 1123–38. New York: Columbia
    University Press, 2007.
Kimbrough, R. Keller. *Preachers, Poets, Women, and the Way: Izumi Shikibu and the Buddhist
    Literature of Medieval Japan.* Ann Arbor: Center for Japanese Studies, University of
    Michigan, 2008.
Kimbrough, R. Keller. *Wondrous Brutal Fictions: Eight Buddhist Tales from the Early Japanese Pup-
    pet Theater.* New York: Columbia University Press, 2013.
Kimura Shigemitsu. *Chūsei shakai no naritachi.* Vol. 1 of *Nihon chūsei no rekishi.* Tokyo:
    Yoshikawa Kōbunkan, 2009.
Kinoshita Keisuke, dir. *Narayama bushi kō.* VHS. New York: Kino on Video, 1996.
Kiriya Kazuaki, dir. *Casshern.* Perf. Iseya Yūsuke and Asō Kumiko. Tokyo: Shōchiku, 2004.
    Film.
Kitami Ken'ichirō. "Ezo—ikitsuzukeru tatakai no kioku." *Gendai no me* 23.1 (1982): 72–75.
Knecht, Peter. "Aspects of Shamanism: An Introduction." In *Shamans in Asia,* ed. Clark
    Chilson and Peter Knecht, 1–30. London: Routledge Curzon, 2003.
Knecht, Peter. "Preface." In *Japanese Demon Lore: Oni, from Ancient Times to the Present,* by
    Noriko Reider, xi–xxvi. Logan: Utah State University Press, 2010.
Knecht, Peter, Hasegawa Masao, Minobe Shigekatsu, and Tsujimoto Hiroshige. "Denshi
    'oni' to 'mushi'—'Kyōu shoya zō Denshibyō kanjin shō ryakkai—.'" Vol. 6 of *Shōdō
    bungaku kenkyū,* 40–95. Tokyo: Miyai Shoten, 2008.

Knecht, Peter, Hasegawa Masao, Minobe Shigekatsu, and Tsujimoto Hiroshige. *"Hara no mushi" no kenkyū: Nihon no shinshinkan o saguru.* Nagoya: Nagoya daigaku Shuppankai, 2012.

Kobayashi Miwa. "Chūsei buyūdenshō to sono kisō—chūsei Watanabe-kaden." *Ritumeikan bungaku* 435–36.09 (1981): 960–74.

Kobayashi Tadao. "Jinkyōron." Vol. 8 of *Gunsho kaidai*, ed. Zoku gunsho ruijū kansei kai, 325–27. Tokyo: Heibonsha, 1971.

Kobayashi Taizō. *GoShirakawa Jōkō: "Emakimono" no chikara de bushi ni katta mikado.* Tokyo: PHP Kenkyūjo, 2012.

Kobayashi Yasuharu. "Saigyō to hangonjutsu saisetsu." In *Bukkyō bungaku kōsō*, ed. Imanari Genshō, 243–55. Tokyo: Shintensha, 1996.

Kōen. *Fusō ryakki.* Ed. Keizai Zasshisha. Vol. 6 of *KT*, 451–847. Tokyo: Keizai Zasshisha, 1897.

Kojima Noriyuki, Naoki Kōjirō, Nishimiya Kazutami, Kuranaka Susumu, and Mōri Masamori, eds. *Nihon shoki.* 3 vols. Vols. 2–4 of *SNKBZ*. Tokyo: Shogakukan, 1994.

Kokumin tosho kabushiki gaisha, ed. "Otogi zōshi." Vol. 19 of *Kōchū nihon bungaku taikei*, 5–648. Tokyo: Kokumin Tosho, 1925.

Kōma Miyoshi, trans. *Sankaikyō: Chūgoku kodai no shinwa sekai.* Tokyo: Heibonsha, 1994.

Komatsu Kazuhiko. "Biwa o meguru kaii no monogatari." In *Yōkai bunka kenkyū no saizensen*, ed. Komatsu Kazuhiko, 214–28. Tokyo: Serika Shobō, 2009.

Komatsu Kazuhiko. *Fuku no kami to binbōgami.* Tokyo: Chikuma Shobō, 1998.

Komatsu Kazuhiko. *Hyōrei shinkō ron.* Tokyo: Kōdansha, 1994.

Komatsu Kazuhiko. *Ijin · ikenie.* Vol. 7 of *Kaii no minzokugaku.* Tokyo: Kawade Shobō, 2001.

Komatsu Kazuhiko. "Ijinron—'ijin' kara 'tasha' e," 175–200. Vol. 3 of *Iwanami kōza gendai shakaigaku.* Tokyo: Iwanami Shoten, 1995.

Komatsu Kazuhiko. *Shinpen oni no tamatebako.* Tokyo: Fukutake Shoten, 1991.

Komatsu Kazuhiko. *Shuten Dōji no kubi.* Tokyo: Serika Shobō, 1997.

Komatsu Kazuhiko. "Supernatural Apparitions and Domestic Life in Japan." *Japan Foundation Newsletter* 27.1 (1999): 3.

Komatsu Kazuhiko. *Yōkaigaku shinkō.* Tokyo: Shōgakukan, 2000.

Komatsu Kazuhiko, ed. *Nihon yōkai taizen.* Tokyo: Shōgakukan, 2003.

Komatsu Kazuhiko, ed. *Oni.* Vol. 4 of *Kaii no minzokugaku.* Tokyo: Kawade Shobō, 2000.

Komatsu Kazuhiko and Naitō Masatoshi. *Oni ga tsukutta kuni Nihon.* Tokyo: Kōbunsha, 1990.

Komatsu Kazuhiko and Tokuda Kazuo. "Taidan Muromachi no yōkai—tsukumogami, oni, tengu, kitsune to tanuki." *Kokubungaku kaishaku to kyōzai no kenkyū* 50.10 (2005): 6–33.

Komatsu Shigemi, ed. *Hikohohodemi no Mikoto emaki, Urashima myōjin engi.* Vol. 22 of *NET*. Tokyo: Chūō Kōronsha, 1979.

Komatsu Shigemi, ed. *Kibi daijin nittō emaki.* Vol. 3 of *NET*. Tokyo: Chūō Kōronsha, 1977.

Komatsu Shigemi, ed. *Kōbō daishi gyōjō ekotoba.* Vols. 5 and 6 of *ZNET*. Tokyo: Chūō Kōronsha, 1982–83.

Komatsu Shigemi, ed. *Kuwanomidera engi, Dōjōji engi.* Vol. 13 of *ZNET*. Tokyo: Chūō Kōronsha, 1982.

Komatsu Shigemi and Akiyama Ken, eds. *Gaki zōshi, jigoku zōshi, yamai no sōshi, kusōshi emaki.* Vol. 7 of *NET*. Tokyo: Chūō Kōronsha, 1977.

Komatsu Shigemi, Kanazawa Hiroshi, and Kanzaki Mitsuharu, eds. *Nōe hōshi ekotoba, Fukutomi sōshi, hyakki yagyō emaki.* Vol. 25 of *NET*. Tokyo: Chūō Kōronsha, 1979.

Komatsu Shigemi and Murashige Yasushi, eds. *Haseo zōshi, Eshi no sōshi.* Vol. 11 of *NET*. Tokyo: Chūō Kōronsha, 1977.

Komatsu Shigemi, Nakano Genzō, and Matsubara Shigeru, eds. *Kitano Tenjin engi.* Vol. 21 of *NET*. Tokyo: Chūō Kōronsha, 1978.

Komatsu Shigemi, Ueno Kenji, Sakakibara Satoru, and Shimatani Hiroyuki, eds. *Tsuchigumo zōshi, Tengu zōshi, Ōeyama ekotoba*. Vol. 19 of *ZNET*. Tokyo: Chūō Kōronsha, 1984.

Kominami Ichirō. *Seiōbo to tanabata denshō*. Tokyo: Heibonsha, 1991.

Komine Kazuaki. "Hyakki yagyō emaki and Parody." *Ajia bunka kenkyū bessatsu* 16 (2007): 11–19.

Komine Kazuaki. "Kaidai: Kibidaijin monogatari." In *Daitōkyū kinen bunko zenpon sōkan: Chūko chūsei hen*, vol. 1, ed. Inoue Muneo, 14–18. Tokyo: Kyūko Shoin, 2007.

Komine Kazuaki. "Kibi no daijin nittō emaki to sono shūhen." *Rikkyō daigaku nihon bungaku* 86.7 (2001): 2–15.

Komine Kazuaki. *Setsuwa no mori: Chūsei no tengu kara isoppu made*. Tokyo: Iwanami Shoten, 2001.

Komine Kazuaki. "Supensā-bon *hyakki yagyō emaki* ni tsuite—kotobagaki wo chūshin ni." *Chūsei bungaku kenkyū* 23.08 (1997): 69–79.

Komine Kazuaki. "*Yabatai-shi*" *no nazo: Rekishi jojutsu to shite no miraiki*. Tokyo: Iwanami Shoten, 2003.

Komine Kazuaki. "Yōkai no hakubutsugaku." *Kokubungaku kaishaku to kyōzai no kenkyū* 41.4 (1996): 80–87.

Kondō Yoshihiro. *Nihon no oni: nihon bunka tankyū no shikaku*. Tokyo: Ōfūsha, 1975.

Konishi Mizue. "'Hachikazuki' to hisame—joseishi kara mita otogi zōshi." *Osaka Shoin Women's University, Faculty of Liberal Arts, Collected Essays* 41 (2004): 37–54.

Kose Natsuko. "Kentōshi wa Chūgoku de nani o shiteita no ka." In *Dai Kentōshi-ten: Heijō sento 1300-nen kinen*, ed. Nara Kokuritsu hakubutsukan, 296–99. Nara: Nara Kokuritsu hakubutsukan, 2010.

Koyama Hiroshi. *Kyōgenshū*. Vol. 43 of *NKBT*. Tokyo: Iwanami Shoten, 1961.

Koyama Hiroshi and Satō Ken'ichirō, eds. *Yōkyoku shū*. Vols. 58 and 59 of *SNKBZ*. Tokyo: Shōgakkan, 1997–98.

Koyama Toshihiko. *Genji monogatari o jiku to shita Ōchō bungaku sekai no kenkyū*. Tokyo: Ōfūsha, 1982.

Koyama Toshihiko. "Otogi zōshi ni miru joseizō—ōchō bungaku kara no juyō to henyō." *Kokubungaku: Kaishaku to kanshō* 50.11 (1985): 85–93.

Kubo Noritada. *Dōkyō no kamigami*. Tokyo: Hirakawa Shuppan, 1986.

Kubota Osamu. "Ryōbu shintō seiritsu no ichi kōsatsu." *Geirin* 26.1 (1975): 2–20.

Kuranishi Yūko. *Kibi Daijin nittō emaki: Shirarezaru kodai chūsei issen nenshi*. Tokyo: Bensei Shuppan, 2009.

Kurano Kenji and Takeda Yūkichi, eds. *Kojiki, Norito*. Vol. 1 of *NKBT*. Tokyo: Iwanami Shoten, 1958.

Kurihara Takashi. "Amewakahiko setsuwa to yūbe—'asobi' no kōzō o chūshin to shite." *Kokugakuin zasshi* 89.2 (1988): 58–70.

Kuroda Akira. *Chūsei setsuwa no bungakushiteki kankyō*. Osaka: Izumi Shoin, 1987.

Kuroda Akira. "Genpei jōsuiki to chūsei Nihongi." In *Chūsei setsuwa no bungakushiteki kankyō zoku*, 205–312. Osaka: Izumi Shoin, 1995.

Kuroda Akira. "Tsurugi no maki oboegaki—Tsuchigumo zōshi o megutte—." In *Taiheiki to sono shūhen*, ed. Hasegawa Tadashi, 311–29. Tokyo: Shintensha, 1994.

Kuroda Hideo. *Kibi Daijin nittō emaki no nazo*. Tokyo: Shōgakukan, 2005.

Kuroda Hideo. *Otogi zōshi*. Tokyo: Perikansha, 1990.

Kuroda Hideo. *Rekishi to shite no otogi zōshi*. Tokyo: Perikansha, 1996.

Kuroda Hideo. *Zōho sugata to shigusa no chūsei-shi*. Tokyo: Heibonsha, 2002.

Kuroda Taizō. "Ban Dainagon emaki kenkyū." In *Kokuhō Ban Dainagon emaki*, ed. Kuroda Taizō, Shirono Seiji, and Hayakawa Yasuhiro, 308–42. Tokyo: Chūō Kōron Bijutsu Shuppan, 2009.

Kuroda Taizō, Shirono Seiji, and Hayakawa Yasuhiro, eds. *Kokuhō Ban Dainagon emaki*. Tokyo: Chūō Kōron Bijutsu Shuppan, 2009.

Kuroita Katsumi, ed. *Azumakagami*. Vol. 33 of *KT*. Tokyo: Yoshikawa Kōbunkan, 1965.

Kuroita Katsumi, ed. *Nihon kiryaku*. 2 vols. Tokyo: Yoshikawa Kōbunkan, 2000.

Kuroki Kaori. "Yoshika zō no henshitsu to 'Tenjin engi'—oni no tsukeku o megutte." *Kokubungaku kō* 104.12 (1984): 10–19.

Kurosawa Kōzō. "Ryōiki no satsugyūsaishinkei setsuwa: Naraiwashima no hanashi ochūshin ni." *Dōshisha kokubungaku* 9.2 (1974): 1–13.

Kushida Ryōkō. *Shingon mikkyō seiritsu katei no kenkyū*. Tokyo: Sankibō Busshorin, 1964.

Kuwabara Hiroshi. *Otogizōshi*. Tokyo: Kōdansha, 1982.

Kuwata Tadachika. *Daimyō to otogishū*. Tokyo: Yūseidō, 1969.

Kyōgoku Natsuhiko. *Jorōgumo no kotowari*. Tokyo: Kōdansha, 1996.

Kyōgoku Natsuhiko. *The Summer of The Ubume*. Trans. Alexander O. Smith. New York: Vertical, 2009.

Kyōgoku Natsuhiko. *Ubume no natsu*. Tokyo: Kodansha, 1994.

Kyōgoku Natsuhiko and Tada Katsumi, eds. *Yōkai gahon · Kyōka hyakumonogatari*. Tokyo: Kokusho Kankōkai, 2008.

Kyōraku Mahoko. "Heian jidai no Josei to shukke sugata." In *Jendā no nihonshi*, ed. Wakita Haruko and B. Hanley, 27–58. Tokyo: Tokyo daigaku Shuppankai, 1995.

Kyoto daigaku bungakubu kokugogaku kokubungaku kenkyūshitsu, ed. *Tsukumogami*. Vol. 10 of *Kyoto daigaku zō Muromachi monogatari*, 231–82, 337–47. Kyoto: Rinsen Shoten, 2001.

Kyoto daigaku fuzoku toshokan, ed. "Tsukumogami." 2000. Accessed May 2008. http://edb.kulib.kyoto-u.ac.jp/exhibit/tsuroll/indexA.html and http://edb.kulib.kyoto-u.ac.jp/exhibit/tsuroll/indexB.html.

Kyoto furitsu sōgō shiryōkan, ed. *Tōji hyakugō monjo*. Vols. 1–2. Kyoto: Shibunkaku Shuppan, 2004–5.

Kyoto National Museum. "Kokuhō jūniten zō." In *Kaiga no ohanashi*. October 1998. http://www.kyohaku.go.jp/jp/dictio/data/kaiga/47juniten.htm.

Kyūsojin Hitaku. *Nihon kagaku taikei: Bekkan 4*. Tokyo: Kazama Shobō, 1980.

LaFleur, William. "Sattva-Enlightenment for Plants and Trees." In *Dharma Gaia: A Harvest of Essays in Buddhism and Ecology*, ed. William LaFleur, 136–44. Berkeley: Parallax, 1990.

Levy, Howard S., trans. *Translations from Po Chü-i's Collected Works*. Vol. 1. New York: Paragon Book Reprint Corp., 1971.

Li, HuoXong. "'Kiki' seiritsu ni okeru 'oni' to iu hyōgen oyobi sono hensen ni tsuite." *Minzokugaku kenkyū* 51.4 (1987): 417–31.

Li, Michelle Osterfeld. *Ambiguous Bodies: Reading the Grotesque in Japanese Setsuwa Tales*. Stanford, CA: Stanford University Press, 2009.

Lillehoj, Elizabeth. "Transfiguration: Man-Made Objects as Demons in Japanese Scrolls." *Asian Folklore Studies* 54.1 (1995): 7–34.

Mabuchi Kazuo, Kunisaki Fumimaro, and Inagaki Taiichi, eds. *Konjaku monogatarishū*, vols. 1–4. Vols. 35–38 of *SNKBZ*. Tokyo: Shōgakukan, 1999–2002.

Makino Tozuho, ed. "Otogi zōshi: moji to e to monogatari to." *Kokubungaku: kaishaku to kyōsai no kenkyū* 39.1 (1994): entire issue.

Marra, Michele. "The Buddhist Mythmaking of Defilement: Sacred Courtesans in Medieval Japan." *Journal of Asian Studies* 52.1 (1993): 149–65.

Mashimo Miyako and Yamashita Katsuaki. "Hoki shō." Vol. 3 of *Nihon koten gisho sōkan*, ed. Fukazawa Tōru, 163–95. Tokyo: Gendai Shinchōsha, 2004.

Mashimo Miyako and Yamashita Katsuaki. "Hokinaiden kin'u gyokuto shū (shō)." Vol. 3 of *Nihon koten gisho sōkan*, ed. Fukazawa Tōru, 99–162. Tokyo: Gendai Shinchōsha, 2004.

Mass, Jeffery P. *The Origins of Japan's Medieval World: Courtiers, Clerics, Warriors, and Peasants in the Fourteenth Century.* Stanford, CA: Stanford University Press, 1997.

Matsumoto Ryūshin. "Minkan setsuwa kei no Muromachi jidai monogatari— 'Hachikazuki' 'Izu Hakone no honchi' hoka—." *Shidō bunka ronshū* (October 1968): 1–62.

Matsumoto Ryūshin. "Otogi zōshi no honbun ni tsuite." *Shidō bunko ronshū* 2 (March 1963): 171–242.

Matsumoto Ryūshin, ed. *Muromachi jidai monogatari taisei*, 2 *hoi*, supp. vols. Tokyo: Kadokawa Shoten, 1987–88.

Matsumoto Ryūshin, ed. *Otogizōshi-shū.* Vol. 34 of *Shinchō nihon koten shūsei.* Tokyo: Shinchōsha, 1980.

Matsumoto Yoshio. "Tsuchigumo ron." *Shigaku* 25.4 (1952): 434–55.

Matsumoto Yuriko. "Chūsei ni okeru mamakotan no ichi kōsatsu—'Hanayo no hime' no seiritsu—." *Denshō bungaku kenkyū* 17 (February 1975): 26–48.

Matsunami Hisako and Iwase Hiroshi, eds. *Tanabata ·Tsuru no sōshi.* Vol. 54 of *Izumi Shoin eiin sōkan.* Osaka: Izumi Shoin, 1986.

Matsuo Ashie. "Heike monogatari Tsurugi no maki kaisetsu." In *Heike monogatari*, vol. 4, ed. Ichiko Teiji, 406–7. Vol. 45 of *Nihon no koten.* Tokyo: Shōgakkan, 1987.

"Matsurowanu monodomo no hanran—Ezo · yami no tsuchigumo · Kibi · Iwai." *Gendai no me* 23.1 (1982): 72–84.

Matsuzaki Hitoshi. "*Kanhasshū tsunagi-uma* kyakuchū yoteki." *Nihon bungaku kenkyū* 31 (1996): 59–70.

Matsuzaki Hitoshi. "*Kanhasshū tsunagi-uma* ron." *Kabuki: Kenkyū to hihyō* 19 (1997): 107–24.

Mayer, Fanny Hagin, ed. and trans. *The Yanagita Kunio Guide to Japanese Folk Tales.* Bloomington: University of Indiana Press, 1986.

McCormick, Melissa. "Tosa Mitsunobu's Ko-e: Forms and Function of Small-Format Handscrolls in the Muromachi Period (1333–1573)." PhD dissertation, Princeton University, Princeton, NJ, 2000.

McCullough, Helen Craig, trans. *Classical Japanese Prose: An Anthology.* Stanford, CA: Stanford University Press, 1990.

McCullough, Helen Craig, trans. *Kokin wakashū: The First Imperial Anthology of Japanese Poetry.* Stanford, CA: Stanford University Press, 1985.

McCullough, Helen Craig, trans. *Ōkagami: The Great Mirror.* Princeton, NJ: Princeton University Press, 1980.

McCullough, Helen Craig, trans. *The Taiheiki: A Chronicle of Medieval Japan.* New York: Columbia University Press, 1959.

McCullough, Helen Craig, trans. *A Tale of Flowering Fortunes: Annals of Japanese Aristocratic Life in the Heian Period.* Vol. 2. Stanford, CA: Stanford University Press, 1980.

McCullough, Helen Craig, trans. *Tales of Ise.* Stanford, CA: Stanford University Press, 1968.

Mibu Taishun. *Konkōmyōkyō.* Tokyo: Daizō Shuppan, 2006.

Mihara Yukihisa. "Oyasuteyama to fukuun." In *Nihon mukashibanashi jiten*, ed. Inada Kōji, Ōshima Tatehiko, Kawabata Toyohiko, Fukuda Akira, and Mihara Yukihisa, 170–71. Tokyo: Kōbundō, 1977.

Mihara Yukihisa. "Ubasute-yama." In *Nihon mukashibanashi jiten*, ed. Inada Kōji, Ōshima Tatehiko, Kawabata Toyohiko, Fukuda Akira, and Mihara Yukihisa, 110–11. Tokyo: Kōbundō, 1977.

Mills, D. E. "The Tale of the Mouse: Nezumi no sōshi." *MN* 34 (1979): 155–68.

Minamoto Akikane. *Kojidan, Zoku kojidan.* Ed. Kawabata Yoshiaki and Araki Hiroshi. Vol. 41 of *SNKBT.* Tokyo: Iwanami Shoten, 2005.

Minamoto Toshiyori. "Toshiyori zuinō." In *Karonshū*, ed. Hashimoto Fumio, Ariyoshi Tamotsu, and Fujihira Haruo, 13–245. Vol. 87 of *SNKBZ.* Tokyo: Shōgakkan, 2002.

Minemura Fumito. *Shin kokin wakashū*. Vol. 43 of *SNKBZ*. Tokyo: Shōgakukan, 1995.
Miner, Earl. *An Introduction to Japanese Court Poetry*. Stanford, CA: Stanford University Press, 1968.
Minobe Shigekatsu and Minobe Tomoko. *Shuten Dōji e o yomu: matsurowanu mono no jikū*. Tokyo: Miyai Shoten, 2009.
Mitamura Masako. "Shohyō Yang, Xiaojie cho *Oni no iru fūkei*—Haseo zōshi *ni miru shūsei*." *Nihon bungaku* 53.5 (2004): 78–80.
Mitani Eiichi. *Monogatari bungakushiron*. Tokyo: Yūseidō Shuppan, 1952.
Mitani Eiichi. *Monogatari-shi no kenkyū*. Tokyo: Yūseidō Shuppan, 1967.
Mitani Eiichi. *Nihon bungaku no minzokugakuteki kenkyū*. Tokyo: Yūseidō, 1960.
Miya Tsuguo. "Amewakahiko sōshi emaki." In *Tenjin engi emaki, Hachiman engi, Amewakahiko sōshi, Nezumi no sōshi, Bakemono sōshi, Utatane sōshi.*, ed. Shimada Shūjirō, 27–33. Bekkan 2 of *Shinshū nihon emakimono zenshū*. Tokyo: Kadokawa Shoten, 1981.
Miyake Hitoshi. *Shugendō: Essays on the Structure of Japanese Folk Religion*. Ann Arbor: Center for Japanese Studies, University of Michigan, 2001.
Miyata Noboku. "Kenshin no Foruku." In *Ijin • ikenie*. Vol. 7 of *Kaii no minzokugaku*, ed. Komatsu Kazuhiko, 78–110. Tokyo: Kawade Shobō, 2001.
Miyata Yoshihiko. *Kibi no Makibi*. Tokyo: Yoshikawa Kōbunkan, 1961.
Miyazaki Kazue, ed. *Kunisaki hantō no mukashibanashi*. Tokyo: Miyai Shoten, 1969.
Mizuno Yū. *Nyūmon kofudoki*, vol. 2. Tokyo: Yūzankaku, 1987.
Mizuo Hiroshi. *Jaki no saga*. Kyoto: Tankō Shinsha, 1967.
Mizuta Noriko. "Yamauba no yume." In *Yamauba tachi no monogatari josei no genkei to katarinaoshi*, ed. Mizuta Noriko and Kitada Sachie, 7–37. Tokyo: Gakugei Shorin, 2002.
Momo Hiroyuki. "Uwanari uchi kō." *Nihon rekishi* 35.04 (1951): 42–44.
Moore, Jean. "*Senjushō*: Buddhist Tales of Renunciation." *MN* 41.2 (1986): 127–74.
Morita Ryūsen. *Shingon mikkyō no honshitsu*. Kyoto: Rinsen Shoten, 1983.
Moriya Takeshi. *Chūsei geinō no genzō*. Kyoto: Tankō-sha, 1985.
Morosawa Yōko. *Wawashii onnatachi: kyōgen, otogi zōshi ni miru shominzō*. Tokyo: Sanseidō, 1972.
Morris, Ivan, trans. *As I Crossed a Bridge of Dreams: Recollections of A Woman in Eleventh-Century Japan*. New York: Dial, 1971.
Morse, Anne Nishimura, Sarah E. Thompson, Joe Earle, and Rachel Saunders. *MFA Highlights: Arts of Japan*. Boston: Museum of Fine Arts Publications, 2008.
Motoki Yasuo. *Minamoto no Mitsunaka, Yorimitsu: sesshō hōitsu, chōka no shugo*. Kyōto-shi: Mineruva Shobō, 2004.
Mulhern, Chieko Irie. "Analysis of Cinderella Motifs, Italian and Japanese." *Asian Folklore Studies* 44.1 (1985): 1–37.
Mulhern, Chieko Irie. "Cinderella and the Jesuits: An *otogizōshi* Cycle as Christian Literature." *MN* 34.4 (1979): 409–47.
Mulhern, Chieko Irie. "Otogi-zōshi: Short Stories of the Muromachi Period." *MN* 29.2 (1974): 180–98.
Murai Shōsuke. *Higashi Asia no naka no Nihon bunka*. Tokyo: Hōsō daigaku kyōiku shinkōkai, 2005.
Murakami Manabu, ed. *Chūsei shintō monogatari*. Vol. 2 of *Shintō taikei: Bungaku hen*. Tokyo: Shintō taikei hensan kai, 1989.
Murasaki Shikibu. *Genji monogatari*, vol. 2. Ed. Yamagishi Tokuhei. Vol. 15 of *NKBT*. Tokyo: Iwanami Shoten, 1959.
Murasaki Shikibu. *Genji monogatari*, vol. 2. Ed. Abe Akio, Imai Geni, Akiyama Ken, and Suzuki Hideo. Vol. 21 of *SNKBZ*. Tokyo: Shōgakukan, 1995.
Murasaki Shikibu. *The Tale of Genji*. Trans. Royall Tyler. New York: Penguin Books, 2001.

Murashige Yasushi. "'Haseo zōshi' no seiritsu to sakufū." In *Haseo zōshi, Eshi no sōshi*, ed. Komatsu Shigemi and Murashige Yasushi, 74–89. Vol. 11 of *NET*. Tokyo: Chūō Kōronsha, 1977.

Murayama Shūichi. "Kyūtei onmyōdō no seiritsu." In *Engi tenryaku jidai no kenkyū*, ed. Kodaigaku Kyōkai, 359–86. Tokyo: Yoshikawa Kōbunkan, 1969.

Murayama Shūichi. *Nihon onmyōdō-shi sōsetsu*. Tokyo: Hanawa Shobō, 1981.

Murei Hitoshi. "Ryōbu shintō." *Shintō shi kenkyū* 47.3–4 (1999): 174–89.

Muroki Yatarō. *Katarimono no kenkyū*. Tokyo: Kazama Shobō, 1970.

Muroki Yatarō. *Kinpira jōruri shōhon shū*, vol. 1. Tokyo: Kadokawa Shoten, 1966.

Nagafuji Yasushi. *Fudoki no sekai to Nihon no kodai*. Tokyo: Yamato Shobō, 1991.

Nagafuji Yasushi. "'Hizen Fudoki' no san'yakakai—tsuchigumo densetsu o chūshin ni." *Bungei kenkyū* 104 (2008): 1–17.

Nagahara Keiji. "Joseishi ni okeru Nanbokuchō · Muromachi ki." Vol. 2 of *Nihon joseishi*, ed. Joseishi sōgō kenkyū-kai, 137–70. Tokyo: Tokyo daigaku Shuppankai, 1982.

Nagahara Shinobu. "'Ubasute' ni okeru shiseikan." *Kokubungaku kaishaku to kanshō* 69.9 (2004): 90–95.

Nagai Kumiko. "Otōto no ōken: *Hikohohodemi no mikoto emaki* seisaku haikei-ron Oboegaki." *Hikaku bungaku bunka ronshū* 18 (2001): 75–84.

Nagai Yoshinori, ed. *Hasedera genki*. Tokyo: Shintensha, 1978.

Nagasaka Kaneo, ed. *Nihon emakimono shūsei*, vol. 2. Tokyo: Yūzankaku, 1929.

Naitō Masatoshi. "Oni no monogatari ni natta kodai tōhoku shinryaku—'Tamura sandaiki' to 'Tamura no sōshi.'" *Tōhokugaku* 9 (2003): 338–64.

Nakada Norio, ed. *Nihon ryōiki*. Vol. 10 of *SNKBZ*. Tokyo: Shōgakukan, 1995.

Nakai Yuki. "Nyōbō kotoba to kango—'Oyudono no ue no nikki' no buntai ni kansuru ichi Kōsatsu." *Josei shigaku* 4 (July 1994): 72–78.

Nakajima Etsuji. *Gukanshō zenchūkai*. Tokyo: Yūseidō, 1969.

Nakamura Kyoko Motomochi. *Miraculous Stories from the Japanese Buddhist Tradition*. By Keikai. Cambridge: Harvard University Press, 1973. Rpt. Surrey: Curzon, 1997.

Nakamura Shōhachi. *Nihon onmyōdō-sho no kenkyū*. Tokyo: Kyūko Shoin, 1985.

Nakao Masaki. "Studies on the Zoku-honcho-ojo-den." *Journal of Indian and Buddhist Studies* 29.1 (1980): 361–64.

Nakayama Tadachika. *Sankaiki*. 3 vols. Kyoto: Rinsen Shoten, 1965.

Nakazawa Shin'ichi. "Yōkaiga to hakubutugaku." Vol. 2 of *Kaii minzokugaku*, ed. Komatsu Kazuhiko, 79–86. Tokyo: Kawade Shobō, 2000.

Napier, Susan. *Anime from Akira to Howl's Moving Castle: Experiencing Contemporary Japanese Animation*. New York: Palgrave, 2001.

Napier, Susan. *The Fantastic in Modern Japanese Literature: The Subversion of Modernity*. New York: Routledge, 1996.

Nara ehon kokusai kenkyū kaigi, ed. *Ogozi zōshi no sekai*. Tokyo: Sanseidō, 1982.

Nasu Seiryū. *Shingon mikkyō no kenkyū*. Kyoto: Hōzōkan, 1997.

National Institutes for Cultural Heritage, ed. "Tsuchigumo no Sōshi Emaki." In *E-Museum: National Treasures and Important Cultural Properties of National Museums, Japan*. No date given. Accessed January 12, 2013. http://www.emuseum.jp/detail/100257?x=&y= &s=&d_lang=en&s_lang=ja&word=%E5%9C%9F%E8%9C%98%E8%9B%9B% E8%8D%89%E7%B4%99&class=&title=&c_e=&region=&era=&cptype=&owner =&pos=1&num=1&mode=simple&century=.

Neumann, Erich. *Amōru to Pushike: josei no jiko jitsugen*. Trans. Tamatani Naomi and Inoue Hirotsugu. Tokyo: Kinokuniya Shoten, 1973.

Nichūreki. Ed. Maeda ikutokukai sonkeikaku bunko. 3 vols. Tokyo: Yagi Shoten, 1997–98.

Nihon Kokugo Daijiten Dainiban Henshūiinkai, ed. "Shūto iri." Vol. 6 of *Nihon kokugo daijiten*. Tokyo: Shōgakkan, 2001 [1979].

Nishida Naoki. *Ōjōyōshū emaki: Shishō to e no kenkyū.* Osaka: Izumi Shoin, 2000.

Nishio Kōichi, ed. *Senjūshō.* Tokyo: Iwanami Shoten, 1970.

Nishio Kōichi and Kobayashi Yasuharu, eds. *Kokon chomonjū.* Tokyo: Shinchōsha, 1983.

Nishioka Hideo and W. Egbert Schenck. "An Outline of Theories Concerning the Prehistoric People of Japan." *American Anthropologist,* New Series 39.1 (January–March 1937): 23–33.

Nishizawa Shigejirō. *Obasuteyama: kojitsu to bungaku.* Nagano: Shinanoji, 1973.

Noguchi Minoru. *Genji to Bantō bushi.* Tokyo: Yoshikawa Kōbunkan, 2007.

Nojiri Tadashi. "Yoki tenjin no rekishi to shinkō." In *Hatsuse ni masu wa Yoki no kamigaki: Yoki Tenman Jinja no hihō to shinzō,* ed. Nara Kokuritsu Hakubutsukan, Yoki Tenmangūsha, and Asahi Shinbunsha, 5–11. Nara: Nara Kokuritsu Hakubutsukan, 2011.

Nomura Hachiryō. *Muromachi jidai shōsetsu-ron.* Vol. 26 of *Monogatari bungaku kenkyū sōsho.* Tokyo: Kuresu Shuppan, 1999.

Nomura Jun'ichi. "Mukashibanashi to bungaku no aida." In *Mukashibanashi to bungaku.* Vol. 5 of *Nihon mukashibanashi kenkyū shūsei,* ed. Nomura Jun'ichi, 2–19. Tokyo: Meicho Shuppan, 1984.

Nozaki Noriko. "Kyōgen no onna to otoko—'Niku jūhachi' no baai." *Bungei tōkai* 9: 10–12.

Ōba Minako and Mizuta Noriko. *Taidan "yamauba" no iru fūkei.* Tokyo: Tabata Shoten, 1995.

Oboroya Hisashi. *Seiwa Genji.* Tokyo: Hanbai kyōikusha Shuppan sābisu, 1984.

Ōchi Yuriko. "Mukashibanashi no ichi mochīfu <kurayami no naka no tomoshibi> no imisuru mono—minkan bungei no bungeisei o megutte." *Mukashibanashi: kenkyū to shiryō* 6 (1977): 75–85.

Ōchi Yuriko. *Nihon no mamakobanashi no shinsō: Otogi zōshi to mukashibanashi.* Tokyo: Miyai Shoten, 2005.

Ōchi Yuriko. "Ubakawagata setsuwa to Muromachi jidai monogatari." *Mukashibanashi: kenkyū to shiryō* 5 (1976): 93–121.

Ōchi Yuriko. "Ubakawakei mamako-banashi no isō." Vol. 4 of *Nihon mukashibanashi kenkyū shūsei,* ed. Fukura Akira, 325–52. Tokyo: Meicho Shuppan, 1984.

Ōe Masafusa. *Gōdanshō.* Ed. Gotō Akio. In *Gōdanshō, Chūgaishō, Fukego.* Vol. 32 of *SNKBT,* ed. Gotō Akio, Ikegami Jun'ichi, and Yamane Taisuke, 1–254. Tokyo: Iwanami Shoten, 1997.

Ōe Masafusa. "Honchō shinsen den." In *Nihon koten zensho,* ed. Kawaguchi Hisao, 275–396. Tokyo: Asahi Shinbunsha, 1967.

Ōhashi Waka. "*Hasedera genki* yori mita *Kibi daijin nittō emaki.*" *Jissen kokubungaku* 31.3 (1987): 126–36.

Okada Keisuke. "'Hanayo no hime' to minkan denshō." *Nihon bungaku* 26.2 (1977): 63–71.

Okada Keisuke. "'Hanayo no hime' to ubagoromo." *Teikyō daigaku bungaku kiyō: Kokugo kokubungaku* 13.10 (1981): 171–84.

Okada Keisuke. "Otogi zōshi no bukkyō shisō to minkan denshō—'Hachi kazuki,' 'Hanayo no hime,' 'Uhakawa' nit suite." *Kokugo kokubungaku ronkyū* 8 (1976): 145–64.

Okami Masao. "(Zadankai) Otogi Zoshi no sekai." *Bungaku* 44 (1976): 121–48.

Okamura Yumi. "Hachi ya ubakawa no imi nit suite—otogi zōshi 'Hachi kazuki,' 'Ubakawa,' 'Hanayo no hime' o chūshin ni—." *Koten bungaku kenkyū* 1 (November 1992): 32–38.

Okiura Kazuteru. "Nihon rettō no senjūmin · tsuchigumo—sono denshō no chi o aruku." *Kanagawa daigaku hyōron* 42 (2002): 30–52.

Okudaira Hideo. *Otogi zōshi emaki.* Tokyo: Kadokawa Shoten, 1982.

Orikuchi Shinobu. "Haru kuru oni." Vol. 17 of *Orikuchi Shinobu zenshū,* ed. Orikuchi Shinobu zenshū kankōkai, 123–41. Tokyo: Chūō Kōronsha, 1996.

Orikuchi Shinobu. "Okina no hassei." Vol. 2 of *Orikuchi Shinobu zenshū*, ed. Orikuchi Shinobu zenshū kankōkai, 348–88. Tokyo: Chūō kōronsha, 1995.

Orikuchi Shinobu. "Oni no hanashi." Vol. 3 of *Orikuchi Shinobu zenshū*, ed. Orikuchi Shinobu zenshū kankōkai, 9–26. Tokyo: Chūō Kōronsha, 1995.

Orikuchi Shinobu. "Shinodazuma no hanashi." Vol. 2 of *Orikuchi Shinobu zenshū*, ed. Orikuchi Shinobu zenshū kankōkai, 253–92. Tokyo: Chūō Kōronsha, 1995.

Ōshima Tatehiko. "Obasute no denshō." *Nihon bungaku bunka* 1 (2001): 2–18.

Ōshima Tatehiko. "Ubasuteyama no mukashibanashi to densetsu." In *Ronsan setsuwa to setsuwa bungaku*, ed. Mitani Eiichi, Kunisaki Fumimaro, and Kubota Jun, 479–522. Tokyo: Kazama Shoin, 1979.

Ōshima Tatehiko. "Yamauba to Kintarō." In *Tenmei bungaku*, ed. Hamada Giichirō, 33–53. Tokyo: Tokyodo Shuppan, 1979.

Ōshima Tatehiko, ed. *Otogizōshi-shū*. Vol. 36 of *NKBZ*. Tokyo: Shōgakukan, 1974.

Ōshima Tatehiko and Watari Kōji. *Muromachi monogatari siōshishū*. Vol. 63 of *NKBZ*. Tokyo: Shōgakukan, 2002.

Ōshima Yukio, Kobayashi Shōjirō, and Mayumi Tsunetada. *Tawara Tōta monogatari emaki*. Tokyo: Benseisha Shuppan, 2006.

Ōsumi Kazuo. *Chūsei shintō ron*. Vol. 19 of *NST*. Tokyo: Iwanami Shoten, 1977.

Ōsumi Kazuo and Nishiguchi Junko, eds. *Ama to amadera*. Vol. 2 of *Sirizu josei to bukkyō*. Tokyo: Heibonsha, 1989.

Ōtsuki Chifuyu. " 'Amewakahiko sōshi' chōbun kei tekusuto kaigaka ni okeru zuyō no tenkai katei." *Nara ehon · emaki kenkyū* 1.09 (2003): 1–26.

Ōtsuki Chifuyu. " 'Amewakahiko sōshi' kaigaka no tenkai katei—akahi bunko kyūzōbon o chūshin ni." *Bijutsushi kenkyū* 39 (2001): 65–84.

Ōtsuki Chifuyu. " 'Amewakahiko sōshi' shoki chōbun kei shohon keitō no saikō." *Bijutsushi kenkyū* 44 (2006): 23–42.

Ōwa Iwao. *Oni to tennō*. Tokyo: Hakusuisha, 1992.

Owada Tetsuo. *Imagawa Yoshimoto*. Kyoto: Mineruva Shobō, 2004.

Ōyama Kōjun. "Ryōbu shintō ron." *Mikkyōgaku* 9.11 (1972): 47–64.

Oyamachō-shi: Genshi kodai chūsei shiryō-hen, vol. 1. Ed. Oyamachō-shi hensan senmon iinkai. Shizuoka: Oyamachō, 1990.

Oyler, Elizabeth. "The *Nue* and Other Monsters in *Heike* Monogatari." *Harvard Journal of Asiatic Studies* 68.2 (December 2008): 1–32.

Ozawa Masao and Matsuda Shigeho, eds. *Kokin wakashū*. Vol. 11 of *SNKBZ*. Tokyo: Shōgakukan, 1994.

Philippi, Donald D., trans. *Kojiki*. Princeton, NJ: Princeton University Press, 1969.

Plutschow, Herbert. *Matsuri: The Festivals of Japan*. Surrey: Japan Library, 1996.

Putzar, Edward D. "The Tale of Monkey Genji: Sarugenji-zōshi." *MN* 18 (1963): 286–312.

Quinn, Shelley Fenno. *Developing Zeami: The Noh Actor's Attunement in Practice*. Honolulu: University of Hawaii Press, 2005.

Rambelli, Fabio. *Buddhist Materiality: A Cultural History of Objects in Japanese Buddhism*. Stanford, CA: Stanford University Press, 2007.

Reider, Noriko T. "Animating Objects: *Tsukumogami ki* and the Medieval Illustration of Shingon Truth." *Japanese Journal of Religious Studies* 36.2 (2009): 232–57.

Reider, Noriko T. " 'Hanayo no hime,' 'Blossom Princess': A Late Medieval Stepdaughter Story and Provincial Customs." *Asian Ethnology* 70.1 (2011): 59–80.

Reider, Noriko T. *Japanese Demon Lore: Oni, from Ancient Times to the Present*. Logan: Utah State University Press, 2010.

Reider, Noriko T. "Ōeyama Shuten Dōji: A Voice of Other and Carnivalesque." *Japanese Studies* 28.3 (2008): 383–94.

Reider, Noriko T. "Shuten Dōji: Drunken Demon." *Asian Folklore Studies* 64 (2005): 207–31.

Reider, Noriko T. "*Tsukumogami ki*: The Record of Tool Specters." *Japanese Journal of Religious Studies* supplement 36.2 (2009). [Online-only supplement: 1–19]. http://www.Nanzan-u.ac.jp/SHUBUNKEN/publications/jjrs/jjrsMain.htm.

Reider, Noriko T. "Yamauba: Representation of the Japanese Mountain Witch in the Muromachi and Edo Periods." *International Journal of Asiatic Studies* 2.2 (July 2005): 239–64.

Reischauer, A. K. "Genshin's Ojo Yoshu: Collected Essays on Birth into Paradise." *Transactions of The Asiatic Soceity of Japan,* second series 7 (1930): 16–98.

Rimer, Thomas J., and Jonathan Chaves, trans. *Japanese and Chinese Poems to Sing: The Wakan rōeishū.* New York: Columbia University Press, 1997.

Robinson, Richard H., and Willard L. Johnson. *The Buddhist Religion,* 4th ed. Belmont, CA: Wadsworth, 1997.

Rodd, Laurel Rasplica, trans. *Kokinshū: A Collection of Poems Ancient and Modern.* Princeton, NJ: Princeton University Press, 1984.

Rubins, Karen. "Tsuchigumo." In *The Mammoth Book of Best New Manga,* vol. 2, ed. ILYA, 163–84. Comic book. New York: Carroll and Graf, 2007.

Ruch, Barbara, ed. *Engendering Faith: Women and Buddhism in Premodern Japan.* Ann Arbor: University of Michigan Press, 2002.

Ruch, Barbara. "Kumakusu to otogi zōshi, soshite jendaa." *Otogi zōshi: moji to e to monogatari to. Kokubungaku kaishaku to kyōsai no kenkyū* 39.1 (1994): 30–35.

Ruch, Barbara. "Medieval Jongleurs and the Making of a National Literature." In *Japan in the Muromachi Age,* ed. John W. Hall and Toyoda Takeshi, 279–309. Berkeley: University of California Press, 1977.

Ruch, Barbara. *Mō hitotsu no chūseizō: bikuni, otogi-zōshi, raisei.* Kyoto: Shibunkaku, 1991.

Ruch, Barbara. "Nara ehon to kisen bungaku." In *Ogozi zōshi no sekai,* ed. Nara ehon kokusai kenkyū kaigi, 17–29. Tokyo: Sanseidō, 1982.

Ruch, Barbara. "Transformation of a Heroine: Yokobue in Literature and History." In *Currents in Japanese Culture,* ed. Amy Vladeck Heinrich, 99–116. New York: Columbia University Press, 1997.

Ruch, Barbara. *Zaigai nara ehon.* Tokyo: Kadokawa shoten, 1981.

Ryūtei Tanekazu. *Shiranui monogatari.* 3 vols. Ed. Takada Mamoru. Tokyo: Kokusho Kankōkai, 2006.

Sadakata Akira. *Buddhist Cosmology: Philosophy and Origins.* Trans. Gaynor Sekimori. Tokyo: Kōsei Shuppan, 1997.

Sadler, A. L. "The Heike Monogatari." *Transactions of The Asiatic Society of Japan* 46.2 (1918): 1–278; 49.1 (1921): 1–354.

Saeki Junko. "Otogi zōshi ni okeru danjo kankei." In vol. 3 of *Onna to otoko no jikvū: Nihon joseishi saikō,* ed. Okano Haruko, 379–89. Tokyo: Fujiwara Shoten, 1996.

Sakakibara Kunihiko, Kazuyoshi Fujikake, and Kiyoshi Tsukahara eds. *Otogi zōshi sōsakuin.* Tokyo: Kasama Shoin, 1988.

Sakakibara Satoru. "*Ōeyama ekotoba* shōkai." In *Tsuchigumo zōshi, Tengu sōshi, Ōeyama ekotoba,* ed. Komatsu Shigemi, 144–60. Vol. 19 of *ZNET.* Tokyo: Chūō Kōronsha, 1984.

Sakakibara Satoru. "Suntory bijutsukan-bon 'Shuten Dōji emaki' o megutte." *Kokka* 1076 (1983): 7–26; 1077 (1983): 33–56.

Sakamoto Tarō, Ienaga Saburō, Inoue Mitsusada, and Ōno Susumu, eds. *Nihon shoki,* vols. 1 and 2. Vols. 67 and 68 of *NKBT.* Tokyo: Iwanami Shoten, 1967 and 1965.

Sakurai Tokutarō, Hagiwara Tatsuo, and Miyata Noboru, eds. "Kitano tenjin engi." In *Jisha engi,* 141–68. Vol. 20 of *NST.* Tokyo: Iwanami Shoten, 1975.

Sanari Kentarō. *Yōkyoku taikan,* vol. 3. Tokyo: Meiji Shoin, 1931.

Sanjōnishi Sanetaka. *Sanetaka kōki*, vol. 2. Ed. Takahashi Ryūzō. Tokyo: Zoku gunsho ruijū kanseikai, 1931.

Sasaki Kaoru. *Chūsei kokka to shūkyōkōzō: Taisei bukkyō to taiseigai bukkyō no sōkoku.* Tokyo: Yoshikawa Kōbunkan, 1988.

Sasaki Kizen. *Kikimimi no sōshi.* Tokyo: Chikuma Shobō, 1964.

Sasaki Kōji. "Otogi zōshi 'Komachi sōshi' ron." *Kokubungaku: kaishaku to kanshō* 60.8 (1995): 60–65.

Satake Akihiro. *Kogo zatsudan.* Tokyo: Iwanami Shoten, 1986.

Satake Akihiro. *Shuten Dōji ibun.* Tokyo: Heibonsha, 1977.

Satake Akihiro, ed. *Kokinshū chū: Kyōto daigaku zō.* Kyōto: Rinsen Shoten, 1984.

Sato, Hiroaki. *Legends of The Samurai.* New York: Overlook, 1995.

Satō Yukiko. "'Shiranui-tan' no tsuchigumo nit suite." *Kokugo to kokubungaku* 83.5 (2006): 29–38.

Schumacher, Mark. "Hachibushū." In *A to Z Photo Dictionary: Japanese Buddhist Statuary: Gods, Goddesses, Shinto Kami, Creatures and Demons.* 1995–2014. http://www.onmark productions.com/html/hachi-bushu.shtml.

Schumacher, Mark. "Jūnishin." In *A to Z Photo Dictionary: Japanese Buddhist Statuary: Gods, Goddesses, Shinto Kami, Creatures and Demons.* 1995–2014. http://www.onmark productions.com/html/12-devas.shtml.

Schumacher, Mark. "Rokudō." In *A to Z Photo Dictionary: Japanese Buddhist Statuary: Gods, Goddesses, Shinto Kami, Creatures and Demons.* 1995–2014. http://www.onmark productions.com/html/six-states.shtml.

Schumacher, Mark. "Shitennō." In *A to Z Photo Dictionary: Japanese Buddhist Statuary: Gods, Goddesses, Shinto Kami, Creatures and Demons.* 1995–2014. http://www.onmark productions.com/html/shitenno.shtml.

Seki Keigo. *Folktales of Japan.* Chicago: University of Chicago Press, 1963.

Seki Keigo. *Mukashibanashi to waraibanashi.* Vol. 8 of *Minzoku mingei sōsho.* Tokyo: Iwasaki Bijutsusha, 1966.

Seki Keigo. *Nihon mukashibanashi shūsei.* 6 vols. Tokyo: Kadokawa Shoten, 1950–58.

Seki Keigo. "Types of Japanese Folktales." *Asian Folklore Studies* 25.2 (1966): 1–220.

Senshū University. "Tanabata no sōshi." *Senshū University: Library and Facilities.* Accessed March 29, 2014. http://www.senshu-u.ac.jp/libif/lib/gallery/w07_tanabata.html#suHeader.

Setsuwa kenkyūkai, ed. *Meihōki no kenkyū*, vol 1. Tokyo: Benseisha Shuppan, 1999.

Shiba Kayono. "Fujiwara no Hōshō kō—sono 2 men-sei to setsuwa keisei." *Ochanomizu joshi daigaku jinbun kagaku kiyō* 46.3 (1993): 85–97.

Shiba Keiko. "Josei tachi no kaita edo zenki no joshi kyōkunsho." *Edoki onna kō* 2 (1991): 22–41; 3 (1992): 4–24.

Shibata Hōsei. "*Tsukumogami* kaidai." In vol. 10 of *Kyoto daigaku zō muromachi monogatari*, ed. Kyoto daigaku kokugogaku kokubungaku kenkyūshitsu, 392–400. Kyoto: Rinsen Shoten, 2001.

Shibata Minoru. *Chūsei shomin shinkō no kenkyū.* Tokyo: Kadokawa Shoten, 1966.

Shibusawa Tatsuhiko. *Shikō no monshōgaku.* Tokyo: Kawade shobō shinsha, 1977.

Shillony, Ben-Ami. *Enigma of The Emperors: Sacred Subservience in Japanese History.* Kent, GB: Global Oriental, 2005.

Shimada Shūjirō. *Tenjin engi emaki, Hachiman engi, Amewakahiko sōshi, Nezumi no sōshi, Bakemono sōshi, Utatane sōshi.* Bekkan 2 of *Shinshū nihon emakimono zenshū.* Tokyo: Kadokawa Shoten, 1981.

Shimauchi Keiji. *Otogizōshi no seishinshi.* Tokyo: Perikansha, 1988.

Shimazu Hisamoto. *Rashōmon no oni.* Tokyo: Heibonsha, 1975.

Shimazu Hisamoto, ed. "Hanayo no hime." In *Otogi zōshi*, 55–98. Tokyo: Iwanami Shoten, 1936.

Shimura Midori. "Heian jidai josei no mana kanseki no gakushū—jūisseiki goro ochūshin ni." In *Kyōiku to shisō*. Vol. 8 of *Nihon joseishi ronshū*, ed. Sōgō joseishi kenkyūkai, 111–39. Tokyo: Yoshikawa Kōbunkan, 1998.

Shinbo Tōru. "Tsukumogami emaki." In *Otogi zōshi emaki*, ed. Okudaira Hideo, 87–88. Tokyo: Kadokawa Shoten, 1982.

Shinbo Tōru and Kaneko Keizō. *Yōkai emaki*. Tokyo: Mainichi Shinbunsha, 1978.

Shinoda, Chiwaki. *Ryūjashin to hataorihime: Bunmei o orinasu mukashibanashi no onnatachi*. Kyoto: Jinbun Shoin, 1997.

Shirane, Haruo, ed. *Traditional Japanese Literature: An Anthology, Beginnings to 1600*. New York: Columbia University Press, 2007.

Shirane, Haruo, ed., and Burton Watson, trans. *The Demon at Agi Bridge and Other Japanese Tales*. New York: Columbia University Press, 2011.

Shun, Ai. "Chōsen hyakki yagyō shō (dai jūichi wa) tsukumogami." *Tōitsu hyōron* 431.7 (2001): 100–103.

"Shuten dōji-e jō, chū, ge." *Nihon bijutsu kyōkai hōkoku* supplement 176 (1904): 1–20; supplement 177 (1904): 21–29.

Skord, Virginia Susan. "Monogusa Taro: From Rags to Riches and Beyond." *MN* 44.2 (Summer 1989): 171–98.

Skord, Virginia Susan. *Tales of Tears and Laughter: Short Fiction of Medieval Japan*. Honolulu: University of Hawaii Press, 1991.

Sonshun. *Hokekyō jurin shūyōshō*, vol. 4. Kyoto: Rinsen Shoten, 1991.

"Spirit of a Spider." In *Nōgaku: Japanese Nō Plays*., ed. and trans. Beatrice Lane Suzuki, 87–92. London: John Murray, 1932.

Steven, Chigusa. "Hachikazuki: A Muromachi Short Story." *MN* 32 (1977): 303–31.

Stone, Jacqueline I. *Original Enlightenment and the Transformation of Medieval Japanese Buddhism*. Honolulu: University of Hawaii Press, 1999.

Sudō Maki. "'Tsuchigumo zōshi' seiritsu no haikei o megutte." *Setsuwa bungaku kenkyū* 37.6 (2002): 62–80.

Sugano Hiroyuki. *Wakan rōei shū*. Vol. 19 of *SNKBZ*. Tokyo: Shōgakukan, 1999.

Sugawara no Takasue no musume. *Yowa no nezame*. Vol. 26 of *SNKBZ*, ed. Suzuki Kazuo. Tokyo: Shōgakukan, 1996.

Sugiura Minpei. "Machishū no mijuku to otogi zōshi no unmei—'Sasayaki take' to 'Menoto no sōshi.'" *Bungaku* 32.12 (1964): 1340–51.

Sugiura Minpei. *Sengoku ransei no bungaku*. Tokyo: Iwanami Shoten, 1965.

Suzuki, Beatrice Lane, ed. and trans. *Nōgaku: Japanese Nō Plays*. London: John Murray, 1932.

Tachibana Kenji and Katō Shizuko, eds. *Ōkagami*. Vol. 34 of *SNKBZ*. Tokyo: Shōgakukan, 1996.

Tachibana Ritsu. "Tōyō daigaku toshikan zō 'Amewakahiko' (kadai) shōkō." *Bungaku ronsō* 62.02 (1988): 108–25.

Tahara, Mildred M. *Tales of Yamato: A Tenth-Century Poem-Tale*. Honolulu: University Press of Hawaii, 1980.

Takagi Ichinosuke, Takagi Masakazu, Yoshikawa Kōjirō, and Ogawa Tamaki, eds. *Heike monogatari*. Vol. 32 of *NKBT*. Tokyo: Iwanami Shoten, 1959.

Takagi Masakazu. *Haku Kyoi*. 2 vols. Vols. 12 and 13 of *Chūgoku shijin senshū*. Tokyo: Iwanami Shoten, 1958.

Takagishi Teru. "'Amewakahiko sōshi emaki' to Muromachi Tosa-ha emaki no tenkai." *Setsuwa bungaku kenkyū* 46.7 (2011): 99–110.

Takahashi Mariko. "Otogi zōshi 'Hanayo no hime' to minkan shinkō—ubakawa, hachi, yamauba o chūshin ni." *Kokubun* 42 (March 1975): 22–32.

Takahashi Masaaki. *Bushi no seiritsu bushizō no sōshutsu*. Tokyo: Tokyo daigaku Shuppankai, 1999.

Takahashi Masaaki. *Shuten Dōji no tanjō: Mō hitotsu no nihon bunka.* Tokyo: Chūō Kōronsha, 1992.

Takahashi Rumiko. *Inuyasha.* 56 vols. Adapt. Gerald Jones; trans. Mari Morimoto. San Francisco, CA: VIZ Meida, 2003–11.

Takahashi Rumiko. *Inuyasha.* 56 vols. Tokyo: Shōgakukan, 1997–2009.

Takao Koishi. "Chūsei no jokunsho ni tsuite." *Kateika kyōiku* 28.6 (1954): 78–82.

Takasaki Fujihiko. "Fudō riyaku engi." In vol. 30 of *Shinshū nihon emaki zenshū,* ed. Takasaki Fujihiko and Minamoto Toyomune, 50–57. Tokyo: Kadokawa Shoten, 1980.

Takei Akio. *Kitano tenjin emaki o yomu.* Tokyo: Yoshikawa Kōbunkan, 2008.

Takeuchi, Melinda. "Kuniyoshi's Minamoto Raiko and the Earth Spider: Demon and Protest in Late Tokugawa Japan." *Ars Orientalis* 17 (1987): 5–38.

Takeya Yukie. *Fujisan no saijinron.* Tokyo: Iwata Shoin, 2006.

Takeya Yukie. *Fujisan no seishinshi: Naze Fujisan o sanpō ni egaku no ka.* Kanagawa: Seizansha, 1998.

Takigawa Seijirō. "Tsuchigumo to Takeru to Hayato to hito to." *Kokugakuin zasshi* 69.10 (1968): 33–36.

Takita Yōji, dir. *Onmyoji.* Perf. Nomura Mansai. Tōhō, 2001. Film.

Tanaka Chisei. "Ōbakuzan Manpukuji no susuharai nit suite." *Ōbaku bunka* 116 (1996): 123–27.

Tanaka Takako. *Gehō to aihō no chūsei.* Tokyo: Sunagoya Shobō, 1993.

Tanaka Takako. *Hyakki yagyō no mieru toshi.* Tokyo: Shin'yōsha, 1994.

Tanaka Takako. "Otogi zōshi no onnatachi—'jūban no monoarasoi' hoka." *Kokubungaku: kaishaku to kyōsai no kenkyū* 39.1 (1994): 82–87.

Tanaka Takako. *Seiai no nihon chūsei.* Tokyo: Yōsensha, 1997.

Tanaka Takako. "*Tsukumogami* to chūgoku bunken." In *Setsuwa bungaku to kanbungaku.* Vol. 14 of *Wakan hikaku bungaku sōsho,* ed. Wakan hikaku bungakkai, 199–214. Tokyo: Kyūko Shoin, 1994.

Tanaka Takako. *Zusetsu hyakki yagyō emaki o yomu.* Tokyo: Kawade Shobō Shinsha, 1999.

Tanigawa Ken'ichi. *Kajiya no haha.* Tokyo: Kawade Shobō Shinsha, 2005.

Taniguchi Katsunori. "Hokinaiden no shūkyō sekai." *Bukkyō daigaku daigakuin kiyō* 33.3 (2005): 33–48.

Taniguchi Kōsei. "Kibidaijin emaki—GoShirakawa-in seiki no kentōshi shinwa." In *Dai Kentōshi-ten: Heijō sento 1300-nen kinen,* ed. Nara Kokuritsu hakubutsukan, 270–75. Nara: Nara Kokuritsu hakubutsukan, 2010.

Terui Takeshi. Leaflet to DVD. Kanze Yoshimasa, dir. *Noh to hana no futaya: Noh Tsuchigumo, Kyōgen Kane no ne.* Perf. Kanze Yoshiyuki and Nomura Mansai. Tokyo: Japan Traditional Cultures Foundation, 2008.

Tochiyama Michiko. "'Ulalume' to Haseo sōshi to gōsei seimei Ulalume." *Osaka Ōtani daigaku eigo eibungaku kenkyū* 34 (2007): 19–37.

Todorov, Tzvetan. *The Fantastic: A Structural Approach to a Literary Genre.* Ithaca, NY: Cornell University Press, 1973.

Toelken, Barre. *The Dynamics of Folklore.* Logan: Utah State University Press, 1996.

Tōin Kinsada. *Sonpi bunmyaku.* 4 vols. Vols. 58–62 of *KT.* Tokyo: Yoshikawa Kōbunkan, 2007.

Tokoro Isao. *Miyoshi Kiyoyuki.* Tokyo: Yoshikawa Kōbunkan, 1970.

Tokuda Kazuo. "*Haseo zōshi emaki* to mukashibanashi *Hanataka ōgi*—'mori mukashibanashi' no ittan." In vol. 19 of *Mukashibanashi—Kenkyū to shiryō,* ed. Mukashibanashi gakkai, 11–24. Tokyo: Miyai Shoten, 1991.

Tokuda Kazuo. "Kitano Shatō no geinō—Chūsei kōki, kinsei shoki." *Geinō bunkashi* 4 (1981): 1–22.

Tokuda Kazuo. *Otogizōshi kenkyū.* Tokyo: Miyai Shoten, 1988.

Tokuda Kazuo. "*Sumiyoshi monogatari* zakki—Muromachi bungei no shiten kara." In *Shindō-bon Sumiyoshi monogatari no kenkyū*, ed. Kobayashi Kenji, Tokuda Kazuo, and Kikuchi Hitoshi, 385–405. Tokyo: Kasama Shoin, 1996.

Tokuda Kazuo, ed. *Otogi-zōshi hyakka ryōran*. Tokyo: Kasama Shoin, 2008.

Tokuda Kazuo, ed. *Otogizōshi jiten*. Tokyo: Tokyo-dō Shuppan, 2002.

Tokue Gensei. *Muromachi Geinōshi ronkō*. Tokyo: Miyai Shoten, 1984.

Tokyo Daigaku Shiryō Hensanjo, ed. *Dainihon kokiroku: Gaun nikkenroku*. Tokyo: Iwanami Shoten, 1961.

Tokyo kokuritsu hakubutsukan, Nagoya Boston bijubutsukan, Kyūshū kokuritsu hakubutsukan, Osaka shiritsu hakubutsukan, Boston bijutsukan, NHK, and NHK Puromōesdh, eds. *Bosuton Bijutsukan Nihon bijutsu no shihō*. Tokyo: NHK Puromōshon, 2012.

Tomohisa Takefumi. "Sumiyoshi Monogatari kara Otogi zōshi e." *Bungaku* 44 (1976): 1176–87.

Tōno Haruyuki. *Entōshisen: Higashi Ajia no nakade*. Tokyo: Asahi Shinbunsha, 1999.

Tonomura, Hitomi. "Coercive Sex in the Medieval Japanese Court: Lady Nijō's Memoir." *MN* 61.3 (2006): 283–338.

Torii Fumiko. *Kintarō no tanjō*. Tokyo: Bensei Shuppan, 2002.

Tsuchihashi Yutaka. *Nihongo ni saguru kodai shinkō: Fetishizumu kara shintō made*. Tokyo: Chūō Kōronsha, 1990.

Tsuda Sōkichi. *Bungaku ni arawaretaru waga kokumin shisō no kenkyū: Bushi bungaku no jidai*. Vol. 31 of *Tsuda Sōkichi zenshū*. Tokyo: Iwanami Shoten, 1966.

Tsuda Sōkichi. *Nihon koten no kenkyū*. Vol. 1 of *Tsuda Sōkichi zenshū*. Tokyo: Iwanami Shoten, 1963.

Tsujita Gōshi. "'Tsuna Kintoki' no kanōsei—Shimokeno-shi to Sakata-shi no hazama." *Koten isan* 53.9 (2003): 85–95.

Tsunoda Ryūsaku. *Sources of Japanese Tradition*. 2 vols. New York: Columbia University Press, 1964.

Tyler, Royall. *Granny Mountains: A Cycle of Nō Plays*. Ithaca, NY: Cornell University Press, 1978.

Tyler, Royall. *Japanese Tales*. New York: Pantheon Books, 1987.

Tyler, Royall. *The Tale of The Heike*. New York: Viking, 2012.

Uegaki Setsuya, ed. *Fudoki*. Vol. 5 of *SNKBZ*. Tokyo: Shogakukan, 1997.

Uekusa Nobukazu, ed. *"Sen to Chihiro no kamikakushi" o yomu 40 no me*. Tokyo: Kinema Jumpōsha, 2001.

Ueno Kenji. "'Tsuchigumo no sōshi' ni tsuite." In *Tsuchigumo zōshi, Tengu zōshi, Ōeyama eko-toba*. Vol. 19 of *ZNET*, ed. Komatsu Shigemi, Ueno Kenji, Sakakibara Satoru, and Shimatani Hiroyuki, 106–13. Tokyo: Chūō Kōronsha, 1984.

Umehara Takeshi. "Haseo no koi." In *Chūsei shōsetsushū*, 35–58. Tokyo: Shinchōsha, 1993.

Umehara Takeshi. "Haseo's Love." In *Lotus and Other Tales of Medieval Japan*, trans. Paul McCarthy, 35–54. North Clarendon, VT: Charles E. Tuttle, 1996.

Umezu Jirō. "Kaisetsu." Vol. 18 of *Nihon emakimono zenshū*, ed. Tanaka Ichimatsu, 3–22. Tokyo: Kadokawa Shoten, 1968.

Unno Kazutaka. "Ryōbu shintō ni okeru seirigakuteki chishiki." *Nihon kosho tsūshin* 906 (2005): 3–6.

Urabe Kanekata. *Shaku Nihongi*. In vol. 8 of *Shintei zōho Kokushi taikei*, ed. Kuroita Katsumi, 1–356. Tokyo: Yoshikawa Kōbunkan, 1965.

Ury Marian. "The Ōe Conversations" *MN* 48.3 (1993): 359–80.

Ury Marian, trans. "Stepmother Tales in Japan." *Children's Literature: Annual of The Modern Language Association Division on Children's Literature and the Children's Literature Association* 9 (1981): 61–72.

Ury Marian. *Tales of Times Now Past.* Ann Arbor: Center for Japanese Studies, University of Michigan, 1979.

Wada Hidematsu and Tokoro Isao. *Shintei kanshoku yōkai.* Tokyo: Kōdansha, 1983.

Wakao Itsuo. *Oni densetsu no kenkyū: kinkōshi no shiten kara.* Tokyo: Yamato Shobō, 1981.

Wakimoto Jūkurō. "Bungaku oyobi emaki to shite no Haseo zōshi." *Bijutsu kenkyū* 45 (1935): 409–21.

Wakita Haruko. *Chūsei ni ikiru onnatachi.* Tokyo: Iwanami Shoten, 1995.

Wakita Haruko. "Chūsei ni okeru seibetsu yakuwari buntan to joseikan." Vol. 2 of *Nihon joseishi*, ed. Joseishi sōgō kenkyū-kai, 65–102. Tokyo: Tokyo daigaku Shuppankai, 1982.

Wakita Haruko. *Nihon chūsei joseishi no kenkyū.* Tokyo: Tokyo daigaku Shuppan, 1992.

Wakita Haruko. *Women in Medieval Japan: Motherhood, Household Management and Sexuality.* Trans. Alison Tokita. Tokyo: University of Tokyo Press, 2006.

Waley, Arthur. *Translations from the Chinese.* New York: A. A. Knopf, 1941.

Walthall, Anne. *The Weak Body of A Useless Woman.* Chicago: University of Chicago Press, 1998.

Wang Zhenping. *Ambassadors from the Islands of Immortals: China-Japan Relations in the Han-Tang Period.* Honolulu: University of Hawaii Press, 2005.

Washio Junkei. *Kokubun tōhō bukkyō sōsho*, vol. 9. Tokyo: Meicho Fukyūkai, 1992 [1926].

Watanabe Tamotsu. "Tōkute Chikamatsu monogatari (7) tsuchigumo densetsu—Kako Norinobu sichihaka meguri." *Shinchō* 99.11 (2002): 336–45.

Watase Junko. "'Kumogiri' kō—tsuchigumo setsuwa no keisei to kanseki." *Koten isan* 53.9 (2003): 74–84.

Watson, Burton, trans. *Po Chü-i: Selected Poems.* New York: Columbia University Press, 2000.

Watson, Burton, trans. *The Essential Lotus: Selections from the Lotus Sutra.* New York: Columbia University Press, 2002.

Yamada Yoshio, Yamada Tadao, Yamada Hideo, and Yamada Toshio, eds. *Konjaku monogatarishū*, vol. 4. Vol. 25 of *NKBT.* Tokyo: Iwanami Shoten, 1962.

Yamaguchi Yoshinori and Kōnoshi Takamitsu, eds. *Kojiki.* Vol. 1 of *SNKBZ.* Tokyo: Shōgakukan, 1997.

Yamanaka Yutaka, Akiyama Ken, Ikeda Naotaka, and Fukuda Susumu, eds. *Eiga monogatari.* 3 vols. Vols. 31–33 of *SNKBZ.* Tokyo: Shōgakukan, 1995–98.

Yamashita Hiroaki. *Taiheiki.* 5 vols. Tokyo: Shinchōsha, 1977–88.

Yamashita Tarō. *Hokuō shinwa to Nihon shinwa.* Tokyo: Hokuhu Shuppan, 1991.

Yanagita Kunio. "Hito bashira to matsuura sayohime." In *Ijin • ikenie.* Vol. 7 of *Kaii no minzokugaku*, ed. Komatsu Kazuhiko, 9–27. Tokyo: Kawade Shobō, 2001.

Yanagita Kunio. *Nihon mukashibanashi meii.* Tokyo: Nihon Hōsōkyōkai Shuppan, 1971.

Yanagita Kunio. "Oyasute-yama." In vol. 21 of *Teihon Yanagita Kunio-shū*, 294–305. Tokyo: Chikuma Shobō, 1970. Rpt. of Tokyo: Asahi Shinbunsha, 1945.

Yanagita Kunio. "Yama no jinsei." Vol. 1 of *Shinpen Yanagita Kunio-shū.* Tokyo: Chikuma Shobō, 1978.

Yanagita Kunio and Ōmachi Tokuzō. *Kon'in shūzoku goi.* Tokyo: Kokusho Kankōkai, 1975.

Yanase Kiyoshi, Yashiro Kazuo, Matsubayashi Yasuaki, Shida Itaru, and Inui Yoshihisa, eds. *Shōmonki, Mutsuwa ki, Hōgen monogatari, Heiji monogatari.* Vol. 41 of *SNKBZ.* Tokyo: Shōgakukan, 2002.

Yang, Xiaojie. *Oni no iru kōkei: Haseo zōshi ni miru chūsei.* Tokyo: Kadokawa Shoten, 2002.

Yang, Xin. "The Ming Dynasty." In *Three Thousand Years of Chinese Painting*, ed. Richard Barnhard, 197–250. New Haven, CT: Yale University and Foreign Language Press, 1997.

Yasufuku Junko. "Amewakahiko monogatari to josei no kokoro no hattatsu." *Osaka kyōiku daigaku kiyō* 43.2 (1995): 251–58.

Yoden Mitsuru. "'Jūban no monoarasoi' oboegaki—senjūka no sesshu." *Shikoku daigaku kiyō* 6 (1996): 189–95.

Yokoi Kiyoshi and Gosukō-in. *Muromachi jidai no ichi kōzoku no shōgai: Kanmon nikki no sekai.* Tokyo: Kodansha, 2002.

Yokomichi Mario and Omote Akira, eds. *Yōkyokushū.* Vol. 41 of *NKBT.* Tokyo: Iwanami Shoten, 1963.

Yokota Takashi. "*Hasedera genki* no seiritsu nendai." *Nihon bungaku* (February 2010): 1–8.

Yokota Takashi. "Hasedera to Tenjin shinkō." In *Hatsuse ni masu wa Yoki no kamigaki: Yoki Tenman Jinja no hihō to shinzō,* ed. Nara Kokuritsu Hakubutsukan, Yoki Tenmangūsha, and Asahi Shinbunsha, 12–13. Nara: Nara Kokuritsu Hakubutsukan, 2011.

Yokouchi Hiroto. "Chōgen ni okeru Sō bunka—Nihon Bukkyō saisei no kokoromi." *Asia yūgaku* 122.5 (2009): 25–34.

Yokouchi Hiroto. *Nihon chūsei no Bukkyō to Higashi Ajia.* Tokyo: Hanawa Shobō, 2008.

Yokoyama Shigeru. *Kojōruri shōhon shū.* 10 vols. Tokyo: Kadokawa Shoten, 1964–82.

Yokoyama Shigeru and Matsumoto Ryūshin, eds. *Muromachi jidai monogatari taisei.* 13 vols. Tokyo: Kadokawa Shoten, 1973–85.

Yokoyama Tarō. "Noh *Tsuchigumo.*" In vol. 3 of *Chōjū chūgyo no bungakushi: Nihon koten no Shizenkan,* ed. Suzuki Ken'ichi, 173–94. Tokyo: Miyai Shoten, 2012.

Yoshida Atsuhiko. *Mukashibanashi no kōkogaku.* Tokyo: Chūō Kōronsha, 1992.

Yoshida Shūsaku. "Jingū kōgō denshō—Jungū kōgō to tsuchigumo, hashiro kumawashi." *Hikaku bunka* 2.3 (2005): 81–98.

Yoshida Wataru. "Tsukumogami emaki ni miru hijō jōbutsu gi no shisō." *Nenpō nihon shisōshi* 4.3 (2005): 58–60.

Yoshikawa Yūko. "Umare kiyomari no minkan setsuwa—kirō tan no shūkyō minzoku." *Setsuwa denshōgaku* 6.4 (1998): 117–36.

Yumemakura Baku. *Onmyōji.* Tokyo: Bungei Shunjū [bunko-bon], 1991 [1988].

Yumemakura Baku. *Onmyōji: namanari-hime.* Tokyo: Bungei Shunjū [bunko-bon], 2003 [2000].

Yumemakura Baku and Amano Yoshitaka. *Kitan sōshi. Asahi bunko.* Tokyo: Asahi Shinbunsha, 2006 [2001].

Zipes, Jack. *The Irresistible Fairy Tale: The Cultural and Social History of A Genre.* Princeton, NJ: Princeton University Press, 2012.

Zoku gunsho ruijū kanseikai, ed. *Gunsho kaidai,* vol. 8. Tokyo: Zoku gunsho ruijū kanseikai, 1981.

About the Author

Noriko T. Reider is professor of Japanese at Miami University, where her research focuses on the supernatural in Japanese literature. She is the author of *Japanese Demon Lore* and *Tales of The Supernatural in Early Modern Japan*. Her articles and reviews have appeared in *Asian Ethnology, Japan Forum, Film Criticism, Japanese Journal of Religious Studies, Marvels & Tales: Journal of Fairy-Tale Studies*, and the *International Journal of Asian Studies*, among many others.

Index